ETHICAL THEORY
Strategies and Concepts

AUDREY COHEN COLLEGE LIBRARY
75 Varick St. 12th Floor
New York, NY 10013

ETHICAL THEORY
Strategies and Concepts

Bernard Rosen
Ohio State University

Mayfield Publishing Company
Mountain View, California
London • Toronto

Copyright © 1993 by Mayfield Publishing Company
All rights reserved. No portion of this book may be reproduced in any form or by any means without written permission of the publisher.

Library of Congress Cataloging-in-Publication Data

Rosen, Bernard
    Ethical Theory / Bernard Rosen
      p.   cm.
    Includes index.
    ISBN 1-55934-088-6 (pbk.)
    1. Ethics. I. Title.
BJ1012.R567   1992
170—dc20   92-15891
                                                                                                                                                                                                 CIP

Manufactured in the United States of America

10 9 8 7 6 5 4 3 2 1

Mayfield Publishing Company
1240 Villa Street
Mountain View, California 94041

Sponsoring editor, James Bull; production editor, Carol Zafiropoulos; text design, Jean Mailander; cover design, Steve Naegele. This text was set in 11/12 Janson by ExecuStaff and printed on 50# Finch Opaque by Maple-Vail Book Manufacturing Group.

Ethical Theory: Strategies and Concepts is a revised edition of *Strategies of Ethics* © 1978 by Houghton Mifflin.

Contents

To the Instructor xi
To the Student xiii

CHAPTER ONE *Introduction* 1

Asking Ethical Questions: A Descriptive Ethics Questionnaire 4
Taking an Ethical Stand 8
    Key to the Descriptive Ethics Questionnaire 8
        A Theory of Value 10
A Survey of Normative Ethics 12
    The General Scheme of Arguments in Ethics 13
    Scheme R and the Ethical Theories 14
    Exercises: Identifying Moral Judgments and the Evidence that Supports Them 18
Arguments 19
    Exercises: Arguments 22
Theories and Phenomena 22
    Theories 22
    Phenomena 24
    Evaluating Theories 24
    Exercises: Evaluating Reasons and Theories 26
Moral Phenomena 27
Knowledge, Truth, and Justified Belief 29
    Knowledge 29
    Truth 30

Justified Assertion   30
Definitions   31
    Stipulative Definitions   31
    Reportive Definitions   32
A Look Back; A Look Ahead   33
    Exercises: Sharpening Your Critical Skills   35

CHAPTER TWO   *Psychologically Based Theories*   39

Egoism   40
Psychological Egoism Defined   42
    Some Phenomena for Theories of Motivation   42
    Benefit or Good   43
    Sole/Primary Motive   44
    Empirical Claim   45
    Voluntary Action   45
    Summary of Psychological Egoism   46
Nonempirical Psychological Egoism   46
    Willing and Wanting   46
    Opposing Views: Psychological Altruism   50
    Opposing Views: Psychological Realism   53
    The End Reached as Motive   54
    Summary of Nonempirical Psychological Egoism   56
    Exercises: Sharpening Your Critical Skills   56
Empirical Psychological Egoism   57
    Summary of Empirical Psychological Egoism   62
    Exercises: Theories of Motivation   63
Ethical Egoism   64
    "Increases"   65
    'Good' or 'Benefit'   67
    MO   67
    Summary of Ethical Egoism   70
    Exercises: Definitions of Moral Notions   70
The Connection Between Psychological and Ethical Egoism   70
The Most Plausible Versions of Ethical Egoism   74
    Summary of the Most Plausible Versions of Ethical Egoism   77
Ethical Egoism Evaluated   77
    Other People   77
    Counterexamples   82
    Too Wide a Theory   85
A Summary of Egoism   85
    Exercises: Practice in Critical Analysis   87
Cognitive Developmental Theories   88

CHAPTER THREE Utilitarianism 99

Direct and Indirect Utilitarianism   102
Nature of the Good, Whose Good, and Who Acts   103
Calculating the Greatest Good   104
    The Problem of Quantifying What's Valuable   105
    The Problem of Knowledge   105
    Limiting the Notion of Consequences   109
    Summary   111
    Exercises: Applying Utilitarianism   111
Utilitarianism Evaluated   112
    Reasons in Favor   112
    Counterexamples   113
    The Problem of Justice   118
    Exercises: Critical Analysis of Utilitarianism   122
Egoism and Utilitarianism   122
Appendix to Chapter 3: Justice   125

CHAPTER FOUR Rule Deontology 131

Distinctions Old and New   132
Multiple Categorical Rule Theories   133
    Egoism and Utilitarianism Combined   133
    The Ten Commandments   135
    Exercises: Working with Rules   138
Multiple Prima Facie Rule Theories   138
    Noncategorical Rules: A Solution, a New Problem   143
    A Rule for Determining Stringency?   147
    Counterexamples   149
    Exercises: Prima Facie Rules   150
Single-Rule Theories   150
    Agapism   150
    Kantianism   152
    Ethical and Cultural Relativism   158
A Look Back; A Look Ahead   167
    Exercises: Evaluating Various Deontological Theories   168

CHAPTER FIVE Nonrule Theories 171

Summary and Constitutive Rules   172
    Exercises: Constitutive and Summary Rules   175
The Claims of the Nonrule Theories   176
Intuitionism   176

Existentialism   180
Pragmatism   181
   Moral Negotiation: A Pragmatist Method for Handling Disagreement   186
Virtue Ethics   190
   Exercises: Basic Units of Morality   194
        Nonrule versus Rule Theories   195
Comparison of Theories of Obligation: A Summary   196
Appendix to Chapter 5: Rule Theory General Arguments   199

CHAPTER SIX   Value   211

Intrinsic Value   212
   Intrinsic Disvalue   214
   The Notion of 'Leads To'   214
   Moral and Nonmoral Value   215
   The Value Sense of 'Value'   215
   Value and Obligation   218
   Exercises: The Various Value Notions   219
An Outline of Theories of Value   219
Categorical Direct Rule Theories   220
   Hedonism   220
   A Theory of Happiness   230
   Other Candidates   232
The Problem with Monistic Value Theories: A Summary   232
   Exercises: Problems of Intrinsic Value   233
A Single Indirect Rule Theory: Relativism   234
   Carryover from Obligation Relativism   235
   Value Relativism Evaluated   237
   Exercises: Value Relativism   239
Pluralism: Multiple-Rule Theories—Prima Facie and Categorical   239
   The Counterexample Problem   240
   The Decision-Procedure Problem   241
   Obligation versus Value in a Pragmatic Theory   246
   Working with a Pragmatic Theory   247
Taking a Stand; Looking Ahead   248
   Exercises: Evaluating Value Theories   249
Appendix to Chapter 6: Meaninglessness and Futility: An Application of the Tools of Moral Philosophy to a Traditional Problem   251

CHAPTER SEVEN   Metaethics   263

The Nature of Normative Ethics: A Review   263
Basicness   264

M and Moral Realism   271
    How Many Places Does the Predicate Have?   272
    To What Kind of "Thing" Does *M* Answer? Realism and
        Antirealism   273
The Moral Connection   277
    Logical Connection   278
    Nonlogical Necessary Connection   279
    Causal Connection   280
    Noncognitive Connection   281
    Moral Connection   284
    Other Views of the Connection   285
Human Nature and Moral Philosophy   286
Free Will   288
Related Normative Concerns   290
    Skepticism, Amoralism, Nihilism   290
    Social and Political Theory   294
    Religion   295
    Other Ideologies   296
Paradigms   297
A Final Word   298

Index   299

To the Instructor

Since the book from which this text has grown was published in 1979, the teaching of university ethics courses has gone through some changes. Lower level ethics courses are now often applied ethics courses with some normative ethical theory. This development has led many philosophy departments to offer a separate course for majors and for those interested in ethical theory. *Ethical Theory: Strategies and Concepts* is appropriate for those who want a more thorough and rigorous examination of normative ethical theories.

I have tried to make the book current in every respect, but events move more swiftly than the presses. By the time this book appears, the map of the world will look much different from the way it did when the book went to press. The Soviet Union is gone, and a new Europe is emerging. The pro-choice and pro-life movements in the United States have taken up direct action as well as political lobbying. It is hard to predict the direction this confrontation will take. Teachers and students should rely as much as possible on current events for moral examples since applying theories to ongoing events is a good way to master them.

Responding to the important new literature on motivation and cognitive development, Chapter 2 is an examination of normative ethical theories that depend on psychological theories. The chapter raises the issue of whether females see morality differently than males. Some think females and males have a different conception of morality but, as you will see, the empirical research does not seem to support that claim. The views of Lawrence Kohlberg are set out and critically evaluated.

Chapter 5 now discusses virtue ethics, existentialism, intuitionism, and pragmatism as distinct normative ethical theories. The material in Chapter 6 has a new framework: monism and pluralism. The methodology for finding the "complex" with the greatest value is tied to the pragmatic methodology set out in Chapter 5.

For help in preparing this new volume, I am indebted to the following reviewers for their insightful suggestions: Linda Bomstad, California Polytechnic State University, San Luis Obispo; Sterling Harwood, San Jose State University; Kathleen Moore, Oregon State University; Anita Silvers, San Francisco State University; Mary Sirridge, Louisiana State University; and Becky White, California State University, Chico. While I accepted many of their suggestions, others set me to thinking about the material in ways that led to changes of a different sort than those suggested. Thus these changes are also due to them.

Nancy Christoff provided invaluable help after high-tech methods of scanning the original version of the book turned out to be more time consuming than typing it into my "Mac." Dana Wrensch offered technical support in the printing of the manuscript when it was sorely needed. She also offered the moral support needed to produce the moral philosophy. Alana Shindler gave me needed encouragement at crucial times as well as helping with the research.

The contributions of several reviewers of the original version continue to be evident in this new one. My thanks to John Dreher of the University of Southern California, Fred Hombach of the College of DuPage, and Andrew Oldenquist of Ohio State University. Most of all, thanks must go to the hundreds of students who have brought this book into existence both with specific criticisms and suggestions and, more generally, as a result of their desire to learn, coupled with a refusal to accept something unless they could really understand how it "went." The book represents a philosopher's attempt to say what he thinks is true in such a way that it will be helpful to everyone, not just to other professional philosophers.

To the Student

This is a book for those who have wondered about the moral life of human beings. You may think morality is an illusion, you may think it reflects a higher nature of humanity, or you may think it is as much a part of being human as reason itself. Whatever your view, this book is intended to help you clarify what you believe and become aware of alternative views that have interested others. I describe a number of different approaches to explaining morality, but, more importantly, I provide the tools for evaluating such approaches. The tools are primarily those of the philosopher, but at times I have borrowed from the psychologist, the anthropologist, and even the biologist and the physicist. I have a strategy concerning morality that I think is correct, but that is not what should be of primary importance to readers. In writing this book, I have intended chiefly to give you a chance to understand the different theories concerning morality and then to choose from among them the one you think is best.

In the first chapter you will find two questionnaires designed to help you to locate where you are now—that is, determine what kinds of theories you are now inclined to hold. Determining your present position does not "lock" you into that position, but it allows you to place yourself in a tradition. It is the rare person who holds a completely consistent view concerning moral phenomena, and you will probably discover one or more inconsistencies in your responses to the questionnaires. No matter: It is better to discover that your present views are inconsistent and choose to work at resolving those inconsistencies than to adopt a consistent view that does not really reflect your own views. In addition, the first chapter lays out the basic philosophical tools you will need in your work as an ethical strategist and tells you something about the theories that will be considered in the book.

Almost everyone holds a normative ethical theory—a theory about how we arrive at justified moral judgments concerning things, actions, and people. The problems of normative ethics are as old as the human race, and the record of theories is almost as old as the oldest writings we have. There are those who think that what philosophers are concerned with, even in normative ethics, has very little to do with our own moral life. I do not share that view. My view—and the one presented here—is that the theories designed by philosophers arise from the problems of individual human beings and are constructed to help solve those problems. The primary emphasis in the book is on normative ethical theories although the last chapter, on metaethics, outlines problems that have bothered mostly philosophers. The most esoteric concerns of metaethics are importantly, though perhaps only distantly, related to everyday moral concerns.

If you already know something about moral philosophy, you will want to know what is new and different about this book, but you will also want to be reassured that the views that have been most important in the history of thought are not left out. The view of normative ethical theories as explanations for a set of phenomena and as tools for deriving singular moral judgments is new in this work. In addition, the use of a general scheme to allow direct comparisons of theories in their "bare bones" state is, as far as I know, not to be found elsewhere. Further, the use of questionnaires that enable readers to discover what kinds of views they hold on the topics and theories examined is unique. And the view of value and the method of setting up and evaluating the rival theories of value differ from anything now in print. These are some of the things that are new.

But the theories presented are not so new. The book includes theories that people who are just beginning to think about morality are inclined to hold, and includes them in the forms in which beginners tend to hold them. This means that sometimes a certain argument is presented because it is taken seriously by students although not by professional philosophers. The book also presents theories that are thought to be finalists in the competitive marketplace of ideas—finalists, that is, as judged by philosophers. There will be disagreement about which views belong in the final selection and disagreement about which versions of those views are best. Yet, if you think there is a better version of ethical egoism, say, than the one presented in Chapter 2, then the method of presenting theories advocated here should enable you to state this view without any difficulty. You should be able to see which, if any, of the criticisms considered apply to your new version. (If you think you have a version of a view that escapes all the criticisms, you might just send it along to me. I would certainly be interested in seeing it.)

Ethical theory is not an easy subject. Yet many students who read the book in manuscript form found that, once they had mastered the elementary material—especially that in the first two chapters—they did not have a great deal of difficulty with the material in Chapters 3 through 6. The material in the last chapter is more difficult. Still, since this book will usually be used in a course, those who have questions will have access to a teacher who can explain whatever they do not understand. If questions and explanations lead to further discussion, the book will have fulfilled its purpose. *Ethical Theory: Strategies and Concepts* is not designed to bring about a consensus, but rather is meant to stimulate thought and discussion.

CHAPTER ONE

Introduction

Everyone is familiar with moral phenomena. People must constantly choose among competing ends based on the supposed greater value of one, or they have to weigh duty to other people against their own right to happiness. We say of the actions of criminals or some politicians that they are wrong or that the person involved should have known better. We say of ourselves that we ought to have written a paper or studied for an examination, but that instead we were lured away by a movie. Usually we notice such behavior and make the corresponding judgments without consciously formulating a theory, for it is easy to make judgments about shortsightedness, about the pain or joy of other people, about the shape of certain objects, or about the distance of one object from another. If we needed to, however, we could consciously formulate a theory that would allow us to make those judgments more easily and accurately. Having a method that will enable us to make such judgments becomes particularly important when we are faced with difficult moral problems, because it is important that we address these before they become pressing. In the midst of trying to decide whether to continue medical treatment for a loved one whose recovery is doubtful is not the time for choosing the means to make a moral decision. Moral philosophy addresses this concern.

Everyone has been exposed to some kind of theorizing about moral phenomena. We typically teach children to accept apparently simple moral theories that we present as rules, such as "Always do unto others as you would have them do unto you." Most parents teach their children to act from rules, such as "Do not lie," "It is wrong to take what doesn't belong to you," "It is wrong to promise to do something and then not do it," and "Potato chips aren't good for you." Accompanying such rules usually are instructions on how to use them. Before long a child supposes that morality consists of a set of rules to be followed or broken, as the case may be. This impression, whether consciously formulated or not, can be said to be a theory in moral philosophy. It is a theory about the phenomena the child is aware of. As a child grows older, theories about moral phenomena change; they become more complex, incorporating such observations as parents lying; persons they admire stealing; and almost everyone, including themselves, breaking promises or eating forbidden foods such as potato chips.

Most students of physics are aware of the phenomena of physics long before they formally study the subject in school. Parents explain that all things fall (except the ones that don't, of course) and that stones thrown in a certain way will break windows and perhaps even heads. Because their science education begins early, most children grow up with a reasonably accurate understanding, or theory, of physics. Of course, when they take their first physics course, most people soon learn that their theory of physics is not really adequate. From the beginning, though, physics students are willing to assume that there are correct theories in physics, to accept that their own views probably are inadequate, and to believe that their teacher will lead them to a more adequate position. This is not true of students' attitudes about moral philosophy.

One reason for this different attitude toward moral philosophy might be the belief of many students that, unlike in physics, there are no correct theories in moral philosophy. Alternatively, some think they know exactly what is true about ethics, and anything in their ethics course that is inconsistent with that belief is clearly mistaken. Others believe there is no such field as moral philosophy—that morality is a "matter of taste." Many think it important to deny there are "moral absolutes." They believe that, although we can acquire knowledge in physics, we cannot acquire moral knowledge.[1]

When skeptics question the possibility of acquiring physical knowledge, physicists usually ignore them. Suppose you claim that gravity, for example, is just the discredited occult view that there is "action at a distance." Your friendly neighborhood physicist, in response, is likely to suggest you go elsewhere with such metaphysical speculation. The physicist knows how the equations work, is aware of and can use the standards of evidence, and knows achieved results in the field. Physicists only rarely respond to skeptical questions about the foundation of physics.

Philosophers, by contrast, attempt to respond to all genuine questions about the foundation of their subject matter and take seriously all versions of skeptical arguments. If physicists get into trouble and can't answer a question about

---

[1] Some of these moral skeptics are general skeptics; they think we fail to have knowledge in all subject matters. Credit has to be given for a consistent stand, though general skepticism is a difficult position to maintain.

the implications of a position, they can say, "that's the job of the philosopher. Why not go to the philosophy department?" Philosophers, however, have no one to send their critics and skeptics to; philosophy is, traditionally, where the intellectual buck stops. Accordingly, in this book many skeptical arguments will be considered and a large number of competing theories will be examined. Some of you will be impatient to get on to the questions or theories that interest you, and you can do that simply by using the table of contents or index. You might find it advantageous, though, to curb your impatience. Following a systematic approach will result in a more secure background from which to pursue your interests and will give you a better understanding of the subject matter in general. It is, of course, up to each of you to choose the course best suited to your ends.

As author, I take positions on the various issues in this book, and it would be intellectually dishonest of me not to point out that one or more of the positions seems better supported by evidence and that others are inadequate. (Such honesty is also an obligation of anyone writing a basic book in physics.) In addition, however, competing positions will be outlined, and the supporting evidence for those positions will be presented. Competing theories are usually not part of physics books. Some people will think the explanation for this is that we have discovered what is true in physics but have made no such discoveries in moral philosophy. Again, though, we shall have to see about that.

The main purpose of this book is to provide readers with the tools and information they need to select the normative and metaethical theories in moral philosophy that work best for them. The tools are a theory placement test plus standards of what good arguments and good theories are. The information consists of an outline of the most important theories, the philosophical information needed for an understanding of those theories, and various strategies for evaluating each theory as it is presented.

As an apprentice ethical strategist, you need certain tools that will enable you eventually to construct your own theory of ethics. These strategist's tools are the subject of this chapter. After finishing the chapter you should be more aware of the ethical theory or theories you have been holding until now.[2] You should also have acquired the means whereby you can begin consciously to adopt a theory. It may well be the same theory you held before studying moral philosophy, or it may be one that is radically different. My main intention is not to lead you to the "truth" (although I must obviously fulfill my intellectual obligation and tell you where I think it is) but to give you the means to find it yourself. This is so even if it should turn out that the only truth is that there is no truth at all in moral philosophy.

---

[2] It is not unusual for people to hold more than one theory, often theories that are inconsistent and often without realizing the inconsistencies. You should discover if this is true of you.

ASKING ETHICAL QUESTIONS: A DESCRIPTIVE ETHICS QUESTIONNAIRE

The first step is to find out where you are now. For that purpose you will find following a questionnaire designed to show you the position you now hold. The questionnaire consists of many statements—some specific, some general. Try to respond to as many of the statements as you can. You may be tempted to give what you think to be "correct" responses in terms of your friends, your church, your parents, or someone else. Resist that temptation and put down only what you believe is correct at this time. Don't worry about what you may later decide is correct and, for now, don't worry about inconsistency. Most of you will be swayed first one way, then another. This is to be expected. It is far better to respond according to your real beliefs than to make something up in an attempt to be "philosophical." Don't look ahead to find the answers; the answers lie with you. If you are not honest with yourself, you will benefit significantly less than you would otherwise.

After you have completed the questionnaire, you can turn to the answer key, which follows it. The key is not a key in the usual sense—namely, something that tells you the right answer—but it will enable you to interpret what you have done. However, because an adequate understanding of your position requires your understanding of most of this book, you should not consider these current results as the final word. Examine the main theories in normative ethical theory before you make up your mind about which positions are best (or at least the best at that time). In responding to the questionnaire, use the code SA for strongly agree, A for agree, D for disagree, SD for strongly disagree, and CA for can't answer (either because you don't sufficiently understand the statement or because you just can't make up your mind). Try to keep down the number of CAs.

1. The only motive people have in doing anything is to get something for themselves. Even when they help others, it's only because it makes them feel good.
2. Only if you would agree to allow everyone to do what you are doing is your action morally permissible or right.
3. What makes an action obligatory is that it leads to the greatest good for the greatest number. Motives are irrelevant.
4. The only thing that counts in determining whether someone did the right thing or not is the motive. The results of the action are irrelevant.
5. Since we can always turn out to be wrong about a factual claim (for example, we think there are nine planets in the solar system, but perhaps there are ten), we don't really have knowledge about such matters.
6. The only thing that is *worth* pursuing is pleasure.

7. A good will can't be used for any bad end, but everything else can. So a good will is the only thing that is good in itself.
8. No one knows what is right or wrong, or good or bad.
9. Whenever you justify a specific moral judgment, such as "Slavery in the United States was wrong," you have to refer to a general rule or principle, such as "All slavery is wrong."
10. Things of value in our society should be distributed only to those who can afford them as a result of their success in competing in our economic system.
11. Moral judgments are an expression of personal taste. Just as "Hot fudge goes well with banana ice cream" is a question of personal taste, so is "Slavery in the United States was a morally bad institution."
12. Those and only those actions commanded by God are our moral obligations; those actions forbidden by God are wrong. To know your obligations you need to know what God commands and forbids.
13. Sometimes when you claim that a person did something wrong, you do so on the basis of the person's motives.
14. Hitler's motives, let us suppose, were to improve European civilization, to eliminate crime, to reduce unemployment, and to restore a sense of pride in Germans. In spite of these good motives, his actions with respect to the Jews and Slavs were wrong.
15. When we claim to know something (for example, that the earth is roughly a sphere), we are justified when we have good enough evidence.
16. The things that have value are the things that a society's members believe to have value.
17. Pleasure is a short-lived experience that comes and goes, but happiness is a fairly stable and long-run condition. The only thing that is worth having for itself and not just for what it leads to is happiness, not pleasure.
18. When you come right down to it, you can't ever really tell whether you are doing the right thing in a given instance.
19. Things of value should be distributed to each individual according to need (and we should receive from each individual according to that person's abilities).
20. There are some statements that we suppose are clearly and objectively true, although not necessarily true. "There are nine planets in the solar system" is an example of such a statement, even though, of course, we must allow the possibility that we are mistaken in making this statement and might have to take it back. Moral judgments are like

that; we suppose they are objectively true, although we have to allow the possibility that we are mistaken.

21. Lots of factors enter into our moral rules, such as amount of good produced, and such special relations as friendship and the repayment of debts. To figure out the rightness of an action you have to weigh all the positive and negative applications of these rules.

22. If you want to see whether or not you have a moral obligation to do something, find out what would happen if you did it and what would result if you didn't. The only things that matter are the likely consequences of your action. Motives are irrelevant.

23. When I say that an action is right or obligatory, I say so only because I perceive that the action will be good for me in some way.

24. Although consequences count in determining that someone did the right or the wrong thing, motives also count. It isn't a matter of just one or the other; motives and consequences are both relevant.

25. There are some specific moral judgments, such as "Slavery in the United States in the eighteenth century was wrong," that we are more certain of than any general rule or principle, such as "All slavery is wrong."

26. Many things are produced in our society that are desired by most people. These things should be distributed equally, numerically when possible, and on the basis of each waiting a turn if a numerical equality is not possible.

27. If you follow the Ten Commandments, you are acting in a morally proper way; if you do not, then you are not. That's all there is to morality.

28. When anyone voluntarily does something, the motive is always to give pleasure to others.

29. If someone sees a person drowning and is motivated to try to save the person, then, whether the effort is successful or not, the action is equally morally praiseworthy.

30. If a naked human being is placed on the moon with no oxygen, then, without a doubt, that person will be dead in a very short time.

31. When anyone voluntarily does something, the motive always is to get pleasure for himself or herself.

32. The institution of slavery in the United States was morally bad.

33. It is very difficult, and often impossible, to know what we ought to do in specific circumstances, but we can at least know the moral principles that apply.

34. Things of value in our society should be distributed on the basis of merit.
35. Our moral obligations are solely a function of what the majority of people living in our society suppose are our moral obligations.
36. Sometimes the consequences of an action have to be taken into account when you judge that someone performed a morally right action.
37. Even though no one can know any factual matter with certainty, we still have knowledge of many factual matters.
38. Some people think that love has value by itself, but its value is just the pleasure one derives from being in love and loving.
39. Things of value in a society should be distributed fairly—that is, in a way that each person would agree to before knowing what his or her place will be in that society.
40. To determine whether or not you did the right thing in a situation, you must find out if you performed the action out of love. If you did, then the action is right; if you did not, then it isn't.
41. Some actions have no appreciable effect on me. For example, a soldier in a far off war killing a small child just for sport does not affect me. Such actions may nevertheless be wrong.
42. No one can really have evidence for anything. It's all a matter of personal preference.
43. Pleasure has a value that is independent of the things it may lead to, but so do other things, such as friendship, freedom, and peace.
44. It is very difficult to know the right thing to do, but sometimes, at least, we do.
45. The only reason it is wrong for a drunken parent to beat a small child to death is that when I hear about it, I feel bad.
46. It may have been that slavery in the United States led to more good than bad overall, but it was still wrong to keep slaves.
47. To say that something is true is just to say that the majority of persons living in your society accept it as true.
48. We all have our own moral opinions, and only about those can we be certain of correctness or acceptability.
49. Some of our motives are to help others.
50. Sometimes actions are right or wrong because of their effect on me, and sometimes they are right or wrong independent of their effect on me.
51. It has happened, on occasion, that a stranger asked directions, and I gave them. In some of these instances, the stranger received valuable

information, and my motive in giving that information was to help the stranger and not to help myself or to provide myself with anything of value.

52. An action is right or obligatory to do when it stems from a good character trait such as honesty or empathetic caring. Any use of moral rules is secondary and after the fact.

TAKING AN ETHICAL STAND

Now that you have filled out the questionnaire, you are understandably eager to know what you did, to have revealed to you what your responses commit you to in the way of positions and theories. In order to make such a commitment intelligible, however, even in a most casual way, we must say something about the subject we shall be studying and the gross divisions within it. The section following the interpretation of the questionnaire is intended to do that. After you have gone through that, the classification of responses to the questions will make more sense. However, one of the purposes of this book is to explain in greater detail the various ethical theories, so don't be surprised if complete understanding is not reached immediately.

Key to the Descriptive Ethics Questionnaire

The following will be based on the assumption that you agreed (A) or strongly agreed (SA) with the statements. If you disagreed (D) or strongly disagreed (SD), then we can say that you hold the denial of the view stated.

1. Psychological egoism (Chapter 2)
2. The "universalizability" principle (If you agree to this, then you are inclined to hold to some kind of rule theory. See Chapter 4.)
3. Utilitarianism (Chapter 3)
4. A formalist deontological theory of obligation (Chapter 4)
5. General skepticism and an endorsement of the argument from possibility (Chapter 1)
6. Hedonism (Chapter 6)
7. Kantian theory of value, inconsistent with statement 6 (Chapter 6)
8. Moral skepticism (Chapter 7)
9. Basic rule theory claim (Chapters 4 and 5)
10. A theory of distributive justice—competition as the test of merit (Appendix to Chapter 3)
11. Noncognitivism—emotivism (Chapter 7)

12. Theological voluntarism (Chapter 4)
13. A denial of teleological theories of obligation, inconsistent with statement 3 (Chapter 4)
14. A denial of formalist deontological theory of obligation (This instance is inconsistent with statement 4. See Chapter 4.)
15. A denial of general skepticism (Agreement with this is inconsistent with statement 5. See Chapter 1.)
16. Value relativism (Chapter 6)
17. Aristotelian theory of value, happiness as the only thing of intrinsic value (Chapter 6)
18. Moral skepticism, specifically with regard to obligation (Chapter 7)
19. A theory of distributive justice—communism (Appendix to Chapter 3)
20. A form of cognitivism, moral judgments as contingent truths (Chapter 7)
21. A prima facie theory of obligation (Chapter 4)
22. A teleological theory of obligation (This is inconsistent with statements 4, 13, and 18. See Chapters 2 and 3.)
23. Ethical egoism (Chapter 2)
24. A nonformalist deontological theory of obligation, inconsistent with statement 4 especially but also with statements 3 and 22 (Chapter 4)
25. An intuitionist theory of obligation (Chapter 5)
26. A theory of distributive justice—equalitarianism (Appendix to Chapter 3)
27. Ten Commandments theory of obligation (Chapter 4)
28. Psychological altruism (Chapter 2)
29. Denial of a teleological theory of obligation, inconsistent with statement 22 (Chapter 4)
30. Denial of general skepticism, inconsistent with statement 5 (Chapter 1)
31. Psychological hedonism, a form of psychological egoism (Chapter 6)
32. An instance of moral knowledge or justified judgment, inconsistent with statement 8 (Chapter 7)
33. A rule theory of obligation, inconsistent with statement 25 (Chapter 4)
34. A theory of distributive justice—meritarianism (Appendix to Chapter 3)
35. Obligation relativism, inconsistent with almost every other theory of obligation (Chapter 4)
36. Denial of a formalist deontological theory of obligation, inconsistent with statement 4 (Chapter 4)
37. Denial of general skepticism, with a denial of certainty, inconsistent with statement 5 (Chapter 1)

38. An instance that supports hedonism (see statement 6), inconsistent with statement 43 (Chapter 6)
39. A theory of distributive justice—Rawlsianism (Appendix to Chapter 3)
40. Agapism as a theory of obligation (Chapter 4)
41. Denial of ethical egoism, inconsistent with statement 23 (Chapter 2)
42. Evidence skepticism, inconsistent with statements 30 and 37 (Chapter 1)
43. Denial of hedonism, inconsistent with statement 6 (Chapter 6)
44. Denial of obligation skepticism, inconsistent with statement 18 (Chapter 7)
45. An instance of ethical egoism (The denial of this is inconsistent with some versions of statement 23. See Chapter 2.)
46. A denial of utilitarianism, inconsistent with statement 3 (Chapter 3)
47. Truth relativism (Chapter 1)
48. Subjectivism (Chapter 7)
49. Denial of psychological egoism, inconsistent with statement 1 (Chapter 2)
50. Denial of ethical egoism, inconsistent with statement 23 (Chapter 2)
51. Denial of psychological egoism, inconsistent with statement 1 (Chapter 2)
52. Virtue ethics theory (Several versions of this kind of theory are found in Chapter 5.)

It is important to understand that many of you will have chosen positions that are inconsistent; this is not just a quirk of a few. Inconsistency is quite natural at this stage, for many theories appeal to different people for different reasons. What is important, however, is to understand exactly why the theories are inconsistent; once you know why, then you will also understand that no matter how tempting a set of inconsistent views might be, you must not subscribe to both of them. At this stage in the investigation, though, you should only note that you tend to hold inconsistent views and not try to determine which view to give up. You may finally want to give up both views and adopt some third position, or you may wish to attempt some method of reconciling the two views that now appear inconsistent.

This questionnaire describes the position or positions you are inclined to hold now. It does not dictate what position you must hold at the end of the investigation. When you have finished with this book, you may wish to return to the questionnaire and see what changes have been wrought.

A Theory of Value

We indicate something is valuable by using terms such as 'good', 'valuable', and 'intrinsically valuable'. Part of everyone's ethical theory is a theory of value, a theory about the kinds of things that are valuable. One popular, though we shall show badly flawed, theory of value is *hedonism*. When someone claims that pleasure is the only thing that is worth pursuing, that person is embracing hedonism. In addition to a general claim expressing a theory of value, people sometimes want to identify specific ends, things, and relations they think are valuable. Vices such as treachery and mendacity are thought of as bad character traits, whereas loyalty and honesty are labeled as good character traits.

The following exercise will give you an opportunity to make preliminary decisions about some specific kinds of things you think are good and bad, although by the end you may well claim that some of the general things you chose in the descriptive ethics questionnaire are valuable.

At any given time, every person has a number of goals or ends. A goal or end is something you seek to achieve, whether material, spiritual, political, personal, public, or private. Goals need not be long run or final, although some of your goals may be of this type. On a sheet of paper you are to list any three goals you now have. For example, you may wish to lose ten pounds, to get to class on time, to play touch football on Sunday, or to start a revolution. Simply list any three goals that come to mind across the top of a sheet of paper. A list of three such goals might be:

1. Lose ten pounds.
2. Get to class on time.
3. Play touch football on Sunday.

Some of the goals we attempt to achieve we seek primarily, or perhaps even solely, because of what they lead to. For example, the woman who cuts a crisscross in her leg after being bitten by a rattlesnake does so in order to draw out some of the poison. The poison is usually drawn out in order to prevent death; the woman may or may not seek to draw out the poison for any other reason. Furthermore, the prevention of death, whether sought for some other reason or not, obviously leads to the attainment of, or makes possible the attainment of, other ends. At any rate, we can all usually recognize the end of a chain of goals, and we can say, "This is a goal I seek for itself and not only for the things it might lead to." Beginning with the three goals you listed at the top of the sheet, construct a chain of goals. It does not matter if the same goal appears in more than one chain; feel free to draw as many branches as seem necessary. At the beginning, one chain might appear as in Figure 1-1. You might expect the other goals in the figure to have chains leading from them, and for the items listed in the first chain to go beyond what is presented; they could. Figure 1-1 is shown only to give you an idea of how to go on.

After finishing your chains, construct a list of two kinds of items. First, list all the ends of the chains. Second, list any goals on the chain that you suppose are valuable no matter where they lead. (If some such goals occur

12   Introduction

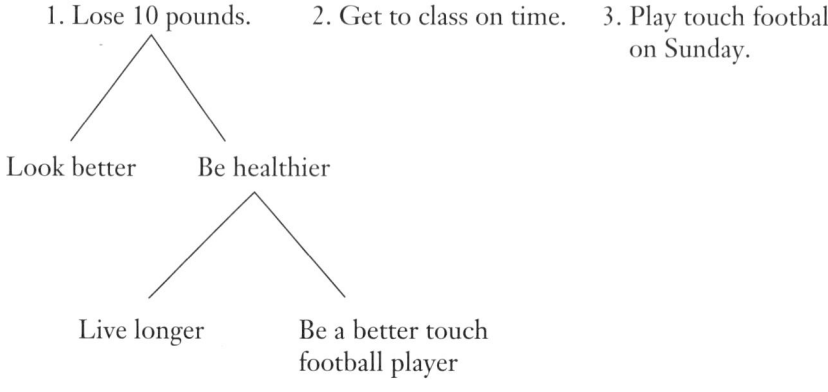

FIGURE 1-1 A Chain of Goals

to you now that you did not put in any chains, you can list them also.) For example, considering only chain 1, we might add:

  a. Live longer
  b. Look better
  c. Be a better touch football player
  d. Be healthier

Try now, with a separate list, to rank the preceding goals—the most important first, the second most important second, and so on. For example, considering the list presented earlier, we might have:

  1. b
  2. a
  3. c
  4. d

There is no key to this kind of questionnaire, as there was to the first one. However, some clarification can be effected by applying the material in Chapter 6, the chapter on value theory. At the end of that chapter, you will be asked to examine your values questionnaire to determine which theory of value best explains what you have written down. You should not attempt such an explanation without reading Chapter 6.

A SURVEY OF NORMATIVE ETHICS

As you build your own theory of ethics, you will want to have a means to compare and contrast the catalogued ethical theories and to compare your own developing view with the views of others. This section introduces a tool that not only will facilitate presentation and comparison of theories but also will help to explain what the main concerns of ethical strategists are. This tool, which we'll call *Scheme R*, will thus provide an approach to the field of normative ethics as a whole.[3]

The General Scheme of Arguments in Ethics

A standard format will be used throughout this book to present the steps in ethical reasoning and the thinking that underlies normative ethical theories. This format is called Scheme R because the letter R stands for the word *rule*—namely, the rule that is captured by the first statement in the scheme. Consider the following:

1. If any x is F, then x is M.
2. This specific x is F.

Therefore, 3. This specific x is M.

The x is a variable that is replaced by the name of any kind of individual: a person, an action, a specific institution, and so on. One instance of x is 'Socrates', and another is 'drinks hemlock'. F and M are property variables, but F will usually be used for nonmoral predicates and M for moral or normative predicates. If we replace all the variables in the scheme with the English words set out here we get the following:

1. If anyone (x) dies rather than give up the most firmly held beliefs (F), then that person (x) is a good person (M).
2. Socrates is a person who died rather than give up his most firm beliefs. (S is F.)

Therefore, 3. Socrates is a good person. (S is M.)

1. If anyone (x) holds another person as a slave (F), then he is doing what is morally wrong (M).
2. Simon Legree held another person as a slave. (SL is F.)

Therefore, 3. Simon Legree did what was morally wrong. (SL is M.)

The first premise of each of these arguments is a *general moral judgment*, which is usually called a moral rule or principle, and the third statement is a

---

[3]Those who hold to a virtue ethics theory (see Chapter 5), will deny this general scheme is the best way to represent their view. I recognize this and will discuss it at greater length at that time. Nevertheless, this general scheme will help us to understand the vast majority of normative ethical theories.

singular moral judgment. The second premise is a claim about a specific person who does the kind of thing mentioned in the first premise. The primary concern of normative ethical theories is to provide a means for arriving at *justified* singular moral judgments.[4] A normative theory, when complete, should address other concerns, too. It should discuss and explain topics such as justice, punishment, freedom and responsibility, and rights (moral, legal, and political).

Scheme R and the Ethical Theories

Normative ethics has two main divisions; theory of obligation and theory of value. In terms of Scheme R, we can see the concerns of each of these areas in Figure 1-2.

Nonmoral uses of moral terms or predicates are just as common as their corresponding moral use or sense. "It is best to enter the Post Office from the front," would not in most instances contain 'best' in a moral sense. Similarly, the 'ought' is not a moral term in "You ought to put your car in neutral when pushing it." These uses are not difficult to distinguish in practice from such uses as "You ought to help those who are in need." We can distinguish the moral from the nonmoral senses in almost every context without difficulty. In any particular instance in which there is some difficulty, we can clear it up by examining more of the context or by asking a few questions.

A normative ethical theory is concerned primarily with the justification of the third statement of the general scheme—singular moral judgments. How do we find justified singular moral judgments? Do they exist at all? What if there is disagreement about such judgments? These are some of the questions that arise. We shall examine some of the theories that purport to explain how we arrive at *justified* instances of statement 3 of the general scheme.

According to *teleological* theories of obligation, all relevant substitution instances of F are consequences (or likely consequences) of x. According to deontological theories of obligation, not all relevant substitution instances are consequences.[5] *Formalists* maintain that none of the values of F are consequences;

---

[4]To say this is not to suppose that a virtue ethics theory is ruled out by this scheme. A virtue ethics view proposes that character traits such as truthfulness and caring or kindness are the basic elements of one's ethical theory. Such views will be examined in Chapter 5. Views that claim that the rules are not basic but are themselves justified by something else will also be examined in Chapter 5. Both of these kinds of views, though, will propose a means for arriving at justified moral judgments.

[5]*Teleological* comes from the Greek *telos*, meaning "end" or "purpose." Thus, the purpose or consequence of x is F. *Deontological* comes from the Greek *deon*, meaning "that which is obligatory." Since teleological theories of obligation are concerned only about the value of the likely consequences of actions, they are often called *consequentialist* theories. Teleological theories about plants invoke an aim of a conscious intelligent being who designed the plants so as to have leaves, roots, and other parts. This sense of teleological is related to teleological normative ethical theories, but the end is not consequences, but a goal or end of a being.

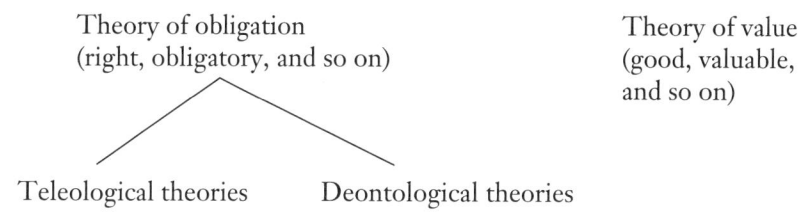
FIGURE 1-2

and *nonformalists* contend that some of the values of *F* may be consequences, but other instances replace *F* as well. A simple teleological theory would specify *F* as 'brings about good consequences for me', and *M* as 'I have a right to do'. This results in an instance of statement 1 of Scheme R that claims "If any action brings about good consequences for me, then I have a right to do it." Similarly, in one deontological theory, *F* would be specified as 'is an instance of keeping a promise', and *M* as 'is obligatory'. This would result in a quite different instance of statement 1 of Scheme R: "If any action is an instance of keeping a promise, then it is obligatory." The second statement, part of a formalist deontological theory, does not mention consequences; the first statement, part of a teleological theory, mentions only consequences. Much more will be said later about these two kinds of theories and how they differ.

We can construct a tree of the views distinguished thus far that may help you keep the relations straight (Figure 1-3).

So far we've been examining Scheme R for its ability to help us generate singular judgments from general rules, but we haven't taken note of the fact that there are different types of rules. Some rules are rules of thumb that are useful but, as we all recognize, dispensable. For example, the rule "If there is a certain characteristic sound present, then there is an automobile close by," is a pretty good way of determining whether or not there is a car nearby. If you use this rule, you will be right most of the time, although sometimes—as when a recording of a car is played or when the car has an electric motor or when you have impaired hearing—the rule will lead you astray. The rule is not *required* in order to determine that a car is present, for there are other ways of finding this out. Furthermore, as shown, using the rule doesn't always lead to success in determining that a car is present.

In contrast with this kind of rule, consider the rule "If the black king is in check and there is no chess move that will change this situation, then black is checkmated." There is never an occasion when the first part of the rule, the *antecedent*, is fulfilled and the *consequent*, the last part, is not. This rule is one of the defining characteristics of the game of chess, or, to use the terminology we shall be using from now on, this rule suitably generalized is a *constitutive rule* of chess. Such rules are required to justify the judgments

16 Introduction

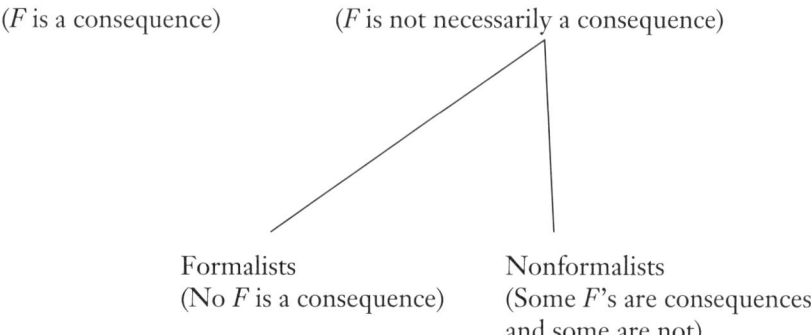

FIGURE 1-3 Normative ethics

falling under them. You can use the rule directly, as we just did, or you can use it indirectly. For example, suppose someone tells you that black has been checkmated. If the person knows something about the game, you can take that as very good evidence that the game is over. However, someone—the person who told you or whoever told that person or whoever told *that* person— at some point must have recourse to the rule that justifies the judgment.

Some philosophers have claimed that rules are always required to justify singular moral judgments, and some have denied this. Those who make the former claim are called *rule theorists*, and those who deny it are called *nonrule theorists*. Some nonrule theorists hold to a virtue ethics theory but others hold to a *pragmatic* or an *existentialist theory*. Rule theorists are those who claim that rules, instances of statement 1 of Scheme R, are always required to justify singular moral judgments, instances of statement 3. Virtue and pragmatic theorists, in contrast, are those who claim that we derive the moral rules from a different means of arriving at singular moral judgments. This distinction will be explained in greater detail when it is used in a substantive way in Chapters 4 and 5. The purpose now is only to allow you to see the position you adopted in the questionnaire. This distinction is, in my view, one of the most basic and important in moral philosophy, although many philosophers do not agree with me.

Among those who hold rule theories, some think that individual rules hold good no matter what else is true, and some do not. A rule that holds good no matter what else is true is a *categorical rule*, whereas a rule that can be overridden by another rule of the same type is a *prima facie rule*. There is a lot more to this distinction, but for now, let's look at a few examples just to help us along. On the one hand, the rule concerning checkmate is one that is true regardless of what else is true, either on or off the chessboard. Someone may wish you to waive the rules, to stop playing chess, but then we recognize this by saying that we aren't really playing chess anymore. On the other hand, the rule "If a batter swings and misses the ball three times, then he is out" can be overridden by the rule "If the pitcher touches his mouth before delivering the ball, then the batter will be awarded first base." As you can imagine, the situation in moral philosophy is much more complicated, but this gives you some idea of how to contrast a prima facie rule with a categorical rule.

One final distinction—between indirect moral rules (or metamoral rules) on the one hand and direct (or primary) moral rules on the other will allow us to point out all the main divisions in normative ethical theory. *Indirect moral rules* are rules that pick out the primary moral rules we apply directly to situations. For example, one indirect moral rule might be "Choose those direct moral rules which, when generally acted on by all or most, will lead to the greatest good for the greatest number." This rule, by itself, does not tell you whether it is right to tell the clerk at the small grocery store that she has given you too much change. However, it should enable you, so some claim, to pick out a rule such as "Honesty is the best policy" or "Always be honest in word and deed."

To see how this is supposed to work, let's go through the various steps a theory containing indirect moral rules suggests when we are in doubt. Suppose you are in a neighborhood grocery store and the clerk gives you too much change. A *direct rule* theory might suggest some rule such as "Always do what will maximize the greatest good for the greatest number." In this instance, you could calculate roughly that the greatest good would result from keeping the money, for the loss is small to the store but the gain means a lot to you—relatively speaking. You could conclude that you don't have a moral obligation to return the money. The indirect rule theorist, however, would say that you didn't calculate correctly, for you must consider what is likely to happen if people generally acted in terms of the rule about keeping change when it would benefit them and not hurt others too much. This could lead to a decrease in the overall good instead of an increase.

Put in the general scheme, the two positions look something like this.

Direct (or primary) moral rule theory
1. If any action leads to the greatest good for the greatest number, then it is morally obligatory to do it. (direct moral rule)
2. The action of keeping the store's money leads to the greatest good for the greatest number. (purported factual claim)

Therefore, 3. It is morally obligatory to keep the store's money. (singular moral judgment)

Indirect (metamoral) rule theory
1. If all or most people generally acting from a direct moral rule x (DMRx) leads to the greatest good for the greatest number, then x is a correct direct moral rule. (indirect moral rule)

2. "If any action is one of being honest in word or deed, then that action is obligatory," is a direct moral rule that, if generally acted from, leads to the greatest good for the greatest number. (purported factual claim)

Therefore, 3. "If any action is one of being honest in word or deed, then that action is obligatory," is a correct direct moral rule.

4. If any action is one of being honest in word or deed, then that action is obligatory (from statement 3). (direct moral rule)
5. Returning the money to the store clerk is being honest in deed.[6]

Therefore, 6. returning the money to the store clerk is obligatory. (singular moral judgment)

The preceding, considerably simplified example, should show how direct and indirect moral rule theories differ, on occasion, with respect to singular moral judgments. More important, it should show you *why* the two kinds of theories differ. When we examine specific theories, we will develop a fuller explanation of the two kinds of theories and we will see how some of them actually work. For now, the purpose is to show the main kinds of theories so that you can have a preliminary understanding of the positions you took on the descriptive ethics questionnaire.

Exercises: Identifying Moral Judgments and the Evidence That Supports Them

1. Identify the singular moral judgments in the following list, and construct arguments of the sort represented by the examples of Scheme R. Identify the nature of the other judgments.
   a. When the light is red, you are permitted to make right turns when the traffic is clear.
   b. All instances of telling the truth are right.
   c. Telling the three-year-old terminally ill with leukemia that Christmas never comes in August is wrong.
   d. Ted Kennedy does not have an obligation to run for president.
   e. The United States did the right thing to engage in Operation Desert Storm so as to drive the Iraqis out of Kuwait.
   f. Moral obligations are a function of social mores.
   g. The right way to go is to take I-73.

(continued)

---

[6]This might be somewhat confusing because the rule, in statement 4, talks about honesty in word *or* deed, but statement 5 talks only about honesty in deed. If one is *either* honest in word *or* honest in deed, then one has fulfilled the moral rule. You can, of course, fulfill both. If you ask whether Jones had cream or sugar in his coffee, I can correctly say yes if he had either one or if he had both.

> (continued)
>
> 2. From a current newspaper or periodical journal, choose what appears to be a moral judgment. Identify singular moral judgments and any moral rules used. Reconstruct, as best you can, the argument for the singular moral judgment.
> 3. Describe, as best as you can remember it, a moral disagreement you had with someone in the recent past. Lay out the evidence you each presented, making clear what moral rules were employed. Identify any indirect moral rules used or confirm that only direct moral rules were used. Make clear what relevant factual claims, if any, were in dispute.

Much of the material that follows is not the primary subject of this book, but it is essential nevertheless. These are the most general tools used to explain and assess the theories examined in the rest of the book. If, later on, you forget about a procedure or begin to lose the direction a discussion is taking, you should return to this chapter to get your bearings. To avoid losing your bearings in the first place, though, it would be wise now to become familiar with the material in this chapter, including the sections that follow.

You will see many arguments and theories in this book, so naturally you will need some tools to help evaluate them. Let us, accordingly, begin by examining arguments in general.

ARGUMENTS

An *argument* consists of two sets of statements in a relation. One set, the *premise(s)*, is presumed to support the other, the *conclusion(s)*. There are two main types of argument: *deductive* and *inductive*. Some people believe that *immediate inferences* are a third type. Good deductive arguments are called *valid*. A *valid deductive argument* is one whose premises provide conclusive evidence for the truth of its conclusion. If the premises of a valid deductive argument are true, then its conclusion cannot at the same time be false. Here are two commonly used forms of valid deductive argument (the form of an argument is what is revealed when the content is abstracted):

Affirming the Antecedent	*Denying the Consequent*
If p then q.	If p then q.
p.	Not-q.
Therefore, q.	Therefore, not-p.

Two invalid argument forms exist that look very much like the valid argument forms but they cannot be used to justify their conclusions.

Affirming-the-Consequent Fallacy
If p then q.
q.
___
Therefore, p.

Denying-the-Antecedent Fallacy
If p then q.
Not-p.
___
Therefore, not-q.

One can show that an argument form is invalid by showing that there is at least one clear case (substitution instance) in which the premises are true (T) and the conclusion is false (F). This is easily done. For example,

T. If Patrick Swayze is a woman, then Patrick Swayze is a mammal.

T. Patrick Swayze is a mammal.
___
Therefore, F. Patrick Swayze is a woman.

This argument shows that some arguments of the affirming-the-consequent fallacy form have true premises and a false conclusion. Therefore, arguments of that form do not meet the requirements of a valid deductive argument. This is also true of arguments of the denying-the-antecedent fallacy form. For example,

T. If Patrick Swayze is a woman, then Patrick Swayze is a mammal.

T. Patrick Swayze is not a woman.
___
Therefore, F. Patrick Swayze is not a mammal.

More argument forms will be introduced as they are needed, and they will be explained at that point. No one will become a logician as a result of working with just a few argument forms, but familiarity with them will enable you to organize your arguments more effectively. Since the only way to become familiar with argument forms is to use them, you should try putting some arguments into the forms just described.

We have called good deductive arguments valid. Good inductive arguments will be called *acceptable*, or *strong*. An inductive argument is acceptable when its premises make its conclusion more probable than not. The higher the degree of probability, the more confidence we can have in the conclusion.[7] This suggests one important difference between valid deductive arguments and acceptable inductive arguments: The conclusions of acceptable inductive arguments can turn out to be false. This supposed liability, though, is more than offset

___
[7]It would be rational to inoculate your child against measles if the chances of preventing measles was much greater than 99% and the probability of a serious adverse reaction was less than 1%.

by the fact that only inductive arguments extend our knowledge. The primary way we justify new claims about the world is by induction.

There are acceptable inductive argument forms, but they cannot be relied on in the mechanical way valid deductive argument forms can, and they do not allow fallacies to be described and detected as readily as the deductive forms do. The following forms should give you a good start in coming to an understanding of what inductive arguments are:

Enumeration	*Statistical Syllogism*
Z percent of the observed members of F are G.	Z percent of F are G. x is F.
Therefore, Z percent of F are G.	Therefore, x is G.

When an inductive argument is of an acceptable form, it may not yet be acceptable, for it may have been "misused." For example, suppose one runs an *enumeration* of the sex of shoppers in a large department store, but the observation point is the men's toilet. On grounds independent of this argument we know very few women are to be found in a men's restroom, so the sample is not well chosen. Such statistics are called *biased*. In addition to using biased statistics, one can go wrong by having insufficient numbers included in the observation group. If we wish to draw a conclusion about the entire student body at Ohio State University (54,000), it would be inadequate to sample just the students in the front row of one class.

When we use a *statistical syllogism* argument, we must be careful that the percentage is higher than 50 percent; the higher it is over that, the stronger the argument. If we find that 80 percent of the students in a class wear or carry watches, then we can justifiably conclude that the first person on the aisle in the second row has a watch.[8]

Notice that we do not include the statement of probability in the conclusion of inductive arguments any more than we include any statement of certainty in the conclusion of deductive arguments. If you have a tendency to forget what kind of argument you are using, it might be a good idea to include some kind of marker, but this is *not required* in either case.

Immediate inferences will be discussed when they become relevant. Some philosophers believe that "I think therefore I am" is a clear instance of such an inference.

---

[8]We typically are interested in positive conclusions. A percentage considerably under 50 allows a negative conclusion to be drawn. Suppose, for example, that a survey shows that 12 percent of people are left-handed. Using this as a first premise and using a second premise that tells us that Dan Quayle is a person, we can conclude that Dan Quayle is not left-handed. However, were we to use George Bush as our specific instance in that second premise, we would arrive at the false conclusion that George Bush is not left-handed.

> *Exercises: Arguments*
>
> 1. Separate the premises from the conclusions in each of the following valid deductive arguments, and then lay the arguments out as shown in the preceding section. Identify each argument.
>   a. If Madonna is a woman, then Madonna is a human being. So she is a human being since she is a woman.
>   b. Today is Wednesday, since yesterday was Tuesday, and if yesterday was Tuesday then today is Wednesday.
>   c. Since there is snow on the ground that is not melting, the temperature is below 0° Celsius.
>   d. It is true that if you can't put this argument into standard form, you do not fully understand how to do such things. But you do understand fully how to do such things, so you can put this argument into standard form.
> 2. Separate the premises from the conclusion in each of the following invalid deductive arguments, and then lay out the arguments as shown in the preceding section. Identify each argument.
>   a. If Jones is dead, then his heart is not beating. So, Jones is dead, because his heart is not beating.
>   b. If rain is falling and not freezing, then the temperature is above freezing. Since rain is not falling (and freezing), the temperature is not above freezing.
>   c. If Anna is a man, then Anna is mortal. Since Anna is not a man, she is not mortal.
> 3. For each of the invalid arguments in exercise 2, construct a counterexample of the same form that is a clear instance of an argument with true premises and a false conclusion.

THEORIES AND PHENOMENA
Theories

In the most general sense, *theories* are explanations of phenomena. Because there are many different kinds of phenomena, there are many different kinds of theories to explain them. The same event, for example, can fall under many different action types and thus have many different kinds of explanation. Suppose a student falls from a balcony as a result of another student's push. We can give a physical, psychological, teleological, legal, or moral explanation. No doubt many other kinds of explanation can be given as well.

The physical explanation would enable us to explain why the chair the student fell on broke, why it took only a few seconds for the descent, and other physical matters. We would provide the appropriate covering laws, and we would relate those laws to other laws if asked to do so. We might also give an explanation of the state of mind of the fellow student who threw him off the balcony. We might also give a psychological explanation. We might point out that this student had an extremely hostile attitude toward those who fall asleep in class, and that the student who was thrown off the balcony had indeed fallen asleep. This hostile attitude might in turn be explained by other psychological laws that apply to such behavior. A teleological explanation would be made in terms of an end achieved by the action—for example, the person was prevented from continuing to snore in class, or this was a dramatic lesson to others who might think of falling asleep in class. A legal explanation might consist of distinguishing murder from lesser grades of homicide. If we gave a moral explanation, we might say that the person who fell asleep was not morally guilty of anything that deserved the kind of punishment he received. We might add that the person who threw him off the balcony was not morally justified and, in fact, is morally blameworthy, for having done the action.

The preceding are all different kinds of explanations of an event that occurred. They are all apparently consistent, and they complement each other. If someone wanted the fullest possible explanation of an event, then all the explanations listed above, plus many others, would be required. Usually, of course, what we want is some particular kind of explanation, and the longer kind of multiple-theory explanation would not be the point of the request. If I ask the newspaper carrier why the paper did not arrive, I am not interested in the ancestors of the printers. So different types of explanations are appropriate depending on the problem at hand or the interests of those who want the explanation.

My view is that ethical theories offer an explanation of moral phenomena.[9] Ethical theories are best understood when we see them in operation. We shall examine several of these theories as well as see how they apply in subsequent chapters. For now, though, we can say that normative ethical theories are not teleological in that we are looking for an end set by some being, and they are not to be identified with some existing scientific theory, such as a sociological theory. Ethical theories attempt to explain sets of phenomena in a characteristic way you will become familiar with in the course of studying such views. A systematic way to begin our explanation is to explain what phenomena are and then give examples of the explanations ethical theories give of them.

[9]The explanation-of-phenomena approach is one way to explain ethics, but it is not the only way. One could claim to know by intuition, for example, which normative ethical theory is the best. A popular approach used today is choosing a theory or set of principles without the knowledge of how you might personally benefit. These other approaches will be discussed in the course of this book. Some of these other approaches are compatible with the explanation-of-phenomena approach, but some are not. That too will be noted when these other approaches are discussed.

Phenomena

One fairly neutral way of describing *phenomena* is as those elements accepted at the beginning of an inquiry or investigation. We are aware of phenomena and then try, via a theory or a group of theories, to explain what we are aware of. Phenomena are thus not unassailable beliefs or necessary truths; they may not even be truths at all.

Included among phenomena are purported facts and theories. If the theory that explains the purported fact is correct, then the fact is not only a purported fact, but it *is* a fact—a truth, if you want speak that way. If the germ theory of disease is correct, then it is a fact that measles is caused by the presence of certain microorganisms in the body. Before the virus that caused AIDS (HIV) was found, we used the germ theory to direct our search for the explanation of this disease. How do we know that this theory, or any theory, is correct? We'll take this issue up shortly also.

One phenomenon we may wish to explain is the seeming flatness of the earth that we observe when we climb to a high place and look out. One theory that explains this phenomenon is that the earth is flat, that it is shaped like a pancake. If this theory were correct, then it would be a fact that the earth is flat, and the earth would look the way it does from a high place because it is that way. However, another theory explains the same phenomenon—namely, that the earth, although actually spherical, looks flat both because it is very large in relation to the projections above its surface and because observers are relatively small. These two additional phenomena, which may of course be questioned, allow us to explain why the earth looks flat even though it is a sphere (with only slight irregularities).

The lesson to be learned here is that accepting something as a phenomenon is not the same thing as accepting it as a fact, for what we start with is not always what we are justified in holding at the end of an investigation. All theories begin with the phenomena in the area in which the inquiry occurs, so to say this is not to say anything exciting or revolutionary; and it is not to say anything specific about the nature of phenomena or facts either, for that would not be appropriate in a work of this nature. What phenomena are chosen at the beginning of an investigation might, of course, prejudice the investigation. A list of the important moral phenomena will be presented shortly. Although I do not believe that this list prejudices your choice of the best theory, you should be on guard.

Evaluating Theories

In order to evaluate theories, we need some tools of evaluation. The following are commonly used criteria for the acceptability of theories:

1. The theory explains the phenomena adequately and without use of *ad hoc devices*.

2. In comparison with rival theories, the theory is simpler, is more fruitfully related to theories in other areas, and does a better job of explaining the phenomena.
3. There are positive reasons in favor of the theory.
4. Serious objections can be adequately answered.

The criteria are stated in a general way for it is important that you recognize these criteria as those that everyone does, in fact, use in every area. If you think other criteria should be added, then chances are they would be welcome.

To understand the criteria better, let's consider an example. Suppose someone claims that the theory that best explains the phenomenon—apparent fact—that the room spins after a person turns thirty-three times on one heel is that turning thirty-three times on one's heel causes the room to spin. When we point out that the room is attached to the rest of the house, our friend claims that the whole house is caused to spin. Notice that this is not a consequence mentioned within the theory itself, nor is it a natural consequence of anything in the theory. It is just something that is added on when the original theory gets into trouble. Thus, it is called an *ad hoc addition*, something added on after the fact to explain this one case.

Our next step might be to point out that the house is attached to its foundation, which is attached to the lot, and so on. Finally, our friend might respond by saying that the whole universe spins as a result of a person's turning. This is one move that would keep the theory in contention with rivals, such as a theory concerning the fluid in the ear. Most of us are familiar with this view, a theory that does not require any ad hoc devices to explain the phenomenon of the room's turning. The seeming-room-spinning fact is only apparent in this view; it is not something that actually occurs. The assumption of the universe spinning, though, requires that parts of it move faster than the speed of light. This assumption is contrary to extremely well-supported theories in physics and would require us not only to reject large parts of physics but to posit as yet undiscovered physical forces. So, the world spinning theory does not fit in well with theories in other areas. For these and other reasons you no doubt can think of, the standard physiological explanation does a much better job in explaining the phenomenon of the room spinning than its universe spinning rival.

All of us can provide additional reasons to support the standard physiological theory, but we are hard-pressed to think of any reasons in favor of its rival. In addition, there seems to be no satisfactory way for the world spinning theory to respond to the serious objections raised. We can always construct answers, but these turn out to be ad hoc or create more problems than they solve.

The conclusion is that theories are to be rejected when they don't do as good a job as rivals, not that they don't do the job at all. Anyone can make a theory consistent with the phenomena; a simple way is to use ad hoc devices. In this way, one can "prove" anything. One can prove that Dan Quayle became vice president because he is Richard Nixon's illegitimate child. One could maintain with consistency that Karl Marx was really a secret capitalist while John Stuart Mill was a defender of paternalism. What one does when "proving" a theory in this minimal sense is just to get it on the playing field with other theories. In this instance, because the theories picked for the purpose of example are clearly bad ones, it is easy to see why they are properly rejected. The trick is to be able to distinguish the better of two theories when both are at least "pretty good." This kind of skill can only be obtained with practice, so you are urged to practice. In addition, the rest of this book will be concerned with the evaluation of rival theories in moral philosophy and related areas. You will have ample opportunity to follow evaluations, and you will be urged to join in on occasion.

Finally, we must understand that the criteria are stated generally, that the application in a specific area requires the expertise of practitioners in that area.

Exercises: Evaluating Reasons and Theories

1. Construct an absurd but consistent theory about the phenomenon of rain. Briefly compare it with the presently accepted theory.
2. Evaluate the following theory of motivation:

   > Human beings have two motives, to be comfortably warm and to have enough food. All other ends are sought only as a means to one or the other of these two goals.

   After you have criticized the theory, fix it up so that objections are "met"—even if you have to use ad hoc devices. After fixing up the theory, reevaluate it.
3. Suppose someone offers as a theory of motivation that the sole motive of humans is to consume petroleum products. A criticism is offered to the effect that recycling, fuel-efficient cars, and the increased use of passive solar heat is evidence against this theory. The counterresponse is that people know the supply of petroleum is limited, and that if we want to increase the consumption of petroleum overall we must decrease consumption now. In the meantime we will discover more petroleum and more people will be able to afford petroleum products.

   Evaluate the counterresponse.
4. Special Creation, or Scientific Creationism as it is also called, is the view that the species of plants and animals we now observe were all created at one time about ten thousand years ago. The

   (continued)

> *(continued)*
>
> earth and everything on it was created by a divine being in one short period of time. The fossils we find are the result of the flood at the time of Noah. The contrasting view maintains that the earth is about four billion years old. The present species evolved from other, now extinct, creatures of usually different species. This view, evolution by natural selection, is sometimes coupled with the view that a divine being created the universe and sometimes it is not. Thus, the issue of whether a divine being created the universe or the earth is not part of the disagreement between the two rival views.
>
> Evaluate these two competing theories. Be sure to say what the phenomena are that both theories are attempting to explain.

MORAL PHENOMENA

Because we say we are going to examine ethical theories, and because theories explain phenomena, we must have some phenomena before us to explain. Following is a list of some of the more important moral phenomena that ethical theories attempt to explain. After presenting the list and saying what it is and is not, I shall say something more about how the explaining is done and about the nature of ethical theories.

1. Some moral and value judgments (for example, "Eating animals is morally permitted," "Eating animals is morally forbidden," "Pleasure is good") are justified and some are not. (A complete list of such judgments can't be given; even a partial list would be too long for this work.)

2. Reasons support moral and value judgments. Reasons are given; some of them are taken to be effective, and some are not. When the reasons are thought to be effective, the judgment is held to be justified.

3. General statements, usually called *moral principles*, are used to support or justify moral and value judgments about specific actions or things. For short, we can call moral judgments about specific actions or things *singular moral or value judgments*.

4. There is moral disagreement. This kind of disagreement most often is between persons, but it can also be between groups of people, cultures, and nations. The disagreement is sometimes about moral or value principles, but sometimes it involves only singular moral or value judgments.

5. Circumstances and particular characteristics of people are relevant to the justification of singular moral and value judgments. No one can have an obligation to save a person drowning in the Pacific Ocean while residing in central Ohio. The mother of a child has an obligation to feed her infant but not the child of someone about whom she knows nothing and who lives in a city hundreds of miles away.
6. None of us is morally responsible for what is beyond our control or power to bring about or to prevent. This is one aspect of the "ought implies can" principle.
7. There is a close relation between the acceptance of moral judgments and what is often called *emotive force*. Human beings are not indifferent to moral judgments in the way many are indifferent to nonmoral judgments. It is common to be indifferent to "Mars has two moons," but not to "It is wrong for me to betray my friend."
8. People are inclined to act from what they accept as their obligation and feel guilty if they do not.
9. People are inclined to pursue what they suppose is valuable and be disappointed if they cannot secure it.

This is a partial list of the moral phenomena that any adequate ethical theory will address. It should be emphasized that the list is not complete, and the items on it are not undeniable truths. If you have other items to add, doing so is philosophically permitted. Many of you will think that one or more of the items are not facts, but only apparent facts. I claim only that this is a list of some items we can use for our starting place—the list that our competing normative ethical theories will attempt to explain.

Some have claimed that all the moral phenomena are linguistic or, at least, judgmental. In this view, not only would the list of moral phenomena contain "Jones judges that *x* is good," but it would contain only statements within quotation marks. However, I see no more reason to restrict the phenomena of ethical theories to the language of morals (what is in quotation marks) than to restrict the phenomena of physics to the language of physics (what is in quotation marks). The language of morals is as important as the language of physics; in each case, we are allowed to talk about the subject matter. On some occasions the subject matter is the language itself—perhaps more often in ethical theory than in physical theory—but this difference in quantity does not appear to justify a claim of a difference in quality.

Jones's saying, "This action is morally wrong" is a moral phenomenon, but it is difficult to understand why, outside some particular theory, people thought it was the only kind of phenomenon. One can understand, within the context of a particular theory of meaning, for example, why moral statements would be the only subject matter of ethics. However, the kind of theory of meaning that would support this (for example, meaning is what a term refers to) is no longer current. Until someone comes up with an argument with some weight, we shall suppose that moral phenomena include at least the kinds of things listed.

The phenomena, as the starting point of any investigation, are not described by incorrigible propositions by which any theory is tested. This is just the kind of position that the general account of phenomena is meant to rule out. Phenomena are not facts, and they are not accounts of the way things or perceptions appear to us; they are not sense data reports, or any other kind of very secure, or perhaps even certain, statements that some claim is the foundation of our knowledge. A phenomenal report is always corrigible. Theories about phenomena are always corrigible.

KNOWLEDGE, TRUTH, AND JUSTIFIED BELIEF
Knowledge

It is generally agreed that there are at least three conditions for knowledge. If person a knows h:

1. a accepts h.
2. h is true.
3. a has proper evidence for h.

Evidence (item 3 in the list) can be understood as the result of arguments or a theory that is better than its competitors. For example, we have evidence that the shortest distance between two points on the surface of the earth is part of a great circle. This is directly supported by the theory that the earth is a sphere, plus some knowledge of the properties of spheres. We hold, on most occasions, to a view that vision is a reliable means of gaining information and knowledge about the world. This kind of view is not usually thought of as a theory; but without any distortion, we can say that it is ("seeing is believing") and understand how this theory provides us with a great deal of evidence. We say the ball is red because we see it; its shape is circular because we are looking directly at it; and so on.

In addition to such theories as these, there are, of course, theories we are most inclined to think of when we use the term *theory*. Theories such as the germ theory of disease, the theory of atomic weights, the theory of evolution, and the gas laws are clear instances. Insofar as these kinds of theories are justified and we use them successfully in other areas of science and technology, they provide us with evidence for the claims we make. It is not an exaggeration to say that most of our schooling consists of coming to understand and apply various theories in different areas of human concern.

Straightforward deductive and inductive arguments also give us evidence. The previous discussion of these types of arguments will help you in understanding their nature. In addition, the use of many such arguments in the course of this book will help to make their use clearer.

Truth

Truth will be understood as involving a relation between whatever *h* is about and *h*. If *h* is "The earth is a sphere," then *h* is true when the earth is a sphere. To say this is not to present a theory of truth such as the correspondence theory or a pragmatic theory.

We can establish without difficulty that truth and acceptance are different. If truth and acceptance were the same, we would have no effective way of explaining many errors of acceptance. But, as a few examples will show, there is an effective way of explaining such errors. For example, Columbus accepted that he had reached India but he accepted what was false. Hegel thought there were exactly seven planets in the solar system, but he was mistaken. Everyone reading this has made mistakes that are explained by saying that you accepted something that was false.

It should be pointed out that on some matters it is always possible that we are mistaken. Some *h*'s are *necessary* truths (for example, 2 + 2 = 4, affirming the antecedent); some—the ones about which we can always be mistaken—are *contingent* truths (for example, the earth is a sphere, Columbus is the capital of Ohio). One way to distinguish the two kinds of *h*'s is to point out that the denial of a contingent truth is not a contradiction, whereas the denial of a necessary truth (or at least of most necessary truths) does result in a contradiction. It is always (logically) possible that a contingent truth is not true—even when it is true. If someone points out that we may be mistaken about a contingent *h*, this is only to say that it is a contingent *h*; it does not show that we do not know *h*. For one thing, the same possibility of being *correct* holds. Since the possibilities exist on both sides, the mere possibility can't show anything. An *h* can be known when it is true; it is not true because it is known.

None of us can "have" truth in the way in which we can have evidence. A person can show us evidence but not the truth of the matter. For a person to *know* an *h*, that *h* has to be true. The person does not have to *know* that the *h* is true; it need only *be* true.

Justified Assertion

Because people are bothered considerably by truth—and in order to say anything helpful we would have to enter into a metaphysical discussion about the nature of truth—we'll content ourselves with focusing on being justified in asserting an *h* when the first and the third conditions are fulfilled.

Unless someone can come up with some new meaning for the phrase, we shall assure that the expression "It is true for" is usually the same as acceptance. So, when we say that it was true for the person who jumped off the cliff wearing wings, that flapping would result in flying, it is the same as saying the person believed this would happen. But, alas, instead of flying there was a crash. Those who believe that cancer is cured by burning incense believe it, but they are mistaken. If you are tempted to say that it is true that cancer is thus cured or that flying takes place, then you ought to find where you disagree with the claims in the section entitled "Truth," on page 30. "Who," though, "is to say?" Those who have the proper evidence. Those who have the better theory. These claims can be made even though we could turn out to be mistaken.

One moral phenomenon related to "true for" concerns the people who have the courage of their moral convictions. The person who risks a job by standing up for the belief that it is wrong to discriminate on the basis of race or sex is morally praiseworthy. But we usually withhold this moral praise if we think the person's moral beliefs are mistaken. We know that David Duke is sincere in standing up for what he thinks is the correct position of the NAAWP (National Association for the Advancement of White People), but if we think that this kind of position is not correct then we don't think he is morally admirable. We can say, "It is true for David Duke that it is morally required to separate the races," but we can also disagree with this view. If we disagree, then we might even think that Duke is morally reprehensible.

DEFINITIONS

There are many theories of definition that can be adopted and used with success. The following way of treating definitions has been found to work well with the rest of the material presented and to make sense of a great deal of what philosophers and nonphilosophers have done with definitions. As far as can be determined, however, no relevant philosophical issues are decided merely by adopting this theory of definition. According to this view, there are two main kinds of definition: *stipulative* and *reportive*.

Stipulative Definitions

There are two kinds of stipulative definition: *strange* and *familiar*. A constructed term whose meaning is independent of existing use is a *strange term stipulation*. *Xerox* is a term made up from existing ancient Greek words, but did not occur in any existing language when it was adopted. I could make up a word—for example, *donk*—and stipulate that it is to mean "a very stubborn person." Since no disputes revolve around this term and its meaning, we might find it useful to adopt it. However, the claim that *bird* means "animal that flies" is objectionable because bats are not birds and ostriches are. A proposed change in a familiar term requires justification for we have no reason to reject an established meaning unless we have some justification for doing so. *Fish* previously meant, roughly, "animal that lives in the water." But as a result of a biological theory, we now find a new meaning superseding the old. This is reflected in the dictionary definition, "Any of various cold-blooded, completely aquatic vertebrates having gills, commonly fins, and typically an elongated body usually covered with scales."[10] The old meaning has become less frequent and will no doubt die out within a relatively short time. A new definition is replacing the old one—a definition based on a new taxonomical theory.

Sometimes both the old and the new meanings continue to fulfill the needs of language users. Since Newton, *force* has had at least two noncompeting uses that are usually distinguished by context. We accept Newton's definition of *force* because of his theory—his set of acceptable physics hypotheses. Sometimes nontheoretical arguments are presented for accepting a new definition of a familiar term; for example, the new definition is precise and the old one imprecise, or the new meaning will allow us to capture something correctly (for example, the notion of "emotive force") and yet allow us to describe a familiar phenomenon (moral action).

Reportive Definitions

There are two types of reportive definitions: *unmodified* and *modified*. *Unmodified usage reports*, as found in most dictionaries, are almost sheer reports of how a term is used in a given language. Some tidying up of such reports is necessary because usage varies according to person, place, and time. Thus, 'modified' and 'unmodified' are terms of degree and do not represent a hard and fast distinction. An unmodified report by itself cannot solve significant problems about the application of a term. For example, 'justice' is defined in the *American College Dictionary* as "1. the quality of being just. . . . ." If we wondered whether 'just' was correctly applied in a situation, or wanted to know the nature of justice, we would not be helped by such a definition. When a usage report is interpreted, the result is a *modified usage report*. F. C. Sharp gives a good example of this kind of modification.

> The subject matter of our studies is still the man on the street. It is what he means by 'right' that interests us. And the difficulty we face is that he cannot tell us. Ask him to define the term, and he will not even understand what you are driving at. The difficulty, however, is not one peculiar to the

---

[10] *The American College Dictionary*, ed. Clarence L. Barnhart (New York: Harper, 1951): 456. I checked to see if the definitions might have changed in the years but found exactly the same definition, word for word, in the unabridged edition of *The Random House Dictionary of the English Language*, ed. in chief Jess Stein (New York: Random House,1973): 536.

vocabulary of ethics. Since John Smith cannot tell you what he means by 'cause', 'probably', or 'now', he cannot give a really satisfactory answer to so apparently simple a question as "what is 'money'?"

When we had been told that this milk was very hot, this tool very heavy, this glass very easily broken, and that we had been very naughty, the meaning of 'very' dawned upon our minds, not in the sense that we could define it but that we could use it intelligently. It is in precisely this same way that we can discover what the layman means by the fundamental terms in the moral vocabulary. We watch his use of them. Thereupon, proceeding one step farther than the child, we generalize our observations and in doing so form a definition.

It is indeed a curious fact that men can go through life using words with a fair degree of definiteness and consistency with no formulated definition before the mind but it is a fact. "I cannot define 'poetry'," says A. E. Housman, in effect, "but I know it when I see it. In the same way a terrier cannot define a rat, but he knows one when he sees it."[11]

Sharp proposes a theory to explain what he finds in unmodified usage reports. The acceptability of his definitions is not a function of the unmodified reports alone, but also of the ability of the theory to account for and explain those reports. Explaining the reports is not the same thing as accepting the reports as facts or truths, for some claims of the unmodified reports are false. The claim that money is always tangible is an accurate report of what many if not most people say, but it is not true. In this instance, the best explanation of the phenomenon would reject this phenomenon as a fact.

Important definitions are supported by acceptable theories, though some of them begin with reports of usage and others do not. The origin of a theory and its corresponding definition is, of course, less important than its acceptability.

A LOOK BACK; A LOOK AHEAD

This first chapter has laid the foundation for an examination of the major theories of normative ethics. In this chapter the basic tools of the ethical strategist were presented, and you were given an overview of the area of normative ethics, as well as some help in discovering what your own tentative or initial position is. No one should feel irreversibly committed to any position, for the whole point now of reading the rest of this book is to compare all the theories to see which one seems to do the best job. You will have a difficult time in doing this if you have determined that you will stick by a theory for all time and as a consequence won't examine seriously the evidence in favor of the theories

---

[11]F. C. Sharp, *Good Will and Ill Will* (Chicago: University of Chicago Press, 1950): 156.

we will examine. The best advice is to suspend judgment about which theory is correct until you have at least carefully considered the main rivals. It may be that even after you have done that, you won't want to make up your mind. Your unwillingness would be understandable. However, at some time you *will* want to make up your mind. This book is designed to help you accomplish that.

There are some who disagree with me about the nature of moral philosophy, as well as disagreeing about which normative ethical theory is the best one. However, the framework provided appears to me, as well as to many who don't hold the same normative theory that I do, to be neutral with respect to what is the correct normative ethical theory. You can accept the framework and still consistently disagree with the normative ethical theory defended in this book. In short, no major metaethical or normative ethical questions are begged simply by accepting this way of setting up theories for discussion. For example, to agree that there are moral phenomena is not to say that they represent facts, and to say that there are moral rules is not to say what kind. These are the kinds of tasks to be performed in the rest of the book.

In Chapters 2 and 3 we shall consider the two main orders of teleological views: egoism and utilitarianism. In Chapter 2 we shall also examine theories that seek support in psychological theories. In Chapter 3 you will find a discussion of theories of justice. In Chapter 4 the survey of deontological theories will begin with the rule deontologists. The survey will be completed in Chapter 5 with an examination of nonrule theories such as virtue ethics views and the view I think is the best.

Chapters 2 through 5 cover theories of obligation, and the only mention of value is general, and neutral with respect to theories of value. In Chapter 6 theory of value is covered. This vast area can be covered in one chapter because we shall have prepared ourselves by the chapters on theories of obligation. The kinds of "moves"—that is, variations on theories, and the kinds of criticisms found in theories of obligation are found also in theory of value, and so we shall borrow freely from the earlier chapters.

In the last chapter we shall take a look at the main issues in the area of metaethics. The emphasis in terms of number of pages devoted to these issues is not as great as that given to normative ethics. However, those who want to find an acceptable theory for themselves in normative ethics will finally have to confront the issues of cognitivism–noncognitivism, definism–nondefinism, and such. Enough material is presented, though, so that the student of moral philosophy can see what the problems and main arguments are.

But we've gotten ahead of our story. One of the views most widely held in ethical theory circles is that the correct normative ethical theory is somehow based on the correct theory of human psychology. It is to this cluster of views, beginning with ethical egoism, that we turn next, in Chapter 2.

Exercises: Sharpening Your Critical Skills

1. Following you will find a theory of obligation and its supporting evidence. This is not a theory you or anyone else will be tempted to hold, for it is absurd almost on its face value. The purpose of the evaluation is to sharpen your critical skills so that when you evaluate theories you are inclined to take more seriously, you can do it more effectively. Please follow carefully the directions in the evaluation for they are designed to separate out different kinds of issues.

    Statement of the theory of *epistemism*:

    > There is only one rule of obligation, and it is the following direct moral rule: "If any action results in a net gain of knowledge, then that action is right."

    a. **Evaluation of reasons in favor:** Critically evaluate the two following proposed reasons in favor of the theory, but do not evaluate the theory directly yet.

    Reason 1: No action of a person can be said to be morally right or obligatory unless that person performs the action knowingly. The more one knows what one is doing, the better the chance of doing what is right or fulfilling one's obligations. This shows the relation between right and obligatory action on the one hand and knowledge on the other.

    Reason 2: Knowledge leads to control over misery and suffering and makes it likely that we shall be able to eliminate hunger. Since we know it would be right to eliminate such evil things, that is evidence that the gaining of knowledge is right.

    b. **Response to criticisms:** Following are two proposed criticisms of epistemism, each followed by a proposed response to the criticism on the part of a defender of epistemism. For now, address yourself not to the criticism itself (it may or may not be any good) but only to the quality of the *response* proposed by the defender of epistemism.

    Criticism 1: There are many instances of increasing knowledge that are apparently not right. The Nazis' human experiments are one kind of counterexample, and the knowledge of the total number of underpants owned by persons in the front row of a class is another.

    (continued)

(continued)

> *Response 1:* The Nazi experiments did increase knowledge, but they also inflicted pain. Since the amount of knowledge gained did not justify the pain and suffering inflicted, the action was not right. The knowledge concerning underwear, similarly, does not represent enough good of other kinds, such as the elimination of suffering, to justify the claim that the action is right.
>
> *Criticism 2:* There are kinds of actions that are apparently right and have nothing to do with increasing knowledge. The hero who throws himself on a grenade is apparently doing what is right, but there is no net increase of knowledge.
>
> *Response 2:* The person who is killed does not experience a net increase of knowledge, of course, but the people who are saved do. They now better appreciate life and how to preserve it. This is true of all instances of right action; the overall amount of knowledge is increased.
>
>   c. **Overall evaluation:** Now that you have evaluated the reasons in favor of and the quality of responses to criticisms, you can evaluate the theory overall. Look again at the criteria for theory evaluation in the section on theories and phenomena (pages 24–25), and apply each to epistemism.
> 2. Everyone is aware of arguments, judgments, and other kinds of moral opinions that are expressed. Describe what you take to be the most common normative ethical theory with which you disagree, state the reasons in its favor given by its proponents and the usual criticisms and responses, and then offer your own evaluation of the theory.
> 3. Describe a disagreement you have had with someone about a moral matter, either about some specific situation or some general judgment or principle. Were there any normative ethical theories involved in the dispute? What, in your opinion, was the key element in the dispute?
> 4. There are some topics about which there is likely to be moral disagreement. Find one of the following on which there is a fairly even split in your class, and have each side present its reasons. You might want each side to appoint a secretary to write the reasons decided on by the group, the criticisms of the other side's views, and perhaps even the responses of the group to the criticisms offered of its own position. The list is meant to be

(continued)

(continued)

   suggestive; everyone should be asked to supply additional suggested topics.
   a. Capital punishment
   b. Abortion (on demand before the end of the twelfth week of pregnancy)
   c. Hunting for sport
   d. Laws regulating the sale and possession of now illegal drugs such as marijuana, cocaine, heroin, and crack
   e. Mandatory HIV testing for health-care professionals
   f. Use of animals for experimentation
   g. Euthanasia
   h. Universal health care
5. Is the definition of 'stipulative definition' given on page 31 a reportive or a stipulative definition? (If you say it is a stipulative definition, indicate which kind and why you say what you do.)

RECOMMENDED READING

Feldman, Fred. *Introductory Ethics*. Englewood Cliffs, NJ: Prentice-Hall, 1978.

Frankena, William R. *Ethics*. 2d ed. Englewood Cliffs, NJ: Prentice-Hall, 1973. In Chapter 1, Frankena proposes a different view concerning the nature of normative ethical theories than the one presented here.

Gert, Bernard. *Morality: A New Justification of the Moral Rules*. 2d ed. New York: Oxford University Press, 1988. In this work Gert has a much simpler view of what normative ethical theories are about.

Salmon, Wesley C. *Logic*. 3d ed. Englewood Cliffs, NJ: Prentice-Hall, 1973. This book should supply you with any additional logic material and explanations you might need.

Warnock, G. J. *The Object of Morality*. London: Methuen, 1971. In Chapter 1 Warnock presents three different views of what ethics is, none of which appears to be the view taken in this book.

CHAPTER TWO

Psychologically Based Theories

Normative ethical theories are explanations of moral phenomena that consist, in part, of a device that generates justified singular moral judgments. The criterion of acceptability of such theories is whether they fit in with—and perhaps receive support from—good, established theories in other areas. Psychological theories that purport to tell us how humans think and feel have been a favorite of ethical theorists for more than 2500 years. Plato discusses such a theory in his *Gorgias,* though the most influential discussion of these theories is found in Thomas Hobbes's work.[1] Many contemporary authors have been influenced by the theories of the Swiss psychologist Jean Piaget.[2] In this chapter, we shall examine such theories, including the more recent ones of Lawrence Kohlberg and Carol Gilligan. We also look at the concepts and philosophical strategies we will need to use throughout the book to examine all ethical theories.

Psychological theories do not themselves contain components of ethical theories but are thought to support such theories. Whether this is so is what we need to determine. For each pair of theories we will ask three questions: (1) Is the psychological theory a good one *within psychology*? (2) Is the ethical theory actually supported by the psychological theory? (3) Is the ethical theory a good one? Clearly, if the answer to the first two questions is positive, we would have significant and strong evidence for a positive answer to the third question. To see these relationships more clearly, let PT = psychological theory

---

[1] See, for example, Thomas Hobbes, *Leviathan* (Oxford: Oxford University Press, 1984). Translated from the Latin by Howard Warrender.
[2] Jean Piaget, *The Moral Life of the Child* (London: Routledge & Kegan Paul, 1932).

and NET = the chosen normative ethical theory. The arguments we shall examine will have the following form:

If PT, then NET.
PT.

Therefore, NET.

The second premise is the assertion of the psychological theory. Philosophers are not the best judges of psychological theories, which, after all, are developed by psychologists. Accordingly, I shall defer to the expertise of psychologists insofar as any theory is presented within that discipline. The first premise is appropriately examined by philosophers because a connection is proposed between a psychological and an ethical theory. Is the claim of such a connection justified? The psychological theory may not be a good one, in which case the argument fails. The argument may also fail because there is no defensible connection between the psychological theory and the ethical theory. However, even if we show that the first and second premises are not justified, the NET may yet be the best one as compared with its rivals.

EGOISM

Egoism is often the first view people adopt when they consciously attempt to formulate an ethical theory. It is tempting to say that the right thing to do is what increases my own good, or that everyone really wants what is best for themselves. We hear such statements as "Look out for yourself or no one else will" and "I'm number one when it comes to doing good." Unfortunately, the view most persons want to adopt is much more difficult to state clearly than it appears at first for in reality this view is actually composed of two different kinds of theories: an ethical theory and a theory of motivation. These two theories may be related, as we shall see shortly, but they are certainly not the same. In order to evaluate egoism clearly, we must first distinguish egoism as a theory of motivation from egoism as an ethical theory. The former view is called *psychological egoism* and the latter, *ethical egoism.*

To see the difference between the two views, consider them as represented schematically:

Psychological Egoism
1. If any person *a* performs a voluntary action, then person *a*'s sole motive for performing that action is self-benefit.
2. Helping an elderly person across the street is a voluntary action performed by person *a*.

Therefore, 3. Person *a*'s sole motive in helping the elderly person across the street is self-benefit.

Ethical Egoism (one version)
1. If any person *a* performs an action that increases person *a*'s own good (benefit), then that action is right.
2. Eating proper foods is an action that increases person *a*'s own good (benefit).

Therefore, 3. Person *a*'s eating proper foods is a right action.

In the first set of statements, the claims are about motives; in the second, about actions being right. There is a common element—benefit, or good, is mentioned in both sets of statements—although it occurs in the consequent of the first statement representing psychological egoism and in the antecedent of the first statement representing ethical egoism. However, it is clear that in the statement of psychological egoism there is no term concerning such notions as *right, obligation,* or *duty.* In the statements representing ethical egoism there is no mention of motives at all, but there is a term in theory of obligation. In the first statement of psychological egoism there is a proposed connection between *benefit for me* and *motive for action,* whereas in the first statement of ethical egoism there is a proposed connection between *good* (benefit) *for me* and *right action.*

Since the second statements in each case are subsidiary, it will be simpler to refer to the first statements as the statement of the theory. The third statements are, of course, derived from the first two via the deductively valid argument of affirming the antecedent.

Most people who are inclined to be egoists adopt a certain strategy when the distinction between psychological and ethical egoism is pointed out. They suppose that indeed there are two different views but that the psychological view offers the evidence for the ethical theory. If we use PE to stand for psychological egoism and EE to stand for ethical egoism, we can see the relationship proposed in the following argument:

1. If PE, then EE.
2. PE.

Therefore, 3. EE.

The defense of ethical egoism in terms of this model requires that we establish the truth of two different kinds of statements. The second premise requires that we establish the truth of a psychological theory of motivation, and the first premise claims that there is a relation between that psychological theory and an ethical theory. If either of the premises should turn out to be unjustified, then the conclusion is not warranted in this argument. Of course, the conclusion may be warranted on other grounds; when we show that an argument fails, we do not thereby show that the conclusion of that argument is false. Because the preceding argument is valid (being an instance of affirming the antecedent), we must look into the truth of the premises. We shall begin with the second premise.

The order of business in this section is as follows:

- Psychological egoism defined
- Nonempirical psychological egoism
- Empirical psychological egoism
- Ethical egoism
- The connection between psychological and ethical egoism
- The most plausible versions of ethical egoism
- Ethical egoism evaluated
- A summary of egoism

PSYCHOLOGICAL EGOISM DEFINED

The first general statement of psychological egoism can be put informally so as to make it more intuitive. We shall return to the formal statement later for purposes of evaluation. Sometimes it is said that we are all selfish, or that selfishness is the basis of all our actions. This is one way of stating psychological egoism, although it is also misleading. Often we want to contrast desirable and undesirable character traits—virtues and vices—and we use the term 'selfish' to describe a vice. Those who wish to defend psychological egoism, however, use the term as descriptive of a fact of human nature, something that is true of all human beings. Thus, using the term 'selfish' as part of an explanation of psychological egoism is not a good idea.

Another statement of psychological egoism might help us to understand the view more easily: "The sole or overriding motive of human beings is to increase their own interests." This is equivalent to the first formulation, and, if it is clearer, you may want to work with it.

Some Phenomena for Theories of Motivation

In keeping with the methodology proposed in the first chapter, we must have some phenomena before us as we begin our investigation into a theory of motivation. The following short list is not intended to be complete; anyone reading this will want to add other phenomena. Additions are acceptable as long as they are not themselves theories of motivation.

1. Quite often we act for our own benefit.
2. Sometimes we act for the benefit of others.

3. Sometimes we act not for the benefit of any particular people but, for example, for the benefit of nonhuman animals, the environment, or to create beautiful things.
4. Often we are mistaken about our motives.
5. Sometimes we change our minds about what our motives were at a given time.
6. If there is a conflict between being able to benefit ourselves and being able to benefit others, we sometimes choose to benefit ourselves and sometimes we choose to benefit others.
7. The motives we have are influenced by what we take to be of value.
8. Sometimes people act contrary to what they believe is to their benefit.

Remember, to say that these are the phenomena of motivation is not in any way to say that they are truths or facts. The correct theory of motivation may actually be incompatible with many of these phenomena and, consequently, they would have to be rejected as facts and no longer even included in the phenomena. The phenomena are the starting place of our investigation, not the stopping place. However, as part of our evaluation of a theory, we must see what kind of a job it does in explaining the phenomena. When a given phenomenon is rejected by a theory, it must be rejected without the use of ad hoc devices or illegitimate assumptions.

Benefit or Good

The terms 'benefit' and 'good' were used in the formulation of egoism. 'Benefit' is used in a nontechnical sense and is probably clear as it stands. For this discussion, the term 'good' will not be specified any further—although it will be helpful to say something about how one would go about specifying it.[3] Many people think that the only thing that is good is pleasure, others think that power is the only good thing. More often, though, people are inclined to think that a variety of things are good—they suppose that pleasure is good, as well as power, freedom, love, friendship, and so on. Those who maintain that the sole or overriding motive of all voluntary action is to secure good for oneself (or to secure what is to one's own benefit) need not, in making this claim, commit themselves to any particular view about what, exactly, is good. At some point, they may want to take a stand on what is good, but they need not do so now. Because we cover good and value in Chapter 6, it would be premature and unwise to say much more about this topic now. However, if the nature of value is significant in terms of your stand on egoism, then perhaps you should skip ahead and read Chapter 6 first. In the following discussion,

---

[3]The full discussion of theories of value occurs in Chapter 6.

though, nothing will be assumed concerning the *nature* of good or other things that might benefit people. It will not be assumed that any given thing is or is not of value, nor will it be assumed that there is exactly one thing of value or that there are a variety of things of value.

Sole/Primary Motive

The theory of psychological egoism states that the sole or *primary* motive anyone has is self-benefit. If, however, the claim is made that only one of many competing motives is to benefit ourselves, then the view is not psychological egoism. This expanded view is quite compatible with views that suggest that self-benefit is unimportant and frequently overridden by other motives, such as doing good for others (without regard for our own benefit). Psychological egoism has to make a stronger claim than just that one among many motives is to benefit ourselves. For example, psychological egoism could claim that other motives either are not primary motives or are always overridden by the motive to benefit ourselves.

Someone could claim that we have a motive to help others but that it is not a primary motive. If we are on a bridge under which a drowning person floats and we could reach down and, without danger to ourselves, pull the person out, then we would do so. This is an example of a motive independent of self-benefit. However, should self-benefit come into conflict with any of these other motives, then it would always override the other motives. In a conflict situation, the motive that determines our action is the egoistic one. This can be called the *primary motive* version of psychological egoism, but it is not widely held. Furthermore, and much more seriously, it does not straightforwardly support ethical egoism. For this latter reason, we shall not interpret psychological egoism in this fashion.

There are some additional difficulties with this primary motive view. In almost every situation, even where nothing concrete is to be gained for ourselves, our reputation is at stake. It might happen that a woman saves a drowning child and before anyone can get her name, she slips away. However, if this did occur, there is reason to believe that a certain amount of good is lost to the rescuer. She loses an enhanced reputation, personal satisfaction, not unlikely financial reward, and so on. If the overriding motive is always self-benefit, then we would expect that the rescuer would stay for the reward. It is not clear, then, that there would ever be a situation in which the egoistic motive was absent.

It would seem, therefore, that it makes no practical difference whether we say that the sole motive is self-benefit or that the overriding or primary motive is always self-benefit. However, the sole motive version clearly supports ethical egoism—and that is the point of talking about psychological egoism.

Empirical Claim

Those who claim that psychological egoism is a correct theory of human motivation are committed to the view that it captures *the* law of human motivation. It is a law of nature that if anyone performs a voluntary action, then the motive is to bring about good for oneself. It is a law of nature in the same way any law in, say, physics is a law of nature.[4]

Psychological egoism is a claim about the constitution of human motives. When we are told that this is the nature of human motives, we are also being told that we will always observe humans acting in this manner (when we are properly instructed) and that other views about human action are not correct. It is unlike a claim about numbers or a claim about geometry. In those areas, we need not observe anything in the world to determine whether a theorem is correct; we need only consult the appropriate axiom system and see if the rules of inference allow the derivation. The kind of claim made is more like the claim that the earth is a sphere, that humans evolved from other species, or that $E = mc^2$. This means that evidence from observing human behavior can either confirm the view or disconfirm it. It is, clearly, a view that is falsifiable by the gathering of evidence.

In spite of the fact that psychological egoism is a falsifiable view, there are many who offer what appears to be a nonempirical defense. Usually such people are willing to admit that the view is falsifiable, and this enables the discussion to proceed, though reminders of the falsifiable nature of the view are sometimes needed. In contrast, though, there are those who claim that the view is not falsifiable, that it is not an empirical theory, and that it is true simply because of human nature or the nature of the concepts involved in motivation. This kind of view will be examined more closely shortly.

Voluntary Action

Nothing fancy or mysterious is meant by voluntary action. We are talking about those actions that, as we sometimes say, are willed by the person and not forced by external factors. A person who inadvertently steps off the edge of a cliff does not voluntarily perform the action of falling, nor does that

---

[4] Many laws of nature are stated statistically and not in a simple deterministic fashion. The Ideal Gas Laws are of this type, as are some genetic principles. However, psychological egoism would not make much sense if it consisted of the claim that we acted from self-benefit 75 percent of the time. If this is not the primary motive view just discussed, we would wonder about the motive the other 25 percent of the time when we perform voluntary actions. Is it concern for others? That, though, would allow a choice of our motives or it would be "pure chance," something over which we have no control. If we have a choice of our motives, then psychological egoism as stated is not correct. If we have no control, we have a mystery about our motives that psychological egoism is to correct.

person even perform the action of stepping off the edge voluntarily. The two actions are nonvoluntary since the person did not act knowingly even if not forced into either action. Suppose, to continue, that electrodes are placed in your brain at certain strategic places, an electric current is run through causing certain muscles in your body to relax, and the result is that your bladder empties. Since this would be embarrassing at a party, it would be something that you would try mightily to prevent. However, if you failed to prevent it, then you would have performed an involuntary action. The "spring of action" would have come not from you but from whichever of your enemies was pushing the buttons—the action was willed by your controller and not by you.

The kinds of actions that we will, that are not performed as a result of someone else's willing or without any willing at all, are the *voluntary actions*. Some of you may wonder whether there are really any such things as voluntary actions on the grounds that there are causes that result in our acting independently of anything we will. Others of you will be tempted to say that our own will is determined by events and factors beyond our own control, and so there are really no voluntary actions after all. These are legitimate concerns. For now, though, let us not raise these problems and instead stay with psychological and ethical egoism.

Summary of Psychological Egoism

Psychological egoism is a psychological theory of motivation that is neutral with respect to which things will benefit us and which things are of value. It claims that egoistic considerations are the sole or overriding motive for all voluntary action, and that as an empirical view purporting to have discovered the law of motivation, it is falsifiable. In exception to this view, some people claim that psychological egoism is a correct theory of motivation and, in support, they provide nonempirical evidence.

NONEMPIRICAL PSYCHOLOGICAL EGOISM

The statement of both nonempirical and empirical psychological egoism is the same regardless of one's grounds for holding the view, but for each the evidence in its favor and the willingness to consider counterevidence are different. In what follows, a sampling of the arguments and the counterarguments of psychological egoism as a nonempirical view will be presented.

Willing and Wanting

Often we hear the claim that in voluntary action we always do what we want to, and so we always act to increase our own good. If we didn't want to do something, then we wouldn't do it, it is claimed, and so we did it to satisfy the want. When we do something to satisfy a want, then we are doing something for our own good. Thus, it is concluded, psychological egoism is established.

This argument is stated in a loose and informal way, but that is the only way the argument can have any plausibility at all. To see this, let us draw some distinctions that are not very controversial but that will help us to state the argument more precisely.

Some actions we do because we will to do them (our voluntary actions) and some actions we do independently of any willing. Examples were given of such actions, but consider a few more. I write the word 'will' because I will to do it, but my eyes just blinked independently of any act of will on my part. So there are voluntary actions that we will and actions we don't will that are not voluntary. In addition to this distinction, there is also the distinction between those actions that follow our *inclinations* and those that do not. Many of you awaken early, jump out of bed, and set about your tasks immediately, but many of you do not. You drag yourself out of bed with great effort when, apparently, your inclination is to sleep a bit longer. This is a common experience for human beings: Often we act contrary to our inclination to do something.

In the informal statement of the argument, the claim that we always do what we want is ambiguous. It might mean any of the following:

1. We always will our voluntary actions.
2. We always will to do what we are inclined to do.
3. We always will to do what we calculate will benefit us in the long run.

If the argument, however it goes, is based on claim 2, it should not be accepted. Claim 2 is obviously not true: Very often we will to do something we are not inclined to do—something that is perhaps contrary to our inclination to act. At the moment this is being written, I am inclined to go for a walk in the bright sunshine of a summer morning before it gets too warm. However, I remain seated at my Macintosh making the world safe for correct psychological theories. Many of you, as you read what I took such pains to write, are inclined to go to the movies, to drink beer, to read a novel, or to go to sleep; but if you have read this far, you have not acted on these inclinations. Our acting according to what we will rather than what we are inclined to do is a phenomenon that any theory of motivation, including theories not based on empirical evidence, must take into account and explain. Failure to explain this phenomenon adequately is evidence against the theory or against that part of it which makes the claim.

Some of you will, at this point, be inclined to say that perhaps claim 2 is really true, even though it does not seem to be true. There is always a possibility when we make claims about the world that such claims are not true, but such possibilities do not prove anything. There is the same possibility, just considering mere possibility, that claim 2 is false as there is that it is true. There is some actual evidence, though, that claim 2 is false. If you state that claim 2 is true, you must present some actual evidence that it is. It will do no good, by the way, to suggest that it is possible that the evidence showing that claim 2 is not true is not actually evidence at all. Although this possibility is cheerfully admitted, as long as there is an equal possibility that the evidence *is* actually evidence, this possibility shows nothing.[5]

Someone might claim, although I don't know how such a claim would be made good, that if psychological egoism (PE) is correct, then claim 2 can be shown to be true; that is, the truth of claim 2 follows from the truth of psychological egoism (PE → claim 2). Let us suppose for a moment that this is so. If it is so, then it requires that we establish the correctness of psychological egoism on some grounds other than claim 2. You cannot use claim 2 as an essential part of the evidence for psychological egoism and then defend claim 2 by using psychological egoism. If claim 2 is the evidence required to establish psychological egoism, then you don't yet have available that psychological theory to defend the claim when it is attacked. If you could establish the correctness of psychological egoism independently of claim 2, then, of course, you could use the theory to establish and defend claim 2. But if you could do that, then you wouldn't need claim 2 to establish psychological egoism.

There were three interpretations of "We always do what we want," the second of which has been considered. So now let us consider the first: "We always will our voluntary actions." There are two closely related problems with this statement as support for psychological egoism. First, it appears to have no content. And second, it appears to be neutral with respect to theories of motivation. When the notion of *voluntary action* was introduced, it was explained in part via the notion of *willing*.[6] In brief, voluntary actions are those actions that we will to do. If we substitute into claim 1 the analysis of voluntary action, then we have the following statement:

---

[5] Because the attempt to use possibilities is made so often, perhaps a more formal presentation is in order. The possibilities are true of observable events in the world, so they can be called *empirical possibilities*. When it is said it is possible that some empirical claim, p, is true, it is usually meant either that it is not a logical contradiction or logically impossible that p is true, or that it is not contrary to any known empirical law or truth. It is logically possible that unsupported objects near the surface of the earth will not fall, but it is contrary to what we have reason to believe is true in physics. We could say it is logically possible but physically impossible.

The claim in the preceding paragraph seems clearly to be a claim of logical possibility. Both an empirical claim and its denial (contradictory) are logically possible. We cannot show one of them to be true or false by pointing out that it is logically possible. To claim that one of them is physically impossible is, at this point, to beg the question of what is true in the area of psychology, for that is what we are in the midst of trying to determine.

[6] Voluntary action could have been explained without using the notion of *willing*. We could have used the (ambiguous) term 'want' to express the notion of an action that is within our power. If this had been done, the ambiguity of claim 1 and claim 2 would still be present, but of course it would be phrased in different language.

1′. We always will those actions that we will.

Claim 1′ is a statement that no one would quarrel with, for it says nothing about *what* we will, and it says nothing about whether, in fact, we will at all. In short, it doesn't say anything that appears to have any content. If it doesn't have any content, then it cannot be used to defend or support psychological egoism—a specific theory of motivation. Claim 1′ does not disallow the possibility that we will some actions that are contrary to our own interests. If we will them, then they are voluntary actions not motivated by self-benefit. And if this is the case, we have shown that psychological egoism is not correct.

Once again the temptation will be to say that there are no voluntary actions in which we will anything other than what we suppose is to our own benefit. This is, however, simply another way of stating psychological egoism. If one could establish this claim independently of claim 1 and, as we have to, independently of claim 1′, then we would be entitled to make that claim. However, again, this cannot be done if claim 1 is the basis for establishing psychological egoism. Similar considerations apply to any suggestions about the possibility of being mistaken.

Suppose we interpret the statement that we always do what we want as:

3. We always will to do what we calculate will benefit us in the long run.

Can this interpretation support psychological egoism? By itself, as it stands, it is compatible with the denial of psychological egoism, for it may be that we will to do that which will benefit us in the long run and we also will what will benefit others in the long run. The problem arises as to what happens if there is a conflict between the benefit to ourselves and the benefit to others. The psychological egoist must maintain that if there is a conflict, then we always will what is to our own benefit.

In evaluating claim 3, we can point out, first, that there is apparently no such calculation done by human beings. When we act to rescue someone who is drowning, we seem to think about the person and not about what the long-run effects might be. We don't calculate the chances of there being a hidden camera taking the whole rescue down for posterity or the likelihood of the person being saved rewarding us. Here again I can speak from my own experience. On two occasions I have rescued drowning people and on each occasion the lack of forethought was (or at least appeared to be) later on astonishingly evident. The same kind of experience is reported by most war heroes—they simply do not, as far as they can tell, think of the consequences of their action on them at all.

If the psychological egoist wishes to claim that all of us, on almost every occasion, do calculate in this way, then some positive evidence that this occurs must be presented. It is always possible, when we are speaking of motivation, to be mistaken. But this fact by itself does not support the claim of the psychological egoist any more than it supports the claim of someone who wants to deny that particular theory of motivation. So there is reason to suppose that claim 3 is false, and as yet no reason to suppose it is true. Furthermore, some supporters of psychological egoism use claim 3 as another way of stating the theory of psychological egoism. Of course, if we could establish that psychological egoism is correct, then we could establish that it is correct in that statement of it also. This is, though, precisely the task the egoist has to perform—namely, to present evidence that psychological egoism is indeed correct.

The conclusion of this discussion of the three interpretations of "We always do what we want" is that one nonempirical argument fails to establish psychological egoism as a correct theory, and so provides no evidence at all for its correctness. We are not entitled to conclude that psychological egoism is not correct, for we do not establish that a theory is mistaken, or even worse than another, simply by discrediting one proposed bit of evidence in its favor. We have to look at more evidence, and we also have to examine its competitors in the area of nonempirically based theories. The next argument to be considered does introduce a competitor for the first time.

Opposing Views: Psychological Altruism

Some people defend psychological egoism by attacking another view. The other view, which we shall call *psychological altruism* is seen by such people to be the polar opposite of psychological egoism.

Psychological Altruism
1. If any person *a* performs a voluntary action, then person *a*'s sole motive for performing that action is to benefit others.
2. Scratching his head when it itches is a voluntary action performed by person *a*.

Therefore, 3. Person *a*'s sole motive in scratching his head when it itches is to benefit others.

This statement of psychological altruism in (1) should be compared with the one for psychological egoism on page 40. In both cases, an example in the second statement was chosen that results in a conclusion that goes contrary to the phenomenon. In each case, though, the defender of the theory in question should be able to explain why such cases are not an embarrassment. The psychological altruist can say that the person who scratches the itch relieves a discomfort all right, but that is only the beginning of the story. If the itch is not scratched, then the discomfort would grow worse, the person would be unpleasant to others, and he would not do his job as well. All this would clearly reduce the amount of good that could be done for others. What this shows, so the psychological altruist claims, is that the action was done for the purpose of securing the good of others.

Most of you reading this "defense" of psychological altruism won't know whether to be amused or outraged, for the defense simply consists of making the theory consistent with the phenomenon, which can be done for any self-consistent theory. However, this is a "defense" of the same quality one often finds for psychological egoism. We are told that the reason the elderly person is helped across the street or, to take a real case, I turn off the headlights of a parked car is that guilt would otherwise follow. Those who feel guilt suffer. Therefore, the action is done in order to avoid the suffering—that is, to benefit self. In both cases the explanation is imaginative but seems not to be supported by any independent external evidence. The temptation to use the psychological theory you are defending to provide the evidence for that defense must, of course, be overcome. The theory itself cannot be used to rescue evidence used to establish the theory as correct, nor can it be used to "defeat" counterevidence by asserting its own correctness and then stating that if it is indeed true, the counterevidence would not really be counterevidence. We'll return to this point again shortly.

Psychological altruism is not an acceptable theory of motivation. If we refer to the criteria for the acceptability of theories, we find that there are few reasons in its favor. It can be admitted that some, perhaps many, actions we perform are apparently performed to increase the good of others. The phenomenon of actions performed for the benefit of others must be explained by any adequate theory of motivation; and psychological altruism, by virtue of its explanation of this phenomenon, merits some support. However, at least as many actions appear to be done not for the benefit of others but for our own benefit.

One of the criteria of acceptability is how well the theory can respond to criticisms. As just pointed out, one obvious criticism of psychological altruism is that there are numerous counterexamples. When I am alone in my room and feel thirsty, the fact that I drink some water does not suggest that the benefit of others was in any way in my mind. This counterexample constitutes a denial of psychological altruism, as can be seen in the following formulation:

> not-1. Drinking a glass of water when thirsty is a voluntary action of person *a*, and the sole motive in performing it is not to increase the good of others (instead the motive seems primarily or solely to increase person *a*'s own good).

This is a counterexample to the statement of psychological altruism. It is called a *counterexample* because it is an example or instance of an action that falls under the theory but goes counter to it. If someone claims that any object when unsupported and near the surface of the earth falls, we can show a counterexample to this view if we can present one such subject that does not fall. Such counterexamples are evidence against a theory—and, except in those situations in which the theory is still the best one around, one counterexample is usually enough to reject the theory.

The defender of psychological altruism can, as we have seen, make the theory consistent with the phenomena represented by the counterexamples. However, this is done only by employing ad hoc devices. Is there any reason to think that the person did think primarily or solely of others when she scratched her head or drank the water? There doesn't seem to be any, except the desire to make those instances of the phenomena consistent with the theory. Only after such examples are presented are mechanisms such as unconscious desires or motives brought in. If the psychological altruist claims that people have unconscious motives primarily or solely to benefit others, is there any reason (independent of trying to save the theory) for accepting such a claim? The answer seems to be no.

Therefore, psychological altruism does not seem to have good reasons for acceptance. In fact, there are good reasons for rejecting psychological altruism; the theory doesn't seem to be able to respond adequately to those criticisms without employing ad hoc devices. We, and the psychological egoist, are apparently justified in rejecting psychological altruism as an acceptable theory of motivation. Does this rejection, though, justify the conclusion that psychological egoism is correct or even a better theory than psychological altruism? The answer to both parts of this question seems also to be no; but let us look at each part separately.

It is a general truth of logic that if a proposition is false, then its negation is true. This is clear of propositions that simply have a negation in front of them. "Today is Monday," has "It is not true that today is Monday" as its negation. From knowing that it is false that today is Monday, we can conclude it is not true that today is Monday. But from this same knowledge we cannot conclude that today is Wednesday or Saturday. The key, then, is to select the correct statement as the negation. For example, the negation of the claim "If anything is human, then it is immortal" ("All humans are immortal") is "Some humans (for example, Socrates) are not immortal." The negation is *not* "If anything is human, then it is mortal" ("All humans are mortal"). The negation of the claim "If anything is a swan, then it is white" is "Some swans are not white" and not "If anything is a swan, then it is not white." Given that there are swans, it cannot be true that if anything is a swan, then it is white and also be true that if anything is a swan, then it is not white. However, from the falsity of one you cannot conclude the truth of the other—since, as is the case here, both statements can be false. There are some white swans; and there are some swans, in Australia, that are black.

Psychological egoism and psychological altruism stand in relation to one another as do the first and third statements about swans. Both cannot be true and, further, both can be false. Such statements, called *contraries*, do not contain an inference of truth to one statement from the falsity of the other. The following presentation may make this clearer:

Original statement
The flag is red.

Contradictory
The flag is not red.

Contrary
The flag is blue.

Or, consider this example: (Original Statement) Socrates is a dog; (Contradictory) Socrates is not a dog; (Contrary) Socrates is human.

Thus, even if we were to establish, as we apparently have, that psychological altruism is not correct, we cannot then infer the correctness of psychological egoism. It may very well be that both theories are incorrect.[7] For this latter reason, we cannot even conclude that psychological egoism is a better theory than psychological altruism, for they may be equally bad in relation to a third and better theory. This is what is argued in the following section.

Opposing Views: Psychological Realism

The results of our discussion of psychological altruism should lead us to consider yet other theories. As was the case with the claims about swans, the truth, in terms of a theory of motivation, may lie somewhere in between the two theories we have considered thus far. It is true that some swans are white and some are not white but instead black. The corresponding theory with respect to motivation would be that some of our voluntary actions aim to benefit ourselves and some to benefit others. In addition, there may be motives that have nothing to do with benefiting ourselves or other persons at all. For example, we may be motivated to save certain animal species, to improve the wilderness, to love God, or to seek the truth—these are all as much phenomena as any that concern benefiting ourselves or others. Because it allows for these other motivations, this third theory seems to do better than either egoism or altruism. However, this third theory, because it covers greater motivational possibilities, does not permit the simple explanations of the other theories. But since we are not considering these views as scientific theories but rather as kinds of commonsense views that we formulate without doing formal empirical research, this is not much of a criticism.

We need a name for this third theory, so let's call it *psychological realism*. This view, to repeat, does not pretend to do the job that psychologists want

---

[7]To see the structure of the fallacy more clearly, let PE = psychological egoism, PA = psychological altruism. The claim, "If not-PA, then PE," is not justified since not-PE may also be true. This is what is argued in this section: that both PA and PE are incorrect.

a theory of motivation to do. For the purpose of our discussion, though, this shortcoming is not so bad, for both psychological egoism and psychological altruism are equally weak—neither allows predictions, fruitful connections with other areas of science, and so on. All three of the theories are grossly deficient as scientific theories. Thus, the fact that one of them is deficient from an empirical point of view is not sufficient reason to reject it and to accept one of the others.

Because we now have three theories to consider, we can make some comparisons that we could not make before. It has been argued that psychological altruism can be supported as well as psychological egoism. This is not to say that psychological altruism can be adequately supported, but rather that, however you assess the strength of psychological altruism, you should make the same assessment of psychological egoism. All the moves that the psychological egoists have open to them in defending their theory are open to the psychological altruists also. If the moves are effective in one case, they must be judged effective in the other. If, conversely, the moves are deficient in one area, then they must be judged equally deficient in the other. This symmetry of effectiveness suggests a scale of acceptability, as well as the place of both psychological altruism and egoism on it. Since psychological altruism is clearly close to the bottom of any scale, and psychological egoism is to be put in the same place (wherever that is), then it too is to be placed close to the bottom. If we suppose that the scale is from 0 to 100, then we might indicate the placement of the theories considered so far as follows (PE stands for psychological egoism; PA, for psychological altruism; and PR, for psychological realism):

```
0   10   20   30   40   50   60   70   80   90   100
|PE
|PA                                |PR
```

This argument can be put briefly as follows:

1. If two theories are equally placed on a scale of acceptability, and one of them is very low on that scale, then the other one is low on the scale of acceptability.
2. PE and PA are equally placed on a scale of acceptability, and PA is very low on that scale.

Therefore, 3. PE is very low on the scale of acceptability.

The End Reached as Motive

Often one hears a defender of psychological egoism assert that whenever we do something such as turning off someone else's car lights in a parking lot, we gain satisfaction from it. Gaining this satisfaction, they claim, is the motive for performing the action. As usually presented, the evidence to support the claim that it was the satisfaction and not the benefit to the other person that motivated us is that we did indeed receive some satisfaction from our action. There are several points worth making about this set of claims.

First, it is not obvious that one always does gain satisfaction. In my own case, it seems false that when I turned off the car lights I gained any satisfaction. Being as honest as I can, and reflecting as coolly as I can, I cannot say that I experienced any short-run or long-run phenomenon that can correctly be called satisfaction. This is not to say that introspection is the best method of determining one's motives, for I and others have been wrong in the past about motives introspected. It is to say, however, that someone who claims to know what my motives are in a given case, or generally, must come up with some reason to support that claim. By this time it should be clear that psychological egoism, the very theory to be supported by the argument we are now considering, cannot be used to support the claim that my motive was to secure my own satisfaction. The theory has not yet been established. In fact, we are considering this evidence precisely because we are attempting to establish this theory. Furthermore, if the theory had already been established, we wouldn't need the argument we are now considering.

Second, even if we suppose it to be true that every time someone performs a voluntary action they receive satisfaction, this would not, by itself, establish that the motive in performing the action was to achieve that satisfaction. That action leads to many other states for me and for others—it leads to a prevention of the unhappiness of the person whose lights were on; it leads me to be about a half a minute later arriving at my office than usual; it leads me to present the example to classes and then to write it down here; and so on. In addition, every action leads indirectly to death. What justifies the selection of only one of these ends as *the* end that motivated me to perform the action? If the only justification for that claim is psychological egoism, then the theory cannot be supported by the argument since the argument requires the theory to support it.

Finally, every action leads to a large number of consequences for the performer of the action as well as for the people and things upon whom and for which the action is performed. If the argument is any good, it establishes that we are motivated to do whatever results from the action—whether we had that consequence in mind or not. This argument would allow us to conclude that expending energy is the motive for performing the action, that pushing knobs is the motive for performing the action, and so on. If one is justified in claiming that satisfaction is the motive, then one is equally justified in claiming that shutting a car door is the motive. But, of course, one is actually not justified in making the silly claim that shutting a car door is the motive.

Often, when this kind of counterargument is presented, the defender of psychological egoism claims that our motive (to achieve satisfaction) is unconscious, and that if we did not get satisfaction from this action, then we would not perform it. However, whether the motives are unconscious or not, there is still no more reason to think we are motivated primarily to achieve self-satisfaction than primarily to achieve satisfaction for others. This is just the kind of claim that establishing psychological egoism as a correct theory would support. So it is difficult to see how the claim can be used to support the theory. Also, there are other motives alleged to move me to action—namely, the good of the other person. If this is rejected as a motive, then some reason must be given for the rejection. The reason for the rejection could be that psychological egoism is the best theory of motivation, but this has not yet been established. In fact, this is precisely the task at hand for the psychological egoist—the one as yet to be completed in a satisfactory way.

Summary of Nonempirical Psychological Egoism

It has been shown in this section that if we use either nonempirical or not formally empirical methods (such as scientists use), we do not seem to be able to establish psychological egoism as a correct theory of motivation. It does not compare favorably with at least one other such theory of motivation—the theory here called psychological realism. There are, in addition to the arguments and counterarguments presented here, a large number of other arguments you may want to examine.[8] Enough has been done here, however, to show you the way such arguments move, and to prepare you to evaluate the next argument of this type that you encounter. Let us now turn to the empirical evidence for psychological egoism to see if the theory fares any better.

Exercises: Sharpening Your Critical Skills

1. Present counterexamples to the following false claims:
   a. If anything is a human, then that thing is male.
   b. All women are mothers.
   c. If anything lives in the ocean and has a backbone, then it is a fish.
   d. If a proposition p is possibly true, then p is true.
   e. Whatever a person does immediately after deciding what to do is the explanation of that person's motive in acting.

(continued)

---

[8] See the Recommended Reading section at the end of this chapter.

> *(continued)*
>
> 2. Offer criticisms of the following arguments. What mistake is being made?
>   a. Since the light was not green, it was red.
>   b. This must be a triangle, since it is not a square.
>   c. If students are not to be excluded from the University Senate, they must hold a majority of seats in that body.
> 3. There is no way to exhaust all the arguments presented in favor of any view, especially a view that is as difficult to pin down as psychological egoism. Present an argument different from any presented here in support of the nonscientific version of psychological egoism, and critically evaluate it. (If you think it is a good argument, please send a copy of it to me so I can consider it in a later edition.)
> 4. What is wrong with the following claim: "Psychological egoism is correct, but not as stated. What is correct is that most of the time people are psychological egoists"?

EMPIRICAL PSYCHOLOGICAL EGOISM

Remember that we are in the process of examining the evidence in support of psychological egoism. We are, as you recall, doing that because some people maintain that psychological egoism supports an ethical theory—namely, ethical egoism. They argue (with PE standing for psychological egoism and EE for ethical egoism) that

If PE, then EE.
PE.

Therefore, EE.

We have examined the nonempirical evidence for psychological egoism and found that it offered no substantial support for that psychological theory of motivation. Now we shall consider the kind of evidence the psychologists use in their work by presenting a brief survey of the scientific evidence for and against this theory of motivation.

Psychologists and others in the social and behavioral sciences are frequently disturbed by what they take to be the intrusion of philosophers into an area in which they have no expertise. Everyone should rest assured that this author intends to do no more than report what psychologists have done. I do this not because psychologists are better at this kind of investigation than anyone else (although this is likely to be true), but because they are the ones who have, in fact, done the research.

A survey of the literature reveals a preponderance of experimental evidence in support of the claim that there are altruistic motives; that is, in the terms introduced so far, there are motives for action in addition to increasing one's own benefit. One of these motives, as indicated by the studies examined, is to increase the benefit of others. Since this is not a psychology book, this section will be brief; you should examine the literature identified in the list of recommended readings at the end of the chapter for further information.

Justin Aronfreed is a good person to begin with because he develops clear distinctions between psychological and ethical egoism and also sets up understandable experiments. "When we say that an act displays altruism, we assert that the choice of the act, in preference to an alternative act, is at least partly determined by the actor's expectation of consequences which will benefit another person rather than himself."[9] However, Aronfreed also agrees that this fact, if it is one, is compatible with the act having some beneficial consequence for the actor. That is, he is not committed to the view that we earlier called psychological altruism. Aronfreed also specifies that there is a need for reinforcement of altruistic behavior. This requirement is the same as for any other kind of learned behavior, but it does not warrant the conclusion that the action is performed solely for the sake of the reinforcement. If you are inclined to think the sole motivation is the reinforcement, then you should look again at the section on nonempirical psychological egoism for a discussion of this kind of argument.

Aronfreed describes many experiments, but a fairly lengthy explanation of one should be sufficient. In this experiment, a group of 125 girls was divided into three groups: one had 57 girls, one had 37 girls, and one had 31 girls. The girls in the largest group

> were exposed repeatedly to a very close temporal association between the agent's expressive cues of pleasure and their own direct experience of the agent's physical affection. Whenever the agent's choice between the levers activated the red light, the agent smiled while staring at the light, and at the same time uttered one of four exclamations in a pleased and excited voice. All of the exclamations were roughly equivalent to *"There's the light!"* The agent then hugged the girl as if expressing a pleasurable reaction to the light. In the group of 57 there were hugs, in the 37 only the expression of pleasure and in 31 no response to the light.[10]

---

[9]Justin Aronfreed, *Conduct and Conscience* (New York: Academic Press, 1968), 138.
[10]Ibid., 144.

Next, each girl was given a choice of pulling a lever that would produce candy for herself or the red light for the agent.

> The [child] is . . . in a situation where her empathetic and altruistic dispositions could be tested by her repeated choices between an act that produced candy for herself and an act that produced only observably pleasurable consequences for another person. . . . The majority of the children who had been exposed to the basic social conditioning paradigm actually chose to produce the light for the agent more frequently than they chose to produce candy for themselves; whereas children from both of the control groups typically chose the candy-producing lever more frequently.[11]

Aronfreed stresses the importance of empathy as a requirement for altruistic behavior. If the girls did not see the agent as having the kind of experience they had when they were pleased, then it is likely they would not have chosen to bring about what they thought pleased the agent. We are able to empathize readily with other people, and perhaps even with many types of animals. It is, however, difficult to empathize with mosquitoes and amoebas.

The experiment seems clear. It indicates, says Aronfreed, that children sometimes act from altruistic motives. If this is true, then they don't always act from the motive of self-benefit. The girls could have always chosen candy for themselves, but on many occasions they did not. This voluntary action is incompatible with the claim that the only motive in voluntary action is self-benefit. As you will find from an examination of the literature in the Recommended Reading section as well as from our continuing discussion, this incompatibility is found not just in this one experiment, but in many experiments of the same type. These results indicate that psychological egoism, taken as a scientific theory of motivation, does not fare very well; the experimental evidence shows that the theory is not acceptable.

However, psychological egoists, whether of the empirical or nonempirical variety, do not accept this evidence as sufficient. They say that the reward for each girl was the agent's pleasure, that the alternative of getting the candy for herself would have produced less benefit (in the form of pleasure) than the action of activating the red light. This kind of response should be quite familiar, for it is just the move made earlier in the nonempirical discussion. On the one hand, it is certainly possible that the girls acted solely or primarily because they received pleasure from the fact that the agent received pleasure. On the other hand, it is possible they did not, but instead acted to secure the benefit of the agent. In terms of possibilities alone, the two views are the same. However, in terms of what we observe in the experiment, there is at least some reason to suppose that the first possibility is not supported by the evidence.

---

[11]Ibid., 145. It should be noted that even without the reinforcement a large number of the girls aimed at benefiting another a significant number of times. If psychological egoism were correct this would not happen.

Moreover, the usual way of supporting the first possibility is to use psychological egoism as evidence. However, once again, psychological egoism is the view in question, so we cannot assume its correctness in the middle of the argument. Finally, those who work in the field give an interpretation of the results of the experiments that appears to be inconsistent with psychological egoism. This fact alone does not guarantee that the experimenters are correct, for it would not be the first time that experimenters badly interpreted the results of their own experiments. The burden of proof, however, lies with those who make the claim that the experimenters are mistaken. Until such time that the experimenters are proven wrong, we would be justified in maintaining that they are correct and that altruistic motives do indeed exist.

In *Altruism and Helping Behavior*,[12] seventeen contributors discuss a variety of studies, from controlled laboratory experiments to the observation of people acting in noncontrolled environments. On the whole, these authors find that altruistic behavior, in the sense discussed here, does exist. Some of the authors allow the possibility of entirely egoistic explanations of the same phenomena, but they suggest that such explanations are implausible. Many of the authors find that a variety of motives direct altruistic actions. In a study on kidney donors, for example, the authors, Carl Fellner and John Marshall, suggest that the donors were motivated by

> (a) their belief in the "good" they were doing for the recipient, saving a life, (b) their positive relationship with their physician, both actual and symbolic, (c) the positive emotional reinforcement from the recipient and family, and (d) the considerable attention paid to them by friends, acquaintances, news media, etc.[13]

The first motive (a) is most clearly identifiable as altruistic—and, if any is egoistic, the last (d) is the most likely candidate. Psychological egoists contend that all the motives are actually egoistic, even though they may not appear to be so at the time. However, once again, it is up to the psychological egoist to establish the truth of that claim. The burden of proof lies with the challenger.

Scientists working in this area sometimes take notice of the kinds of moves mentioned here, but more often they do not. Sometimes, though, the language used by psychologists seems to be more applicable to the kinds of claims made here. Consider the following as an example:

> A wealth of recent laboratory experiments on altruistic behavior clearly indicates that, under certain circumstances, people will help others who are in need, despite the absence of an externally administered reward for the

---

[12] J. Macaulay and L. Berkowitz, eds., *Altruism and Helping Behavior* (New York: Academic Press, 1970).
[13] Ibid., 280. Carl H. Fellner, John R. Marshall, "Kidney Donors."

altruistic person. We now find that people will actually learn an instrumental conditioned response, the sole reward for which is to deliver another human being from suffering.[14]

These authors are clearly saying that there are some solely altruistic actions, the motives involved apparently having to do only with rewards for other people. In case anyone doubts that these authors had philosophical positions in mind, the following passage should dispel any questions:

> Classical political philosophers, such as Hobbes, Locke, Rousseau, and Comte, as well as their modern descendants, have found it essential to address themselves to the problems of selfishness and altruism in human nature. Ample psychological evidence is available to indicate that man is neither wholly selfish nor wholly altruistic in his behavior. It has not previously been demonstrated, however, that the roots of altruistic behavior are so deep that people not only help others, but find it rewarding as well. . . . Our research demonstrates that instrumental behavior can be learned and maintained solely through the rewarding function of altruism.[15]

A search of the literature in 1991 revealed the same kind of consensus among psychologists that altruistic motives do exist. A few citations should suffice.

In an article looking for sex-linked differences in altruistic behavior, hypothetical and actual situations were examined by Rosemary S. L. Mills, Jan Pedersen, and Joan Grusec.[16] Concerning the hypothetical stories they concluded:

> An altruistic choice was made 75% [of the time] by both women and men, with the distribution uniform across the three stories. . . . There was no difference between women and men in the distribution of other and self choices for any of the stories. . . . [17]

Sometimes psychologists do evaluate egoistic explanations of altruistic behavior. One such study explains altruism as an attempt to prevent sadness to oneself. The abstract of a paper tells us what is at stake.

> This experiment investigated altruistic vs. egoistic interpretations of the effect of empathetic concern on helping. The empathy-altruism hypothesis posits that empathic concern arouses an altruistic motivation to relieve the distress

---

[14]R. F. Weiss, W. Buchanan, L. Alsstatt, and J. P. Lombardo, "Altruism Is Rewarding," *Science* 171 (March 26, 1991): 1262.

[15]Ibid., 1263. The authors will be relieved to hear that very few philosophers follow any of the cited authors in their theory of motivation.

[16]Rosemary S. L. Mills, Jan Pedersen, and Joan Grusec, "Sex Differences in Reasoning and Emotion About Altruism," *Sex Roles* 20, nos. 11/12 (1989): 603–621.

[17]Ibid., 615, 616.

of another person; the negative state relief interpretation proposes that the effect of empathic concern is mediated by sadness, which produces an egoistic motivation to reduce one's own unpleasant state. Male ($n = 96$) and female ($n = 96$) Ss first listened with an imagined or observed set to another person's problem and then were given an opportunity to help that person with the same problem or with a different problem. Consistent with the empathy-altruism hypothesis, imagine-set Ss helped more often than did observe-set Ss for the same problem but not for a different one. In addition, only empathic concern associated with the specific problem related to helping. Although sadness was related to helping, it did not account for the effect of empathic concern.[18]

The details of the study need not concern us, but interested readers might examine this and other empirical studies to assure themselves that I have presented this issue accurately and as it is examined by psychologists. In an extraordinarily cautious statement, the authors of this last study tell us:

> The findings of the present study, we believe, add substantial weight to Batson's position that altruistic motivation may exist under some conditions and that all motivation for helping is not necessarily egoistic.[19]

In less cautious language, the authors are saying their experiment supports the claim that altruistic motives do exist. This is inconsistent with psychological egoism's claim that all motives are egoistic.

Once again, psychological experiments and statements should not be expected to clear away empirical psychological egoism. Egoism's defenders will claim that the motive in performing the action is the reward or the pleasure received from seeing another person benefit, or to prevent a bad state such as sadness. If egoism's defenders are in the empirical realm, let us see their studies. If they are engaged in nonempirical theorizing, let us see their response to this preceding critique.

Summary of Empirical Psychological Egoism

The material presented here is only a small part of the available empirical evidence showing that psychological egoism is not an adequate empirical theory of motivation. For more detail, you may want to follow up on some of the references cited. This section, though, allows us to conclude that empirical

---

[18] John F. Dovido, Judith L. Allen, and David A. Schroeder, "Specificity of Empathy-Induced Helping: Evidence for Altruistic Motivation," *Journal of Personality and Social Psychology* 59, no. 2 (February 1990): 249.

[19] Ibid., 259.

evidence does not support psychological egoism. Furthermore, given that many psychologists agree that motives vary, what we have called psychological realism seems to be the most supportable theory. The nonempirical case for psychological egoism is discredited; and now, so is the empirical case.

Exercises: Theories of Motivation

1. Choose some recent general work in psychology and read the entries under motivation in the index or table of contents. Does what is said address itself to the issue of psychological egoism? What is the position taken?

2. In the discussions of psychological egoism and altruism, nothing was said about motivation toward bad consequences for oneself or others. If we suppose bad consequences to be the polar opposite of good consequences, or benefit, then we can construct two additional principles of motivation:

   Psychological masochism: If any person *a* performs a voluntary action, then person *a*'s motive for performing that action is self-harm.

   Psychological maltruism: If any person *a* performs a voluntary action, then person *a*'s motive for performing that action is to harm others.

   If we consider each of these two principles as representing a theory of motivation, we can evaluate them in the same way that we did PE, PA, and psychological realism. Present such an evaluation. Can all of these theories be equally good/bad?

3. Argue either in favor of or against the following claim: "Psychological masochism and psychological maltruism each explain some phenomena. Those phenomena are not explained by psychological realism, and thus we have to adopt another theory of motivation or else fix up psychological realism." In part, this exercise requires that you address the issue of whether human beings are sometimes motivated to do harm to themselves or to others.

4. Evaluate the truth of, and indicate the place of, the following proposed principle: "If something reinforces action, then that something is a motive of action." Is the principle acceptable? If it were acceptable, would it support psychological egoism more strongly than psychological altruism? Does it support psychological maltruism?

ETHICAL EGOISM

Since the examination of psychological egoism is now complete, it is time to see if there is any relation between it and ethical egoism. Egoists usually claim that psychological egoism supports ethical egoism, and, accordingly, the psychological view is presented first to provide the required support for the ethical theory. However, the ways in which the psychological theory support the ethical theory are not clear, partly because of the multiplicity of views that have gone under the title of "ethical egoism." The first task is thus to state clearly what ethical egoism is, so we may then consider any relation of support between it and psychological egoism. This consideration is worthwhile for two reasons, even though the last section concluded that psychological egoism does not fare well as a theory of motivation. First, further evidence might very well change our views about psychological egoism. Second, when we see what kind of relation there is between the two kinds of egoism, we might not want to offer psychological egoism as a support for ethical egoism.

To remind the reader, ethical egoism is schematically represented as follows:

1. If any person a performs an action that increases person a's own good (benefit), then that action is right.
2. This particular action increases person a's own good.

Therefore, 3. This particular action is right.

This representation, however, is not sufficiently general either to capture all the versions of ethical egoism or to represent a complete theory of obligation. A theory of obligation covers not just actions that are right, but also actions that are obligatory (duties), actions we have a right to do, actions that are morally better than others, actions that are morally worse than others, and so on. These different predicates represent different kinds of judgments about actions, and, as such, they are some of the phenomena a theory of obligation will attempt to explain. So, to indicate that as broad a range of phenomena as possible should be explained by our ethical theory, we can say that we need to have a more complete ethical theory. If we let MO represent any term in our theory of obligation, including 'right' and 'obligatory', we can generate the following more general statement:

1. If any person a performs an action that increases person a's own good (benefit), then that action is MO.
2. This particular action (whatever it is) increases person a's own good (benefit).

Therefore, 3. This particular action of person a (whatever it is) is MO.

In keeping with the function of a theory of obligation, this general statement of the theory of ethical egoism allows us to arrive at justified singular moral judgments (instances of statement 3). This is the main function of a normative theory of obligation, and a theory should be judged in terms of how well it performs this function.[20] Let us now explain some of the crucial terms in this general statement.

"Increases"

The statement establishes a distinction between an action that does, in fact, increase a person's own good and one that only seems to increase that person's own good. It may seem to someone that it will be beneficial to take a shortcut across a field on the way home. However, if the person sinks into a quicksand pit, then it's obvious that the person made a mistake. We don't want to saddle anyone with the view that it is obligatory to do what merely appears to be of self-interest. If this were the case, it would be obligatory for the person to take the shortcut—to take the turn that leads into the quicksand—or, in the case of a student, to write in "none of the above" on a true/false exam, even when none of these actions is actually in the interest of the person—and even when they are contrary to the person's interests. This is certainly one way to interpret ethical egoism—but since it results in such a weak position, we will not interpret it that way here.

There is another reason to avoid interpreting the statement as claiming that what appears to be in your interest determines, say, obligations. The usual way of interpreting ethical egoism is as a *teleological normative ethical theory*—that is, as a theory that restricts the information in the antecedent of the first statement to consequences of actions. Specifically, for egoism, this means the

---

[20]The most general scheme for an ethical theory is

If any x is F, then that x is M.

This x is F.

Therefore, this x is M.

The F is replaced with whatever the theory suggests as the appropriate nonmoral predicate, and the M is replaced with what is claimed to be the appropriate moral or value predicate. The actions of persons are referred to by x; the characteristics of those actions that increase the good of the people performing them are referred to by F; and some term of obligation, such as 'right' or 'obligatory', by M. The logical terms 'if' and 'then' are never replaced. For those who demand a more symbol-laden general scheme, the following is offered:

$(x)(Fx \rightarrow Mx)$.

Fa.

∴ Ma.

The first line here captures the first statement of the general scheme.

consequences of an action insofar as they affect me. The problem with talking about what seems to be a consequence of an action is that a seeming consequence is often not an actual consequence, and, moreover, no *seeming* consequence of an action is a consequence of that action at all.[21]

A consequence of an action is something that occurs as a result of that action. For example, one usual consequence of drinking water, under normal circumstances, is that the water quenches your thirst. This occurs whether it seems to you beforehand that it will or not. The consequence is independent of what seems to you to be a consequence. What seems to you to be a consequence is not regularly related to an event in any causal way and can occur independently of any cause of that event. A seeming consequence is something that is true of the person to whom it seems to be a consequence. If, in contrast, a consequence is true of the world, then we have good evidence that a seeming consequence (of an action) is not any kind of consequence (of the action) at all. If it is not, then we do not want to classify as a teleological theory an ethical theory that concerns only seeming consequences.

However, we do not want to say that the increase in benefit is properly limited only to what actually does occur independently of what the agent knows and has evidence for. Many actions have consequences a person does not know about and could not reasonably be expected to know about. Suppose, for example, you are walking along a beach and pass over a fortune in Spanish gold buried long ago by a pirate. If you had dug a hole at that place and recovered the gold, this would no doubt have been to your advantage since, under most circumstances, the discovery would have benefited you greatly. However, we would not be justified in claiming that you failed to fulfill your obligations by passing by without digging because there is no reasonable way that you could have known the gold was there. There are many actions that could be beneficial to you but that are not obligatory. The same kinds of examples could be generated for other moral predicates in theory of obligation. For example, suppose you step on a fly that, if it had lived, would have fatally bitten you. There is no obvious sense in which you have performed a morally right action.

It seems, therefore, that if we are to be fair to the egoist, we must find some position between the seeming interests and the real interests of a person. One good candidate for such a middle ground is *the set of actions likely to lead to beneficial consequences for you, given what you know*. Each of us is in possession of a certain amount of knowledge, and each of us has to act on what we know at that moment. (Keep in mind that you may want to restrict our knowledge to those items we are justified in accepting at a given time, given the evidence on hand. Nothing fancy is meant by 'knowledge'.) The egoist's claim, for example, is that obligatory actions are those actions likely to benefit the person,

---

[21] What seems so to me is something true of my "psyche." Nothing in the world need be affected by what seems to me to be so. If a child thinks that wishing his parents dead caused their deaths, this does not justify the claim that it was the wishing that caused the fatal car crash.

given the knowledge available to that person. So the general statement's reference to 'increasing the benefit' will be understood in this manner, and not as referring either to what the person merely believes will increase his interest or to what in fact will increase his interests.

'Good' or 'Benefit'

Once again, the terms 'good' and 'benefit' will not be further specified. What is to your benefit may be restricted to power, or it may include pleasure as well as power, or only pleasure, or these plus freedom, and so on. You may, for the time, plug in whatever you suppose is of value or whatever you suppose does benefit you. Later on, in Chapter 6, we shall examine theories of value and draw some specific conclusions about what is good.

MO

In the consequent of the general statement of ethical egoism, MO is only a partially specified term, since it refers to some predicate or other in the area of theory of obligation. A number of terms can replace MO and mean quite different things. To claim that one *has* a right to express whatever opinions one wishes is far different from saying that *it is* right to express whatever opinions one wishes. You no doubt have the right to claim that milk tastes best when chocolate syrup is added, but you are not ordinarily doing something morally right when you express this opinion. You have the right to drink milk with scotch whiskey and chocolate syrup, but this does not turn the action into one that is right. Each person has the right to get up at night to get a drink of water, but this is not usually an action that is right. In general, different roles are played by different predicates of moral obligation. Because different roles are played by these two predicates that share the letters in 'right', it would prevent confusion if we used *permitted* for 'right to'. 'Permitted' is an alternative way to express this notion, as in "We are permitted to adopt children." Accordingly, henceforth 'permitted' will be used in place of 'right to', and 'right' will be used to talk about actions that are positively evaluated.

Even though different roles are played, significant relationships among such predicates are not precluded. There have been many attempts to define all the moral predicates of obligation via one that is taken as a *primitive*. This attempt at finding basic or primitive predicates is a common phenomenon in all areas. Of course, such definitional theories or taxonomies must be seen as attempts to provide a simpler theory of the relation of moral predicates to one another and should be evaluated accordingly.

Our purposes now will be served by noting two things: First, some predicates cannot serve as the primitive for defining all others, and, second, insofar as an ethical theory cannot allow for the use of a predicate or predicates, that theory is deficient—especially if there are other theories that can account for the applications of those predicates. One predicate that apparently cannot be used to define all the other predicates is 'right to'. However, there is a way of defining this predicate in terms of 'obligation' that enables us better to understand both predicates (=df means "is defined as").

> Person *a* is permitted to do action B.   =df   Person *a* has no obligation not to do action B.[22]

Supposing, for the moment, that we understand roughly what we mean when we talk about obligations, then this definition does help. To say that person *a* has a right to or is permitted to take a drink of water in the middle of the night is equivalent to claiming that he or she has no obligation not to take such a drink. If I am not permitted to cut off the head of the person in front of me at a movie so that I can see better, then I have an obligation not to do so. If you are permitted not to attend a Prohibition Party lecture, then you don't have an obligation to do so. If a mother is not permitted not to buy food for her children, then she has an obligation to buy the food for them. These four examples expand the definition and exhaust the possible combinations. More abstractly, the combinations are as follows:

permitted	=df	no obligation not to
not permitted to	=df	obligation not to
permitted not to	=df	no obligation to
no permission not to	=df	obligation to

This is one way to show that 'obligation' and 'permission' can be interdefined. In terms of generating the other, it would not matter which of the notions we took to be the primitive. However, neither of these notions can be used to define the notion of *right action*. A simple proof of this consists of presenting some right actions that are neither obligatory to do nor obligatory not to do. Consider the class of actions that are, as we say informally, over and above the call of duty (or obligation). (In more formal language, such actions are called *supererogatory*.) The soldier who throws himself on a grenade in order to save the others sharing his foxhole is doing something that has positive moral

---

[22] A number of different moral notions go under the heading of *rights*. If the claim is that a person has a right to scratch his or her head, this is one sense of the term, the one we shall concentrate on in this section. However, when we claim a right to free speech, this is not the same sense of 'right to'. Here we mean that if anyone prevents us from speaking, he or she is doing what is wrong; in the other use of 'right to', interference is sometimes acceptable and sometimes not. I have a right to win the race, but all my competitors have a right to win the race also. The competitors are not violating obligations or being immoral if they win.

Moral rights that require others to act or to forbear are, in a sense, stronger than the ones that do not. The former involve *right action* or *obligation*. It will be assumed that those alternative terms can be used in place of 'right to', and this procedure will be used to prevent confusion.

worth. It is an action that is apparently right, but it is not apparently obligatory. If the soldier scrambled out of the foxhole instead of throwing himself on the grenade, this would not justify a claim that he had failed to fulfill an obligation, for he does not have an obligation to sacrifice himself for his soldier colleagues. The person who travels a half hour to return a book you dropped has no obligation to do this, but is doing what is right. These examples show that the following definition is mistaken because it does not adequately take into account important phenomena:

Person a's action X is right = df Person a has an obligation to do X.

This proposed definition is not acceptable because supererogatory actions do exist. When you stop to help someone who has a flat tire, open a door for someone whose arms are full, go out with someone who is lonely, or turn off someone's car lights, your actions are right—but they are not, apparently, obligatory. The name may be fancy, but actions of this sort are familiar to us all.

Some people think there is another kind of counterexample that consists of obligatory actions that are not right. Suppose you agree to meet someone at the Empty Wallet restaurant at 8 P.M., and you're there on time. Here, it might be claimed, is fulfillment of low-level obligation and yet the action doesn't have enough positive value for it to be called morally right. Your fulfillment of what we might call your ordinary obligations is no reason (as yet) for calling such actions right. It may be that if you fail to meet your obligations, you are doing what is wrong; but it does not follow from this that if you do meet your obligations you are doing what is right. This can be captured, again more formally, as follows:

1. If person a is obliged to do X, then not doing X is wrong.
2. It is not true that if person a does X and X is obligatory, then person a's doing X is right.

These examples are included here to show that there is no way to derive the rightness of an action from its being obligatory, even if it is true that not to act in this instance would be wrong.[23]

If this line of reasoning is correct, then there is a whole area in theory of obligation that cannot be explained or accounted for by use of the notions of *permission* and *obligation*. Thus, as we shall argue later with respect to ethical

---

[23] One cannot define *right action* via the negation of *wrong action*. A proposed, but incorrect, definition of that sort would be the following:

Person a's action B is right = df Person a's action B is not wrong.

There are, of course, numerous counterexamples to this. It is not wrong to tie your left shoelace before your right, but it is usually not morally right to do so. It is not wrong to put ketchup on pea pods and beef served with brown rice, but it is not morally right either. It is not wrong to take a deep breath of clean air when you walk in the woods, but it is not morally right to do so. There are, as everyone can easily see, many more examples of this sort.

egoism and its basis in psychological egoism, if a theory can account for only part of the phenomena, it is to that extent deficient. Furthermore, if another theory can account for these additional phenomena, then the first theory is seen to be yet more deficient and most likely unacceptable.

Summary of Ethical Egoism

There are a variety of notions in theory of obligation; some of these notions can be taken as basic and others can then be defined in terms of them. Some notions, though, cannot be used to define all the rest. One that cannot is *permission*, and another is *obligation*. It will be argued that the only version of ethical egoism that can be supported by psychological egoism is one that replaces MO with *permission*. This will show, in turn, that insofar as you hold ethical egoism because of psychological egoism, your ethical theory will be deficient. It is not an endorsement of psychological egoism to argue that it can support ethical egoism; it is only to say that *if* psychological egoism is correct, then one version of ethical egoism is correct.

Exercises: Definitions of Moral Notions

1. This section suggested that the consequences of actions be specified as the likely consequences, given what a person knows. Contrast this view with the specification of consequences as "the consequences person *a* calculates will occur, given what person *a* knows."
2. Show what is wrong with the following proposed definitions of moral terms:
   a. wrong action $=df$ a nonobligatory action
   b. obligatory action $=df$ action we have a right to do
   c. right action $=df$ action that is not wrong *and* that we are permitted to do
3. Explain what 'wrong' means in the first line of exercise 2.

THE CONNECTION BETWEEN PSYCHOLOGICAL AND ETHICAL EGOISM

The usual strategy for the egoist is to attempt to establish psychological egoism and then to show that the psychological theory supports the ethical theory. In the most general form, this strategy is represented as:

If PE, then EE.
PE.

Therefore, EE.

So far, the second premise has been examined and the conclusion is that psychological egoism is found wanting as a psychological theory of motivation. The first premise, the purported connection between the psychological and ethical theory, is what we shall now examine.

It was earlier shown that psychological egoism purports to have discovered the law of human motivation. Such a law would be a law of nature and, insofar as it is, any conclusions we can draw about other laws of nature apply to it. For example, it is often said that if someone is an unsupported body near the surface of the earth, he or she *must* fall, or it is *impossible* for them not to fall. Terms such as 'must', 'possible', 'impossible', 'can', 'may', and the like are *modals*. The sense of the modal and the justification for its use in such statements is almost always, if not always, dependent upon the corresponding law. In fact, the significance of the modal seems to be exhausted by referring to the appropriate law. When we say that a person must fall, we do not in such contexts suggest the person has a moral obligation to fall or that it would be prudent to fall. If a person's grip on a tree limb slips, resulting in a fall, there is nothing the person can do either to stop the falling or to alter it in any significant way. It may be strange to use modals in connection with laws that describe the way the world is, but it is a common enough practice and does no harm as long as we continue to understand that natural laws *describe* the world and do not prescribe how it *ought* to be.

It has been argued that psychological egoism is not a correct theory. But if psychological egoism is correct, then people can no more refrain from acting in what they perceive to be their own interests than an unsupported body can refrain from falling.[24] This suggests the following argument in support of the "permission" version of ethical egoism.

Argument A
1. If psychological egoism is correct, then no one can ever do anything except act in a self-interested way.
2. Psychological egoism is correct.[25]

Therefore, 3. No one can ever do anything except act in a self-interested way.

---

[24]You must supply the fuller context for the falling example. You are an unsupported body near the surface of the earth; so you aren't in orbit, you're not resting on a helium-filled balloon, and so on.

[25]Contrary to what has apparently been established.

Argument B

4. If (3) (No one can ever do anything except act in a self-interested way), then no one has an obligation to act in a non–self-interested way.

5. (3). (No one can ever do anything except act in a self-interested way.)

Therefore, 6. No one has an obligation to act in a non–self-interested way.

Argument C

7. If (6) (No one has an obligation to act in a non–self-interested way), then each of us is permitted to do what is in our own interest.

8. (6). (No one has an obligation to act in a non–self-interested way.)

Therefore, 9. Each of us is permitted to do what is in our own interest.

This series of arguments may look imposing at first, but it is actually only three separate affirming-the-antecedent arguments. In each of the arguments after the first, the second premise—the one that affirms the antecedent—is the conclusion of the argument preceding it. (The numbers in parentheses indicate where the statement is located in the earlier argument so you can find your way more easily.) The challenge, though, is not to present a *valid* argument but to present a *sound* argument, an argument that has true premises as well as being valid. You will be able to work through the preceding series of arguments and convince yourself of its validity in a relatively short time, but the truth of the premises requires more careful attention.

The first premise, (1), claims that if the proposed law presented by the psychological egoist is an actual law of nature, then, just as is true of any law of nature, things that fall under it *must* act in the way described. In this instance, people must act in their own interests.[26] That is, they can do nothing except act in their own interests. Premise (2), however, should not be taken as an affirmation of psychological egoism, but rather as an illustration that, based on the *assumption* that psychological egoism is correct, one can establish one version of ethical egoism. The value of this is great, even though the argument can be only a hypothetical one based on the (mistaken) assumption that psychological egoism is correct.

In argument B the first premise, (4), uses the conclusion of argument A as the antecedent and, for the first time, introduces a term of obligation into the consequent. The justification for this premise is part of the "ought implies can" principle. Very simply put, if you are obliged to do something, then you must be able to refrain from doing it. Some examples will help. If someone claims that you are obliged to be a champion swimmer, you can show that

---

[26]Remember, though, that this sense of 'interest' is not what might, in fact, turn out to be a person's interests, which are the interests of the person given the knowledge the person has.

you are not so obliged by presenting evidence indicating that you have limited endurance—perhaps even a heart condition. More clearly, you can show you have no obligation to save a drowning person by establishing that you can't swim. You cannot be obliged to love your neighbor as you love yourself if human nature does not allow this. The complementary principle involves essentially the same considerations. If you cannot stop your hair from growing, then you have no obligation to stop it. Suppose the floor gives way and you fall from the balcony of a theater. You notice that you will land on a small child if you continue to fall, but obviously you can do nothing about it. No one can accuse you of failing to meet your obligations when you do indeed land on the child, for you could do nothing other than fall in just that way.

The second premise of argument B is the conclusion of argument A. Its justification is that it is the conclusion of a valid deductive argument, even though, because of the second premise of argument A, that argument is not sound.

The third argument, argument C, contains the definitional connections between the notions of *obligation* and *permission* noted on page 68. The second premise of that argument is the conclusion of argument B.

The three arguments together constitute an argument showing how one can move from psychological egoism to ethical egoism, even if the ethical view is an incomplete one. And this is the main problem such a defense of ethical egoism has—namely, it results in a theory of obligation that leaves out all phenomena having to do with right and wrong actions. If this point has become obscured, then you should review the section titled "MO" on page 67.

Another criticism of this stance is that there are no positive obligations in the resulting theory. To get a positive obligation from a permission to do something, you would need to establish that no one has a permission not to do something (see the definitions in the section titled "MO" on page 68). Do you have an obligation to feed your child? Such an obligation could be established only if we could show that you have no permission not to do so. However, we can't establish this obligation by showing that you can't do anything other than feed your child. Attempting to establish the obligation in this way would show only that you have permission to feed the child, not that you have no permission not to do so. Because the only thing one can show, given the strategy of using psychological egoism to support ethical egoism, is that one has permission to do something, then the whole area of phenomena involving positive obligations is left unexplained.

One can say, of course, that such phenomena as right and wrong actions, supererogatory actions (those above and beyond the call of duty), and positive obligations are all illusory. This may be so, but if it is, then one needs some positive evidence to support the claim. The need for positive evidence becomes very pressing indeed when there are other competing theories that can account for the phenomena and do themselves have some reasons in their favor. The desire for this kind of superiority has led egoists to adopt a broader version of ethical egoism—in fact, many different versions of ethical egoism have been suggested. Now that we have looked at how one version of ethical egoism may be supported by psychological egoism, we shall examine some other versions of ethical egoism independently of any support they might derive from psychological egoism.

THE MOST PLAUSIBLE VERSIONS OF ETHICAL EGOISM

A large number of views could go under the title of "ethical egoism," but we need examine only the most plausible versions, the ones people have been most inclined to hold. We hope the plausible versions and ones most commonly held are the same, but if a view is not examined here that you think is more plausible, you will find the means here to state and evaluate it.

We have argued that egoism presents at least two different sets of moral notions: those having to do with obligations and rights and those having to do with right actions. We established the difference through a presentation of actions that are right but not obligatory, and vice versa. One clear way to proceed, then, is to establish these two areas of egoism as the minimum number that should be included in a theory of obligation.

> If any person *a* performs an action that increases person *a*'s own good (benefit), then that action is right.

> If any person *a* performs an action that increases person *a*'s own good (benefit) more than any other available action, then that action is obligatory.

In addition to the use of 'right' versus 'obligatory' in the preceding statements, another difference has been built in. Right actions are those likely to benefit you, given the knowledge you have. Accordingly, many actions in a given situation are right, but only one such action is obligatory. The obligatory action is the one most likely to maximize what benefits you, given the knowledge you have. By stating the difference in this way, we can incorporate both *right* and *obligation* into one egoistic theory and arrive at a more complete view.[27]

---

[27]There is a drawback. From certain points of view, this way of accounting for obligations seems deficient. A few examples will illustrate this. When playing music, you may find that you enjoy the music more when the volume is turned up. If there are no decompensating factors, such as great inconvenience in turning the volume up, then the preceding rules would suggest an obligation to do so. Obviously, no such obligation exists. Furthermore, how wide does the consideration of our interests have to be? Suppose it casually occurs to you as you read the paper that it is quite certain that the stock market will go up in the next few months and that auto stocks in particular are quite likely to go up. Are you then obliged to buy such stocks? More examples of this type are presented later in the text.

Assuming that these two rules together represent a reasonable statement of ethical egoism, we still must take into account the distinction between direct moral rule theories and indirect, or metamoral, rule theories. Recall that a direct moral rule allows the derivation of a singular moral judgment, whereas a metamoral rule allows the derivation of a direct moral rule. Put into the general scheme, the rules concerning *right* for the two positions are contrasted as follows:

Direct Moral Rule Ethical Egoism
1. If any person *a* performs an action that increases person *a*'s own good (benefit), then that action is right.
2. This particular person *a* performs this particular action that increases person *a*'s own good.

Therefore, 3. This particular action is right.

Indirect or Metamoral Rule Ethical Egoism
1. If any person *a* performs an action from a rule R that, when regularly acted from by person *a*, increases person *a*'s own good (benefit), then R is a direct moral rule of moral rightness.
2. This particular person performs an action from a rule R that, when regularly acted from by person *a*, increases person *a*'s own good (benefit).

Therefore, 3. R is a direct moral rule of moral rightness.

The preceding contrast is more easily understood through an example. Suppose for a moment that ethical egoism is a correct ethical theory and that some person is faced with a decision about whether to lie about why he was late. The truth is that our friend, *a*, was engrossed in reading magazines at the drugstore and forgot about his date with *b* until, with a start, he came back to reality and saw that he would be an hour late. Should he tell *b* the truth, or should he tell her that he stopped to help an accident victim to the hospital? Using direct moral rule ethical egoism, he can conclude that lying would be right, for by lying he will avoid all the unpleasantness as well as the decline of his status in *b*'s eyes. However, if a person regularly acted on a rule R of the form "If you have broken a promise or not fulfilled an obligation to someone, then lie about what happened," it is not likely that he would thereby increase his own good. Such people are usually found out—usually sooner than later. This results in distrust and rejection of subsequent explanations and leads, in turn, to all manner of damage to that person's interests—in ways that are obvious to all. Thus you could conclude that even though in a particular instance it might be to your advantage to lie, it is nevertheless not in your interest to adopt a rule to that effect. On the contrary, it is to your advantage to adopt a rule that requires truth-telling, for then the bad consequences will not come about. In their place will be the good consequences of an enhanced reputation, an increase in the likelihood of your attaining a respectable and secure place in society, and so on.

Someone might suggest that this distinction is really just the distinction between long-run and short-run interests. It might be in your short-run interest to lie, but not in your long-run interest. However, this is really not that distinction, for in certain cases you may be able to get away with lying, and thus, insofar as that individual action is concerned, it would be in his long-run interest to lie. Nevertheless, it is not in your long-run interest to adopt such a policy when it is likely that you will be found out. In this sense, it is in your interest in the long run to be an indirect ethical egoist rather than a direct ethical egoist.

The ethical egoist will want to explain as many of the moral phenomena as possible, so we will want to allow for explaining wrong actions—those we have an obligation not to do. So far we have talked only about actions that are right and actions that are obligatory. It is relatively easy, though, to provide the principles that cover negative notions once we understand that *right* and *wrong*, for example, are contrary notions. The principles concerning right and wrong actions would appear as follows:

> If any person *a* performs an action that increases person *a*'s own good (benefit), then that action is right.
>
> If any person *a* performs an action that decreases person *a*'s own good (benefit), then that action is wrong.

There are interesting and important questions about the relationship between a decrease of benefit and *positive disbenefit*, but such questions need not be answered to understand these relations. Similarly, the principles concerning obligation to and obligation not to perform some action would appear as follows:

> If any person *a* performs an action that increases person *a*'s own good (benefit) more than any other available action, then that action is obligatory.
>
> If any person *a* performs an action that decreases person *a*'s own good (benefit) more than any other available action, then that action is obligatory not to do.

In spite of the number of different notions and the different-looking principles in which they occur, only one kind of consideration is really involved in these principles—self-benefit. Because this is so, we shall say that the ethical egoist has only one principle, although perhaps a more precise statement would be that there is only the one source of obligation, right, wrong, and so on. In this text we shall concentrate on only one or two of the notions on the assumption that similar comments will apply to the others.

Summary of the Most Plausible Versions of Ethical Egoism

Ethical egoism seems to require at least two different rules: one having to do with *obligation* and its related notions and the other having to do with *right* and its related notions. At least two kinds of positions can be generated after we have interpreted all the variables and unclear parts of the statement—namely, the direct and the indirect (metamoral) rule versions. An apparent but unstated assumption is that the various forms of egoism are rule theories; rules are required to justify the singular moral judgments that fall under them.

ETHICAL EGOISM EVALUATED

Now that the main positions are before us, let us evaluate them by use of the criteria of acceptability. We cannot use psychological egoism as a support for ethical egoism because psychological egoism does not fare well as a theory of motivation. Thus, we must look elsewhere for support. It is apparently true that at least some actions are right because they increase our own interests. Insofar as there are such phenomena and the theory before us accounts for them in a direct manner, we have some evidence in favor of that theory. Admittedly, this does not constitute a great deal of evidence, especially if the theory cannot adequately account for many phenomena that other theories can. This seems to be the position so far of the two versions of ethical egoism previously laid out.

In the following sections, I shall present and evaluate some of the standard criticisms of ethical egoism, doing my best to avoid ad hoc assumptions, and avoiding any examination of competitors. If some of the criticisms do not apply to both the direct and the indirect versions, then I will make that clear.

Other People

What about other people? This question results in a series of puzzles that egoists must face and a series of questions they have great difficulty in answering. Is it true that other people should, if they want to adopt the correct ethical theory, hold one of the versions of ethical egoism? The answer to this question must be yes, for the following reasons. If the theory were true for only one person, then it would scarcely recommend itself as a theory covering all or a significant number of moral phenomena. Moral phenomena extend backward in time and across the whole planet, wherever and whenever there have been human beings. In the face of this, it is an odd suggestion, to say the least, that the only phenomena worth explaining are those concerning one person. This would be the same as saying that there is a correct theory of motivation—perhaps psychological egoism—but that it applies only to one person. Such a theory would fare very poorly compared with other theories with a range wider than just one person.

Furthermore, if you are *the* person, you would have to explain why other people are excluded. Suppose your neighbor also adopts ethical egoism and then claims you have chosen the wrong person—it should be her instead of you. There seems to be no reason why you should be the chosen person. It is probably an entirely arbitrary choice on your part, with nothing to justify such a limit.

This would lead the ethical egoist to agree that the first statement in the general scheme should be read as it is written: "If *any* person a. . . ." We have, therefore, proposed a moral standard for *all* human beings. Only in this way can the ethical egoist present a theory that will even be in the running when a final decision is made as to which of the competing theories is best. In this form, the theory is more reasonable; but now, other problems arise.

One such problem concerns actions that advance the interests of one person at the expense of the interests of another. Suppose, for example, that a race is to be run in which only one person can win. It benefits a to win, and, thus, for person b to win the race is not right. However, since the theory is equally accessible to person b, she can say the same thing. Thus, for person b to win the race is right, and for person a to win is not right. This situation justifies the conclusion that the same action—for example, person a's winning the race (coming in first)—is both right and not right. Such a conclusion is an extreme embarrassment to a theorist and cannot be allowed to stand. If this situation isn't remedied, the theory will never rank very high among ethical theories.

Ethical egoists have attempted to respond to this criticism in a variety of ways. One common response is to say that it is true for person a that his winning the race is right but that it is also true for person b that *her* winning the race is right. This response, though apparently clear, is ambiguous between the following two different claims.

1. Person a accepts (believes) that his winning the race is right (as does person b for herself).
2. Ethical egoism is a correct ethical theory when it applies to person a but not correct when it applies to anyone else.

Let us consider the first response. Earlier, in Chapter 1, the notion of *acceptance*, or *belief*, was discussed in connection with *knowledge* and *truth*. It was argued there that neither acceptance and truth nor acceptance and knowledge could be equated because people accept many items that are not true and they accept many that they are not warranted in accepting. You may accept that Calcutta is the capital of India, but you are mistaken. It is not true that Calcutta is the capital of India and no one can justifiably claim to know that it is.[28] If someone claims to accept ethical egoism, he or she can be saved from a contradiction in the following way.

When *a* claims that the action is right, he is saying only that he accepts that it is right; *b* is making the same kind of claim. It is then true of both *a* and *b* that they accept different propositions:

1. Person *a* accepts that his winning the race is right and that *b*'s winning the race is not right.
2. Person *b* accepts that her winning the race is right and that *a*'s winning the race is not right.

These two statements can both be true, for now their truth depends on what the people accept as true and not what really is true.

To see this more clearly, consider two other claims that persons *a* and *b* might disagree about:

1. Person *a* accepts that the earth is a sphere.
2. Person *b* accepts that the earth is pie shaped.

Both of these claims can be true as long as they are claims that persons *a* and *b* really do accept. The truth of this acceptance can be discovered by administering a lie detector test, or by some other appropriate means. One thing, though, that would not be relevant here would be to establish whether or not the earth is a sphere. This fact is totally irrelevant to the truth or falsity of either of the two preceding statements.

The two claims are not part of a theory about the shape of the earth; they are about the mental states of people. Similarly, acceptance claims about morality are themselves not part of an ethical theory.[29] In terms of this model, the interpretation of ethical egoism results in something that is not primarily an ethical theory.

Furthermore, if we persist, claiming that all an ethical theory does is tell us what we accept, it would be difficult to explain why any such theory is needed and what light it sheds on moral phenomena. Such a theory cannot help us arrive at any justified singular moral judgments, for there are apparently no such things. There are only the judgments we accept. Thus, there can be no actual disputes between people. Once it is pointed out that each

---

[28] Some circumstances exist under which you could conceivably be justified in making a knowledge claim like this, but such occurrences are very rare indeed. You may have purchased a defective world atlas or been told that Calcutta was the capital of India by a drunk geography teacher. However, these occasions are rare and, even in these cases, the proposition is not true.

[29] Of course, this is not to say that theories about the shape of the earth and ethical theories are the same in essential respect. They may or may not be the same, but that need not be discussed here. Beliefs are something theories may have to explain, but they are not part of a theory's statement or any part of its working apparatus. Later on, we shall compare different kinds of theories with ethical theories, but not now.

person is merely calling attention to what he or she believes when making a moral judgment, then each person can agree that the discussion is over. Although such a theory may turn out to be true, it does not appear that it will. Anyone maintaining that the theory is true must provide us with some reasons—independent of the theory—to support the claim.[30] However, such a theory appears to provide us with little or no explanation of the phenomena, and in the absence of any reasons to accept it, we would be foolish to do so.

Finally, some judgments that people make (and accept) apparently are not correct. Therefore, contrary to the theory, judgments do exist in addition to those merely accepted by a person. For example, Hitler accepted that he was doing what was morally acceptable, if not right, when he killed six million Jews and Slavs in World War II. The same is true of at least some of the National Guard troops at Kent State University, when they killed several students there. It is especially true of many slave owners in the United States in the seventeenth, eighteenth, and part of the nineteenth century. What seems to be true is that such people were *mistaken,* not merely that they and we had different beliefs.[31] The fact that we can argue with such people and provide support for own views supports this interpretation to some degree. Later, in Chapter 7, we shall examine the question of what kind of support moral judgments can have; for now, we can report that they seem to have some kind of support and that this apparent support is one of the phenomena to explain. A theory that simply rejects a whole range of phenomena without any reason is in trouble.

This brief discussion raises a whole range of questions, such as "Who is to say which person is correct when moral judgments differ?" and "How can I tell if I am correct?" These are the very questions with which we began our substantive discussion, and they are a few of the questions that an ethical theory is supposed to handle. The fact that they arise here naturally is not surprising. But their appearance does not mean that there is not an answer. (Of course, there may be no answer, and perhaps we shall wind up holding a theory similar to the one being examined. But such a choice should be made only when all other major theories have been examined and found not to be as good as this one. Until that happens, we can tentatively say that this theory doesn't seem to be a very good one.

Finally, to end the discussion of 'true for me' interpreted as acceptance, consider what an individual might mean by the claim, "I am an ethical egoist." Sometimes a person making such a claim means that he or she accepts some version of psychological egoism; and, as we know, it takes a while to straighten that out. However, if you have made it this far, you can already do that

---

[30]In Chapter 7, such a theory will be examined at greater length. In reality, it is a theory in metaethics and will be discussed in that context.

[31]Remember, though, that what *seems* to be so is not *always* so. We may finally conclude that there are no moral disputes in this sense, and something like ethical egoism is correct.

(straighten it out) for yourself or your friends without any great difficulty. Sometimes, though, the person claiming to be an ethical egoist may mean that she or he always tries to act in such a way as to maximize self-interest. This is an interesting claim for someone to make, but what is gained by making it is not clear. No psychological or ethical theory is supported by it or related to it in any clear way. If someone makes this claim, we can simply point out many actions that are not directed primarily toward self-interest. All of us have opened doors for strangers whose arms were loaded with packages, given directions to people we never expected to see again, and so on. Of course, anyone who makes this kind of claim will reject these as counterexamples, but the rejection is usually made on the basis of some general theory of motivation. Which one do you suppose is likely to be used?

A person who claims to be an ethical egoist may be expressing a great determination to stick to that point of view, or expressing a firm belief that it is a correct ethical theory no matter what. In either case, the claimant must come forward with a defense of the theory, especially in relation to other theories. What we must do, as scrutinizers of ethical theories, is examine the kind of defense the person presents. If no defense is forthcoming, the person must be placed with that group of people who maintain a view regardless of how good or bad it is and regardless of how good or bad rival views are. These are difficult people to deal with in any area, so no special problem is posed in moral philosophy by their existence. However a geologist would appropriately treat such people when they stubbornly hold to a geological theory that says the earth is about ten thousand years old is likely an appropriate way to treat them when they stand by their egoism theory in moral philosophy.

Let us now consider the interpretation of 'true for' as an attempt to escape inconsistencies; that is, let us consider the interpretation that ethical egoism is a correct ethical theory when it applies to person *a* but not correct when it applies to anyone else. This claim, if substantiated, would allow us to escape an inconsistency, for it would show that person *b*, for example, is mistaken when she claims that her winning the race is right. Only person *a* is correct in making this claim. So while it is right for *a* to win the race, it is not right for *b* to win. Thus, we have avoided a situation in which it is both right and not right for *a* to win the race.

There are several problems with this interpretation; but since such mistakes are by now familiar, they will be covered quickly. First, it is difficult to see how *a* or any other person could justify choosing himself as the only person whose interest has to be taken into account. Without such a justification, the choice appears arbitrary and capricious. If all others are equally justified, then the original problem of an inconsistency reappears. Second, interpreted in this way, the theory becomes very narrow, covering only a small part of the total area a theory can cover. It would leave out all the phenomena involving relations among people other than *a*. It would, for example, provide no basis for judging that if *b* tortures person *c* for no reason, that such an action is not right.

It would make it impossible to make justified judgments about events that occurred before *a* was born—and after *a* dies, so will all of morality.[32] At this point you should be able to supply additional criticisms that will add to the evidence discrediting this interpretation.

To summarize this section, the various senses of 'true for' arose in the context of wondering how the ethical egoist would handle other people. In allowing everyone to use the theory as correct, we found ourselves committed to inconsistent claims. To get out of this difficulty, we introduced the expression 'true for'. However, this expression does not seem to be able to save the day; the criticism generated by the problem of other people (justifiably) using the theory remains. This criticism, in brief, poses a dilemma. If the theory applies to all people, then apparently inconsistent judgments are equally justified. If the theory applies to only one person, then it is woefully incomplete, and the choice of the person who gets to use the theory is arbitrary. Such arguments are complex because the various interpretations of key notions have to be taken up. If you got lost the first time through, you may wish to go through again, now that you have the overall strategy in mind.

Counterexamples

Counterexamples are examples drawn from the phenomena that go counter to a general claim. The general claim "If anything flies, then it is a bird" can be shown to be false by the justified claim "This thing flies, and this thing is a bat." The general claim "If anything is a human, then it is male" can be refuted by showing that "Elizabeth is human, and Elizabeth is female." What we shall be looking for are counterexamples to one or more of the direct moral rules or the indirect or meta-moral rules that the egoist maintains are part of the correct ethical theory. Let us consider first the direct moral rule version.

> If any person *a* performs an action that increases person *a*'s own good (benefit), then that action is right.

> If any person *a* performs an action that increases person *a*'s own good (benefit) more than any other available action, then that action is obligatory.

Let us consider the rule concerning *right* first. The United States endorsed the institution of human slavery from its inception until 1865. Before the United States was founded as a country, slavery had been permitted in the colonies for about 150 years. There were hundreds of thousands of slave owners and millions of slaves during that time. Some of these slave owners, no doubt,

---

[32]As usual, there is always a possible response. Person *a* could say that such actions are wrong because they make him feel bad when he hears about them (or some such move). However, at this stage, you can no doubt handle such ad hoc moves yourself.

did not do very well as managers of plantations, factories, or other businesses in which their slaves worked. Others, though, did very well indeed, living a life of luxury and enjoying the best and tastiest fruits available. Not only did they live well and prosper, but many families did so for generations. The reference group for our counterexamples will be that considerable group of slave owners who lived very well indeed, became respected members of their communities, and died still being honored by their fellow citizens. There is little question that the activity of keeping slaves was to their interest. This enables us to state the following counterexample(s):

> This person *a* (and thousands like him) performed the action of keeping slaves, which increased person *a*'s own good (benefit), and that action is not right.

If this claim is accepted, then we have a strong reason for thinking that the egoistic rule concerning *right* is not acceptable. Notice that it is not just one case that is being relied on, for then the force of the counterexample would not be nearly so great. In addition, there are many counterexamples involving different kinds of actions and additional millions of persons. It is to the interest of generals, usually, that they wage war, but war is not usually right. It is to the interest of the pimp that he solicit for his prostitute, but in a large percentage of such cases it is not right. It is to the interest of the seducer who is not at all interested in his or her sex partner as a person to practice the art of seduction, but it is not usually right. You can join in at this point and add many more such counterexamples.

Counterexamples, if they are effective, are strong evidence against the acceptance of direct rule ethical egoism. As presented, the proposed counterexamples address themselves to the rightness of actions, but the same counterexamples apparently apply to the "ought" rule also. It is not obligatory for the slave owner to keep slaves, even though it may be, given the alternatives available to him at the time, the one that would maximize his interests. If the action is not right, then it would appear that it is not obligatory. In this instance, to make the point even stronger, it appears obligatory not to keep slaves. The same kinds of comments apply to the other proposed counterexamples. Once again, you are advised to construct your own counterexamples so as to begin actively to do philosophy.

Egoists will deny the effectiveness of the proposed counterexamples drawn from the moral phenomena. They will claim that such apparent counterexamples are not counterexamples at all—and we can expect that a certain number of proposed counterexamples *will* turn out not to be counterexamples. However, responses to proposed counterexamples must be to the point; they cannot simply assume the correctness of the theory and then dismiss the counterexamples because they are not compatible with the theory. If the proposed counterexamples were not incompatible with the theory, they couldn't be used as counterexamples. As a reminder, if this procedure could be used freely, then any theory whatsoever could be "defended." Someone might claim, for example, that all humans are male. When we present Elizabeth as a proposed counterexample, that person could claim that Elizabeth cannot be a human being because she is not a male. Given the correctness of the theory "If anyone is human, then that person is male," such a response would indeed be perfectly plausible and effective. However, when we are examining whether such a view is correct, the view itself cannot be brought into play to counter a proposed criticism. If this were permissible, then any theory could be shown to be immune to criticism.

If the ethical egoist wishes to show that proposed counterexamples are not actually counterexamples, he or she must provide a positive argument to that effect, independent of the theory. Failing this, the egoist should admit the counterexamples as powerful criticisms of the theory. However, because there is no time limit on responses to criticisms, we cannot say the counterexamples are absolute, indisputable proof that egoism is incorrect. This is especially true if all the other theories we shall consider do a worse job than egoism in responding to such criticisms.

Finally, you are reminded that counterexamples are drawn from the phenomena. They are not God-given, intuitive, final truths that we must all accept. They are, instead, simply those items that appear to be facts when we begin our investigation. We should all be prepared to give up any one phenomenon that can be shown to be unreasonable, given other things we know. The other side of that is that we would be foolish to give up something as part of the phenomena simply because it is inconsistent with someone's chosen theory.

Do the kinds of counterexamples proposed apply to the indirect rule theories as well as to the direct rule theories? If they do, then we are saved a great deal of time and trouble in our evaluation. And it does seem that with a small amount of modification the same examples can be used. Consider the rule a slave owner might adopt for himself: "If buying and keeping slaves will make me rich and a respected member of the community, then it is right." In many parts of the United States in the eighteenth century, this rule, if acted from, would have significantly benefited the actor. Recall that one of the indirect rules of such a version of ethical egoism is the following:

> If any person a performs an action from a rule R that, when regularly acted from by a, increases a's own good (benefit), then R is an acceptable direct moral rule of moral rightness.

This proposed direct rule that the slave holder can adopt and act from seems to fit the indirect, or metamoral rule. So, it is an acceptable direct moral rule. However, as was established, it is not acceptable as a direct moral rule of moral rightness. Once again, what it means to say that it is not acceptable, is that there are a significant number of counterexamples that can be directed against it. And, once more, the egoist cannot respond by pointing out that the proposed counterexamples are not consistent with the theory and must, for that reason alone, be rejected. If the counterexamples should be rejected, then some other reason must be given.

Too Wide a Theory

The two kinds of egoist theory—the direct and the indirect rule versions—apparently would classify many actions as right or obligatory that are not. Simply put, the theory seems to turn every prudent action into a right action, and the most prudent action into an obligation. This point, as with most others, is best understood via actual examples. It will most likely benefit each of us if we continue to breathe, and yet, that does not seem to be an action that is morally right. However, using the direct moral rule version of ethical egoism, that action is right. Each of us can supply many counterexamples of this kind. For example, it will benefit most people if they keep both eyes open when they walk down the street, if they don't eat too fast, if they look to the right and to the left before they cross the street, if they have health insurance, if they determine fairly accurately the balance in their checking account, and so on. In most circumstances, though, these actions are not morally right. The same kinds of examples can easily be generated with respect to *obligation*.

The earlier counterexamples show that apparently wrong actions exist that, in terms of the theory, would be called right. The preceding examples illustrate some morally neutral actions that, given the theory, would be called right. To achieve a kind of completeness, you may want to find a class of apparently right (or obligatory) actions that the theory would classify as morally neutral or wrong. To do this, you might want to examine common courtesy. We have some obligation, it would seem, to treat others in a courteous manner and not to cause them needless suffering. If treating someone this way would not likely lead to some benefit for ourselves, then according to ethical egoism this kind of action would either be morally neutral or wrong (if it actually led to some decrease in benefit to ourselves). At this stage, since evidence has piled up against ethical egoism, we will leave this exercise to those who have a special interest in counterexamples of this type.

A SUMMARY OF EGOISM

The discussion of egoism requires a distinction between the psychological view—psychological egoism—and the ethical theory. The psychological theory is thought to support the ethical theory although the method of support beyond the following general scheme is difficult to determine:

> If psychological egoism is correct, then ethical egoism is correct.
> Psychological egoism is correct.
>
> ---
>
> Therefore, ethical egoism is correct.

If PE, then EE.
PE.

Therefore, EE.

We first stated, as clearly as possible, the psychological theory. Next, we examined the two different kinds of proposed support for it: the nonempirical and the empirical. We found that nonempirical support is not adequate, that at least one other theory—psychological realism—is better supported, and that at least one other theory—psychological altruism—is as well supported. We found the theory of psychological altruism unacceptable, and if psychological egoism is no better a theory of motivation than psychological altruism, then it is not acceptable either. The empirical evidence available does not support psychological egoism. Experimental evidence exists that illustrates nonegoistic or altruistic primary motives in human beings, even though it may be true that no one would act from altruistic motives if they were not rewarded for so acting.

Although we found psychological egoism wanting as a theory of motivation, we nevertheless explored the relation of support between that psychological theory and ethical egoism. We found a connection between psychological egoism and the part of theory of obligation that deals with the notions of *right to* or *permission* and *obligation*. This connection does little good for the ethical egoist, though, for the psychological theory is apparently not justified, and the ethical theory supported by it is not a complete theory.

An examination of ethical egoism completed the chapter. First, we described and explained that view more carefully. We pointed out that there would have to be at least two sets of rules, one having to do with *permission* and *obligation* and the other with *right* and its attendant notions. We also noted the difference between an egoistic theory that applies its rules directly to actions and situations—direct rule egoism—and one that applies its rules to other rules—indirect rule ethical egoism. Finally, we levied three broad types of criticism: one arising from the problem of other people, one having to do with counterexamples, and one stemming from the egoist's apparent inability to distinguish between prudence and morality.

In response to many of the criticisms, especially that of the counterexamples, the temptation will be to claim that counterexamples work only because we have restricted the interests we are considering to just one person. If, instead of considering just the interests of the slave owner, we had included the interests of the slaves as well, it might be suggested, then, the counterexamples would not work. When we consider the sorry state of the slaves, we see that overall the interests of everyone are not furthered by slavery. This may be, but if we extend the range of consequences to include everyone, then we have given up egoism in favor of another teleological view—namely, utilitarianism. This is a natural move for people to make when egoism appears deficient.

These people will want to maintain that consequences—and only consequences—are what counts, and yet they want to consider the consequences for everyone. In a very rough way, that is the statement of utilitarianism, the normative ethical theory considered in the next chapter.

Exercises: Practice in Critical Analysis

1. "If an action is not right, then it is not obligatory" ("If an action is obligatory, then it is right"). Present considerations for or against the truth of this claim, in either of the forms presented.
2. One difficulty we face in analyzing theories is learning how to expose inadequate responses to criticisms—and especially inadequate responses to proposed counterexamples. Show what is wrong with the responses to the proposed counterexamples (shown in **bold** print) in the following:
    a. *View:* If I accept an action as right, then that action is right.
    Proposed counterexample: The action of my rescuing a child from a fire was right, and you did not learn about it until much later.
    Response: **It was right then only because I was going to accept it as right later.**
    b. *View:* If any person is a woman, then that person is a mother.
    Proposed counterexample: Martha Graham is a woman, but she is not a mother.
    Response: **Martha Graham is not really a woman because she is not a mother.**
    c. *View:* If any book is more than 500 pages long, then it is worthless.
    Proposed counterexample: The Columbus, Ohio, telephone book is useful, and it has more than 1000 pages.
    Response: **The telephone book is useful, but it is actually a large number of different books: one consists of all the listings under A, one consists of all the listings under B, and so on. None of these books is more than 500 pages long.**
3. Each of the following theories proposes exactly one direct rule of obligation. Criticize them.
    a. If any action consists of reducing disease (directly or indirectly), then that action is right.
    b. If any action maximizes jobs (directly or indirectly), then that action is right.
4. Each of the following theories proposes exactly one indirect rule of obligation. Criticize them.

(continued)

(continued)

> a. If any person *a* performs an action from a rule R that, when regularly acted from by person *a* increases the number of walls in the world, then R is a direct moral rule of moral rightness.
> b. If any person *a* performs an action from a rule R that, when regularly acted from by person *a* increases the gross national product of the United States, then R is a direct moral rule of moral rightness.
>
> 5. Many more different versions of ethical egoism exist than have been presented in this chapter. If you know of a version that is significantly different from any of the ones discussed here, present and evaluate it.
> 6. Suppose we change one thing about ethical egoism—either the direct or the indirect view—stipulating that when you calculate what will be of benefit to you, you don't know anything about yourself except that you are a member of our society: "No one knows his place in society, his class position or social status, nor does any one know his fortune in the distribution of natural assets and abilities, his intelligence, strength, and the like"[33] Now attempt to formulate ethical egoism and then describe what differences have been made in the theory. Are any criticisms now answerable? Do any new ones occur to you?
> 7. One normative ethical theory that has most of the defects of ethical egoism plus some additional ones is *subjectivism*. This can be taken as a direct rule view.
>
>> If any action *X* is one preferred by person *a* over any alternative, then *X* is right.
>
>> Criticize this view. State and criticize an indirect version of subjectivism.

COGNITIVE DEVELOPMENTAL THEORIES

The general form of support between a psychological and a normative ethical theory is:

If PT, then NET.
PT.

Therefore, NET.

---

[33] John Rawls, *A Theory of Justice* (Cambridge: Harvard University Press, 1971), 12.

Although no psychologists defend psychological egoism and use it, in turn, to defend ethical egoism, some influential psychologists do defend cognitive developmental theories, arguing that such theories do support a normative ethical theory. The thinker whose work spawned much of the contemporary literature with this viewpoint is Jean Piaget. Piaget proposes that the cognitive ability of a child to reason logically develops as the child matures. Before this maturation, little can be done to teach children the difference between, say, volume and height. Young children will judge that a tall, narrow container holds more water than a short, wide container because the water level is higher in the first. And pouring a certain volume of liquid from one container to another to show that the amount of liquid does not change makes no difference to their ability to judge which container holds more water; they will still pick the tall, narrow one. Piaget proposes that there are developmental stages in moral development just as there are for logical development.

American psychologist Lawrence Kohlberg has been the most influential thinker using Piagetian-type strategies. His detailed version of Piaget's views has provided a useful alternative to the less structured and less rigorous moral education programs commonly found.

> A cognitive-developmental theory of moral development holds that there is a sequence of moral stages for the same basic reasons that there are cognitive or logico-mathematical stages, that is, because cognitive structural reorganizations toward the more equilibrated occur in the course of interaction between the organism and the environment.[34]

Kohlberg is saying here that the same reasons given to explain why children are able at a later age to handle certain mathematical concepts they could not handle at a younger age can be used to explain the development of moral reasoning. That is, a moral problem that could not be handled at an earlier age can be handled at a later age because of maturation and interaction with the environment. Note that this ability is acquired naturally—it is not taught. At the earlier stage, Kohlberg says, the children are not in what he calls *equilibrium* concerning that moral problem. Developmental psychologists use this same kind of reasoning to explain why children are able to solve problems in logical thinking at a later age without being taught logic.

Without an adequate logical theory, Kohlberg believes, we cannot determine if someone is reasoning logically. For example, we cannot say that someone is not reasoning adequately because that person has committed the fallacy of

---

[34]Lawrence Kohlberg, "From Is to Ought: How to Commit the Naturalistic Fallacy and Get Away With It in the Study of Moral Development," in *Cognitive Development and Epistemology*, ed. T. Mischel (New York: Academic Press, 1971), 183. The discussion in this book on Kohlberg closely follows that presented in B. Rosen "Kohlberg and the Supposed Mutual Support of an Ethical and Psychological Theory," *Journal of Social Behaviour* 10, no. 3, (1978): 195–210.

denying the antecedent unless we have an adequate logical theory that recognizes this fallacy. Similarly, in order to make a determination of adequate moral reasoning we must have an adequate normative ethical theory. However, there is no widespread agreement about what an acceptable normative ethical theory is. The theory that Kohlberg chooses as acceptable has elements from both Kant and John Rawls. Although we won't examine Kant until later and will only indirectly mention Rawls, neither of those theories need be set out in order to evaluate whether Kohlberg's strategy of supporting his ethical theory with his psychological theory is acceptable. We shall argue, though, that elements of his ethical theory have been illegitimately added to his cognitive developmental psychological theory. In the following quote, elements flagged with an asterisk are the parts of his psychological theory that contain parts of his ethical theory. We shall show that other ethical theory parts could replace those flagged and that this would result in a different ethical theory being chosen as the best one. If this strategy is successful, then Kohlberg will be shown to be guilty of begging the question.

> By cognitive-developmental I refer to a set of assumptions . . . . [There are] (a) *stages* of moral development representing (b) *cognitive-structural transformations* in conceptions of self and society . . . (c)* that these stages represent successive modes of "taking the role of others" in social situations, and hence that (d)* the social-environmental determiners of development are *its opportunities for role taking* . . . . [We also assume] (3) an *active* child who structures his perceived environment and, hence, have assumed (f) that moral stages and their development represent the interaction of the child's structuring tendencies and the structural features of the environment, leading to (g) successive forms of equilibrium in interaction. This equilibrium is conceived as (h)* a level of justice with (i) change being caused by disequilibrium.[35]

We shall contend that a psychological theory would still be a cognitive developmental theory if the starred items were replaced by other components. The first passage quoted from Kohlberg (page 89) seems to show that the starred components are not essential to the statement of what a cognitive developmental theory is. To show that the starred items are illegitimately included, we will replace Kohlberg's ethical theory items with a version of ethical egoism. Kohlberg has his own way of stating his ethical theory, and to ensure that methodological questions are not begged, we shall let him state his own views and then parallel his statement with an egoist rival. Kohlberg's statement is given first.

> Stage 6: The *Universal-ethical-principle-orientation*. Right is defined by the decision of conscience in accord with self-chosen *ethical principles* appealing to logical comprehensiveness, universality, and consistency. These principles are

[35]Kohlberg, "From Is to Ought," 183, 184.

abstract and ethical (the Golden Rule, the categorical imperative); they are not concrete moral rules like the Ten Commandments. At heart, these are universal principles of justice, of the *reciprocity* and *equality* of human *rights*, and of respect for the dignity of human beings as *individual persons*.[36]

> There is one indirect moral rule that defines what we are morally permitted to do: We are permitted to act on those direct moral rules that maximize our own benefit. The moral principles are used to justify individual moral judgments. The one indirect moral rule that defines our moral obligations is: We are obligated to do whatever is needed to ensure the primary rights of self-benefit.

Kohlberg adds a theory of justice to his indirect moral rule, so we shall add an extreme laissez-faire capitalist theory of justice to ethical egoism. This view, to be explored more fully in Chapter 3, holds that the relatively scarce things of value are to be distributed to those who can afford to buy them in the market. This contrasts with the Rawlsian view that no one should get more than is needed for a minimum level of living until everyone has at least the minimum level. Because a detailed discussion of these components is not needed now, it will be deferred.

Capitalism-egoism holds that we are each permitted to attempt to maximize our own benefit. To make this possible, we need rules that everyone can follow. I, and each person, will follow these rules because following them is most likely to maximize self-benefit. Each of us engages in role playing so as to compete better with others. No one, however, has a moral claim to a share of what we compete for, as the Rawlsian theory claims.

One additional element in Kohlberg's presentation is a theory about acceptability of normative ethical theories. As we shall see, the criteria differ considerably from those presented in Chapter 1:

> Our notions of moral philosophic adequacy derive then from the notion that moral theories are derivative from the natural structures we term stages. The structures are "natural" not in the sense of being innate, but in the sense of being the sequential results of processing moral experience, not derivatives from particular teaching or particular moral ideologies or theories.[37]

A cognitive developmental theory claims that there are stages and describes how these relate to other cognitive stages. Philosophers also pass through these stages, and their ethical theories are, in some sense, descriptive of the way in which they actually do reason morally. However, a person can be helped to achieve a "higher" stage by someone who has formulated the theory that describes the way we think at that higher stage. Sufficiently mature persons

---

[36]Lawrence Kohlberg, "The Claim to Moral Adequacy of a Highest Stage of Moral Judgment," *The Journal of Philosophy* 70, no. 18 (October 1973): 634, 635.

[37]Kohlberg, "The Claim to Moral Adequacy," 633, 634.

will be able to perform the higher-stage reasoning as described by the moral philosopher. This feature of cognitive developmental theories shows clearly why Kohlberg thinks it is all right, and even required, to assume the correctness of an ethical theory. But this requirement does not, of course, show that Kohlberg has assumed the correct normative ethical theory. It does not show that Kohlberg has not illegitimately included some ethical theory elements in his statement of the cognitive development theory.

Kohlberg's criteria of acceptability should be contrasted with the more general ones discussed in Chapter 1. In the following list, Kohlberg's criteria are on the left and our more general ones are on the right:

Kohlberg List	Our List
1. Differentiation	1. Explains phenomena adequately and without ad hoc devices
2. Integration	
3. Reversibility	2. Better than rival theories
4. Consistency	3. There are positive reasons in favor of the theory
5. Universality	
6. Prescriptivity	4. Serious objections can be adequately answered
7. Autonomy	
8. Equilibration	

Kohlberg does not seem to have an exhaustive list of acceptability criteria, but the list given here is close to exhaustive and certainly contains the important criteria. These criteria apply either to the whole theory or to what the theory makes possible, or to the judgments that result from the theory's application. For example, a theory passes the criterion of differentiation when it is able to distinguish the moral from the nonmoral, and also when it contains within it clear distinctions among the many moral notions (such as right action and obligatory action). A theory is autonomous when it does not provide for, or perhaps, allow for its own reduction to theories in other areas (as we shall see ethical relativism apparently doing in Chapter 4). Integration appears to be the theory's capacity to relate all the moral notions that the criterion of differentiation requires us to differentiate. It also seems to require us to explain how the lower stages are somehow included or incorporated into the higher—for example, the claim that rights and duties are correlatives: If person a has a duty with respect to b to perform X, then b has a right with respect to a to have X performed. Not all of the criteria are of equal importance, and not all need be discussed. Kohlberg feels that prescriptivity is implied by criteria 3 to 5, and it may be that equilibration is also implied by some set of the others. A moral judgment and, thus, one assumes, the structures or theory that was applied (or the person who did the applying) is in disequilibrium when another judgment is inconsistent with it. "A moral situation in disequilibrium is one in which there are unresolved conflict claims."[38] The assumption is that when there are no unresolved conflicting claims, expressed by conflicting judgments, then there is equilibrium. Kohlberg thinks this equilibrium results from applying what he calls principles of justice or fairness, but that claim is not obviously derived from an examination of Kohlberg's notion of disequilibrium.

To contrast Kohlberg's set of criteria with ours, you may need to review the discussion in Chapter 1. One thing those criteria allow us to say is that since the work of Piaget and Kohlberg, one of the moral phenomena is that stages in the development of moral reasoning parallel stages in the development of any reasoning. This, though, is not to say that Kohlberg's account of moral stages is the best one, or that the stages represent "higher" and "lower" levels of moral development.

Although our criteria are not drawn from the subject matter of a particular area, such as physics or moral philosophy, Kohlberg admits that his criteria are drawn from the ethical theory he thinks is correct. Granted that he thinks he has drawn the criteria from the psychological theory "alone," but he also tells us there is no such isolated theory. And, as indicated, parts of the developmental theory are not needed to state what a cognitive developmental theory is. These parts, one now suspects, are the ones imported from the ethical theory. Capitalism-egoism could do the same thing and skew the criteria of adequacy of an ethical theory. Any claim to superiority on such a basis is unacceptable. So, let us now turn to this kind of comparison, using Kohlberg's criteria of acceptability.

The reader needs to keep in mind that capitalism-egoism tells each of us to act on those direct rules that maximize our own benefit, and that differentiation requires us to distinguish various moral notions, such as *right action* and *obligatory action*. The theory has no difficulty in making such distinctions, as our examination showed us. Does capitalism-egoism distinguish moral from nonmoral notions? It could be argued that the nonmoral sphere consists of that which has no impact on me. You may not accept this way of making the distinction, but the nonacceptability does not result from any cognitive developmental theory of psychology but rather from a philosophical or ethical theory disagreement. Kohlberg might say that prudence is not adequately distinguished from moral rightness, but then it would be clear that his criteria contain normative ethical theory components. These criteria, however, would be illegitimate since they would be begging the question against rival ethical theories. The same kind of procedure has to be made available to the capitalist-egoist, who would then tell us that it is a mistake to distinguish prudence from rightness. We could, from the perspective of either theory, distinguish moral and legal rights and obligation from rightness.

[38] Ibid., p. 633.

Reversibility is also composed of two parts; it involves seeing the logical relations between pairs of notions such as right–duty and also seeing yourself in the other person's position, or role playing. The first has been discussed, and the notion of correlatives is easily accepted by the capitalist-egoist. Role playing is explained by Kohlberg in terms of kantian notions such as being a member of the *kingdom of ends*—that is, those beings who ought never to be treated as a mere means—or what Rawls calls the *original position*.[39] Role playing for the capitalist-egoist is explainable as a means of predicting what people will do. If you cannot successfully predict what people will do, you will make mistakes about what they will do, thus seriously hampering your ability to maximize your own benefit. Furthermore, when you put yourself in the position of others, you expand your own view of the world and the things in it. This expansion will enable you to use all those things, including the people, to increase the likelihood of maximizing your own benefit. This response would not please Kohlberg, Rawls, or Kant. Their displeasure, though, would be directed to the normative ethical theory of capitalism-egoism, not to any psychological theory. The capitalist-egoist would no doubt express similar displeasure with Kohlberg's account of role playing.

Universalizability on the capitalist-egoist account would consist of giving everyone a chance to compete so as to maximize self-benefit. I watch you being ruined—perhaps I am the one who ruins you—and think how glad I am that I am not you. I see that this could happen to me—something that gives me great incentive to be shrewd and calculating in my business dealings.

Any of the Kohlberg criteria can be met by the capitalist-egoist in ways that by this time the reader no doubt can supply. To use our more neutral criteria, we need to have the major competitors before us. This provides a good place to leave this discussion, for if Kohlberg wishes to show that his normative ethical theory is best, he must show that it is better than the major competitors already known to us. He cannot claim his theory is best unless we can show that another view is better. When we examine Kant's view, we shall briefly return to Kohlberg's claim.

Before we leave developmental theories, we shall briefly note the views of those who think there are sex-linked differences in moral outlook. The view that biological differences between human females and males explain some differences between the two groups in thinking and organizing the data of the senses is reasonably well established. In *Time* magazine, a summary article noting such differences tells us:

> At the Bowman Gray Medical School in Winston-Salem, N.C., Cecile Naylor has determined that men and women enlist widely varying parts of their

---

[39]The "original position" is described in exercise 6 on page 88. Its role is more fully explained in the appendix to Chapter 3. The "kingdom of ends" is discussed more fully in Chapter 4.

brain when asked to spell words. . . . the neuropsychologist found that women use both sides of their head when spelling while men use primarily their left side. Because the area activated on the right side is used in understanding emotions, the women apparently tap a wider range of experience for their task.

. . . The ability to tell directions on a map without physically having to rotate it appears stronger in those individuals whose brains restrict the process to the right hemisphere. Any crosstalk between the two sides apparently distracts the brain from its job. Sure enough, several studies have shown that this mental-rotation skill is indeed more rightly focused in men's brains than women's.[40]

Sex-linked differences in thinking result from biological differences in the brain, so it is not sheer speculation to think that there might be differences in the way males and females process moral phenomena. However, when mathematics is taught in single-sex classrooms where bias about expectations is not present, the differences between the sexes tend to diminish.

But is there actually a unique female way of morality? Carol Gilligan has been the most influential thinker in drawing attention to this possible aspect of moral development.

> The different dynamics of early childhood inequality and attachment lay the groundwork for two moral visions—one of justice and one of care. . . . Since everyone is vulnerable both to oppression and to abandonment, two stories of morality recur in human experience.
>
> By tracing moral development across two intersecting dimensions of relationship, it is possible to differentiate transformations that pertain to equality from transformations that pertain to attachment and to consider the interplay between problems of inequality and problems of detachment. Observations of sex differences in moral understanding and moral behavior reflect a tendency for these problems to be differentially salient or differently organized in male and female development.[41]

Gilligan and Wiggins maintain that *caring* is more pronounced in girls than boys, but is an equally important aspect of our moral life as justice. Justice and caring are the two parts of our moral life that explain both moral tension and why girls and boys (and women and men) tend to process moral problems differently.

---

[40]*Time*, January 20, 1992, 46. This article reviews a number of findings that were reported in scientific journals. Those interested in more technical studies should consult the original sources.

[41]Carol Gilligan and Grant Wiggins, "The Origins of Morality in Early Childhood Relationships," in *Mapping the Moral Domain*, ed. Carol Gilligan, Janie Victoria Ward, and Jill McLean Taylor with Betty Bardige (Cambridge, Mass.: Center for the Study of Gender, Education and Human Development, 1988), 116.

> When seen in terms of *either* justice or care, the following problems *appear* to have right, if difficult, answers. Seen from *both* perspectives their ethical ambiguity appears. With this shift one comes to a different understanding of the child who is uncertain whether to adhere to standards of fairness or help another child on a test, or the adolescent who is torn between loyalty to particular relationships and loyalty to ideals of equality and freedom, or the adult who wonders in allocating resources whether it is better to respond to the perception of need or to follow principles of justice.[42]

In an earlier work, Gilligan says very much the same thing: Males tend to think in terms of rights whereas females tend to emphasize caring. For this reason, Gilligan pictures the female conceptualizing that

> the moral problem arises from conflicting responsibilities rather than from competing rights and requires for its resolution a mode of thinking that is contextual and narrative rather than formal and abstract. This conception of morality as concerned with the activity of care centers moral development around the understanding of responsibility and relationships, just as the development of morality as fairness ties moral development to the understanding of rights and rules.[43]

There is disagreement about whether such clear sex-linked psychological differences actually exist.[44] An equally attractive hypothesis at this time is that most of the observed intellectual differences between males and females are culturally generated. Even if there are differences in the ease with which boys and girls can visualize or sense emotions, each can do what the other can do. We need to note that the issue of male–female differences is not the focus of this chapter—the issue is whether any psychological theory can support a normative ethical theory. We have argued here that the developmental

---

[42]Gilligan and Wiggins "Origins of Morality," 117.

[43]Carol Gilligan, *In a Different Voice*, (Cambridge, Mass.: Harvard University Press, 1982), 19.

[44]For example, Rosemary S. L. Mills, Jan Pedersen, and Joan Grusec in "Sex Differences in Reasoning and Emotion About Altruism" [*Sex Roles* 20 (June 1989): 603–621] think that empirical research shows some sex-linked differences:

> It has been suggested that the sex difference found with personally generated dilemmas may reflect women's greater experience with relational concerns and hence the greater salience of these concerns for women than for men, rather than a sex difference in the way these issues are judged or construed; indeed, when only this type of dilemma is considered, either similar reasoning has been found in women and men, or a difference has been found only among adults at higher levels of moral development. (605)

The authors cite a number of studies by M. W. Pratt, J. M. Royer, L. J. Walker, and B. de Vries. The empirical research is what properly settles the issue of whether there are such sex-linked differences in moral reasoning or moral outlook. This is not to say that only psychologists engaged in such research are entitled to offer hypotheses, or that psychologists always have well-designed experiments. Philosophers, sociologists, poets, or anyone else is entitled to offer hypotheses and might, in fact, have more interesting ones than psychologists.

psychological strategy of attempting to establish such a connection appears not to work. Gilligan's position can be seen as saying there is a connection, but as disagreeing with Kohlberg about the specifics of the ethical theory supported by the evidence of developmental psychology. When we examine virtue ethics in Chapter 5, remember to ask if there are any peculiarly female virtues. It has been suggested, for example, that females are more oriented toward caring and compassion than boys. Do these studies give us reason to think this is not so? If males have a virtue to a lesser extent than females, should we then work harder to cultivate that virtue in males or should we not try to cultivate it? Obviously this is not the last word on the issue. Those who are interested should examine the latest empirical studies—but keep in mind that empirical studies alone do not generate a normative ethical theory.

RECOMMENDED READING

Aronfreed, Justin. *Conduct and Conscience.* New York: Academic Press, 1968. This book presents some empirical data about egoism from a philosophically sophisticated psychologist.

Card, Claudia, eds. *Feminist Ethics.* Lawrence: University Press of Kansas, 1991. This is a collection of articles by those attempting to work out details of a feminist ethics.

Dovido, John F., Judith L. Allen, and David A. Schroeder. "Specificity of Empathy-Induced Helping: Evidence for Altruistic Motivation." *Journal of Personality and Social Psychology* 59, no. 2 (February 1990): 249.

Gauthier, David P., ed. *Morality and Rational Self-Interest.* Englewood Cliffs, N.J.: Prentice-Hall, 1970. A selection of articles.

———. *Morals By Agreement.* Oxford: Oxford University Press, 1986. This is the detailed working out of a Hobbesian-inspired view.

Gilligan, Carol. *In a Different Voice.* Cambridge, Mass.: Harvard University Press, 1982.

Macaulay, J., and L. Berkowitz, eds. *Altruism and Helping Behavior.* New York: Academic Press, 1970.

Mills, Rosemary S. L., Jan Pedersen, and Joan Grusec. "Sex Differences in Reasoning and Emotion About Altruism." *Sex Roles* 20, nos. 11/12 (1989): 603–621.

Milo, Ronald D., ed. *Egoism and Altruism.* Belmont, Calif.: Wadsworth, 1973. Among other essays, both for and against egoism, you will find the work of Bishop Butler, a must reading for any serious student of egoism.

Rand, Ayn. *The Virtue of Selfishness.* New York: New American Library, 1964. This is a work popular with nonphilosophers but not well thought of by philosophers.

Schlick, Moritz. *Problems of Ethics.* Translated by David Rynin. New York: Dover, 1962. Originally published in 1932. The author attempts to defend ethical egoism. See especially Chapter 2.

Weiss, R. F., W. Buchanan, L. Alsstatt, and J. P. Lombardo. "Altruism Is Rewarding." *Science* 171 (March 26, 1991): 1262.

CHAPTER THREE

Utilitarianism

In Chapter 2 we noted that one way to make up a deficiency of ethical egoism is to extend the range of consequences to more than just one person. We could not establish that the general's waging war was wrong when we took into account just his own interests and benefits, but we could when we considered what would be in the interest of and would benefit everyone. We could then see that war is not, usually, right at all. This is simply an extension of egoism—we still restrict the range of considerations to the consequences of actions, but we have made the range of consequences broader.

> The creed which accepts as the foundation of morals "utility" or the "greatest happiness principle" holds that actions are right in proportion as they tend to promote happiness; wrong as they tend to produce the reverse of happiness.[1]

Stating the most general utilitarian view in the usual manner, we have:

Direct Utilitarianism[2]

1. If any person *a* performs an action that increases the good (benefit) of the greatest number, then that action is right.

---

[1] John Stuart Mill, *Utilitarianism, (with Critical Essays)*, ed. Samuel Gorovitz. (Indianapolis, In.: Bobbs-Merrill, 1971), 18. All subsequent citations are to this edition.

[2] What are here called *direct* and *indirect utilitarianism* are typically called *act* and *rule utilitarianism*. The usual set of terms has two disadvantages: It is not as descriptive and it will be confusing when the contrast and discussion of rule and nonrule theories is presented in Chapter 5.

2. Person *a* performs this particular action that increases the good (benefit) of the greatest number.

Therefore, 3. This particular action of person *a* is right.

1. If any person *a* performs an action that increases the good (benefit) of the greatest number more than any other available action, then that action is obligatory.
2. Person *a* performs this particular action that increases the good (benefit) of the greatest number more than any other available action.

Therefore, 3. This particular action of person *a* is obligatory.

What is useful or has utility is the same thing as what benefits someone or has value; that is, what is good and what has utility are the same thing. Mill supposes that only happiness has value—at least only happiness has value underivatively. We shall explore questions concerning *value* in Chapter 6.

Indirect Utilitarianism
1. If any person *a* performs an action from direct moral rule R that, when generally acted from increases the good (benefit) of the greatest number,[3] then R is a direct moral rule of moral rightness.
2. Person *a* performs an action from a direct moral rule R that, when generally acted from increases the good (benefit) of the greatest number.

Therefore, 3. R is a direct moral rule of moral rightness.

1. If any person *a* performs an action from a rule R that, when generally acted from increases the good (benefit) of the greatest number more than any other available action, then R is a direct rule of moral obligation.

---

[3] If we wanted to restate the phrase 'increases the good (benefit) of the greatest number' so as to emphasize the teleological nature of utilitarianism, we could use 'has good maximizing consequences', or 'has good maximizing consequences for the greatest number'. However, this phrasing does not make for a clear parallel with egoism and would be more difficult to work with later on.

2. Person *a* performs an action from a rule R that, when generally acted from increases the good (benefit) of the greatest number more than any other available action.

Therefore, 3. R is a direct rule of moral obligation.[4]

These general statements of the two main types of utilitarian theory will not be a total mystery if you have worked your way through Chapter 2. However, it will help to remind you of some distinctions already made, and to interpret other parts of utilitarian theory that are in some way ambiguous. The examination of utilitarianism is simpler than that of egoism because utilitarians have not used any psychological theory of motivation to support their ethical theory. Mill did make two relevant psychological claims, but he does not use either as evidence to support his view, as egoists have done to support their view. First, he thinks that people desire only happiness as an end, though he hedges even on this claim. However, he does not use this supposed fact to argue that we have a right to desire our own happiness as an end. Second, Mill thinks there is a social "impulse" in human nature that makes it natural for humans to act to secure the good of others. Mill denies, in short, psychological egoism:

> The feeling of duty, when associated with utility, would appear equally arbitrary; if there were no leading department of our nature, no powerful class of sentiments, with which that association would harmonize, which would make us feel it congenial, and incline us not only to foster it in others (for which we have abundant interested motives), but also to cherish it in ourselves; if there were not, in short, a natural basis of sentiment for utilitarian morality, it might well happen that this association also, even after it had been implanted by education, might be analysed away.
>
> But there *is* this basis of powerful natural sentiment; and this it is which, when once the general happiness is recognized as the ethical standard, will

---

[4]Mill should be taken as the model of what a utilitarian is, for it seems clear that he was the most influential philosopher in that tradition and, in my opinion, the best philosopher within that tradition. There is some evidence that Mill held a version of indirect utilitarianism, and although it is not the purpose of this chapter to argue about how best to interpret him, the following passage seems to support the view that Mill held a version of indirect utilitarianism:

> The corollaries from the principle of utility, like the precepts of every practical art, admit of indefinite improvement, and in a progressive state of the human mind, their improvement is perpetually going on. But to consider the rules of morality as improvable is one thing; to pass over the intermediate generalizations entirely and endeavour to test each individual action directly by the first principle is inconsistent with the admission of secondary ones (*Utilitarianism*, 29).

constitute the strength of the utilitarian morality. This firm foundation is that of the social feelings of mankind; the desire to be in unity with our fellow creatures, which is already a powerful principle in human nature, and happily one of those which tend to become stronger, even without express inculcation, from the influences of advancing civilization. The social state is at once so natural, so necessary, and so habitual to man, that, except in some unusual circumstances or by an effort of voluntary abstraction, he never conceives himself otherwise than as a member of a body; and this association is riveted more and more, as mankind are further removed from the state of savage independence. Any condition, therefore, which is essential to a state of society, becomes more and more an inseparable part of every person's conception of the state of things which he is born into, and which is the destiny of a human being. Now, society between human beings, except in the relation of master and slave, is manifestly impossible on any other footing than that the interests of all are to be consulted. Society between equals can only exist on the understanding that the interests of all are to be regarded equally.[5]

This passage also contains a new argument for Bentham's dictum that each person should count as one when we calculate the overall good.

There is much controversy about how Mill, in Chapter 4 of *Utilitarianism*, used the supposed psychological fact of what people desire, but we shall not get involved in that controversy here. We shall discuss the view of utilitarianism, and specifically the position of Mill, without discussing any psychological theory of motivation.

In this chapter we shall employ the same strategy used in Chapter 2: First, offer clarified versions of the view to be considered and then evaluate the view as clarified.

DIRECT AND INDIRECT UTILITARIANISM

The general statement of each version of utilitarianism contains two separate parts. The direct and the indirect versions of the theory each require one rule for the notions of *obligation* and another rule for those of *right*. Direct

---

[5]Mill, *Utilitarianism*, 34. Mill is not saying here that the social viewpoint of people is the only "force" at work or that it works infallibly to bring people to the position of utilitarianism. People are also, of course, interested in their own good. This element of self-concern allows authors such as Hobbs, Gauthier, and perhaps even Rawls to construct theories that assume people are concerned primarily with their own good.

The cited passage may also be used to help respond to many of the standard criticisms of utilitarianism (see pp. 120 ff). Mill might say it would be psychologically very difficult to view slaves as nonpersons. This would make it psychologically difficult to pursue one's own happiness at the expense of the slave. Is this true? We cannot answer without doing the psychological research needed to defend this point of view.

utilitarianism applies the principle of utility, as we shall call it, directly to the actions that are to be judged right or obligatory; indirect utilitarianism applies the principle of utility to rules and not directly to actions that are to be judged. The same distinction was made in Chapter 2 with respect to egoism and should be somewhat clear. A few examples will serve as a reminder.

Consider just the rules regarding *right*, the first rule in each of the pairs, where the rule is the first statement in the general scheme. Suppose you get $5 too much change from the clerk/owner of a small grocery store, and there is little likelihood that this error will be noticed. Suppose also, as is not unreasonable, that if you keep the money, the resulting overall good will be greater than if it is returned. The grocer will miss it, but, again in our story, you will benefit more from having it since you will treat it as a windfall. The grocer will not know specifically that the $5 was given out by mistake. The profits for that week will be $5 less, but profits fluctuate and the grocer does not know beforehand anyway what the profit is going to be. In this set of circumstances, the greatest good for the greatest number seems to be reached by keeping the money. (We shall have to suppose you will spend it in very much the same way whether it comes from the grocer or from some other source.) If we apply the direct utilitarian rule concerning right ("If any person *a* performs an action that increases the good (benefit) of the greatest number, then that action is right"), then we are lead to conclude that keeping the money is right.

In contrast, the rule from which the person acts, "If you receive too much change, then it is permitted to keep it," probably would not lead to the greatest good (benefit) for the greatest number. If people generally acted from this rule, then clerks would have to be much more careful, they would have to be much more suspicious of their customers, the customers would be annoyed at not being trusted, fewer people would get away with any overpayment, and so on. All these are bad consequences of generally acting from the rule and would enable us to reject the rule, on utilitarian grounds, as one that can justify the singular moral judgment that taking the $5 is right.

NATURE OF THE GOOD, WHOSE GOOD, AND WHO ACTS

Once again, we need not specify precisely the nature of what is good or of benefit to a person. Many utilitarians claim that the only thing of value is pleasure; but many others claim that other things are also of value, including knowledge, virtue, friendship, love, beauty, and freedom. In Chapter 6 we shall examine more carefully the nature of value and what things, if any, have value. For now, if you require a more specific view, plug in your own favorite candidates as we consider the usual distinctions necessary for proper examination of a normative ethical theory.

The expression 'greatest number' seems fairly clear, but there have been some astonishing interpretations of it. One common move is to limit those who are to count as part of the numbers, and then to do your calculating. Many Nazis claimed that they were increasing the amount of good in the world, even though they were causing great suffering among the Jews, Slavs, and many more millions of people. Their claim was that such creatures were not really, or fully, human, and thus their benefit (that is, the benefit of the Jews, Slavs, and the others) did not need to be taken into account when they (the Nazis) determined the morality of their own actions. The same kind of response was found among slave owners and many nineteenth- and early twentieth-century factory owners. In times of war, it is common not to view the enemy as fully human. This may make it easier to fight wars, but it is a difficult move to defend rationally.

Recall that the egoist could not justifiably select the one *person* whose good should be increased; and, similarly, no one can apparently justifiably select the one *group* whose good should be increased. It would then follow that we cannot justifiably restrict the range of whose good is to be considered. The good of all human beings, at least, must be taken into account. If we become aware of additional rational or perhaps even sentient creatures besides humans, we'll have to include them also.

One great advantage of utilitarianism over egoism is that it clearly applies to everyone, in terms of both whose interests have to be taken into account when we calculate the consequences and which people are morally enjoined to act or not. In the passage cited on page 102, Mill makes it clear why the consequences affecting all people are to be taken into account and why all people have rights and obligations. A problem arises for egoism when there is a conflict between two individuals, each trying to achieve self-benefit. This is not a problem for utilitarianism, though, for, in this theory, each person is asked to and finds it natural to seek not the benefit of self alone but of all. This advantage of utilitarianism over egoism is, when we compare the two theories, a strong reason for preferring the former to the latter.

CALCULATING THE GREATEST GOOD

Most utilitarians talk about calculating the greatest good for the greatest number, but few of them suppose there can be some kind of precise and completely quantitative way of doing such calculation. However, those who restrict what is of benefit or value to pleasure, such as Jeremy Bentham, are inclined to think there *is* a strict calculus. They suppose that one can add up the pleasures resulting from some action, subtract the pains and discomforts, and then arrive at a figure that will allow us to conclude either that the action is right or wrong, obligatory or not. Bentham puts it as follows:

Sum up all the values of all the *pleasures* on the one side, and those of all the pains on the other. The balance, if it be on the side of pleasure, will give the *good* tendency of the act upon the whole, with respect to the interests of the *individual* person; if on the side of pain, the bad tendency of it upon the whole.

Take an account of the *number* of persons whose interests appear to be concerned, and repeat the above process with respect to each.[6]

The Problem of Quantifying What's Valuable

For most utilitarians, there is no precise way of calculating the greatest good. They avoid trying to do so because, for one thing, there is no quantifiable standard of what is valuable. We use the standard meterstick to determine whether something is a meter long, but no such standard unit exists for, say, pleasure. Furthermore, most philosophers do not want to restrict to pleasure things of value or of benefit to human beings. Once you include other candidates, such as happiness (as a long-run state in contrast with the short-run state of pleasure), freedom, love, and friendship, then you have added items that are even more difficult to quantify. We talk about "quantities" of love—but only in a general sense. No one supposes that there is a calculus of love available for precise counting and comparing.

Because we want to consider only the strongest views, we shall assume that there is no strict method of calculating the greatest good and that none is needed for utilitarianism to be workable. We must assume, however, that we can estimate or calculate the relative desirability of ends in some rough way. For example, we have to agree that we must be able to compare the value of freedom as opposed to the amount of security desired. If we offer a person a choice of a life with great security but with few material goods or one with many material things but greater insecurity, then we have to assume that a decision can be made between the two. The person making the decision would have to know more about the circumstances—for example, the kind of insecurity—but allowing the possibility for a decision is not difficult. In fact, we make this kind of decision frequently.

The Problem of Knowledge

When the problem of determining what was in a person's own interest arose in the discussion of egoism, we decided to assume neither that the person merely believed an action would be of benefit nor to limit consideration to those consequences that would in fact benefit the person. If we did not do this, on the

---

[6]Jeremy Bentham, *An Introduction to the Principles of Morals and Legislation* (New York: Hafner, 1948), 20.

one hand, we would have the absurdity of claiming that an action is obligatory or right simply because a person believes it will produce benefit—even when there is good evidence to show that the action will be harmful to that person. And, on the other hand, we would be asked to suppose that a person is obliged, say, to perform an action about which she is completely unaware because, in fact, the performance of that action would maximize her benefit.[7] This same problem arises with respect to utilitarianism. We do not want to say, when a person performs an action that he merely believes (perhaps even without evidence) will bring about the greatest good for the greatest number, that the action is right. Suppose someone believes, for example, that it is in everyone's interest to die as quickly as possible so as to join God in heaven—and to this end, poisons the water supply of as many cities as possible. Or, to take a less fanciful case, suppose someone believes that whites are superior to all other types of people and sets about to enslave all nonwhites so as to maximize the greatest good for the greatest number—even, as this person believes, for nonwhites. Is this person performing an obligatory action? This is an apparently clear instance, drawn from the phenomena, of an action that is not obligatory, but one that would be said to be obligatory if we were to interpret utilitarianism in terms of *belief* in the good-maximizing consequences of an act as the determiner of obligation.

Recall, also, that a supposed or believed consequence of an action is not a consequence at all. It is true that someone believes something when that belief exists. Whether, in our example, people will be happier when whites are the master race is another matter, one that may very well be irrelevant to the fact that someone holds that belief. You may want to say that the belief itself is false, but that is irrelevant to whether the person holds the belief. If obligation is a function of what someone believes the consequences of an action are, then the actual consequences are irrelevant to a determination of obligation. However, utilitarianism is usually held as the second of the two main teleological theories of obligation—theories that see obligation as a function of the value consequence of (the likely) actions alone. However, if obligation is seen as a function of what are believed to be the consequences of an action, then the theory is not teleological. So if we interpret the consequences to be what a person believes the consequences to be, we have numerous counterexamples that show that the view is not a teleological view at all.

The other extreme—that obligation or rightness is a function of what the consequences actually are—is also unacceptable. Suppose you take a crucial multiple-choice examination on which the answer to number 17 is: "(d) Either none of the above or the denial or the conjunction of (a) and (c)." The action of circling (d) is, we can easily suppose, the one that in these circumstances will maximize the good for the greatest number. You will do well on the examination, your family will be proud, your chances of getting a good job

---

[7]If this discussion has slipped your mind, turn to page 66 in Chapter 2.

will be increased, and so on. (Suppose also, to "lock up" the case, the grading is done on a noncomparative basis so that others will not suffer on the examination if you do well.) In this set of circumstances, supposing that obligation is a function of what the actual consequences are, then you are morally obliged to circle (d). However, again, this is a pretty clear instance of an action that is not obligatory. It is bad luck not to circle (d); you may curse yourself for not having done so; but it would apparently not be correct to accuse you of moral laxity for not doing so.

Frequently, more fanciful examples help to fix the point more firmly than realistic instances. Suppose that unbeknownst to you a new antibiotic drug is growing in the small piece of mold on your toothbrush. If you were to take that toothbrush to a biology laboratory at 10:45 A.M. on Tuesday, when professors Fisher and Wrensch are discussing the relative merits of dog walking and smoking as methods of stress reduction for faculty, those two, in a desire to stop the conversation, would ask you what you had in your hand. The rest would be history—for this antibiotic will wipe out all diseases and no one will be allergic to it. In terms of the view considered, you would be obliged to perform the action of going to the biology lab with toothbrush in hand, whether you knew where the biology lab was or not. However, once again, this is an apparently clear instance of an action that is not obligatory.

There are countless actions that, if carried out, would maximize the greatest good for the greatest number. This seems to be an incontrovertible truth. However, if obligation is a function of the actual consequences of an action (if it is performed), then all those actions are obligatory, and all those who are in a position to perform the actions except for their ignorance of the nature and significance of those actions are to be morally blamed for not fulfilling their obligations. This is a consequence that a theory of obligation would have great difficulty overcoming, and there is no reason to saddle utilitarianism with this consequence if we can avoid it. Because there is another interpretation that allows utilitarians to escape both this problem and the results of replacing consequences with what are *believed* to be consequences, we shall use that interpretation.

The middle ground, chosen both for egoism and utilitarianism, specifies consequences in terms of what is likely to occur given the knowledge available. For example, given the knowledge available, you cannot predict or even have an inkling that the mold on your toothbrush is a new and important antibiotic. Thus, you have no obligation to take the toothbrush to the biology laboratory, for the knowledge available to you does not contain that item.

Generally, the knowledge available is what we can reasonably expect people in a social setting to have. This is not meant to be a complicated notion, but to approximate the legal requirement and definition of what we can reasonably expect people to know. This means that sometimes a person will fail to fulfill an obligation because of a lack of knowledge and yet will still be held morally accountable and judged to have failed to fulfill an obligation. Suppose a father knows that if he is aware of the needs of his children, then he will know that his obligations to them include the obligation to buy them shoes, to take them for medical treatment, to provide nutritious food, and so on. The father cannot escape his responsibility by deliberately keeping himself in ignorance, for he has an obligation to know these things. His obligation stems from his general obligation as a parent, and the kind of knowledge he is attempting not to have is just the kind required in order that he fulfill that general obligation. A principle is sometimes invoked here to capture this point: We are obliged to know all those things that are required for us to carry out all our genuine obligations. This principle may, at first, seem strange to you; it may even seem to oblige people to do all manner of things. However, if you apply it in a few simple cases, you will see that this is not so.

Some people, because of special knowledge, have obligations most of us do not have. If three people watch a man stagger and subsequently collapse on the street, and one of them is a physician, then it seems clear that the physician has a special obligation stemming from his or her medical knowledge to help the person. A teacher in a classroom has a special obligation to help someone who has a learning disability, whereas people passing in the street outside do not. By contrast, some people, because of knowledge *dis*abilities, have few obligations. A severely mentally retarded person who cannot know or cannot, with any reasonable effort, come to know something, has no obligations with respect to this knowledge. A mentally retarded person who cannot master the notion of pressure point can hardly have an obligation to stop the bleeding of a severely injured person. A case such as this is a simple application of the "ought implies can" principle; for if the person cannot perform the action (because of a lack of knowledge in this case), then that person is not obliged to do so. This contrasts with the father who tries to keep himself ignorant but is capable of knowing about his children's needs. That person continues to have obligations to his children in spite of his ignorance.

The position being developed will also allow the utilitarians to explain a good deal of the phenomena often lumped under the name of "relativism." Some cultures provide information not available in others, training not given in others, and general knowledge not provided in others. One cannot reasonably be expected to know about how to treat those who have received back injuries if that knowledge is not available in one's culture. Thus, obligations will vary from person to person because of different knowledge and abilities, and also from culture to culture because of the differences in the availability of knowledge and the possibility of acquiring skills. This does not make utilitarianism the same as some relativistic view, as we shall see later, but it does allow it to explain many of the same phenomena as a relativistic view. Much more will be said on this topic in Chapter 4.

Limiting the Notion of Consequences

There is a sense, understood by us all, in which the U.S. involvement in Operation Desert Storm in 1991 in Iraq is a consequence of the Revolutionary War in the eighteenth century. If the latter event did not successfully occur, then the former event would not have occurred because there would have been no such country as the United States of America. We can capture this by saying that the Revolutionary War was causally necessary for the U.S. involvement in Desert Storm almost two centuries later. This may not appear to be a very strange claim, but the claim that U.S. involvement in Desert Storm is a consequence of the beginning of life on earth, some two billion years ago, no doubt does seem strange. However, let us restrict our examples to consequences that occur as a result of actions performed by human beings. Some person or people were crucial to the ancestors of those who made the Revolutionary War successful. The actions of these people in reproducing, making use of the sense already explained, can be called causally necessary for the success of the war. In that same sense, then, the successful prosecution of the war is a consequence of the actions of such people in reproducing.

This sense of 'consequence', however, is too broad to be used by the utilitarians. It would require us to calculate—in a rough sense of 'calculate'—the roots and effects of actions indefinitely into the past and future. Even if we could somehow come to know what the consequences of an action would be and what the effects of it were, this would make the practical task of arriving at singular moral judgments impossible. Furthermore, even though there is a sense of 'consequence' and 'effect' in which we can talk about remote events both in the past and the future as consequences, there are other senses of those terms in which it is not appropriate. We usually use shorter-run notions of *cause* and *consequences* in our daily lives. We say that someone died of head injuries, not that the death was the consequence of that person's birth or of the production of a certain car with a bolt that, as a result of lack of service, would fail at a crucial time and bring about the accident. We say that the consequences of a person's flunking a course include having to take the course over again, but not that twenty years later the person would tell a certain joke at a cocktail party.

We shall, accordingly, limit the consequences of actions to those events that result from the actions that one could reasonably predict and that are relatively important in terms of the histories of the people involved. Admittedly this is not a very precise notion, but since it relies on an everyday notion of the limits of consequences, its use seems legitimate. Limiting the consequences to what one can reasonably predict and the relative importance of the prospective consequences is closely related to another kind of limitation. In a commonsense way, there is a temporal and spatial limitation to the actual consequences of actions.[8] The ripples in a pond caused by a rock thrown into the middle spread out but then subside; so, too, do the causal consequences of actions fade out. It may be true theoretically that causal consequences extend indefinitely into the past and the future, but practically we do not view the situation that way. When we talk about the consequences one could reasonably predict, it will never turn out that what can reasonably be predicted is greater than the practical limit of the consequences of an action. Thus we have a connection between what one can reasonably know to be the consequences and the practical limit of those consequences.

However, you may think that, even though we do not have to calculate indefinitely into the future and the past, we still face the practical problem of calculating in each set of circumstances. For example, when we are in a position of having to invite someone we don't like very much to join us at a table in a bar, it is very difficult on the spur of the moment to calculate the benefit to all the parties involved. Action is called for then, and we must act. Many of the really important moral decisions in our lives, as well as many of the trivial moral decisions, have to be made without any time to calculate, and often in circumstances in which calculation is impossible. This problem is an old one for utilitarians, and Mill responds to it by pointing out that although an individual may not have time to calculate or think very much about an individual action, there really has been enough time.

> There has been ample time, namely, the whole past duration of the human species. During all that time mankind have been learning by experience the tendencies of actions; on which experience all the prudence, as well as all the morality of life is dependent. People talk as if the commencement of this course of experience had hitherto been put off, and as if, at the moment when some man feels tempted to meddle with the property or life of another, he had to begin considering for the first time whether murder and theft are injurious to human happiness.[9]

The utilitarians, along with the egoists, think that consequences alone count in determining the rightness of actions. This is not to say that they think motives unimportant. Motives, though, are not important in determining whether an action is right or wrong. One might want to say, along with Mill, that people who have motives of a certain sort are good people, but that is not to say

---

[8]This kind of notion has received attention from philosophers—it has even been given the fancy name of the "ripples and pond postulate." See, for example, J. J. C. Smart, *An Outline of Utilitarian Ethics* (Victoria, Australia: Melbourne University Press, 1961), 19–23. Just as the ripples caused by a stone thrown into a pond have an effective limit, even though they may have no theoretical limit, so do the consequences of actions. This image will perhaps help to fix the notion of the *limit of consequences* a bit better.

[9]Mill, *Utilitarianism*, 29. In this passage Mill also indicates he holds an indirect version of utilitarianism, for he is talking about classes of actions such as killing and theft. These are to be found in direct moral rules such as, "If any action is one of stealing, then it is wrong."

that their actions are *right*. People with good motives may nevertheless perform wrong actions frequently, and those with bad motives may perform right actions almost all the time. Later in the chapter we shall return to this issue and question whether that assumption is correct.[10] For now, however, simply note the difference for the utilitarian in the evaluation of the moral worth of an action and the moral worth of the individual who performs that action. The former is a function of consequences alone and not motives, but the latter is a function of motives.

Summary

Utilitarianism requires that we be able to calculate what is of value, and it especially requires us to be able to determine that one end or course of action is more valuable than another. This does not, however, require a strict calculation, but only that we be able to determine in most cases without great difficulty. Just as was true of egoism, what is of value or benefit will not now be specified. It may be limited to one thing, such as pleasure, or it may include any number of other things, such as love, freedom, and friendship. When utilitarians talk about what is in the interest of the greatest number, they do not mean what someone *believes* is in the interest of the greatest number. Instead, we shall take them to mean that consequences are those that one could reasonably predict will occur given the knowledge that is available. Finally, consequences are not to extend indefinitely into the future, the past, or, into space; they are to be limited to results that could reasonably be predicted and that have a certain degree of significance to the people involved. This, in brief, is how we should understand the key notions of utilitarian theories of obligation.

Exercises: Applying Utilitarianism

1. Choose an incident within your own experience in which you or some other person made a singular moral judgment (of obligation, right, wrong, and so on). Show how the application of direct egoism and direct utilitarianism to this situation would allow the derivation of the judgment, even though it is likely that neither of the theories was actually used in the set of circumstances. If applying the theories gives different results, give reasons for preferring one to the other.

(continued)

---

[10]In Chapter 5 we shall examine virtue ethics theories, those views that suppose that the character trait from which the action is performed determines its moral worth. In a sense, these are motives of action.

> *(continued)*
> 2. Suppose you could choose to be more intelligent or better looking but not both. Which would you choose? How did you make your choice? What kind of calculation did you make?
> 3. What are (were) the consequences of the U.S. involvement in Operation Desert Storm? What are (were) the consequences of George Bush choosing Clarence Thomas as a candidate for the Supreme Court? Does the method of determining consequences in these instances support or undermine the proposed method of determining consequences in this chapter?
> 4. The utilitarian suggests that we divorce the evaluation of actions from the evaluation of agents performing those actions. Without reading ahead, present reasons for agreeing or disagreeing with this position.

UTILITARIANISM EVALUATED
Reasons in Favor

Now that we have a better idea of what utilitarianism is, it is time to evaluate its ability to explain moral phenomena as well as to see why anyone would want to hold such theories. The reasons in favor of utilitarianism are

1. The theory has universal scope.
2. It is held and used by people either directly or indirectly when they consciously and explicitly do moral reasoning.

These two reasons are set out by Mill and have some force. Before examining criticisms of utilitarianism, two things must be pointed out. First, utilitarians posit no psychological theory of motivation to support their view even though, as pointed out above, Mill thinks there is a social impulse. The second claim, which is an empirical claim, requires some explanation about how it supports utilitarianism.

Remember that most theories have few positive reasons for acceptance in their favor; they win out by being able to explain the phenomena best, to answer adequately any criticisms, and to avoid ad hoc explanations. These are the other criteria of acceptability, the most important reasons for accepting a theory. One of the problems with egoism, you will recall, was that its scope was too limited; there seemed to be no way in which the theory could reasonably be applied to other people. A theory of obligation gains acceptability insofar as it can account for such phenomena wherever they occur. This is something utilitarianism is explicitly designed to do, especially as it is interpreted here. Utilitarianism suggests that right action, for example, is a function of the likelihood of good-maximizing consequences for everyone.

You may be tempted to say this aspect of utilitarianism is just a special instance of accounting for the phenomenon better than its rivals, and you would have a good point. However, since the reason is very important in terms of comparing utilitarianism with egoism, it seems worth stating as a separate, positive point. I would not be upset, though, if someone whose philosophic sense is disturbed by this special placement put it in the category of explaining better or accounting for the phenomena better than its rivals.

Counterexamples

At this point we have more carefully specified the nature of utilitarian theories of obligation and have given a brief summary of the reasons in their favor. Now we shall examine some of the objections to utilitarianism. The counterexamples selected will apply to both the direct and indirect varieties of utilitarianism, although we will show, in each case, exactly how the counterexample applies.

Suppose, as evidence indicates, we can provide fresh produce to the American public (and by extension to everyone) if we but pay those who pick the produce a very low wage. This wage allows the pickers to live only at a low standard of living, but it does allow them to live without starving or suffering any fatal diseases. It is true that they do not live with much dignity and the chances of their children escaping such a life are very small, but these are negative factors that must be weighed along with the positive. On the positive side, we have an increase of the quality of life of several million people by a small amount as a result of being able to buy produce for a low price. Although the amount of benefit each person receives is small, there are so many millions of people that the resulting amount of benefit is large.

The amount of disbenefit or disutility that each farm worker receives more than offsets the benefit each individual consumer receives—however, there are very few workers in comparison with the entire population that receives the benefit. Suppose there are about 50,000 farm workers and, again roughly, about 100 million people who consume the products they pick. In order to match the utility produced by the millions, there would have to be 200 times as much disutility to each picker. It is plausible to suppose that there is not that much disutility. Each farm worker gets enough to eat, has a place to sleep, clothes to wear, and all the other basic necessities.

Even if we suppose the amount of utility and disutility to be about the same, the example would still work as a counterexample for then it would, on utilitarian grounds alone, be morally indifferent which way we acted. It would not matter whether we paid the farm workers more or continued to keep the produce prices low. However, let us illustrate this with respect to specific utilitarian views.

Consider, first, direct utilitarianism—the view whose principle of obligation is "If any person *a* performs an action that increases the good (benefit) of the greatest number more than any other available action, then that action is obligatory." The complementary principle concerning right is "If any person *a* performs an action that increases the good (benefit) of the greatest number, then that action is right." The suggestion is that paying the farm workers the low salary does increase the good or benefit of the greatest number. If this is so, then the action is morally right. You must not misunderstand the claim; it is not that it is good business to pay low salaries, or that it is the American Way, or that it is necessary—none of those. The claim is that it is morally right to pay low salaries. Whatever one thinks about farm workers, it is pretty clear, insofar as we report the phenomena, that it does not appear morally right to pay such workers low salaries.

Of course, if one could establish direct utilitarianism, independently of any of these considerations, as a correct theory of obligation, then one could establish the surprising conclusion that paying the farm workers low salaries is right. However, there are no overwhelming reasons in favor of utilitarianism and, thus, this is not a justified conclusion.

It would be a sufficiently powerful criticism of direct utilitarianism to describe actions that are apparently not right but that, according to that view, are right. It would be a stronger conclusion yet to establish that the action of paying low wages to the farm laborers was obligatory. Now, it is not clear that one can establish this, but it is worth a short discussion. One would have to establish that paying low wages is the action that, among all the alternatives, given what we know, is most likely to maximize the good or benefit of the greatest number. This is difficult to establish for we have to consider the alternatives available to us. On the one hand, we could invest in mechanical pickers that, in the not-too-distant future, would replace hand pickers. In the short run, the venture would be costly for the development costs would be very high, but within a fairly short period of time this money would be retrieved by the savings on labor. On the other hand, it is not at all clear, given the lack of success in developing such machines in the past, that such machines either could be developed or that when developed would result in any savings. Furthermore, given the unskilled nature of the labor involved, and the nature of our society, if the farm workers were unemployed, it would work a great hardship on them. This disutility would also have to be included in our calculations. When we add the positive and the negative benefit, it is not clear that this alternative would increase the benefit of the greatest number more than paying the farm workers low wages. You are invited to consider other such alternatives and to decide whether there is a reasonable case to be made that the alternative of paying low wages is the one most likely to maximize the greatest good of the greatest number among all the alternatives available. According to direct utilitarianism, not only is the action of paying low wages right, but it is also apparently obligatory.[11]

Remember that this last criticism is not necessary for the counterexample to be effective. But should the last criticism be effective, it would be very powerful.

A single counterexample by itself does not provide a very strong criticism of direct utilitarianism—or any ethical theory for that matter. If the theory were otherwise strongly supported, we might say, as is sometimes said in the sciences, that that counterexample is just an anomaly. In this instance, the counterexample represents a large class of actions of the same type. The same kinds of considerations apply to paying women lower wages than men for the same work, to paying blacks lower wages than whites, and so on. The reader is asked to flesh out and construct the counterexamples of this type that seem most plausible. As can be seen, moral philosophy is not something esoteric, but something that we all can and must engage in.

Since counterexamples always meet with a mixed reception, it is wise not to depend on just one kind but to offer a variety of kinds. There are people—alas, all too many of them—who find the greatest good and benefit in the suffering of others or in cheating others. Suppose, for example, that a person receives immense benefit in the form of pleasure and enough psychic energy to last the rest of the day from underpaying the paper deliverer. The deliverer, we shall suppose, does not find this out, for the customer is very clever. The action affects no one but the two of them; and since we can calculate the amount of benefit and disutility in just the two instances, it is easy to see that more overall utility results when the deliverer is cheated out of the money. You can fill in more details—such as the deliverer has 100 customers—as you wish.

The action of the cheater is, on direct utilitarian grounds, morally right—and yet it appears to be a pretty clear instance of an action that is not morally right. The same case can apparently be used for the indirect utilitarian view, for the general adoption of the rule "If an action of cheating one person a small amount will benefit the cheater much more than the cheated person is harmed, then cheating that person is permitted," would apparently increase the good or benefit of the greatest number. Remember, though, that the action does not affect very many people.

---

[11]Counterexamples are themselves sometimes controversial. American consumers continue in the 1990s to increase their purchase of Japanese cars. This has led to reduction of the U.S. auto industry, with tens of thousands of workers losing their jobs. However, American consumers are getting supposedly better cars. It is not implausible that the overall good, especially if we include the benefit accruing to the Japanese workers, is increased. Do we as Americans have a special obligation to our fellow citizens to help save their jobs? Is it morally required on utilitarian grounds for the public (through the government) to invest in research and education to help make the U.S. auto industry more competitive?

The presentation of just one person of this type would not be much of a criticism of utilitarianism, but the existence of many such people presents a serious problem to the theory. There is the sadist who gets enormous kicks from sticking pins into people on the subway, the teacher whose day is "made" if one student can be humiliated, the petty bureaucrat who can make it through the whole week by frustrating the aims of a few customers with tons of red tape, the vandal who pulls flowers from flower boxes, and so on. Once again you are invited to try your hand at constructing such counterexamples from your own experience.

Now we shall consider a third counterexample. In this case, the action involves a very small amount of benefit that does not thereby seem to render it morally right. Suppose someone whispers, just loudly enough to be heard by the person two ahead in the line in which they are both standing, "Isn't that person in the blue sweater attractive?" Mightn't this make the person who overhears the compliment feel somewhat better? Now suppose someone does this complimenting as a matter of course and adopts as a rule of action "If you can compliment someone without incurring any responsibilities onto yourself but at the same time cause some benefit to the person complimented, then making your compliment is right." This kind of action, although it may involve only a few people, results in an increase in the amount of good for the greatest number and thus, according to the utilitarian standard, would have to be judged morally right. Yet this kind of action, even if we say that it is kind, is apparently not a morally right action.

Other examples of this type might include scratching someone's back when it itches, returning 3 cents in overpayment to the neighborhood grocer, smiling at the child who is nervously taking a shortcut through your yard, and complimenting your host's food (even when it isn't very good). Doubtless, once again, you can supply still other examples from your own experience since kindly, relatively uncomplicated actions of this sort are abundant.

Finally, as the fourth type of counterexample, consider actions that do increase the benefit of the greatest number but profit the actors in such a way that apparently justifies our withholding the judgment that they have done something morally right. Suppose for a moment that putting the mass-produced automobile within the reach of most citizens in many countries has increased the benefit of the greatest number of people. Certainly, the private car has enlarged people's horizons, provided mobility, freed many from dependence on local merchants, created jobs, provided increased social opportunities and a place to pursue such opportunities in private, and so on. The person whose actions are probably most responsible for this great—and we're saying, beneficial—change in society is Henry Ford, the man who made the assembly line work. It's probably safe to say that Henry Ford's motive in making the assembly line work was not to increase the greatest good of the greatest number, but to make a great deal of money. According to the utilitarians, the motive for an action is irrelevant to whether it has positive moral worth,[12] so Ford's action of mass producing cars, to the utilitarian, would be morally right. However, although we may admire Ford for his cleverness, or despise him for his lack of social awareness, his action of perfecting mass production methods does not seem to be a morally right action.

This same kind of counterexample can be constructed wherever someone has benefited greatly from an action that has also benefited a larger number *and* the person did not have the increase in the benefit of others as a primary motive in acting. This would apply to James Fisk and Jay Gould and the others who developed the railroads in the United States in the nineteenth century, John D. Rockefeller's development of the oil industry, those who made fortunes in armament manufacturing while supporting the justified side in war, and so on. You should work out a counterexample of this type that is most convincing to you.

If the utilitarians are correct, then motives are not relevant to the rightness of actions but only to the goodness of persons, and the preceding purported counterexamples are not actual counterexamples. However, to remind you, utilitarianism has not been established via any strong independent evidence as yet, so the construction of counterexamples from the phenomena is perfectly legitimate. Someone could, of course, provide a strong defense of utilitarianism or work out some new arguments in favor of the view; then we would be justified in rejecting the proposed counterexamples. For now, though, these counterexamples have to be seen as negative evidence, as examples that tend to show that utilitarianism is not a correct theory of obligation. Nevertheless, despite this evidence against the theory—and still more criticisms will be presented as we go on—it would be premature to make a final decision about utilitarianism until we examine all the main theories of obligation.

The proposed counterexamples apply to direct utilitarianism, but it would save us considerable trouble if the same kinds of counterexamples also applied to indirect utilitarianism. With very little change it seems that most of the counterexamples do apply to the indirect form of utilitarianism. To show this, consider how just a few of the counterexamples would have to be changed to apply. Consider the rule "It is morally right to pay low wages to farm workers" or, as we have been saying it, "If any action is one of paying low wages to farm workers, then it is right." Is this a rule that, when acted from by most, leads to the greatest good for the greatest number? If the answer is yes, then we are entitled, given indirect utilitarianism, to conclude that the rule is a direct moral rule. The rule, along with the appropriate second premise, would enable us to derive a singular moral judgment to the effect that paying this group of farm workers low wages is right.

---

[12] Utilitarian moralists have gone beyond almost all others in affirming that the motive has nothing to do with the morality of the action, though much with the worth of the agent. He who saves a fellow creature from drowning does what is morally right, whether his motive be duty or the hope of being paid for his trouble. (Mill, *Utilitarianism*, 25)

This kind of reasoning, which attempts to establish that it is for the greatest good that we pay low wages to farm workers, would also establish, then, that the cited rule, when generally acted from, leads to the greatest good for the greatest number. This is not to say that whenever an action—for example, keeping the $5 the clerk overpaid you—would lead to the greatest good for the greatest number, you are justified in concluding that acting on the general rule that corresponds to that action would lead to the greatest good. In this instance, it does not. However, the examples presented here were chosen because they do seem to apply both to the direct and the indirect versions of utilitarianism. Hopefully, this is clear enough from the discussion, and you can fill in the details of the other kinds of counterexamples to make them apply also to the indirect versions.

Supposing that the preceding claims are justified, then we do not have to construct completely different counterexamples to indirect utilitarianism since, with appropriate changes, the same criticisms apply.

The Problem of Justice

The problem that causes utilitarians the most difficulty is distributive justice. *Distributive justice* is usually contrasted with *retributive justice*. The latter concerns theories of punishment; and the former, theories of the morally proper manner of distributing the relatively scarce things of value. The expression 'things of value' is what is at stake when we talk about benefit, good, utility, and disutility. The utilitarians tell us a right action is one that increases the benefit or value for the greatest number but, according to most philosophers, utilitarians are not adequately able to distinguish among different distributions of the value created.[13] To see this difference, let us begin by distinguishing among various notions of distribution. One distinction exists between the *greatest amount* of value and the *greatest amount for the greatest number*. It might be that we could increase the amount of value by killing some of the people in our society. If, having a barely adequate amount of food, we killed off certain nonproductive old people, we would have fewer people, but these fewer people would eat better. The amount of value would increase, but it would not increase for the greatest number of people. One criticism of utilitarianism has been that it cannot distinguish between these two situations—that in fact it would

---

[13] For now, things of value can be considered tangible things, such as a bag of rice, or nontangible things, such as love or freedom. When we ask, "How shall we properly distribute the things of value?" we are asking how much rice each person should get, whether all or only some of us will be free, and so on. Even when we consider the distribution of nontangible things of value, the question of how properly to distribute them is an important and practical one. Depending on the answers, we will choose certain governments and economic systems. (At the risk of boring you, I ask you to recall that no specific theory of value is being presupposed in this discussion.)

have to allow that it is morally permissible to kill nonproductive elderly people in the name of justice.[14]

Even if we suppose that we do not kill people and that the number of citizens of alternative societies stays constant, still other kinds of distributions of things of value give rise to problems. Imagine a society that has ten people to whom the things of value are to be distributed. Suppose that we measure the things of value by some unit of value V and that there are a total of 100 V's to be distributed in this society. The first of the columns that follow represents the distribution of V's in this society:

Society 1	Society 2	Society 3
10	15	15
10	15	15
10	15	15
10	15	15
10	15	15
10	5	5
10	5	5
10	5	5
10	5	5
10	5	6

The second column shows the distribution in a society that, like the first one, has 100 V's to distribute but that parcels them out differently. The third column shows a distribution like that in society 2 except that it involves 101 V's.

If we compare society 1 with society 2, we see that the total amount of good is the same, 100 V's. However, we all recognize the difference between the two cases. The difference is not in the average amount of V's people receive, for the arithmetical average is the same, 10 V's. It is the distribution that is different.[15] We can characterize the difference in a technical way (see footnote 15), or we can draw attention to relevant differences via nontechnical examples. Suppose that V is food and that the twenty people that make up societies 1 and 2 require rougly the same amount of food. It would seem that

---

[14]This counterexample is not as clear as the others presented. You may wish to defend the utilitarian position when the choice is starvation for all or for only a few. This kind of case is better living for many at the expense of killing a minority, including, however, a substantial number of the elderly.

[15]We could use what are now fairly standard technical terms to make these same distinctions:

Pareto improvement upon an initial distribution [is] . . . any alternative distribution according to which every participant fares no worse than (i.e., fares better or as well as) he does on the initial distribution. We arrive also at the idea of a Pareto *optimal distribution* within a set of alternatives as any distribution within the set that is such that none of the other distributions in the set effect a Pareto improvement upon it. [Nicholas Rescher, *Distributive Justice*, (New York: Bobbs-Merrill, 1966), 13]

in society 2 half the people would be on the edge of starvation and half would live very well, whereas in society 1 this would not be so. Most of us would say there is a moral difference in the way the V's are distributed in the two societies. But utilitarians, so the argument goes, cannot make this distinction within their theory of obligation.

We can make this point more dramatically if we consider society 3 and society 1. Because the total amount of V's is greater in society 3 than in society 1, some would certainly claim that on utilitarian grounds alone, the former is actually preferable to the latter.

The three cases represent three different distributions of things of value; in two of them, the total amount of value is the same. In spite of the same value being present, the choice of a method of distribution will often make a moral difference. If we are asked whether society 1 or society 2 is morally preferable, we all recognize the significance of the question; the societies *are* morally different. As citizens, we would perform such actions as voting, sending money to political candidates, supporting revolutions, writing books and pamphlets, fighting wars, and the like on the basis of our choice of which of these societies is best.[16] When we oppose some of the options, we sometimes do so because we believe them to be morally wrong or to include morally wrong (that is, unjust) ways of distributing society's things of value. For example, society 2 might describe a slave society and society 1 a free society. No one, I think, would say the choice between these two societies is morally indifferent. How the amount of good in those societies is to be distributed is not a morally indifferent choice. Well, you ask, who says it *is* morally indifferent?

The answer to this question highlights the major criticism of utilitarianism. If utilitarianism cannot adequately distinguish the moral worth of different distributions of the things of value, then it cannot adequately account for an important area of our moral life and a significant part of the moral phenomena. Suppose, as utilitarians supposedly do, that as long as the amount of value created is the same, it does not matter whether we choose the distribution of society 1 or that of society 2. If society 2 turns out to be a slave society, that, according to the utilitarian, is irrelevant.

Furthermore, suppose it turns out that a certain kind of slave society produces a slight amount more of good than a corresponding free society. That is, suppose society 3 represents a slave society that will allow the production of the greatest amount of good—even more than in society 1. This is not incredible. Because we must often make decisions about which kind of society we want to build in the future, and if the only considerations we can use are utilitarian ones, we would conclude that society 3 is the best society since it results in more overall good than any other possible alternative. The creation

---

[16]There are, of course, many more options than these three. These three were chosen because they are fairly clear and allow the general point to be made.

of this society would, on utilitarian grounds, be obligatory; and, of course, it would at least be morally right.

Traditionally the claim is that utilitarianism is silent on these questions, for it calls only for the maximization of things of value and has nothing to say about their distribution. But utilitarians often say that the method of distribution does make a difference in the total amount of good produced, and some, especially Mill, try to show that a principle of the just distribution of things of value follows in some way from the principle of utility. However, as the case now stands in the philosophical world, the evidence indicates that the utilitarian is in trouble because of the problem of justice. There is no reason to think that the greatest total amount of good will be produced in a society when there is a just distribution. Societies exist in which that is not true. Before advanced technology, more good may well have been produced by having the institution of slavery than by not having it. The action of keeping slaves would then, on utilitarian grounds, have been morally right.

In Chapter 5 of *Utilitarianism*, Mill makes a valiant attempt to save utilitarianism from this criticism but, again, it is not clear that he succeeds. (In the appendix to this chapter there will be a brief presentation of Mill's view.)

If the criticism is restated in terms of which of two competing societies we should morally prefer, or which is morally better, the point can be made in a sharper way. Of course, we are not in a position to set up a society; as individuals, we do not have the resources or power. However, as members of a democratic society, we are constantly making decisions about which society is best and which one we should create. One of the important considerations in setting up or maintaining a society is determining morally preferable actions, and one of the important moral questions concerns distributing the things of value in the society. A theory of obligation that cannot provide adequate help with this question is deficient.

There is apparently a moral difference between two societies—one, a slave society, and the other, a free society—that create the same amount of value. If there is a moral difference, then there is a moral difference in the worth of the action of setting up one of these societies rather than the other. Most of us would say that in most circumstances the creation or selection of the slave society is morally wrong. However, since the total amount of value created by either action (of creating either society) is the same, on utilitarian grounds our choice of which society to work for is morally indifferent. If it *is* morally relevant to distribute value in one way rather than another, and utilitarianism cannot account for that difference, then as an ethical theory it is importantly incomplete.

The temptation is to use some nonutilitarian grounds to determine which of the distributions is morally preferable. However, if we do this, we abandon utilitarianism as usually understood. Some philosophers suppose a theory of obligation should consist of some version of the principle of utility *and* a principle of justice.[17] Such people do not think a principle of justice can be reduced to, or derived from, a utilitarian theory of obligation. They believe that a theory of justice is independent of what we have called utilitarianism. In the appendix following this chapter you will find the utilitarian account of justice. Examine it carefully to decide if the account overcomes the standard criticisms.

Exercises: Critical Analysis of Utilitarianism

1. Choose some moral issue in which it would make a difference in your final (singular) moral judgment if you adopted utilitarianism rather than ethical egoism. Show how the applying of each of the theories leads to your making different judgments. Now choose an issue in which applying the different theories would make no difference in the singular judgment arrived at.
2. Critically evaluate the following argument: The counterexamples against the various forms of utilitarianism presuppose some other theory that is incompatible with utilitarianism. Of course, if we suppose the correctness of that incompatible theory, we can show that there is something wrong with utilitarianism, but that is true of any theory. So the counterexamples are not effective.
3. Present a utilitarian argument either in favor of or against U.S. involvement in the military operation called Desert Storm.
4. J. S. Mill supposes that ordinary people actually do use utilitarianism as a theory in their moral reasoning, although they frequently do not recognize this fact. "It would, however, be easy to show that whatever steadiness or consistency these moral beliefs have attained, has been mainly due to the tacit influence of a standard not recognized. . . . The principle of utility . . . has had a large share in forming the moral doctrines even of those who most scornfully reject its authority" (*Utilitarianism*, 14, 15). Critically evaluate this claim.

EGOISM AND UTILITARIANISM

The astute among you will have noticed that the criticisms of utilitarianism involving justice also apply to ethical egoism. In fact, there is no reasonable way egoism can even generate a theory of justice; Mill at least presents some

---

[17]William K. Frankena [*Ethics*, 2d ed. (Englewood Cliffs, N.J.: Prentice-Hall, 1973)] holds a version of that theory that we shall examine in the next chapter.

arguments in an attempt to show that utilitarianism accounts for the phenomenon of justice. On this score, then, utilitarianism fares better than egoism. To the extent that utilitarianism can account for the rightness of actions that involve more than one person without any problem of inconsistency, it is also more acceptable than egoism. Evidence suggests that people use some kind of utilitarian standard more frequently than an egoistic one. Furthermore, you should consider what usually happens when the two kinds of considerations clash—when there is an irreconcilable conflict between your own good and that of others. Whichever way the resolution of this conflict turns out, it will provide evidence for one or the other of the two teleological theories.

In terms of the number and seriousness of criticisms, utilitarianism fares better than egoism. However, remember that so far we have examined only two theories of obligation, both of which are teleological; that is, both the egoist and the utilitarian suppose obligation and rightness are a function solely of the consequences of actions. They do disagree, though, about the range of consequences that must legitimately be taken into account: The egoist limits the consequences to one person while the utilitarian extends the range to all human beings. In the next chapter, we shall begin the examination of nonteleological theories of obligation.

RECOMMENDED READING

Acton, H. B., and J. W. N. Watkins. "Negative Utilitarianism." *Proceedings of the Aristotelian Society*, supplement 37 (1963): 83–114. Do we have more of an obligation to relieve suffering than to bring about positive good? If your answer is yes, your utilitarianism will take a different form than otherwise.

Bentham, Jeremy. *An Introduction to the Principles of Morals and Legislation.* New York: Hafner, 1948. Bentham's work most influenced Mill, though the latter's views are not always the same as Bentham's.

Brandt, Richard B., ed. *Justice and Equality.* Englewood Cliffs, N.J.: Prentice-Hall, 1962. Brandt presents a variety of essays on a variety of topics concerning justice.

Lyons, David. *Forms and Limits of Utilitarianism.* London: Oxford University Press, 1965.

Mill, John Stuart. *Utilitarianism (with Critical Essays).* Edited by Samuel Gorovitz. Indianapolis, In.: Bobbs-Merrill, 1971. The text of Mill's *Utilitarianism* is reprinted along with many very good articles about that work and its problems. Mill's major works in ethics are collected in an excellent work titled *Essays on Ethics, Religion and Society* (Vol. 10 of *Collected Works of John Stuart Mill.* Edited by J. M. Robson. Toronto: University of Toronto Press, 1969).

Narveson, Jan. *Morality and Utility.* Baltimore: Johns Hopkins University, 1967.

Rescher, Nicholas. *Distributive Justice.* Indianapolis, In.: Bobbs-Merrill, 1966.

Ryan, Alan. *The Philosophy of John Stuart Mill*, 2d ed. London: Macmillan, 1987.

Sidgwick, Henry. *The Methods of Ethics*. 7th ed. London: Macmillan, 1962. This is a very detailed and carefully worked out utilitarian position by a late nineteenth-century author.

Smart, J. J. C. *An Outline of Utilitarian Ethics*. Victoria, Australia: Melbourne University Press, 1961.

Solomon, Robert, and Mark C. Murphy, eds. *What is Justice?* Notre Dame, In.: University of Notre Dame Press, 1990. This is a good place to find statements of the major current theories of justice.

APPENDIX TO CHAPTER THREE

Justice

Although we cannot fully treat the topic of justice, we should at least outline the main rival theories in order to understand better the issues raised in Chapter 3. The position of each theory must be brief, so if you wish to examine the views in greater detail, you should read from the works quoted or from the ones listed in Recommended Reading for Chapter 3. Because this is a chapter on utilitarianism, let us begin with J. S. Mill's views on justice.

Mill's strategy should be quite familiar to us. First, he lists a set of phenomena that people generally believe to fall within the topic of *justice*. He then attempts to show that utilitarianism can account for these phenomena. For example, he notes that we suppose it unjust to deprive someone of liberty, property, or "any other thing which belongs to him by law."[1] Knowing that certain laws are unjust highlights the injustice of "taking or withholding from any person that to which he has a moral right."[2] We think it unjust for a person to "obtain a good or be made to undergo an evil which he does not deserve."[3] We suppose it unjust to "break faith with anyone . . . [and] to be *partial*—to show favor or preference . . . [where these] do not properly apply."[4]

---

[1] John Stuart Mill, *Utilitarianism (with Critical Essays)*, ed. Samuel Gorovitz (Indianapolis, In.: Bobbs-Merrill, 1971), 43.
[2] Ibid., 44.
[3] Ibid.
[4] Ibid., 44.

These phenomena are, so Mill claims, explained by his view:

> Duties of perfect obligation are those duties in virtue of which a correlative *right* resides in some person or persons; duties of imperfect obligation are those moral obligations which do not give birth to any right. I think it will be found that this distinction exactly coincides with that which exists between justice and the other obligations of morality. . . . Whether the injustice consists in depriving a person of a possession, or in breaking faith with him or in treating him worse than he deserves, or worse than other people who have greater claims—in each case the supposition implies two things: a wrong done, and some assignable person who is wronged. Injustice may also be done by treating a person better than others; but the wrong in this case is to his competitors, who are also assignable persons. It seems to me that this feature in the case—a right in some person, correlative to the moral obligation—constitutes the specific difference between justice and generosity or beneficence. Justice implies something which it is not only right to do, and wrong not to do, but which some individual person can claim from us as his moral right.[5]

If, as Mill supposes, he can give his standard utilitarian analysis of the notions of *obligation* and *right*, then he will have given an account of justice without bringing in some principle independent of the principle of utility. Mill is very careful to give a psychological explanation of how it has happened that justice has a different "feel" to it than ordinary obligations. However, this is not essential to our discussion.

Has Mill succeeded? It is not at all clear how this account of justice adequately responds to the criticisms in the chapter, but that will be left up to you to determine. Now, in very brief fashion, here are some other accounts of justice.

One view that is popular in the United States we can call *competitionism*: "The ethical principle that would directly justify the distribution of income in a free market society is, 'To each according to what he and the instruments he owns produces.'"[6] This principle, as applied here by Milton Friedman, is directed to income policy alone, but we can extend it without difficulty to the level of a general principle of justice. So stated, it might appear as follows:

> If any distribution of things of value is a result of competition in the economic system, then that distribution is just.

There are many problems with an unrestricted principle of this sort. For example, should we allow those who cannot compete (the sick, the mentally handicapped, the poorly educated) to starve? What do we do about those forms

---

[5]Ibid., 47–48.

[6]Milton Friedman, *Capitalism and Freedom* (Chicago: University of Chicago Press, 1962), 161–162.

of competition that lead to the absence of competition? What provisions do we make for national defense? Do we set aside some supplies independently of the market mechanism? These adjustments would require a more complex principle, and it is not at all clear what such a principle would look like. We can say that, as it stands, the principle is inadequate to address these problems; we must await a further statement of it before any final decision can be made.

A view that is also popular would make distribution a function of merit. A general statement of this view might be:

> If any distribution of things of value is on the basis of merit, then that distribution is just.

Most people who hold a theory like this realize the need for some test or further specification of merit. The problem has been that many of the proposed tests of merit are apparently not morally acceptable. Some have claimed that one has merit when one is an Aryan, or a member of the Central Committee, or of noble birth. Obviously, this indicates the need for a test to determine which standards of merit are morally acceptable. One test that might work is to determine if the distribution of things of value under the standard resulted in a just distribution. This, of course, cannot be done because merit is supposedly being used to explain the notion of *just distribution*. Furthermore, we cannot leave the notion of *merit* unspecified because there are competing notions, some of which, at least, are clearly unacceptable.

Another view would distribute things of value equally. As Mill points out in his listing of the moral phenomena, equality is one thing we are concerned about when we discuss justice. A general principle of justice in the equalitarian tradition might be:

> If any distribution of things of value is equal, then that distribution is just.

There have been many attempts to specify *equality*. Some have used numerical equality: We each take numerically the same amount and take turns when there isn't enough to go around. This approach runs into difficulty in a way pointed out by Aristotle long ago. The amount of food that an active woodsman needs is more than that needed by a sedentary clerk, so a numerically equal amount of food for each would sometimes be unjust. Such considerations led Aristotle and others to introduce some notion of *proportional increase* in the amount of value in a person's life:

> Treating people equally does not mean treating them identically; justice is not so monotonous as all that. It means making the same relative contribution to the goodness of their lives (this is equal help or helping according to need) or asking the same relative sacrifice (this is asking in accordance with ability).[7]

---

[7]William K. Frankena, *Ethics*. 2d ed. (Englewood Cliffs, N.J.: Prentice-Hall, 1973), 51.

This statement by Frankena is representative of the sort of position equalitarian philosophers are inclined to move toward. A number of questions about the term 'same relative contribution' remain unanswered, however. Do we accept the judgment of each person as to what his or her own relative contribution should be? Do we accept each person's judgment of what each needs in order for there to be a proportional increase in the good of each? This doesn't appear to be acceptable. So we must also await some further specification of this view.

Is there a communist theory of justice? Those who claim there is begin with these words of Marx:

> In a higher phase of communist society, after the enslaving subordination of the individual to the division of labour, and with it also the antithesis between mental and physical labour, has vanished; after labour has become not only a means of life but itself life's prime want; after the productive forces have also increased with the all-round development of the individual, and all the springs of co-operative wealth flow more abundantly—only then can the narrow horizon of bourgeois right be crossed in its entirety and society inscribe on its banners: From each according to his ability, to each according to his needs![8]

Marx obviously had a certain context in mind when he proposed this principle. It seems clear that we have not reached the point he describes as that point at which the principle of distribution can be put into effect. Shall we conclude that all distributions are now not just? The principle, taken from its context, would be:

> If any distribution of things of value follows the rule "From each according to his ability, to each according to his needs," then that distribution is just.

If we attempted to apply this principle now, before the "springs of co-operative wealth flow more abundantly," either nothing would be just, or severe difficulties would arise. We cannot use 'need' in the sense that individuals now have need, for that would not result in a just distribution. What do we do when some supposed or even real needs are incompatible? These questions would have to be answered in order for Marx to have a complete theory of justice.

As a result of the work of John Rawls, contemporary writers have taken up the topic of justice with enthusiasm. Rawls proposes to set out and defend what he thinks are the indirect principles of justice. Thus, he does not, in setting out these indirect rules, embrace a marxist or a libertarian position, which give us a direct principle of justice. Rawls's indirect rules, though, do eliminate many theories of justice, including libertarianism. His indirect rules are:

---

[8] Karl Marx, *Critique of the Gotha Programme* (Peking: Foreign Language Press, 1972), 17.

First Principle
Each person is to have an equal right to the most extensive total system of equal basic liberties compatible with a similar system of liberty for all.

Second Principle
Social and economic inequalities are to be arranged so that they are both:
(a) to the greatest benefit of the least advantaged, consistent with the just savings principle, and
(b) attached to offices and positions open to all under conditions of fair equality of opportunity.[9]

Rawls's theory is set out in a wonderfully detailed context of economic and political theory, a context it is not possible to re-create here. Those who are interested in contemporary theories of justice need to read what is arguably the most important work on justice in the twentieth century. Here I only note its existence and its importance.

In this short appendix you have seen some of the theories of justice that are available. It is not necessary for you to choose one in order to continue in the investigation of which normative ethical theory is best. You may finally say, as Mill does in effect, that whatever turns out to be the best normative ethical theory will also tell us what is the morally proper way to distribute things of value. However, should that not be so, you may wish to return to this topic later.

---

[9]John Rawls, *A Theory of Justice* (Cambridge: Harvard University Press, 1971), 302. In Chapter 7 I discuss the methodology Rawls proposes as one way of finding the best ethical theory.

CHAPTER FOUR

Rule Deontology

In Chapters 2 and 3 we examined two teleological theories of obligation, theories that restrict the considerations relevant to *rightness* and *obligation* to the value of the likely consequences of people's actions. The following general form of a theory of obligation will help us to contrast this kind of theory with another:

If any *x* if *F*, then *x* is *M*.
This *x* if *F*.

Therefore, this *x* is *M*.

Teleological theories restrict the substitution instances of *F* to the likely value consequences of actions, such as leading to more good for one individual or for the greatest number of individuals. *Deontological* theories of obligation are the negation of such theories—they do not restrict the substitution instances of *F* to consequences. For example, one such theory has the following moral principle: "If any action would be judged by the majority of persons living in a culture as morally right, then in that culture the action is morally right." This form of ethical relativism is not concerned with the consequences of actions; in fact, consequences are irrelevant. Another view, one we shall call *agapism*, maintains that the correct moral principle is "If any action is performed out of love, then it is morally right." This principle too has no reference to consequences.

Not all deontological theories ignore consequences entirely. Some claim that consequences do matter, but only as one of many factors relevant in determining the moral rightness of an action. William Frankena, for example, suggests that we should use two considerations to determine whether an action is right: the amount of good or value resulting from the action and the way in which that value is distributed. For such views, there are at least two rules and, correspondingly, two different kinds of instances of F that are relevant to rightness of actions. In contrast, egoism and utilitarianism claim that only the value that is a consequence of an action is relevant. The complication of bringing in more than one kind of substitution instance of F will require considerable explanation before we can evaluate such deontological theories. In fact, the number of different kinds of rule deontological views is so great that we will need a fairly complicated set of distinctions in order to know which view is being discussed. Fortunately, one set of distinctions has already been introduced and the others can be set out without great trouble.

DISTINCTIONS OLD AND NEW

In Chapter 1 the distinction between categorical and prima facie rules was drawn. A rule that holds no matter what else is true of the action or thing to which it applies is a *categorical rule*. In contrast, a rule that can be overridden by a rule of the same type is a *prima facie rule*. "If you have made three outs, then your side is no longer at bat" is a categorical rule of baseball. No matter what else is true of your team and no matter what else happens, you are no longer at bat. When the antecedent of "If an enclosed plane figure has three straight sides, then it is a triangle" applies to a figure, then no matter what else is true of that figure, it is a triangle. It may be green, drawn in the sand, exist only in your mind, or whatever—but if the antecedent is fulfilled, then so is the consequent, no matter what other predicates apply to it. A prima facie rule is always one of at least two such rules for one rule can't override another unless there is another to be overridden. One theory we shall look at shortly maintains that there is a principle of justice and a principle of beneficence.[1] The second enjoins us to bring about good and the first, to distribute it in a certain manner. 'Prima facie' will be explained further later in this chapter when such theories are examined.

Egoism and utilitarianism not only limit the values of F to consequences but also limit the consequences to only one kind that is to count in determining the rightness or obligation associated with actions. The egoist claims that the only factor is the amount of benefit that I, an individual, receive, whereas the utilitarian claims that the benefit to all is what is important. Even though

---

[1] For our purposes, it would not be misleading to call this theory a version of the utilitarian principle. The problem is that when philosophers talk about the principle of utility, or the greatest happiness principle, they usually have utilitarianism in mind. Accordingly, the reader must note carefully how the principle of beneficence is described.

TABLE 4.1

	Single		Multiple	
Categorical	Direct	Indirect	Egoistic utilitarianism	
	Agapism	Agapism Kantianism Relativism	A Ten Commandments theory	
Prima Facie			Direct	Indirect
			Ross	Frankena

each of the theories has a rule concerning obligation and another concerning rightness, they agree that the difference between rightness and obligation does not revolve around the kind of consideration—the value of the likely consequences—but rather around the kind of action that will bring about the most of those consequences. There are not two kinds of considerations, such as bringing about good and distributing it in a certain way, but only one kind of consideration. Theories maintaining only one kind of factor will be called *single-rule theories*, and those positing more than one factor will be called *multiple-rule theories*. Thus, a theory that maintains both a rule of justice and a rule calling for the maximization of benefit is a multiple-rule theory. As we know, both egoism and utilitarianism are single-rule theories.

The two sets of distinctions—categorical versus prima facie and single-rule versus multiple-rule—cross to generate the chart shown as Table 4-1. The table will be useful in reviewing this chapter, and it will assist you as you begin each section; it charts the different views to be discussed and indicates why certain views are put together.

The discussion begins with multiple categorical rule theories because they are the most obviously flawed and will allow a clear presentation of the strategy we will use to discuss deontological theories.

MULTIPLE CATEGORICAL RULE THEORIES

A theory that maintains that there are at least two categorical rules of obligation or right is a *multiple categorical rule theory*. Two such theories will be examined briefly: One is an attempted combination of egoism and utilitarianism and the other is an interpretation of the Ten Commandments taken as an ethical theory.

Egoism and Utilitarianism Combined

Those who have read the first three chapters will understand quite well the flaws of egoism and see also some of the difficulties in utilitarianism. Some may be tempted to try to make up the deficiencies of the theories by combining them. If one argues, loosely, that egoism has a defect on the side of benefit for oneself, then it seems to make some sense to suggest a theory that simply incorporates both egoism and utilitarianism. If we consider just the direct versions of these theories with respect to *obligation*, then we would have a theory with the following two rules:

> If a person *a* performs an action that increases person *a*'s own good (benefit) more than any other available action, then that action is obligatory.
>
> If any person *a* performs an action that increases the good (benefit) of the greatest number more than any other available action, then that action is obligatory.

A problem immediately arises when we consider those actions to which the two rules apply, but each gives a different result. There are times when an action will maximize your own good, but only at the expense of the good of the greatest number. Consider the typical "con man" who increases his own good only at the expense of others; it may be that certain businesspeople and generals are in a similar position. If such people consider the first rule (egoism), then they are allowed to conclude that an action is obligatory. However, when the second rule is activated, that same action is seen as not obligatory. This is most embarrassing, for when the theory is used to help us arrive at a singular moral judgment to guide our actions, we are told that a certain action is both obligatory and not obligatory. In short, the theory leads to a contradiction—a fatal flaw for any theory.

How could this happen? It happens because the two rules are taken as categorical rules; once the antecedent applies to some situation, the consequent also applies, regardless of what else is true of that set of circumstances.[2] When we activate the first rule, then we, as "con men," conclude that cheating a pensioner out of her monthly paycheck is obligatory; and when we activate the second rule, the conclusion is that the action is not obligatory.[3] We are

---

[2] The reason utilitarianism does not get into trouble from its one rule, even though categorical, concerns the difference between an *absolute* and a categorical rule. The utilitarian rule is not an absolute because its factor is not specific—for example, All killing is wrong. This will become clearer later when the notion of absolutes is more fully spelled out.

[3] The two rules are to be used, of course, with an appropriate second statement of the general scheme to arrive at a singular moral judgment. For example, the "con man," when he is considering cheating the pensioner and uses first the egoism part of the rule, would, we are supposing, reason as follows:

> If any person *a* performs an action that increases person *a*'s own good (benefit) more than any other available action, then that action is obligatory.
>
> Cheating this pensioner out of his or her monthly paycheck will increase my good (benefit) more than any other available action.

> Therefore, cheating this pensioner out of her monthly paycheck is obligatory.

not justified in qualifying the conclusion by saying that the action is obligatory (only) if the rule does not apply, for the rule is categorical.

It is easy to see that such a theory won't work; this is especially easy to see in the theory just examined. However, exactly the same problems arise for any theory having more than one categorical rule. For such theories, conflicts are bound to occur, and since no provision is made for such conflicts, the theory is saddled with contradictions. Thus, this combination of the egoistic and utilitarian principles is not acceptable.

The Ten Commandments

A theory popular among nonphilosophers seems to call for ten different categorical rules. This theory, as you can guess from our discussion of the egoistic-utilitarian theory, would be subject to many more sources of contradiction. In fairness to those who hold this theory, it should be said at the outset that there is clearly a stronger version of that theory—and I shall suggest what it is at the end of the following discussion. At any rate, here are the Ten Commandments, thought by some to capture a theory of obligation:

1. Thou shalt have no other gods before me.
2. Thou shalt not make unto thee a graven image, nor any likeness of anything that is in heaven above, or that is in the earth beneath, or that is in the water under the earth; thou shalt not bow down thyself unto them, nor serve them; for I Jehovah thy God am a jealous God. . . .
3. Thou shalt not take the name of Jehovah thy God in vain. . . .
4. Remember the Sabbath day, to keep it holy.
5. Honor thy father and thy mother. . . .
6. Thou shalt not kill.
7. Thou shalt not commit adultery.
8. Thou shalt not steal.
9. Thou shalt not bear false witness against thy neighbor.
10. Thou shalt not covet thy neighbor's house, thou shalt not covet thy neighbor's wife, nor his manservant, nor his maidservant, nor his ass, nor anything that is thy neighbor's.

The list is no doubt familiar to most of you, but the form is not quite correct for this context. Therefore, let's transform a few of the commandments into

---

Since exactly the same reasoning can be used with a version of the second rule to conclude that the action is not obligatory, we arrive at a contradiction. ("If any person a performs an action that fails to increase person a's good more than any other available action, then that action is not obligatory" is the relevant principle.)

moral rules of the form discussed here. The numbers before the transformed statements refer to the original numbers in the list.

5. If any person *a* honors (is in a position to honor) his mother or his father, then that action is obligatory.
6. If any person *a* kills (is in a position to kill), then person *a* has done what is forbidden (has an obligation not to do).
7. If any person *a* commits adultery, then person *a* has done what is forbidden.
8. If any person *a* steals, then person *a* has done what is forbidden.
9. If any person *a* bears false witness against a neighbor, then person *a* has done what is forbidden.[4]

These translations can serve as models of how to transform the other commandments into the form of the first statement of the general scheme. The transformed statements, in conjunction with an appropriate second premise, would allow the derivation of a singular moral judgment. Notice that I have translated the "shalt nots" and the "shalts" into "obligation not" or "forbidden," and "obliged." The context seems to indicate that obligations are being laid upon us, and not just that we are being told which actions are morally right. However, the same kinds of criticisms apply regardless of the interpretation, so if you want to work with "right" and not "obligation," you should be able to modify the discussion in a relatively easy and straightforward manner.

First, because each of the rules is a categorical rule of moral obligation, we are entitled to offer counterexamples. And further, because the theory maintains that these are all rules of moral obligation and that together they constitute a theory of obligation, then a counterexample to one of them is a counterexample to, and a criticism of, the entire theory.

There are some kinds of killing that are apparently not obligatory not to do; in some instances we are permitted to kill. For example, we are apparently permitted to kill a maniac who is shooting people from the top of a building or inside a restaurant and who cannot in any practical way be stopped short of death. We seem to be permitted to fight and kill in a war that is itself just (as was apparently the case with World War II). More controversial examples might appeal to some of you—for example, whether you are permitted to kill an aged parent who is suffering from terminal cancer and who requests euthanasia. As usual, you are asked to join in and construct your own counterexamples.

Some people maintain that no matter what the set of circumstances and no matter who is involved, no one is ever permitted to kill another. This is

---

[4]The rules apply, of course, to actual and contemplated actions: "If person *a* were to kill, then person *a* would do what is obligatory not to do," or to state this in another way, "If person *a* is in a position to kill, then person *a* is forbidden to kill." This kind of clarification can be carried out for all the rules.

a complicated issue so it is fortunate that it is not necessary for our discussion that we resolve it. We need only enough counterexamples for enough of the rules so that almost everyone is convinced by one. You may be prompted to construct effective counterexamples from your own experience.

Suppose a mother steals a loaf of bread to feed her hungry children when there is no other way for her to get food and the society has more than enough to feed all its members. Does that person not have permission to do that? Consider the theft of a weapon from a person you know is going to use it to rob and maim somebody. Are you not permitted to do that? Suppose you are engaged in a just war and have an opportunity to steal secrets from the enemy. Is there any doubt that you have a right to do so? If not, then some occasions do exist on which you are not obliged not to steal, as Commandment 8 claims; and these represent counterexamples to that purported moral rule.

In addition to counterexamples, of which there are abundant numbers, the theory can be charged with inconsistency in the same way as the egoistic-utilitarian theory was. Suppose, as did many Christians, Jews, and Muslims, that you believe God orders you to convert the "heathen" by force. As history reveals, this requires the killing of large numbers of people. In other words, there are circumstances in which one or more of Commandments 1, 2, and 3 are inconsistent with Commandment 6. If you are to honor God and not take His name in vain, then if He commands you to do something that requires killing, or directly orders you to kill, you are obliged to do it. Activating the sixth moral rule (Commandment 6), in contrast, generates the conclusion that your obligation is not to kill.

Commandment 6 is a fertile source of inconsistency. For example, depending on what it is to honor your parents (Commandment 5), if your parents ask you to honor them by providing a human sacrifice for their anniversary, you can't both fulfill this and not kill. Similarly, suppose that honoring your mother requires you to be at her birthday party, but to do so requires that you travel on the Sabbath. So you can't keep the Sabbath day holy and honor your mother both.

By this time, you should be able to construct situations from your own experience in which two of the rules apply, thus resulting in an inconsistency. There are problems with interpreting some notions, such as *covet* and *vain*, but there should be enough clear examples to satisfy even the most scrupulous observer.

Must we conclude, therefore, that people who believe that the Ten Commandments have anything to do with our moral life are fools? No, of course not! However, anyone who accepts the Ten Commandments literally as ten *categorical* moral rules is attempting to maintain a very awkward ethical theory. Such people are well advised to give up the Commandments as categorical rules; rather they should be interpreted as *prima facie rules*, as rules that have variable weight.

Exercises: Working with Rules

1. Suppose we try to save the egoistic-utilitarian view by specifying what is to happen when the two rules conflict—for example, we say that the utilitarian rule is always to prevail. State what such a theory must say, what the principles would look like, and what kind of rule the conflict-resolution rule is. (That rule, the one that will tell us to follow the utilitarian principle when the two conflict, is obviously not a direct moral rule. What kind is it?)
2. Give some examples of categorical rules from sports or other games. Are there other types of rules within these games? Describe those rules, and try to say what kinds of rules they are.
3. The laws that govern our society are often called *civil laws*. Such laws, as are found in criminal codes, traffic laws, and corporate law, are rules for behavior. Are any of them categorical laws? Are any of them clearly not categorical? Does the Bill of Rights pose any special problems?

MULTIPLE PRIMA FACIE RULE THEORIES

First, we must state clearly what a *prima facie rule* is. In the very brief discussion thus far, we have said that a prima facie rule, as opposed to a categorical rule, can be overridden by other rules of the same type. Whereas categorical rules are of a fixed weight, prima facie rules are variable in weight. Prima facie rules are designed, so to speak, to account for situations in which more than one rule can apply. Prima facie rules are such that a conflict between rules can occur and yet we can continue to hold both (or all) rules as moral rules. If we state more formally the nature of a categorical rule, then we can do the same for a prima facie rule.

A rule R of the form "If any x is F, then x is M" is *categorical* = df Given that x is F, then no matter what other characteristic x has, it is M.

A consequence of this definition is that once x is G, as long as G is not simply not-M, it always follows that x is M. This can be seen clearly if we again consider simple examples in plane geometry. Once we establish that x is an enclosed-plane figure with three straight sides (F), then, no matter what other G we add (red, sides of 5 inches, drawn in ink, and so on), it is still true that x is a triangle.

We can now define what it is for R1, a member of a set of at least two direct moral rules, R1 and R2, to be a prima facie rule.

A rule R1 of the form "If any x is F, then x is M" is *prima facie* = df When x is F, x would actually be M (for example, an actual obligation or duty) if R1 were the only rule, but R1 can be overridden by R2 and so x may not actually be M even though it is F.[5]

To get a less technical explanation of a prima facie rule, let us call upon W. D. Ross, the philosopher who introduced the notion in its modern sense:

> I suggest '*prima facie* duty' or 'conditional duty' as a brief way of referring to the characteristic (quite distinct from that of being a duty proper) which an act has, in virtue of being of a certain kind (e.g., the keeping of a promise), of being an act which would be a duty proper if it were not at the same time of another kind which is morally significant. Whether an act is a duty proper depends on *all* the morally significant kinds it is an instance of. The phrase '*prima facie* duty' must be apologized for, since (1) it suggests that what we are speaking of is a certain kind of duty, whereas it is in fact not a duty, but something related in a special way to duty. Strictly speaking, we want not a phrase in which duty is qualified by an adjective, but a separate noun. (2) '*Prima' facie* suggests that one is speaking only of an appearance which a moral situation presents at first sight, and which may turn out to be illusory; whereas what I am speaking of is an objective fact involved in the nature of the situation, or more strictly in an element of its nature, though not, as duty proper does, arising from its *whole* nature.[6]

This characterization, even though it may not be overly technical, does not present a clear and intuitively understandable explanation of 'prima facie'. When Ross talks about *duty*, he is talking about what here is called one's *actual obligation*. There is, unfortunately, no simple way to explain that notion. An actual obligation, given a specific normative ethical theory, is determined by the final application of the normative ethical theory used. For example, for a normative ethical theory that uses categorical rules, the first application is the final one. For a prima facie theory, in contrast, the final application comes

---

[5]Since we have divided rule theories into two types—categorical and prima facie—there are correspondingly two slightly different ways in which someone can come to have an actual duty. According to the categorical rule theories, someone has an actual duty to perform an action when that action falls under a categorical moral rule. In contrast, according to a prima facie rule theory, someone has an actual duty to perform an action when that action falls under a prima facie moral rule and there is no other prima facie moral rule overriding that one.

[6]W. D. Ross, *The Right and the Good*, (Oxford: Clarendon Press, 1930), 19–20. All quotations from *The Right and the Good* that appear in this chapter are reprinted by permission of the Oxford University Press.

only after the weighing of all the applicable prima facie rules. To see that, we'll need to have some actual rules before us to show how such a theory works. Let us continue with Ross's view:

> (1) Some duties rest on previous acts of my own. These duties seem to include two kinds, (a) those resting on a promise or what may fairly be called an implicit promise, such as the implicit undertaking not to tell lies which seems to be implied in the act of entering into conversation (at any rate by civilized men), or of writing books that purport to be history and not fiction. These may be called the duties of fidelity. (b) Those resting on a previous wrongful act. These may be called the duties of reparation. (2) Some rest on previous acts of other men, i.e., services done by them to me. These may be loosely described as the duties of gratitude. (3) Some rest on the fact or possibility of a distribution of pleasure or happiness (or of the means thereto) which is not in accordance with the merit of the persons concerned; in such cases there arises a duty to upset or prevent such a distribution. These are the duties of justice. (4) Some rest on the mere fact that there are other beings in the world whose condition we can make better in respect of virtue, or of intelligence, or of pleasure. These are the duties of beneficence. (5) Some rest on the fact that we can improve our own condition in respect of virtue or of intelligence. These are the duties of self-improvement. (6) I think that we should distinguish from (4) the duties that may be summed up under the title of 'not injuring others'. No doubt to injure others is incidentally to fail to do them good; but it seems to me clear that nonmaleficence is apprehended as a duty distinct from that of beneficence, and as a duty of a more stringent character.[7]

Ross supposes that there are six prima facie rules of obligation, although he uses the term 'duty' to capture what we mean by obligation. He thinks he has discovered all the prima facie rules of moral obligation although he would be willing to admit as many more rules as someone could reveal by producing counterexamples that show other sources of obligation. Here is a translation of the rules into the familiar form of the first premise of the general scheme:

> 1a. If any person *a* promises (explicitly or implicitly) to perform some action or to abstain from performing some action, then person *a* has an obligation to perform that action or to abstain from that action. (fidelity)
>
> 1b. If any person *a* performs a wrong action with respect to person *b*, then person *a* has an obligation to "undo" the wrong to person *b*. (reparation)

---

[7]Ibid., 21.

2. If any person *a* performs some service (favor) for person *b*, then person *b* has some obligation to person *a*. (gratitude)
3. If any person *a* merits a distribution of pleasure or happiness and person *b* can bring that distribution about (or prevent such a distribution that is not merited), then person *b* is obligated to distribute what is merited (or prevent what is not merited). (justice)[8]
4. If any person *a* can make some person *b* better with respect to virtue, intelligence, or pleasure, then person *a* has an obligation to do so. (beneficence)
5. If any person *a* can make a self-improvement with respect to virtue or intelligence, then person *a* has an obligation to do so. (self-improvement)
6. If any person *a* is in a position to avoid hurting person *b*, then person *a* has an obligation to do so. (nonmaleficence)

By this time everyone should know how each of the rules works in deriving singular moral judgments. All that is required to derive singular moral judgments is appropriate second statements of the general scheme to go with the first statements just presented. For example, an appropriate second statement to go with rule 1a might be "I promised to pay George the $10 I borrowed from him." This allows us to conclude that I have an obligation to pay the money back to George.

Even though the derivation of singular moral judgments may be clear, some of the rules contain parts that are unclear. For example, it is not clear precisely what one is to do when a wrong is 'undone', as rule 1b requires; nor is it clear in rule 2 what kind of obligation person *b* has to person *a*. One would expect that the context would, in most circumstances, allow us to conclude what kind of obligation person *b* has. Thus, if someone rescues you from drowning, you probably would not say that you had an obligation to give that person your entire library or to become an indentured servant for 10 years. Similar contextual considerations hold for the other rules and how they are to be understood. For our purposes, though, some lack of clarity will not hurt. Few of the criticisms trade on such unclarities, and when specific rules are involved in such criticisms, they will be explained more fully.

These rules are not categorical. From the fact that I promised to pay George back the $10, we cannot conclude that no matter what else is true, I have an obligation to pay back the $10.[9] Suppose that George is a fairly wealthy friend who does not need the money right away, and I meet someone on Christmas who cannot buy his children gifts because he has no money. This activates rule 4, and since he can buy the gifts with the $10 and make himself

---
[8]Ibid.
[9]Since the rules are not categorical, from the simple fact that a prima facie rule applies, you cannot conclude that I have an actual duty to pay back the $10.

and his children happy, my actual obligation seems to be to give him the $10. Obviously, I cannot give him *and* George the $10, and I cannot be categorically obliged to do so—it is impossible to have the obligation to do both at the same time. In this set of circumstances, according to Ross, we escape the puzzle by suggesting that the prima facie obligation to give the money for Christmas presents is stronger than the prima facie obligation to pay the money back to George. So my actual obligation is to give the money for the Christmas presents.

This is not to say that I am no longer under a prima facie obligation to pay the money back to George. Even as I give the poor man the money, it is true that I still have the prima facie obligation to give the money to George. This obligation, though, is overridden by the obligation to make the others happier. The next $10 I have is George's, but he will hopefully understand that my obligation to him was not as strong as the obligation to increase the happiness of these other people. This is not to say that no matter who the others were, and no matter who George was, rule 4 would override rule 1a when they conflict.[10] One of the positive features of a prima facie rule theory is that it doesn't commit us to saying that one of the rules is always stronger than another; there is no need to specify a hierarchy of moral rules.[11] One of the problems, as we shall see shortly, is explaining how one knows when one of the rules is weightier than another. About this problem, Ross has this to say:

> For the estimation of the comparative stringency of these *prima facie* obligations no general rules can be, as far as I can see, laid down. We can only say that a great deal of stringency belongs to the . . . duties of keeping our promises, of repairing wrongs we have done, and of returning the equivalent of services we have received. For the rest, "The decision rests with perception." This sense of our particular duty in particular circumstances, preceded and informed by the fullest reflection we can bestow on the act in all its bearings, is highly fallible, but it is the only guide we have to our duty.[12]

However, as indicated, we will discuss this in more detail later.

In any given set of circumstances, one or more of the prima facie rules may apply. The trick is to know which ones do apply and then, as a separate problem, decide which is the more stringent. Ross believes he has discovered all the sources of prima facie obligation, so we should not worry about whether there is yet another source. However, even if there should turn out to be

---

[10] Two prima facie rules conflict when, if each rule was the only one that applied, the person would have incompatible actual duties.

[11] Actually, a fixed hierarchy of rules would be incompatible with a prima facie theory. The rule at the top of the hierarchy would be a categorical rule, something the prima facie theory is designed to replace. The status of the other rules in the hierarchy would be less clear.

[12] Ross, *The Right and the Good*, 41–42. Ross quotes Aristotle's *Nicomachean Ethics*, 1109 b 23, 1126 b 4, concerning perception.

additional rules of obligation, this would not be embarrassing to anyone holding a prima facie rule theory of obligation. All that would be needed would be to add the new rule to the list. Once we have the list of rules, we next determine which ones apply in a given set of circumstances, and finally we determine, of ones that do apply, which are the weightiest. This may seem like a lot of trouble, but it is a fairly easy procedure in most instances.

Other philosophers have thought that two prima facie rules were enough. One such view, held by William Frankena, maintains that the two prima facie principles are those of beneficence and justice:

> What does the principle of beneficence say? Four things, I think:
> 1. One ought not inflict evil or harm (what is bad).
> 2. One ought to prevent evil or harm.
> 3. One ought to remove evil.
> 4. One ought to promote good.[13]
>
> The principle of justice lays upon us the prima facie obligation of treating people equally . . . [that is], making the same relative contribution to the goodness of their lives . . . or asking the same relative sacrifice. . . .
> . . . We can derive all of the things we may wish to recognize as duties from our two principles, either directly as the crow flies or indirectly as the rule-utilitarian does.[14]

Even though Frankena claims he has but two rules, it is easy to see that the principle of beneficence contains four separate rules in it. The two theories of Ross and Frankena are not as different as they might seem at first. However, they do hold different theories of justice, and that, ultimately, will turn out to be a very important difference in choosing between them. In addition, Frankena wants his theory to be both a direct and an indirect theory of obligation. The principle of beneficence is to be used to derive other rules concerning injuries to others and liberty, for example. However, these differences are less important to us now than the common elements. Both theories are prima facie rule theories, and both recognize the problem of the relative stringency of conflicting rules.

Noncategorical Rules: A Solution, a New Problem

A prima facie rule theory, as opposed to a categorical rule theory, allows rules to have exceptions; that is, the rule can apply and yet the person may not have an actual obligation to perform the action that falls under the rule. This is another way of saying the obligation is not categorical, but the point is important enough to make in a few different ways. Many people want to claim

---

[13] William K. Frankena, *Ethics*, 2d ed. (Englewood Cliffs, N.J.: Prentice-Hall, 1973), 47.
[14] Ibid., 47, 52. What Frankena calls *rule utilitarianism* is here called *indirect utilitarianism*.

that there are no absolute moral rules; what they mean is that there are no categorical moral rules. Use of prima facie rules allows one to maintain an essential function for rules and yet avoid the problems of universal exceptionless rules. Nevertheless, there are problems with such theories.

One problem involves a situation when two rules conflict.

> I see no way out of [the problem of conflict].... It does seem to me that the two principles may come into conflict, both at the level of individual action and at that of social policy, and I know of no formula that will always tell us how to solve conflicts between their corollaries.... One can only hope that ... we will ... come to agree on ways of acting that are satisfactory to all concerned.[15]

Neither Ross nor Frankena supposes that there is a hierarchy of rules such that one rule is always stronger than another. There are clear instances in which the principle of justice overrides the principle of beneficence and vice versa. For Ross the situation is more complex since he posits six rules, but the situation is essentially the same. There is no set order to the strength of the six prima facie duties. Frankena hopes that we shall all agree in time if we all come to have the "moral point of view." Ross supposes that at a certain point the issue is left up to "perception"; that is, we just "see" in context which of the principles is stronger. I shall argue that neither of these responses is adequate; and, what is worse, they undermine the very theory the authors are trying to defend.

First, remember that both prima facie rule theorists hold that it is only via the rules that we are able to arrive at justified singular moral judgments. They hold that moral rules are *required* in order to arrive at singular justified moral judgments; without such rules, we have no way of justifying our singular moral judgments. They hold, in short, that there is a set of moral rules that constitute our moral life—that there are moral constitutive rules. If there are ways of arriving at singular moral judgments without the rules the authors maintain are constitutive of morality, then those rules are not constitutive of morality.[16] Furthermore, if it can be shown that the authors are committed to some such method, then that method and not a prima facie theory is what they hold.

Suppose we take Ross and Frankena seriously when they say that in a given set of circumstances we can determine which of two competing prima facie rules and the corresponding obligations is more stringent—that is, which overrides which. Since the two rules of morality are not being used to determine which of the two conflicting rules of morality overrides the other, what

---

[15] Ibid., 53.

[16] If this point has become vague, see again page 16 to refresh your memory concerning the nature of constitutive rules.

basis do we have for making such a determination?[17] We could use some nonmoral basis, such as flipping a coin, but surely that is not acceptable to anyone who supposes that some moral judgments are justified and others are not. What we seem to use (and here it is open to the defender of prima facie rules to offer something else) is the knowledge that in this set of circumstances one of the proposed actions is obligatory and the other is not. However, if we can determine without the use of the prima facie rules that one action is obligatory and the other is not, then the rules cannot be the complete explanation of how to arrive at justified moral judgments. The basis of justified moral judgments cannot be the set of prima facie rules because we have at hand at least some justified moral judgments that are arrived at without the use of the rules. This conclusion, of course, is completely incompatible with a prima facie rule theory.

Let's catch our philosophical breath before we plunge on. The prima facie theory consists of two or more prima facie rules used to arrive at justified singular moral judgments. When two prima facie rules conflict, this conflict is settled either with a rule or without those rules. We showed earlier that the latter is not really a "live" option for the prima facie rule theorist. But, if rules are to be used, are they constitutive rules or summary rules? If one maintains that we can arrive at justified singular moral judgments without the use of prima facie, or some other, constitutive rules,[18] one could maintain that the rules actually used are rules of thumb, inductive conclusions reached by having arrived at many singular moral judgments in just the manner described when there is a conflict between two prima facie rules. We can say that on the whole, in most cases, it is obligatory to try to make someone happier, but not always. This is good moral advice, a good rule of thumb, but it does require there be some means other than the rule of thumb to arrive at judgments that fall under that rule. The rule of thumb, if we put it in the familiar form, looks like this:

> If any person *a* can make person *b* happier, then it is likely that person *a* has an obligation to do so.[19]

This kind of rule cannot serve as the basic method of determining what you are obliged to do. To see that, consider another rule of the same type:

> If any person *a* attends a university, then it is likely that person *a* can read.

---

[17]You might be tempted to think that a third prima facie rule might settle the conflict, but this would not work. First, the prima facie rules are about actions, moral situations, and the like, not about rules. Second, the rule itself cannot state a fixed relationship of overridingness because on some occasions one rule overrides the other, but on other occasions this relation is reversed.

[18]The rules cannot be categorical, but this will be completely argued in the next section.

[19]It would make no difference for this context if we put the term 'likely' in front of the rule.

This is a truth, but we arrived at it by observing that most persons attending universities can read. We performed, if you will, an induction in which we noticed two characteristics that tend to appear together: attending university and being able to read. Such an induction can be represented in the following *induction by enumeration form*.[20]

Person *a* attends a university, and person *a* can read.
Person *b* attends a university, and person *b* can read.
Person *c* attends a university, and person *c* can read.
. . .
Person *n* attends a university, and person *n* can read.

Therefore, if any person *a* attends a university, then *a* can read.

Notice that the term 'likely' is not put into the conclusion of the argument. It is only added afterward, when we must remind the reader where the conclusion came from—that is, what kind of argument supports it.

The conclusion, "If any person *a* attends a university, then that person *a* can read," is drawn from premises that require us to know that someone can read without making use of that conclusion. We must be able to know someone can read without making use of the general statement that we derive from knowing that some people can read and also attend a university. This is true of *summary rules*, rules drawn from inductive arguments such as the preceeding; they presuppose some available method other than the inductive generalization to establish the truth of the premises. We can use the generalization, once we have arrived at it, to offer evidence that some given person can read. We do this kind of reasoning all the time without difficulty. However, we cannot say both that the generalization is the only way we can determine if someone can read and also that the generalization is an induction drawn from past instances, such as was just shown.

Those who maintain that at least two prima facie moral rules are required to justify singular moral judgments cannot therefore also maintain that moral rules are summary rules. We cannot maintain that sometimes we can determine which prima facie rule overrides another without the use of the rules that are part of the prima facie theory, for otherwise we undermine the whole basis of the claim that the prima facie theory is the means required to arrive

---

[20]The enumeration form is not quite of this type, but rather as follows:

All (or most) of the observed *F* are *G*.

Therefore, all (or most) *F* are *G*.

The form goes from observed instances to all instances. A similar form works when the number does not include all instances but does include most of the observed members.

at justified singular moral judgments. So the attempt to provide summary rules as the means to settle the conflict between two prima facie moral rules fails.

A Rule for Determining Stringency?

Suppose that prima facie rule theorists do not claim to be able to determine which of two competing prima facie rules is more stringent without a rule. (As we have just seen, this claim is incompatible with the theory.) Then, they must claim that the conflict between two prima facie rules has to be settled by using a (constitutive) rule. What kind of rule? The rule that is to be used must be either itself a prima facie rule or a categorical rule. However, it is not, as Ross and Frankena both admit, a categorical rule because in some circumstances the first prima facie rule overrides the second and in others the second rule overrides the first. There is no fixed hierarchy of prima facie rules.

Thus, if there is a rule that determines, in this set of circumstances, which prima facie rule overrides the other, then it must be a prima facie rule. If it is a prima facie rule, though, it cannot be a rule of the same set that contains the two that conflict for those rules tell us which actions are obligatory and which are not—they do not tell us which rules to adopt. The prima facie rule that tells us which of the two conflicting prima facie rules overrides the other in a situation must be an indirect or meta-moral rule.[21]

If something is a prima facie indirect moral rule, though, there has to be at least one other such rule—for there is no such thing as one prima facie rule of anything. However, if there are at least two such indirect prima facie rules, then again a situation will arise in which those two conflict. And now we are faced with the same problem we had at the beginning: The conflict of the two indirect prima facie rules is either to be settled with the aid of a rule or without it. As we have seen, it is not possible for a prima facie rule theorist to allow the conflict to be settled without the aid of a rule. Therefore, the rule must be either a prima facie rule or a categorical rule. However, as we have already established it cannot be a categorical rule. Thus is must

---

[21]Can a rule be both a direct and an indirect moral rule? Obviously the very same rule cannot because one applies to actions and the other, as Frankena suggests, to rules. But one could use the same test—for example, maximizing utility—as the test for the moral worth of an action and the moral worth of a proposed direct moral rule. If we were to have both versions of utilitarianism, though, what would we do if there was a conflict between the direct and indirect rule in a given case? If we propose a given procedure to follow—for example, always let the direct rule override the indirect rule—then there will no doubt be counterexamples to this rule taken as a categorical rule. If it is a prima facie rule, then there would have to be another procedural rule, and the entire problem of the conflict of prima facie rules would arise at a different level.

be a prima facie rule. However, it cannot be an indirect rule of the same type as the two that conflict, or else it could not settle the conflict.[22] If it is of a different level, then there is at least one other prima facie rule at that level with which *it* can conflict, and the conflict problem has not yet been resolved but continues on and on in the same way.

It would seem that this problem is not solvable by a prima facie rule theory. It does no good to talk about a moral point of view or what is known by perception, or the hope that in the future everyone will agree. None of these sentiments does away with actual conflicts that cannot be settled by a prima facie rule theory. If there is something called a moral point of view, then *it* and not the structure of prima facie rules is the normative ethical theory we should adopt.

This argument is more technical than any presented thus far, so a short summary revealing the structure of the argument more clearly is in order. In any system of prima facie rules, there are at least two such rules: PF-1 and PF-2. There are, in fact, situations in which PF-1 and PF-2 conflict. Such a conflict must be settled either with the use of a rule or without the use of a rule. It is not compatible with a prima facie theory that the conflict be settled without the use of a rule device within the theory, for otherwise we would have to admit that we sometimes do not need rules at all to arrive at justified singular moral judgments. The rule that is used to settle the conflict must either be a categorical rule or a prima facie rule. It is not a categorical rule because PF-1 and PF-2 have no set "weight"; in some circumstances, PF-1 overrides PF-2 and vice versa.[23] The rule is, then, a prima facie rule. However, the rule is not a rule of the same type, but an indirect rule, or a rule of a "higher" type. Let us call it IPF-1, for indirect prima facie rule 1. Because there are always at least two prima facie rules within a system of such rules, we know that there is an IPF-2. Since prima facie rules are designed to allow for conflicts that do, in fact, arise, a conflict situation will arise with respect to IPF-1 and IPF-2. At this point we are back at the beginning of the argument, which starts with a conflict of two prima facie rules. Thus, we see that the conflict situation leads forever to other conflict situations—something philosophers call a *vicious infinite regress.*

---

[22] You might think that you could claim that the rules are of the same type if the indirect rules are of the same type, "If prima facie rules 1 and 2 conflict, then rule 1 overrides rule 2." However, the rule would then be something like "If indirect prima facie rules 1 and 2 conflict, then rule 1 overrides rule 2." This rule, though, is one of at least two that are about indirect prima facie rules 1 and 2; so the same kind of conflict situation can arise with respect to it and the original, and the same problem of a conflict situation has arisen at this indirect rule level.

[23] This is just another way of noting that there are effective counterexamples to the categorical rule.

Counterexamples

In addition to the main argument against prima facie rules, some counterexamples may be effective.[24] These are the type that show that there are instances of prima facie rules in which the action is not even prima facie obligatory. Recall from the discussion of utilitarianism that some actions (for example, scratching someone else's itch) bring about a small amount of benefit but are not thereby right or obligatory. If those counterexamples hold up, we can't even conclude that actions that fall under one of the purported prima facie rules are prima facie right or obligatory. The counterexamples concerning beneficence are to be found in Chapter 3, on utilitarianism.[25] The principle of beneficence is not equivalent to the principle of utility, but insofar as each claims that the value of the likely consequences is at least one of the factors making for right and obligatory actions, then the same counterexamples would apply to both. Perhaps the same kind of counterexample concerning a principle of justice will round out the case against prima facie theories.

Because Ross and Frankena hold different theories of justice, if we can construct counterexamples that don't depend on one specific principle of justice, we'll be better able to do the job. Suppose the general principle of justice is as follows:

> If any person *a* performs an action that consists of distributing some things of value in manner J, then that action is right (just).

If we consider the same kind of underwhelming value situation just described, we can reach our counterexample. Suppose you have one M&M candy left in your bag on Halloween and ten children appear at your door. Can we say you have performed a just action if you carefully cut the candy into ten pieces? It hardly seems so. What about the man passing out free gum samples to anyone who wants one—regardless of race, religion, national origin, or sex? He does distribute something of some small benefit or value to people, but the action appears to have no positive moral worth. Join in and construct examples from your own experience.

Now we have one complicated criticism of prima facie rule theories and one criticism of the usual type with a twist. If these criticisms are effective, then prima facie theories have serious problems.

At this point, perhaps a word of sympathy is in order. Sooner or later, you are going to reach a state of intellectual fatigue and shock with respect to

---

[24]The main argument against prima facie rule theories is the immediately preceding one. I do not have nearly as much confidence in the argument that follows, for whether it is effective or not depends on the truth of certain things in theory of value. The reader is cautioned to exercise even more philosophical vigilance than usual in reading this section.

[25]See pages 116–117.

theories. As the next one comes up for consideration, the thought arises, "I wonder what will be wrong with this theory?" It is easy to become cynical and skeptical about the possibility of reaching a correct theory because of the emphasis on critical comments. However, if you have been careful, you will also realize that the criticisms are becoming more complicated because the theories are getting better; they are harder to criticize. If, for example, you read through this book and are inclined to pick a prima facie rule theory to defend, you can read Ross, Frankena, or other authors to see what the complete theory looks like. You may yourself be able to construct a viable way to respond to the criticism. This is, after all, a book that shows you the main theories; it does not purport to give you the last word. So be of good cheer as you proceed.

Exercises: Prima Facie Rules

1. State the theory of egoistic utilitarianism as a direct rule prima facie theory with two rules, and then evaluate it.
2. Evaluate the Ten Commandments theory as a direct prima facie rule theory.
3. Suppose we take egoistic utilitarianism to be a two-rule prima facie theory, with the egoistic principle as a direct rule and the utilitarian principle as an indirect rule. Critically evaluate that theory.
4. Explain why it would be a mistake to equate summary rule with prima facie rule.

SINGLE-RULE THEORIES

Egoism and utilitarianism, both the direct and the indirect versions, are single-rule theories. They are teleological theories, though, and the views we are about to consider are deontological theories of obligation. That is, the single rule proposed is not concerned only with the consequences of actions. The multiple prima facie rule theories just examined did, in part, bring in consequences because one of the rules made obligation or rightness a partial function of consequences. However, these single-rule deontological theories do not make obligation a function of consequences at all. It is for this reason that such views are sometimes called *formalistic*.

Agapism

We begin with a brief look at a view Frankena calls agapism. There is both a direct and an indirect rule version of this theory of obligation. The basis of the view comes from such biblical passages as the following:

> Thou shalt love the Lord thy God with all thy heart, and with all thy soul, and with all thy mind. This is the first and great commandment. And the second is like unto it, Thou shalt love thy neighbor as thyself. On these two commandments hang all the law and the prophets. (Matt. 22:37–40)

For now, let us not consider God but rather translate into the appropriate form only the requirement to love our fellow humans.

Direct Agapism

If any person *a* performs an action out of love, then that action is right.

Indirect Agapism

If any person *a* acts on a proposed direct moral rule R that is likely to increase the amount of love in the world, then R is a direct moral rule.

The indirect version talks about increasing the amount of love in the world, and since it does, the most plausible interpretation of this version involves the notion of consequences. The rule directs us to pick those rules to act from which have, as a consequence, an increase in the amount of love in the world. If we take a standard utilitarian view, such as was discussed in Chapter 3, and interpret the things of value as limited to love of fellow humans and perhaps other creatures, then we have indirect agapism. Insofar as this is so, we don't have a different view at all, but simply one version of a utilitarian theory. Therefore, all the criticism of indirect utilitarianism also applies to this version; we do not need to consider it separately.

In direct agapism it is not clear how obligation should be handled. In the indirect version we can make the same moves as we did for utilitarianism. For the direct version, we might say that the action that brings about the most love possible from the alternatives is the obligatory one. We could say that the action done from the greatest love is the obligatory one, but that is highly artificial. Neither of these explanations seems plausible, but since there are other problems with direct agapism, we won't worry about how obligation would be explained.

One could interpret direct agapism, as we did with indirect agapism, as a form of direct utilitarianism. Once again, this results in a view that has already been discussed. So let's try to interpret it as a view that is different from any presented thus far. To do this, we simply state that there is only one source of rightness—love. If someone performs an action out of love, then it is right regardless of the consequences.

This view, set out this baldly, is quite deficient. Many sources of right have nothing to do with love. For example, someone who rescues a drowning person often does not feel any love toward that person. In fact, a rescuer may save someone toward whom he feels no such love; he may even feel the opposite, whether this is said to be hate or a feeling that the person is not a good person, or whatever. It does seem that this is frequently done. If so, then there exists a large class of right actions that are not covered by the moral rule concerning love.

You may be tempted to say that we should simply add another moral rule, whatever it is, to supplement the law of love. However, the view that would result would not be a single-rule theory. Further, and more importantly, the rule added would have to be either a categorical or a prima facie rule. It would make the most sense for the rule to be one of a number of prima facie rules, even though you would then give up agapism as a single-rule theory. If this is your choice, then you need to work on the problems with prima facie theories.

In addition to the class of right actions not covered by direct agapism, some actions fall within the rule that are apparently not right. For example, suppose it is out of a sense of love toward your neighbor that you smile at her in the morning and say hello. This hardly seems to transform the action into one that has positive moral worth, one that is morally right. Suppose that out of a sense of love you torture someone so that he will recant what you take to be a heresy. An action such as this, frequently performed in the history of humankind, especially by Christians, is apparently not right.[26] Such counterexamples are abundant; you can no doubt construct others of the same type from your own experience.

Kantianism

Because the procedure for criticizing theories is well known by now, no more will be done with agapism. You can follow up any interest you have in the subject by consulting the recommended readings at the end of this chapter. Let us now take up the most influential single-rule deontological theory, kantianism, named for its author. Immanuel Kant constructed a very complicated, subtle, and elaborate theory of obligation, so the following discussion does not purport to capture it fully. The intention is to give you an idea of the kind of theory he held and to indicate the kinds of criticisms that have traditionally been directed against it. To see the difficulty in interpreting Kant, let's examine a few passages from him.

> An action done from duty has its moral worth, *not in the purpose* to be attained by it, but in the maxim in accordance with which it is decided upon; it depends therefore, not on the realization of the object of the action, but solely on the *principle of volition* in accordance with which, irrespective of all objects of

---

[26]Here you may want to invoke the distinction between an action being right and a person being a good person. The action is wrong, you may want to say, but the agent is a good person for doing what he believes is right. This can be said, but it does not save the moral theory because it concerns actions that people perform on the basis of certain evidence. The person is, so to speak, already built into the rule.

the faculty of desire, the action has been performed. That the purposes we may have in our actions, and also their effects considered as ends and motives of the will, can give to actions no unconditioned and moral worth is clear from what has gone before. Where then can this be found if we are not to find it in the will's relation to the effect hoped for from the action? It can be found nowhere but *in the principle of the will*, irrespective of the ends which can be brought about by such an action. . . .

But which kind of law can this be the thought of which, even without regard to the results expected from it, has to determine the will if this is to be called good absolutely and without qualifications? Since I have robbed the will of every inducement that might arise for it as a consequence of obeying any particular law, nothing is left but the conformity of actions to universal law as such, and this alone must serve the will as its principle. That is to say, I ought never to act except in such a way *that I can also will that my maxim should become a universal law*. Here bare conformity to universal law as such (without having as its base any law prescribing particular actions) is what serves the will as its principle, and must so serve it if duty is not to be everywhere an empty delusion and a chimerical concept. The ordinary reason of mankind also agrees with this completely in its practical judgments and always has the aforesaid principle before its eyes.[27]

In order, Kant espouses the following views:

1. Consequences (ends attained by the actions) are not the determinants of moral obligation.
2. The moral worth of an action (that it is right or the fulfillment of an obligation) is a function of the direct rule (principle of volition or maxim) from which the action is performed.
3. The direct moral rule must be chosen independently of any desire to achieve an end, or even from any desire regarding the rule itself.
4. The indirect moral rule that determines the direct moral rules cannot have any particular actions or moral rules described within it.
5. The form of the indirect moral rule is, as stated by Kant, "I ought never to act except in such a way that I can also will that my maxim [direct moral rule] should become a universal law."

We can shed more light on these claims by translating them into our usual general form. The rule, an indirect moral rule that Kant calls the *categorical imperative*, would be written as follows:

---

[27]Immanuel Kant, *The Moral Law: Kant's Groundwork of the Metaphysics of Morals*, trans. and analyzed by H. J. Paton (London: Hutchinson University Library, 1948), 66–70.

> If any person *a* performs an action from a direct rule R, where R (1) is willed by person *a* and (2) can be willed to be a universal law of nature, then R is a rule of moral obligation.

The rule is categorical, in roughly the sense just introduced, but it does not apply directly to actions, only to moral rules.[28] Because there is only the one rule, there is no problem of conflict with rules of the same type.

We have seen the words Kant uses to state one version of the categorical imperative, and we have translated that imperative into a rule of the form familiar to us all, but as yet we have no real understanding of how the indirect rule works in selecting direct moral rules. Kant attempts to help us once again, though the help will not be as great as we might like.

> Suppose I seek, however, to learn in the quickest way and yet unerringly how to solve the problem "Does a lying promise accord with a duty?" I have then to ask myself "Should I really be content that my maxim (the maxim of getting out of a difficulty by a false promise) should hold as a universal law (one valid both for myself and others)? And could I really say to myself that everyone may make a false promise if he finds himself in a difficulty from which he can extricate himself in no other way?" I then become aware at once that I can indeed will to lie, but I can by no means will a universal law of lying; for by such a law there could properly be no promises at all, since it would be futile to profess a will for future action to others who would not believe my profession or who, if they did so over-hastily would pay me back in like coin; and consequently my maxim, as soon as it was made a universal law would be bound to annul itself.
>
> Thus I need no far-reaching ingenuity to find out what I have to do in order to possess a good will. Inexperienced in the course of world affairs and incapable of being prepared for all the chances that happen in it, I ask myself only "Can you also will that your maxim should become a universal law?" Where you cannot, it is to be rejected, and that not because of a prospective loss to you or even to others but because it cannot fit as a principle into a possible enactment of universal law.[29]

Here Kant attempts to give us an example of how his indirect rule works. He has chosen an easy enough case to understand, where we can get out of some trouble or solve a problem by promising to do something with no intention of fulfilling that promise. For example, I need money to pay off my

---

[28]Kant notes a similarity between the categorical imperative and the Golden Rule. The latter is best understood as a direct moral rule, "If any action is one that I would judge others have an obligation to do concerning me, then I have an obligation to do for them." Negatively the rule becomes, "If any action is one that I judge is forbidden to do to me then I am forbidden to do it to others." In more familiar forms these are "Do unto others as you would have others do unto you," and "Do not do unto others what you would not have them do unto you."

[29]Kant, *The Moral Law*, 70–71.

gambling debts, so I lie to my friend when I borrow money, saying that I will pay it back next week when I know I can't. The moral rule (maxim) from which I act might be stated as follows:

> If any person *a* performs an action of lying with respect to a promise that enables *a* to get out of a difficulty, then *a* is permitted to perform the action (has no obligation not to perform it).

This is clearly a recognizable direct moral rule and, in conjunction with the appropriate second statement (This person *a* performs . . .), allows us to derive a singular moral judgment (the person is permitted to perform the action). Kant supposes that the categorical imperative, the indirect moral rule, shows that this proposed direct moral rule is not acceptable because it could not be willed to be a universal law. It does not pass the test of the indirect moral rule that he calls the categorical imperative. Why does he think this? Alas, I can't say as clearly as I would like how the indirect rule works, though Kant is clear about how it is *not* intended to work.

Kant does not mean to say that if everyone told lies when they were in trouble and promised to do things that they had no intention of doing, confidence in other people would erode and soon no one would accept any promises made. If he took this approach, he would be offering a utilitarian defense of the direct moral rule; that would make the categorical imperative a version of the principle of utility. If fact, this is just the criticism Mill offers of Kant. So this is *not* how to interpret Kant.

Kant seems to think that there is something *logically* deficient about a direct rule concerning lying. He and many of his followers suggest that there is a contradiction in logic in willing such a rule. However, there appears to be no logical difficulty in adopting the direct moral rule about lying, or in agreeing to allow anyone else in these circumstances to lie also. The inconsistency appears to require two different direct moral rules that *a* wills. Perhaps Kant might think that when *a* tells the friend, "I'll pay the money back next week," the contradictory of the lying maxim is acted from. That maxim is:

> If any person *a* performs an action of lying, then *a* is forbidden to perform the action (has an obligation not to perform it).

This maxim and the lying promise maxim are or can be made contradictory. Why, though, would *a* will this maxim? Here we seem to lose our kantian way and seem to make use of consequentialist considerations. One possibility, though Kant never talks about this, might be that we *presuppose* the second maxim in our ordinary dealings, and that unless *a*'s friend thought that it was operative, no money would be lent. Is that a consequentialist consideration? It is not clear.

Another problem for kantianism is that there may be times when the conditions for a moral rule laid down by the indirect moral rule are met and yet the resulting action from the direct rule is not morally right at all. The proposed direct rule "If any person *a* performs an action that enables *a* to scratch an itch on the head, then *a* has performed a morally right action," seems to pass the test of the categorical imperative. However, no such action has positive moral worth, and one can generate such rules indefinitely.

Someone might suggest that the rule should read that the person is permitted to scratch, and not that the action is right. This would be a way to escape the counterexamples, but it raises another question of how the indirect rule works. Supposedly, any proposed direct moral rule that passes the test of the indirect moral rule gives us a source of obligation. Now, to save the theory, we are told that this is not so, that the rule generates *permission* and not *right* or *obligation*. How then shall we account for such notions? Recall that a theory that can only account for *permission* cannot thereby account for *right*. In addition, the more or less mechanical way of generating out obligations from not having permission not to seems not to be open here because, as the first kinds of counterexamples appeared to show, there is almost no action we aren't permitted to perform.

Other counterexamples the kantian apparently can't handle are what we might call "pseudo-generalizations." Suppose someone wills a moral rule of the following sort: "If any person *a* whose fingerprints are of type such and such performs an action of so and so, then that action is right (or obligatory)." We can demonstrate that this proposed direct moral rule passes the indirect rule, for since you are the only one with those fingerprints, there can be no conflict with any other willing and no contradiction with other direct rules. You may say this is cheating, but there is nothing in the indirect rule that makes this procedure illegitimate.

Kant talks about another notion, the notion of *dignity*, that has greatly influenced contemporary thought. Kant states this notion as if it were just an alternative formulation of the categorical imperative, but it is difficult to follow Kant's reasoning on this. Kant tells us we ought never to treat another merely as a means, but always at the same time as an end. Treating others in this way creates what Kant calls

> a systematic union of rational beings under common objective laws—that is, a kingdom. Since these laws are directed precisely to the relation of such beings to one another as ends and means, this kingdom can be called a kingdom of ends (which is admittedly only an Ideal). . . .
>
> The practical necessity of acting on this principle—that is, duty—is in no way based on feelings, impulses, and inclinations, but only on the relation of rational beings to one another, a relation in which the will of a rational being must always be regarded as making universal law, because otherwise he could not be conceived as an end in himself. Reason thus related every maxim of the will, considered as making universal law, to every other will and also to every action towards oneself; it does so, not because of any further motive or future advantage, but from the Idea of the dignity of a

rational being who obeys no law other than that which he at the same time enacts himself.

. . . That which constitutes the sole condition under which anything can be an end in itself has not merely a relative value—that is, a price—but has an intrinsic value—that is, dignity.

Now morality is the only condition under which a rational being can be an end in himself; for only through this is it possible to be a law-making member in a kingdom of ends. Therefore, morality, and humanity so far as it is capable of morality, is the only thing which has dignity.[30]

It is difficult to see how we can subsume this discussion under the working of the categorical imperative. Each person can determine how to live in an independent way by the maxims or direct moral rules we promulgate. We are self-governing in contrast to following what others (or their instincts) decide. Slavery is immoral because it prevents human beings from realizing what is most valuable about their nature. To deprive someone of their dignity prevents them from using their capacity to be self-governing. The exercise of dignity is thereby to exercise our autonomy. This, however, seems to set out a direct moral rule independent of the categorical imperative.

If any action consists of respecting a person's dignity, then it is obligatory.

If any action consists of violating a person's dignity, then it is forbidden.

Kant appears to think dignity is another way of expressing the one indirect moral rule. Some philosophers agree with Kant, but most think that with the introduction of dignity Kant has formulated a new and important source for a direct moral rule; it is not just the formal requirement for generating other direct moral rules. As just indicated, I find myself in sympathy with this position and remind the reader that even if Kant is correct about this identification, it does not alter the criticism of the function of the categorical imperative. Most of us would agree with the direct moral rule, for autonomy is something we are inclined to think is of intrinsic value. When, for example, we support the aim of the elderly to live independently, we are prizing autonomy. If we oppose mandatory seat belt or motorcycle-helmet laws, we are appealing to autonomy.[31] Autonomy taken as a direct moral rule needs to be examined independently of the categorical imperative.

Is autonomy taken as a direct moral rule itself a categorical moral rule? To show that it is not, we need only show that we are sometimes justified in restricting a person's autonomy. Sometimes we do this for the common good and, on some rare occasions, even for that person's own good. We prohibit

---

[30]Ibid., 101, 102.

[31]When we act for someone else's good without that person's permission, and often against the wishes of that person, we call that *paternalism*. Kant would claim that paternalism toward adults who are rational is not morally permitted. This is still a controversial position.

driving on the left-hand side of the road, for our good and yours, too. We justifiably override your autonomy to secure the common and your specific good. The direct moral rule of autonomy (or dignity) is not a categorical rule but it could be added to our list of prima facie rules. Kant's claims about intrinsic value will have to wait for our discussion of value in Chapter 6.

These are some of the standard problems philosophers have found with kantianism. However, to remind you, the actual view is much more complicated than I have indicated here. For this reason, some of you may wish to pursue Kant's ethical theory further, and this is, of course, what you should do. However, in our brief survey of single categorical rule theories, we shall now proceed to a very popular view, relativism.

Ethical and Cultural Relativism

Relativism is a theory held by many students and social scientists. As is true with most popular theories, it is difficult to get a clear vision of the theory so as properly to evaluate it. In his book, *In Search of Human Nature*, Carl Degler describes the views biologists and anthropologists have had about people of different races.[32] It was widely held in the late nineteenth and early twentieth centuries that some races were biologically superior to others. Franz Boas, whose views Degler discusses at length, had a key role in convincing social scientists to reject the notion that some cultures are superior to others. Boas argued that European culture was one way to respond to the challenges of an environment, but that of the Quakiutal Indians was an alternative. The languages of each were sufficiently rich to be used in social cooperative activities. The music and art were alternatives, not related to one another as better or worse. The same was thought to be true of morality. Those who held a European moral view held one kind of moral view, but other cultures had other perspectives. It would be just as much a mistake to think one of these "moralities" was better than another as to think that one culture's music was better than another. Well, most of us do not want to be on the side of those who claim their culture is innately superior to that of others. In some cultures, it is morally forbidden to engage in sexual relations before becoming part of a stable long-term family unit, and in some, experimental sexual relations are expected and no great moral import is put on this activity. These activities are "governed" by alternative direct moral rules, each seeming to do its job in that culture. So, should we not then adopt a position in ethical theory that holds that there are alternative normative ethical theories in different cultures that are equally good? Not yet, for we are not yet clear enough about what relativism is.

---

[32]Carl N. Degler, *In Search of Human Nature* (New York: Oxford University Press, 1991). See especially Chapter 3. Degler argues for a role for biology, but not the one that has the bad effects we know today as racism and sexism.

Those who hold to relativism feel very strongly about absolutes; they deny the existence of any such things. What are absolutes? One way to understand this notion is as categorical direct moral rules. The Ten Commandments taken as ten categorical direct rules would then be a set of absolutes. We can, though, give a better general characterization of what an absolute is by contrasting direct utilitarianism with an absolutist view. Direct utilitarianism offers us just one rule that "governs" all of morality. Since this rule holds without exception, isn't it an absolute? No, for what relativists object to are direct moral rules that identify specific characteristics of actions in the rules. The general characteristic, *increase overall good*, has to be contrasted with the specific characteristics in the Ten Commandments—for example, killing. The second premise of the general scheme is needed to pick out which action among those available will increase overall good. Significant inquiry is needed to find the action that will increase overall good, but killing, lying, stealing, and so on tell us more directly what to look for. Furthermore, the nature of the good is not closed. One could, as will be argued shortly, use utilitarianism in any culture but argue that how the good is to be achieved sometimes varies by culture. There may be disagreements about what is good or what will bring about some good we agree upon, but still use the one direct moral rule of utilitarianism. Theories such as utilitarianism and egoism use general characteristics in their rules, but those who hold to absolutes use specific characteristics.

A second difference is that there are many direct moral rules in an absolutist normative ethical theory; the theory is a set of specific characteristic direct moral rules. Typically, these rules describe moral prohibitions and requirements for the people of that society. In some cases a hierarchy of stringency of these rules is provided and sometimes not. Any particular list of such direct moral rules would be true of one culture or even true of just one subculture. It is this kind of rule that Kohlberg, as we saw in Chapter 2, is most opposed to. And so are the relativists.

'Absolutism', then, does not pick out the details of a normative ethical theory but is a description of a kind of such theory. Such theories put forward a list of direct moral rules, sometimes based on a religious view, but not always. The direct moral rules contain specific characteristics of actions and not the general kind of characteristics found in egoism and utilitarianism. Any time someone talks about an absolutist theory, we need to ask which set of these specific characteristic direct moral rules the person has in mind. Only when we know this will we have a complete enough theory before us to evaluate.

Many relativists also maintain that the state of knowledge of the people performing actions should have a bearing on whether the actions are right or wrong. But this is something that almost all the ethical theories we have examined agree to and can easily account for. Perhaps it is best for us now to use the usual procedure and state the view in the general scheme. As a normative ethical theory, the view appears first as a direct moral rule theory and then as an indirect moral rule theory.

Direct Ethical Relativism

If any person *a* of culture C performs an action that is believed by the (majority of) people of culture C to be right (or obligatory), then that action is right (obligatory).

Indirect Ethical Relativism

If any proposed direct moral rule R is believed by the (majority of) people of C to be a direct moral rule, then R is a direct moral rule.

As usual, some of these notions need further explanation. What is meant by 'the people of C' are those who have been raised in culture C and have been taught what someone normally would be taught in that culture. For example, someone might have been raised in India but taught in American schools in that country, resided in a neighborhood that had only Americans, and then returned to the United States. That person would be someone who, for a time, is *in* culture C but not *of* that culture. That person would be a person of the American culture.[33]

It does not happen, with the possible exception of extremely small populations, that every person in a culture agrees that an action of a certain sort is right or that a proposed moral rule is indeed a moral rule. So we must interpret the claim that the people of C believe or accept that the rule is a moral rule or the action is right as meaning that a *majority* of people in that culture do so. How much of a majority there must be before the rule is taken as a moral rule is difficult to say, but once again, we should be able to arrive at some agreement about the (rough) percentage who must hold the belief.

Many of those who defend this kind of ethical theory use the expression 'true for' in both of the statements. There is a sense of 'true for', as was mentioned in Chapter 1, that means the same as 'believes' or 'accepts'. There is nothing wrong with using this expression, but there is the danger that those who use it will suppose it to mean the same thing as 'true', or that there is no use for 'true' but only a use for 'true for'. Both these claims are false, as was shown in Chapter 1. So we shall not use 'true for', but it is useful to see how it has been used by those who are fond of it. A related expression 'true of' is more appropriate to what relativists want to say, but it does not support their position. It is true of a person in American culture that they have an obligation to take their children to the emergency room of a hospital when critically ill, but it is not true of those who live in parts of the world where such hospitals are not available. This difference in obligations, though, is a function of how a certain good is to be achieved. If it cannot be achieved by

---

[33]You may think there is some precise set of items that indicate or define one culture rather than another. This does not seem to be so, or at least it is very difficult to pick out such items. All that is necessary to distinguish cultures is some set of items, however vague it might be, that most anthropologists or sociologists can pick out.

a person in, say, Bangladesh, that person has no obligation to achieve it. This is the kind of analysis the utilitarian would give.

Now we have before us the statements of relativism and an explanation of what those statements mean. Why would anyone hold this view? Most frequently, one finds an empirical view being put forward as a defense of the ethical theory. The empirical view is that anthropologists have discovered that moral opinions vary from culture to culture. The Eskimos in traditional culture, we are told, think it is right to put an aged parent on an ice floe and push it out to sea, but we do not. In some cultures they think it is permitted to eat human beings, and in other cultures they do not. This is the kind of exciting information all of us are aware of from television, if from no other source. This position, like psychological egoism, is clearly based on observation; thus it is called an empirical view. Philosophers call this view *cultural relativism* to distinguish it from the ethical theories that we shall call *ethical relativism*. The ethical theories, you may note, allow the derivation of singular moral judgments, but the empirical theory does not. The ethical theory acts as an aid in arriving at moral judgments, whereas the empirical view only records the fact that moral judgments were reached. The empirical view is one that almost all people agree to, for the evidence is very strong indeed. The ethical theory is more controversial, and most do not accept it. However, if the empirical view does support the ethical theory, and the empirical view is correct, then we have good grounds for accepting the ethical theory. First, though, we need a more precise statement of cultural relativism.

> If any person *a* of culture C makes a moral judgment (adopts a moral rule), then that judgment (adoption of the rule) is a result (causal) of person *a*'s being of culture C.

The statement points up something that seems harmless enough—namely, that when we learn moral rules, for example, we learn them from our parents or in school or church. These are people or institutions that "reflect" a certain culture, and it is natural for them to teach children a certain point of view. As we all know, children are very much influenced by their teachers, and they wind up, on the whole, maintaining very nearly the same views as those espoused by their teachers and institutions. This relation is a kind of causal relation; the child is caused to come to hold certain views by cultural and societal pressures.

However, we must not say these causal pressures are always effective. If you throw a ball with a certain force against a pane of glass that has a certain tensile strength, the glass always breaks. When we dip a naked human being in molten steel for 30 seconds, death always occurs. When we push the same naked human being off a cliff, there is an inevitable fall. These are invariant causal relations because the causal forces are very strong. Cultural pressures, although strong, are not this strong. They are difficult to resist, but many persons do resist, holding views that are different and often inconsistent with those expressed by their culture. This is one reason we must talk about the majority of people rather than all of them—many persons resist the pressures and adopt views different from those around them.

So now we have two kinds of views before us: an ethical theory and an anthropological observation about differences between cultures. What connection is there between the two views? Certainly the ethical theory doesn't follow directly from the anthropological view although some persons seem to argue that it does. They appear to argue as follows:

The members of tribe X judge (believe) that action B is morally right.
The members of tribe Y judge (believe) that action B is not morally right.

Therefore, action B is right in tribe X and not right in tribe Y.

If we take this to be a deductive argument, it is clearly invalid, for the conclusion simply does not follow from the premises. To show that a deductive argument is not valid, remember, we need only show that another argument of the same form goes clearly from true premises to a false conclusion. We do not have to choose another argument that is about the same subject matter, for the subject matter or content is irrelevant to an illustration of the validity of an argument. Thus, to show that the preceding argument is invalid, all we need to do is present another argument of the same type that clearly has true premises and a false conclusion. This is easy enough.

Tribe X judges (believes) that burning incense cures measles.
Tribe Y judges (believes) that burning incense does not cure measles.

Therefore, burning incense cures measles in tribe X and does not cure measles in tribe Y.

It is easy to see that the premises of this argument are true, for there are tribes that believe this sort of thing, and yet the conclusion is false. It does no good to complain that the subject matter of the two arguments is not the same, for the subject matter is irrelevant to whether or not the argument is invalid.[34] You may not like the particular example chosen. Choose your own favorite if you want. For example, there are still some who believe that the earth is flat, that diseases are caused by evil spirits, that Dan Quayle is the illegitimate son of Richard Nixon, and so on. Any of these, or any other false belief will do.

These counterexamples show that the argument attempting to go from cultural relativism to ethical relativism, if it is interpreted as a deductive argument, is invalid. The counterexamples neither presuppose that moral judgments

---

[34] You may wish to refresh your memory on this point by reviewing pages 19, 20.

are objectively true nor that they are not. They do not require the existence of moral absolutes, and they do not deny their existence; they are entirely silent on the matter. So, no questions are begged against ethical relativism.

Can there be some kind of inductive connection between cultural and ethical relativism? There is no inductive argument of the usual sort, at any rate, that allows ethical relativism to be drawn from cultural relativism.

One very clear kind of induction that may help us is *enumeration*.[35] In this kind of inductive argument, you establish that two different kinds of phenomena always or very frequently occur together, and conclude that one is the cause of the other or that they will go together always or frequently in the future. For example, drinking 6 ounces of alcohol within an hour goes together with a certain feeling. If we call the drinking AL and the feeling that results within an hour E, for euphoria, we can construct the following argument:

ALa & Ea
ALb & Eb
ALc & Ec
.
.
.
ALn & En

Therefore, for any person n, if ALn, then En [(n) (ALn $\rightarrow$ En)].

In simple English, the argument is that we have observed enough instances of the two phenomena going together to conclude that whenever the one occurs, it causes the other. Drinking alcohol causes drunkenness.

In terms of this model, the argument connecting cultural relativism to ethical relativism would require that we have a series of statements conjoined; the first conjunct would be a statement of cultural relativism, and the second, of ethical relativism. An instance of such a statement would be as follows: "If Jones of the United States judges that George Bush did the right thing in ordering Desert Storm, then Jones's judgment is a causal result of being of U.S. culture." Supposing that Jones did make this judgment, we can, then, by affirming the antecedent, claim that Jones did make the judgment and that the judgment is a causal result of Jones's being of the U.S. culture.[36]

The corresponding statement of ethical relativism would be "If George Bush did the right thing in ordering Desert Storm, which is believed obligatory by the people of the United States, then George Bush did the right thing in

---

[35]See page 20.

[36]More than 80 percent of the people in the United States held this view when President Bush ordered the start of Operation Desert Storm in the Gulf.

ordering Desert Storm." Once again, since we can assert the antecedent, we can claim that the action was believed to be right; and given the correctness of ethical relativism, it also was right.

To illustrate an induction, let us symbolize the cultural relativism statement as CRgb and the ethical relativism statement as ERgb.

> CRgb = George Bush did the right thing in ordering Desert Storm, which is believed obligatory by the people of the United States.
>
> ERgb = George Bush did the right thing in ordering Desert Storm.

The statements can be read either in their if-then form or in the form resulting when we affirm the antecedent and subsequently conjoin the antecedent and the consequent. To generate the induction, we need other moral issues such as capital punishment and abortion, about which the majority of Americans have moral beliefs. If we couple these statements as we showed for the Desert Storm example, we will arrive at a series of statements that appear as follows:

CRgb & ERgb
CRcp & ERcp
CRa & ERa
.
.
.
CRn & ERn

Therefore, if any action is believed by the people of the United States to be right, then that action is right.

In the preceding scheme, 'gb' refers to George Bush ordering Desert Storm; 'cp' to 'capital punishment is morally permissible'; and 'a' to 'abortion is morally permissible'. In each case the CR refers to the moral beliefs of the majority of Americans and ER to what is right. I think that these issues are representative and that the attitudes of the people of the United States are as described. If you prefer other examples, use whatever you wish.[37]

The problem with this kind of argument is that since it requires the establishment of the correctness of ethical relativism, it cannot be used to establish the correctness of that ethical theory. Notice that the premises consist of two independent statements, one an instance of cultural relativism and the other an instance of ethical relativism. We have agreed that cultural relativism is

---

[37] If you have trouble reading the premises, try translating them into full English sentences using the meaning of the symbols provided. Just take your time and do it for each symbolic representation.

a correct view, so we are justified in asserting instances of it. However, ethical relativism is the very theory now under examination; we cannot therefore assume its correctness in the middle of an attempt to determine if it is correct or not. Thus, the right-hand conjuncts of each of the lines are illegitimate. This is not to say that they are false; that has not yet been determined. However, since we have yet to determine the acceptability of ethical relativism, we cannot assume that theory's correctness either. So this kind of argument cannot be used to establish the correctness of ethical relativism.

Someone might say that ethical relativism is the theory that best explains the phenomena brought to our attention by the correctness of cultural relativism. Ethical relativism is, they say, the best theory concerning the phenomena of cultural relativism. However, whether that is so or not is just the question we are attempting to answer. Very likely, we will be able to say in a short time whether this is so or not, but certainly we can't answer the question before we begin the examination.

So the most obvious kind of inductive argument cannot help, and the kind of argument that is most likely to be the best one is not yet quite ready for use.

Another defender of ethical relativism might suggest that it is the best explanation of the fact that there is a higher degree of intracultural agreement on moral matters than intercultural agreement. Let us examine this claim. First, the fact that cultural relativism is correct does not support this claim about differences in cultural agreement and disagreement. In fact, there is an enormous amount of cross-cultural agreement (the recommended readings at the end of this chapter contain several relevant works on this topic). Frequently, what appears to be a cross-cultural disagreement about a moral matter is really much closer to a more basic agreement than you might think. For example, the Eskimo who puts his aged parent on the ice floe agrees with us that parents ought not to be killed. Eskimos also hold that if there is a choice between allowing a small child to die and an aged parent who is no longer contributing to the society to die, then it is better for the aged parent to die. This is a difficult view to maintain, but notice that to get to it we traversed at least two moral agreements. The moral opinion last expressed may also be one that most people agree to, and, if utilitarianism is correct, it is the one they should agree to. However, we shall examine moral agreement and disagreement more closely in the next chapter.

The claim that ethical relativism is the best explanation of intracultural agreement and intercultural disagreements is somewhat dubious because it is not clear that there is more disagreement of the one type than the other. However, let's continue our examination to see if other ethical theories can account for the same phenomenon equally well. Let us consider utilitarianism as a rival, for it has the advantage of being a clearer theory. The utilitarian can account for the different moral judgments—supposing for a moment that they are different—in the following way. First, people may disagree about the calculation of what is to their benefit. A person in a culture that believes that incense cures measles agrees that getting rid of the disease is a good thing, but this person thinks that one course of action does it and we suppose another does it. Do we have a moral disagreement? Yes, in the sense that we disagree about what is the cause and cure for measles. We both agree that good health, say, is a benefit. If we hold an indirect version of utilitarianism, we can say that we agree on the principle of utility as the indirect moral rule, but we might disagree about which of the direct moral rules is picked out by the indirect moral rule. This allows moral disagreement cross-culturally and, as a bonus, seems to account for some of the underlying cross-cultural agreement; yet it does not embrace ethical relativism.

If this reasoning is acceptable, then we cannot say that the best hypothesis to explain intracultural agreement and intercultural disagreement is ethical relativism, for utilitarianism seems to do at least as good a job.[38] In addition, utilitarianism accounts for other phenomena that ethical relativism apparently does not. For example, utilitarians can account for why people change their mind about moral matters—they realize that more or less benefit results from the action. The relativist has no such explanatory mechanism. More will be said on this point in a short time.

The conclusion is that there is no obvious way in which cultural relativism supports ethical relativism. This is not to say that someone will not come up with some way of showing support, but none appears to be available now. Thus, we must consider ethical relativism by itself, without any support from cultural relativism, to see how it fares as an ethical theory.[39]

As has been noted, there are moral disagreements within cultures. This is a fact that ethical relativists have a very difficult time explaining. They could say that subcultures exist within a culture and that each subculture has its own set of moral opinions. However, there are historical instances in which whole cultures have changed moral opinions without any significant outside influence. This is true of the change in moral attitude toward slavery in England and the United States in the early and middle nineteenth century, respectively. People within the culture argued that the action of keeping slaves was morally wrong, and they carried the day. If ethical relativism were correct, this kind of argumentation could not occur. Imagine, if you can, Harriet Beecher Stowe on an

---

[38] Ethical egoism, as another consequentialist theory, could give the same kind of response.

[39] It is interesting to compare the relationship between psychological and ethical egoism with the relationship between cultural and ethical relativism. In the former, the empirical view was found to be false, although we could see some connection between the ethical theory and the empirical theory. Here, in the latter, we find that the empirical theory is correct, but it seems not to offer any support for ethical relativism.

| True | If PE, then EE. | False | If CR, then ER. |
| False | PE. | True | CR. |

Therefore, EE.   Therefore, ER.

antislavery lecture tour of Mississippi in 1850. She delivers, we'll suppose, her standard lecture on the evils of slavery, and at the end asks for questions. Someone in the audience rises and points out that the majority of people in that subculture believe that slavery is morally acceptable. If ethical relativism were a correct ethical theory, the only thing Mrs. Stowe could do would be to apologize for having made such a stupid mistake.

The point can be generalized: If ethical relativism is correct, then anyone who attempts to bring about moral reform is doing something incredibly silly. Those who argued that the U.S. involvement in Desert Storm was morally wrong, supposing ethical relativism to be correct, would have been making a simple error about public opinion. In 1991 the vast majority of Americans believed the war to be morally justified. But even the most enthusiastic supporter of the military action to oust Saddam Hussein from Kuwait agrees that evidence can be presented to show that it was a mistake after all. If the condition of people in Kuwait and Iraq is worse than before the war, if peace and democracy are even more remote in the area, that would be significant evidence of this.

So change in moral opinion and argumentation are phenomena that ethical relativism does not seem to be able to account for adequately.[40] In addition, the standard kind of counterexamples could be presented. What we want to find are kinds of actions that are apparently right or wrong independently of cultures, or actions that have been thought to be right in a culture but are clear instances of wrong actions. For the latter, consider the actions of the Nazis in taking away the civil rights of the Jews. For the former, consider the action of keeping slaves. By this time, you should be aware that counterexamples are not magic; everyone should join in to find the counterexamples that seem most effective.

As an ethical theory, then, ethical relativism does not have much to recommend it. It does not compare favorably with other ethical theories, there are no reasons to accept it, and there are serious criticisms of it.

A LOOK BACK; A LOOK AHEAD

In summary, the deontological single-rule theories suffer from counterexample difficulties as did their teleological counterparts. The counterexamples are not

---

[40]For new moral problems, the situation is even worse for ethical relativism. There is no basis for making a judgment about a new situation, such as Truman faced in using the atomic bomb in 1945 or the U.S. faced when Gorbachev was ousted by a coup in August 1991. When these moral problems exist the public does not yet have a view. For ethical relativism to work, there needs to be a majority view. Since no majority view exists yet for new problems, ethical relativism cannot give a result. Furthermore, every existing issue or problem for which we have a majority view was once a new problem. There is no rational way for ethical relativism to have reached a decision for any moral issue or problem.

the same, but the results appear to be the same. Since there are no single prima facie rule theories, we have exhausted the theories to be considered in this chapter. In the next chapter, we shall finish our survey of the major theories of obligation with an examination of nonrule theories. At that time I will indicate my choice of the best theory among all the ones examined and argue in its favor. However, this fact should not be taken as earthshaking. Everyone should finally pick a theory to defend, for this is not only necessary for our moral life but is the best way to come to decide which theory is best. It is in defending a theory that one comes to understand its strengths and weaknesses. I hope you will do this and will understand the spirit in which I defend the view I think is best.

Exercises: Evaluating Various Deontological Theories

1. Joseph Fletcher is associated with a position called *situationism*. That view has not been discussed directly, but you can get an idea of it from the following two passages:

   > In this moral strategy the governing consideration is the situation, with all of its contingencies and exigencies. The situationist enters into every decision-making situation armed with principles, just as the legalist does. But the all-important difference is that his moral principles are *maxims* of general or frequent validity; their validity always depends upon the situation. The situationist is prepared in any concrete case to suspend, ignore or violate any principle if by doing so he can effect more good than by following it.
   >
   > . . . Nothing is inherently good or evil, except love (personal concern) and its opposite, indifference or actual malice. Anything else, no matter what it is, may be good or evil, right or wrong, according to the situation.[41]

   Is this view best understood as an instance of agapism or a form of utilitarianism? Is it best understood as some third view?

2. Some philosophers and theologians have said that kantianism is just an elaboration of the Golden Rule ("Do unto others as you would have others do unto you"). What are the similarities and differences between kantianism and the ethical theory that would result if you assumed the Golden Rule to be a single-rule theory?

   (continued)

---

[41]Joseph Fletcher, "Love Is the Only Measure," *Commonweal* (January 14, 1966), reprinted in Situationism and the New Morality, ed. Robert L. Cunningham (New York: Appleton-Century Crofts, 1970), 57, 61–62.

(continued)

    Do you have to suppose it to be an indirect rule or a direct rule? Which is more plausible?

3. Show how your favorite form of utilitarianism, kantianism, and relativism would explain the moral phenomenon that a mother (usually) has an obligation to feed her own infant but does not have an obligation to feed the infant of the family down the street. Which of these theories does a better job in explaining this phenomenon?

4. Explain, as best you can, what you think most people have in mind when they deny the existence of moral absolutes. Given the sense of your explanation, show which of the theories examined so far suppose the existence of moral absolutes and which do not.

5. People often note phenomena that lead others to posit ethical relativism to explain them. In the following AP news story, a high school nurse is defending the prohibition on the topic of birth control in the sex education curriculum: "We are teaching the kids abstinence. To be realistic I know children are not (always going to practice it). But we are certainly not going to promote or give out condoms. When you work in a public community, everyone has different morals."[42]

    Present a clear explanation of what is meant by 'different morals'. Use ethical relativism and one additional normative ethical theory you think does at least a reasonably good job in explaining this phenomenom as clarified by you. Which is the better explanation? Why?

RECOMMENDED READING

Fletcher, Joseph. *Situation Ethics: The New Morality.* Philadelphia: Westminster Press, 1966. You might think this is a kind of utilitarian view or a form of agapism.

Frankena, William K. *Ethics.* 2d ed. Englewood Cliffs, N.J.: Prentice-Hall, 1973. The view examined is discussed in Chapter 3.

Harman, Gilbert. *The Nature of Morality.* Oxford: Oxford University Press, 1977.

Kant, Immanuel. *The Moral Law: Kant's Groundwork of the Metaphysics of Morals.* Translated and analyzed by H. J. Paton. London: Hutchinson University Library, 1948.

Ladd, John. *Ethical Relativism.* Belmont, Calif.: Wadsworth, 1973. This is a collection of essays representing many different positions.

Ross, William David. *The Right and the Good.* Oxford: Clarendon Press, 1930.

Wong, David B. *Moral Relativity.* Berkeley: University of California Press, 1987.

---

[42] *The Columbus Dispatch*, August 26, 1991, 5B.

CHAPTER FIVE

Nonrule Theories

All the theories examined so far have been *rule-based theories*—that is, theories that explain justified singular moral judgments by means of moral rules. Rules, on this view, are required to justify singular moral judgments. Without the use of such principles, judgment is just a matter of guessing which alternative is justified. *Nonrule theories*, in contrast, claim that a "device" other than moral rules best explain how we arrive at justified singular moral judgments. Since *nonrule* as a category is defined negatively, it contains a variety of different views. The major views we shall survey are:

1. Intuitionism
2. Existentialism
3. Pragmatism
4. Virtue ethics

Intuitionism can be covered quickly because of well-known problems and also because few defend the view today. Existentialism as a movement has left its mark but also has few active advocates. The two major types of theory examined in this chapter are pragmatic ethics and virtue ethics. These theories offer a method, of course, for arriving at singular moral judgments, but the method does not include the requirement of a rule. In order to understand these claims and be in a position to evaluate the two main types of nonrule theories, it is necessary now to explain at much greater length than in Chapter 1 the difference between rule and nonrule theories. Thus, we begin with the distinction between summary rules and constitutive rules.

SUMMARY AND CONSTITUTIVE RULES

Summary rules are inductions from individual instances. An example presented in Chapter 1 is induction by enumeration. Such rules are often summaries, we say quite naturally, of past singular justified judgments of that type. Such summary rules presuppose a method of arriving at singular justified judgments that is independent of the summary rule. When we put the summary in the form of premise 1 of the general scheme, we can add some statement of probability so that it looks like the following:

If any x is F, then probably x is M.
or
Probably, if any x is F, then x is M.

Usually, we do not put in probability terms, however, because the way the statement is justified tells us what kind it is.

Suppose, for example, we wish to determine how many people in a class wear or carry watches. One way to do that is to take a sample of all the people in the class—perhaps all the people in the first two rows. If we discover that 75 percent of them wear watches, we can conclude, using induction by enumeration, that 75 percent of all the members of the class wear or carry watches. The argument, put in more formal attire, would appear as follows:

75 percent of all the observed members of the class wear or carry watches.

Therefore, 75 percent of all the members of the class wear or carry watches.

Recall that we need not put in a probability term before '75 percent', for the form and nature of the argument tell us already that it is a probability statement. However, we could put in some such term to remind ourselves. We could rewrite the statement in its equivalent form as "If any person is a member of this class, then the probability is .75 that the person wears or carries a watch." If we rephrase the conclusion in this way, it helps us to understand better the nature of the statement.

To arrive at the conclusion that 75 percent of the members of the class wear watches, we must have some method other than the conclusion itself to determine that individual members of our sample wore or carried a watch. To make this clearer, consider the corresponding statistical syllogism:

75 percent of all the members of the class wear or carry watches.
Person a is a member of that class.

Therefore, person a wears or carries a watch.

Notice, again, that we do not include a probability term, or even a degree of probability in the conclusion—although we can if we wish. In both arguments, of course, something may have gone wrong; there may have been a bad sample, or person *a* may be a peculiar subject. For example, person *a* may have taken a vow never to carry a watch to show her belief that time is unreal.

If a conclusion is general and is the result of an inductive argument, it is a summary rule.[1] An individual judgment falling under it—for example, that person *a* wears a watch—need not be justified by reference to the rule that 75 percent of all the members of the class wear or carry watches. In fact, the opposite is true because the general statement depends on some method of determining that individuals wear or carry watches that is independent of the general statement. In this instance, we look at a person's wrist and search her pockets. The justification of the general statement depends on the singular judgments rather than the justification of the singular judgments depending on the general rule.

This approach is compatible with the view that sometimes the only justification available for a singular judgment is the general judgment. If we are at home and the person in question is not before us to examine or question, then we can do no better than to use the general rule. However, it is clear that the basic method is the one we use to determine whether an individual wears or carries a watch—and that method is *not* using the general statement to justify the singular judgment that falls under it.

However, not all general statements or rules are summaries. Another type of general statement we are interested in is a constitutive rule. *Constitutive rules* define a practice; they bring an activity into existence by their existence. Sports are a good example. The game of baseball started with a simple game for which there were already rules; then, so we are told, Abner Doubleday codified the rules. He added a good number of new rules and thereby brought the game of baseball into existence. The game has changed through the years in a number of ways: The uniforms and equipment are quite different; and the training methods, strategy, and economics are far different now from what they were in Abner Doubleday's time. However, another kind of change involves the game more intimately. When it was decided that a walk no longer would be counted as a time at bat, all scorers had to follow the new rule, whether they thought this was the best way to score a game or not. When a "spitter" became illegal, pitchers were no longer allowed to throw the pitch, no matter how much their records would have been improved by its use.

The rules that tell us what a game is and the rules that cannot be changed without a change in the game are the set of rules that define it. These are

---

[1]There are inductive argument forms more important than enumeration for arriving at conclusions. The hypothetico-deductive form (H-D) is perhaps the most important of these forms and plays a prominent role in pragmatism, as outlined later. If H-D is used, any rule arrived at is a summary, though the method of determining individual instances falling under it is not as clear as when we use enumeration. This should be clearer after reading the pragmatic ethical theory section later in the chapter.

the rules that are changed only by some person or group of people who have the authority to do so. When they change the rules of the game, the game has changed. (We should, of course, still call it baseball unless the change was very radical and occurred within a short period of time. If the game evolves, though, as did baseball and basketball, the chances are that we will go on using the same name, even though the game has changed substantially over the years.)

Two kinds of constitutive rules of games should be distinguished: those calling for punishment and those that simply are not a "move" in the game. For example, if a pitcher balks, then any runner on base is allowed to advance one base. The penalty is assessed, and the pitcher continues. The same is true of those pitchers who throw a spitball. However, no catcher who sprays mace in the eyes of a batter is allowed to continue. Sometimes, something happens that is not even mentioned in the rules but that the umpire, as interpreter of the rules, can clearly disallow *because* the rules don't allow for it or *because* it is judged to be contrary to the rules of the game. If a pitcher shoots a base runner to prevent him from reaching first, the umpire will not allow the pitcher to continue this kind of activity, and the batter will not be ruled out—if he is still alive. One kind of constitutive rule calls for a punishment, for the violation is recognized within the rules. The other kind calls for a judgment that the person is no longer even playing the game when that rule is violated.

This point becomes clearer in a game like chess. One can be penalized a pawn if the pawn is moved past a piece that could have taken it. However, moving a king two spaces to avoid checkmate is not a permissible move. It is not that the person is penalized a pawn, or even the queen, for moving the king two spaces; rather, the move is not in the game of chess at all. Of the two kinds of rules, we shall be most concerned with the kind for which there is no provision in the rules for violation. However, both kinds of rules share one feature that makes them constitutive—they must be used to justify any decision falling within their "jurisdiction."

Constitutive rules are required to justify individual or singular judgments that fall under them—namely, statements of the form of the third statement of the general scheme. No consequent of the first statement can be asserted without first having the appropriate first statement and then asserting the antecedent of it.

Suppose that player A in a basketball game hits another player B. The referee is authorized (by the appropriate league to be a referee, and) by the rules to eject player A. If one of the coaches questions the decision, the referee justifies it by citing the appropriate rule (the "one punch" rule). It would do no good for the coach of player A to argue that since she was on her home court and the fans had come to see their team win that player A should not be thrown out. The rules prevail for the game is what the rules say it is.

Constitutive rules are required to justify singular judgments falling under them. From this requirement it seems to follow that there is no other method by which to justify such judgments. Perhaps a contrast with a *strategy rule*, which is a kind of summary rule, will make this clearer: "If you are playing a team that 'presses', then use at least three players to bring the ball down court." This is a basketball rule that, when followed, will increase the likelihood of winning. At the very least, if you do not follow it, you are much more likely to lose. The very fact that you can lose, though, shows that you don't have to fulfill the rule in order to play the game. However, you must fulfill the rule that forbids one player from lifting another up to reach the basket.

One additional consequence of a rule being constitutive is the impossibility of arriving at a justified singular moral or nonmoral judgment that is inconsistent with it. The rules are what make the singular judgment justified; there can be no singular justified judgment (of that type) that is inconsistent with the rule.[2] If you do find a singular judgment that is both justified and inconsistent with a rule, then you know that the rule is not a constitutive rule in that area. It is a purported constitutive rule, but it is *not* a constitutive rule. Constitutive rules can have no counterexamples.

All the ethical theories we have considered so far claim that one or more constitutive rules of morality exist. What we have been doing, in part, by presenting counterexamples, is showing that such purported constitutive rules are not constitutive. The counterexamples come from the phenomena. The theorist who proposes such a rule must be able to show, in some way that is neither ad hoc nor question begging, that the proposed counterexamples fail to be effective.

Exercises: Constitutive and Summary Rules

1. Classify each of the following rules as either constitutive or summary. Present reasons for the classification.
   a. The "Big Ten" team playing in the Rose Bowl next year will be either Michigan or Ohio State.
   b. A barking dog does not bite.
   c. A pass across two lines in hockey is not allowed.
   d. If you want to pick a rose without being pricked by a thorn, wear gloves.
   e. If you can vote in the United States, then you are at least eighteen years old.

(continued)

---

[2] If the rules of the "game" are inconsistent, there is no correct or incorrect way to play—or, if you like, every way is correct. In either case, no game is described, or no *playable* game is described.

(continued)

2. Are all categorical rules constitutive? Are all prima facie rules constitutive?
3. Present a constitutive rule of some activity and a summary rule within that same activity. Present what would be a counterexample to the summary rule if it were taken as a constitutive rule. Explain why you continue to hold to the summary rule in spite of the counterexample.

THE CLAIMS OF THE NONRULE THEORIES

The preceding explanation of the distinction between summary and constitutive rules allows us to state what all nonrule theories hold in common. These elements should become clearer as different versions of nonrule theories are laid out.

1. There are no moral constitutive rules.
2. There is a describable and usable method for arriving at justified singular moral judgments.

The method of each of the nonrule theories gives us what is unique about the view. Arguments against rule theories will be presented within the context of the nonrule theories in which they arose.

INTUITIONISM

Intuitionism as a philosophical movement had its heyday in the first third of the twentieth century. Logical atomism, as propounded by Bertrand Russell and G. E. Moore, maintained that our usual knowledge of the world and of morality was about complexes. When I know that an automobile has an internal combustion engine, I have knowledge about a complex object and my knowledge is inferred from a number of simpler knowledge parts. I see and hear the car, I have read about cars, I look in the engine compartment, and so on. Even these simpler knowledge items, say the logical atomists, are themselves knowledge complexes. When I look at an engine I am aware not only of parts of the engine but of colors and shapes. It is these latter items that I know directly. I know directly that there is a black patch, a certain (oily) smell, a certain feel to the surface, a sound when the engine runs, and heat felt when I move closer. If I did not know of these things without inference, then I would not know there was an engine. Without direct knowledge there would be no indirect knowledge. Most of our knowledge of the world is indirect, so, the defender of direct knowledge concludes, without direct knowledge there would be no knowledge at all.

The principle that logical atomists and almost all defenders of the need for direct knowledge use may be stated as:

> If there are complexes, then there are simples.

According to logical atomists, there are knowledge simples (we can call them sense-data claims) as well as physical simples (e.g., quarks), and metaphysical simples. In morality also there are simples. Moore, in *Principia Ethica*, argues for his view in the following way:

> There are, in fact, only two serious alternatives to be considered, in order to establish the conclusion that 'good' does denote a simple and indefinable notion. It might possibly denote a complex, as 'horse' does; or it might have no meaning at all. Neither of these possibilities has, however, been clearly conceived and seriously maintained, as such, by those who presume to define good; and both may be dismissed by a simple appeal to facts.
>
> . . . The Hypothesis that disagreement about the meaning of good is disagreement with regard to the correct analysis of a given whole, may be most plainly seen to be incorrect by consideration of the fact that, whatever definition be offered, it may be always asked, with significance, of the complex so defined, whether it is itself good.
>
> . . . If we . . . say 'When we think that A is good, we are thinking that A is one of the things which we desire to desire', our proposition may seem quite plausible. But, if we carry the investigation further, and ask ourselves 'Is it good to desire to desire A?' it is apparent, on a little reflection, that this question is itself as intelligible, as the original question 'Is A good?'
>
> . . . anyone can easily convince himself by inspection that the predicate of this proposition—'good'—is positively different from the notion of 'desiring to desire' which enters into its subject . . .
>
> . . . And the same consideration is sufficient to dismiss the hypothesis that 'good' has no meaning whatsoever.[3]

Moore thought that since *good* was a simple, we must directly know of its presence or absence. His argument, the famous "open question," is referenced in the citation for those who are interested in becoming familiar with it. Moore was an intuitionist concerning good and bad, the two simples in the area of morality. At the same time he was a utilitarian, for once the good is known, utilitarianism describes the way we justify what our obligation is:

---

[3] G. E. Moore, *Principia Ethica* (Cambridge: Cambridge University Press, 1954), 15, 16. The first edition of this work was published in 1903; it was never revised.

> Our duty . . . can only be defined as that action, which will cause more good to exist in the universe than any possible alternative. And what is 'right' or 'morally permissible' only differs from this, as what will *not* cause *less* good than any possible alternative. When, therefore, Ethics presumes to assert that certain ways of acting are 'duties' it presumes to assert that to act in those ways will always produce the greatest possible sum of good.[4]

Although Moore was an intuitionist concerning good (we had to know directly that instances were good) he was not an intuitionist concerning *ought*. Some authors heavily influenced by Moore, though, have been intuitionists concerning *ought*. The most influential of these authors is H. A. Prichard.

> The sense of obligation to do, or of the rightness of, an action of a particular kind is absolutely underivative or immediate. The rightness of an action consists of its being the origination of something of a certain kind A in a situation of certain kind, a situation consisting in a certain relation B of the agent to others or to his own nature. . . . by a process which is, of course, merely a process of general and not of moral thinking we come to recognize that the proposed act is one by which we shall originate A in relation B, then we appreciate the obligation immediately or directly, the appreciation being an activity of *moral* thinking. We recognize, for instance, that this performance of a service to X, who has done us a service, just in virtue of its being the performance of a service to one who has rendered a service to the would-be agent, ought to be done by us.[5]

We can explain this quote, suggesting that Prichard thinks that the methodology is:

1. Know the relevant facts.
2. Check to make sure that you are not abnormal.

---

[4]Ibid., 148. I have conducted almost all the discussions using 'ought' or 'obligation' as synonyms for 'duty'. Some people think these notions are not the same, but I shall not make any finer distinction since they are not needed for present purposes. In addition, Moore has a clearly inadequate view of permission and right, for the most common use of 'permission' today, at any rate, is the Hobbesian one of absence of obligation. In addition, Moore's sense of 'right' is not a commonly used one.

[5]H. A. Prichard, "Does Moral Philosophy Rest on a Mistake?" in *Moral Obligation* (London: Oxford University Press, 1957), 7, 8. The essay was originally written in 1912.

W. D. Ross whose prima facie rule normative ethical theory is presented in Chapter 4, claims that we know each of the prima facie rules directly. This position is discussed in Chapter 7. Ross won't be counted here as an intuitionist who is a nonrule theorist since he does hold to the prima facie rule view. There is nothing wrong, however, with characterizing Ross as an intuitionist with respect to the rules of his theory; but in order to keep the contrast here between rule and nonrule theorists, I choose not to use that category.

A somewhat dated but still good discussion of the intuitionists is to be found in R. T. Garner and B. Rosen, *Moral Philosophy* (New York: Macmillan, 1967). See Chapter 5, "Act Deontology."

3. Abstain from using any rule theories to derive the singular moral judgments.⁶
4. Directly know what your obligation is (what is good).

The first claim is very much like any standard requirement of knowledge. Recall, for example, the requirement the utilitarian sets for us: roughly to know all the consequences that are important and relevant to the action. Of course, no one can know all the facts in a given situation, and there are always occasions when you will be mistaken. This is, though, a truth about any ethical theory that does not require us to have infallible knowledge. A theory requiring infallible knowledge would have a more serious defect: We could never apply it because we do not have infallible knowledge about the world and our relation to it. So, whatever the criteria any proposed ethical theory sets up to determine what knowledge is relevant and how much knowledge is needed, the intuitionist theorist can use those criteria.

The requirement of nonabnormality is more important to the intuitionist than, say, to the utilitarian. For example, no one who has such brain damage that no distinction can be made between a person performing an action and the person on whom the action is performed is able to make moral judgments about the people in such a relation. The same comments apply to those under the influence of drugs (for frequently such people are in no position to make judgments about anything, let alone moral matters). However, the description of what is normal and what is abnormal must contain no moral notions. It would not do to sneak a moral judgment or notion into a description of how we are to arrive at singular moral judgments.

"How are we to arrive at singular moral judgments?"
"Simply make sure that you haven't any disabilities."
"What kind of disability?"
"Oh, the kind that prevents you from making justified singular moral judgments."

Such an answer is not enlightening, to say the least. We need a morally neutral description of what a normal or abnormal person is. The one that seems most workable is the one given by those psychologists who are not at that time using any moral notions: A normal person is one who is able to pass the tests for normalcy for knowledge of nonmoral matters.⁷

The third requirement is clear enough: Don't use any of the rule theories. The final claim that Prichard makes is the one most criticized. The intuitionist

---

⁶Alternatively, this could be put as a requirement not to use any mistaken theories to arrive at singular moral judgments. It is not, though, the requirement to use a nonrule theory.

⁷Was Hitler a normal observer in this sense? There is evidence that he was, at least at the beginning of his regime. The problem of what to do about disagreement will be handled shortly; however, the problem cases are no doubt beginning to disturb many of you now.

has a problem about disagreement. We don't have to be relativists to agree that moral disagreements about what is obligatory are common. One person thinks it is forbidden to publish a book that describes how to commit suicide, while another thinks it is permitted or even obligatory. If intuitionism were correct, we would not expect this kind of disagreement to occur. It does seem, though, that equally well-informed and conscientious people do disagree about specific proposed actions. This form of nonrule theory does not have many philosophical resources with which to respond to this criticism.

EXISTENTIALISM

One of the best known anecdotes of Jean-Paul Sartre is about a young man who has to decide whether to go to England to join the Free French Forces or to stay at home with his mother. His older brother had been killed by the Germans in an early offensive of WW II, and his father was a collaborator. He knows that he might not actually fight the Germans but instead do office work. If he leaves his mother, he leaves her without personal support. Sartre considers various ethical theories one might use—a religious view, utilitarianism, and kantianism:

> He was hesitating between two kinds of morality; on the one side the morality of sympathy, of personal devotion and, on the other side, a morality of wider scope but of more debatable validity. He had to choose between those two. What could help him choose? Could the Christian doctrine? No. Christian doctrine says: Act with charity, love your neighbor, . . . To whom does one owe the more brotherly love, the patriot or the mother? Which is the more useful aim, the general one of fighting in and for the whole community, or the precise aim of helping one particular person to live? Who can give an answer to that *a priori?* No one. Nor is it given in any ethical scripture. The Kantian ethic says, Never regard another as a means, but always as an end. Very well; if I remain with my mother, I shall be regarding her as the end and not as a means: but by the same token I am in danger of treating as means those who are fighting on my behalf; and the converse is also true, that if I go to the aid of the combatants I shall be treating them as the end at the risk of treating my mother as a means.[8]

There is no rule that one can use to choose which course to take. Indeed, claims Sartre, it goes the other way. By choosing the course one thereby makes a choice of moral rule. "No rule of general morality can show you what you ought to do: no signs are vouchsafed in this world."[9] Well, how does one make a choice? In the *existentialist* view, one simply chooses on the basis of

---

[8] Jean-Paul Sartre, "Existentialism as a Humanism," in *Existentialism from Dostoevsky to Sartre,* ed. Walter Kaufmann (New York: Meridian Books, 1957), 295, 296.
[9] Ibid., 298.

the particularity of that situation. Sartre also has a view about being true to the kind of person one is, an essential part of understanding his full view. There is, though, no further rational part of the decision.

Those who criticize the existentialist position complain of its lack of rationality. No choice can be said to be unjustified and, of course, none justified. If there are bases for moral decisions, even nonrule bases, this kind of position is less desirable because of the absence of guidance.

PRAGMATISM

Among the most important philosophers in the American *pragmatist* tradition are C. S. Peirce, William James, and John Dewey. James's ethical views were influential, but since he holds a version of utilitarianism, we won't focus on him. Peirce was an influential pragmatist but wrote no important ethics works, so we shall not look at his ethical theory. Dewey's ethical writings are both pragmatic and influential, so we shall examine his view. There is significant disagreement about his actual position, however, so I shall note that what follows is at least one way to interpret Dewey, though I think it is the best interpretation. If it should turn out to be more my view than Dewey's, that is O.K. I shall nevertheless call the view spelled out in this section "pragmatism." I am aware that this is not the only way a pragmatist might formulate a normative ethical theory, and I do not want to suggest that this view is the only one that could legitimately be called a pragmatic view. On the other hand, I do think that what follows is indeed the view of one of the most important pragmatists—Dewey—and it is also the view that I adopt.

According to the pragmatists, a belief is a disposition to act in certain ways in certain circumstances. To have the belief that putting a dollar in the machine will secure a drink is to have the disposition to put the money in the machine when one has that end. If action is not successful in the appropriate circumstances, the belief from which we acted becomes suspect. That is, we no longer are in the settled state that is belief, but fall into a state of what Peirce calls "doubt." The action on the belief stops and a search for a new belief is instituted—this search is called "inquiry." If it is my habit to buy a drink every day at 3:00 P.M., and if the action that usually results in securing the drink does not succeed I search for hypotheses that would account for this. The dollar is perhaps torn or crumpled. No. Perhaps the price has been raised again. No. Perhaps the machine is out of the selected drink. Yes. Well then another machine must be found. When something in the situation needs to be completed—for example, to secure a drink—and the usual way of accomplishing this is not effective, that is a problem situation. As we shall see Dewey elaborating on this, the problem is not accurately described just in terms of an unsettled state; it is not just that the person is dissatisfied, or distressed. There is something about the environment in relation to the person that is the problem. The problem is part of the situation. The problem is, in a sense that will be made clearer, an objective fact.

People don't spend much time thinking about the problem of how to secure drinks because they have typically worked out a general method of solving such problems. Because of having had such problems in the past, I rely on a higher-level belief or plan of action about how such problems are solved. I pick a specific instance of the plan of finding alternative machines and walk a block to another machine, thus solving the problem. We constantly formulate hypotheses or theories about which kinds of actions are likely to succeed because we know from past experience that when we have a supply of alternative solutions to problems, we are more likely to solve problems when they arise.[10] For the same reason, we also lay in a stock of specific solutions to problems that have not yet arisen. At home we teach our children these stock solutions in the form of rules such as "Look to the right and look to the left before you cross the street." We also teach moral rules, the direct moral rules such as "Lying is wrong" and "Honesty is the best policy." These rules are the ones we teach our children and that we ourselves use. So far Dewey sees no problem in this description of our moral life. The rules, though, are definitely limited.

> Principles exist as hypotheses with which to experiment. Human history is long. There is a long record of past experimentation in conduct, and there are cumulative verifications which give many principles a well earned prestige. Lightly to disregard them is the height of foolishness. But social situations alter; and it is also foolish not to observe how old principles actually work under new conditions, and not to modify them so that they will be more effectual instruments in judging new cases. . . . the choice is not between throwing away rules previously developed and sticking obstinately by them. The intelligent alternative is to revise, adapt, expand and alter them. The problem is one of continuous, vital readaptation.[11]

The new notion concerns principles as hypotheses. A hypothesis on which we act is successful when we reach the end at which we aim or solve our

---

[10]Peirce calls this 'feigned doubt'; see, for example, CP 5.394 [*Collected papers* (Cambridge: Harvard University Press, 1960)]. Peirce has an embarrassing problem in his early essays, for he chides Descartes for not knowing what doubt is. Descartes thinks we can just doubt anytime we want, but in Peirce's view doubt only occurs when our plan of action fails. It is also true, though, that we imagine that we are in doubt in order to work out alternative plans of action. It is what the military does in war gaming and sports coaches do in game preparation. In defense of Descartes, one could say that Descartes was not in actual doubt but was, as he insists, only feigning doubt. Peirce would likely reply that it is only real doubt that shows anything about our knowledge or lack of it.

[11]John Dewey, *Human Nature and Conduct*, ed. Jo Ann Boydston (Carbondale: Southern Illinois University Press, 1988), 164,165. (The text was originally published in 1922, four years after a series of lectures at Stanford on which the book is based. The similarity to Mill's description of what he calls secondary rules should be clear.

problem. A problem situation is not correctly described solely in terms of one's beliefs of the situation, or one's affective attitudes toward it, or in terms of just the physical description of the problem. The problem situation is true of someone in relation to his or her environment, given the chosen ends. The ends are not the final ends of one's life, not the *summum bonum*, the ends are those one is aiming at in this set of circumstances. They are, for this reason, called by Dewey 'ends-in-view'.

The proposition involved in this problem situation is sometimes indicated to be the conclusion one reaches as a result of affirming the antecedent of the kind of conditional statement we have seen repeatedly in direct moral rules. That is, 'person X is in problem situation Y', as instantiated for this problem situation. Perhaps the following captures the Dewey practical syllogism:

P1. If person X is in problem situation Y (not able to buy a drink), then X should do Z (walk a block to the next machine).

P2. X has the problem of not being able to buy a drink.

Therefore, C. X should walk a block to the next machine.

It is not easy to tie Dewey down on what a proposition is, though what he says in a much later work is somewhat clearer.

> Judgment may be identified as the settled outcome of inquiry. It is concerned with the concluding objects that emerge from inquiry in their status of being conclusive. Judgment in this sense is distinguished from Propositions. The content of the latter is intermediate and representative and is carried by symbols; while judgment, as finally made, has direct existential import.[12]
>
> Propositions . . . are what are affirmed but not asserted. They are means, instrumentalities, since they are the operational agencies by which beliefs that have adequate grounds for acceptance, are reached as end of inquiry.[13]

Sometimes, the conclusion of the moral reasoning scheme is what Dewey calls the "proposition." It is a plan of action to change the problem situation. It might be better if we construed the entire set of claims—the two premises and the conclusion—as the proposition, because the premises state the problem and isolate the factors whose change would result in a solution to the problem. In the preceding passages, a judgment is distinguished from a proposition although in "The Logic of Judgments of Practise," a proposition is a kind of

---

[12]John Dewey, *Logic: The Theory of Inquiry*, volume 12 of *John Dewey: the Later Works, 1925–1953*, ed. Jo Ann Boydston (Carbondale: Southern Illinois University Press, 1988), 123. The work was originally published in 1938.

[13]John Dewey, "Propositions, Warranted Assertability, and Truth," *The Journal of Philosophy* 38, no. 7 (1941). Reprinted in *Dewey and His Critics*, ed. Sidney Morgenbesser (Lancaster, Pa.: Lancaster Press, 1977), 271.

judgment.[14] At any rate, when someone reaches or constructs a judgment, this is a plan of action. It is something that results in action; thus, it "has direct existential import." One acts so as to change the situation in which one finds oneself.

The conditional statements that are about moral matters are, when successful in solving our problems, generalized and used as direct moral rules.[15] We then use these direct moral rules to solve our problems. They become beliefs or plans of action that we use when the situation which gave rise to their use occurs again. In Peirce's terms—which Dewey borrows—this becomes a habit. Habits are rules, both for action and for inference in Peirce's scheme, that Dewey adopts as his own. Dewey, however, emphasizes two other elements that Peirce does not: the conflict of habits and the role of impulse or desire. It is important to explain how Dewey's view is completed, but it will be clearer if we contrast his view with that of Mill's.

Mill's remedy for two conflicting direct moral rules (DMRs) is to bring in the principle of utility as either an indirect moral rule or as a direct moral rule to settle the issue. The principle of utility works by allowing us to choose the rule that, when followed, results in an action that is likely to increase overall good. In both "The Logic of Judgments of Practise" and *Human Nature and Conduct*, Dewey rejects the view that any one state, or experience, or whatever, is the good.[16] Thus, Dewey apparently has no indirect moral rule to settle a conflict of DMRs. This is a significant difference between Mill and Dewey. Because the direct moral rules, in Dewey's view, are all hypotheses to be adopted or given up depending on their usefulness in solving our problems, Dewey qualifies as a nonrule theorist.

When two DMRs conflict in a real-world situation, we have a philosophical problem that requires inquiry. For example, my mother cooks a meal for my birthday, but it tastes terrible. She asks me, "How does it taste?" In the past, I have used two DMRs to solve moral problems that conflict in this situation:

If any action is one of truth telling, it is obligatory.

If any action prevents harm to another, it is obligatory.

---

[14]"A practical proposition is binary. It is a judgment that the given is to be treated in a specified way; it is also a judgment that the given admits of such treatment, that is, admits of a specified objective termination." [John Dewey, "The Logic of Judgments of Practise," *The Journal of Philosophy* 12, no. 19 (September 16, 1915). This article is reprinted in *Dewey and His Critics*, ed. S. Morgenbesser (Lancaster, Pa.: Lancaster Press, 1977), 569.

[15]The generalization is from one instance, so to speak, so it is not an enumeration. The whole scheme of proposing a solution to a problem and then seeing if the outcome is what is predicted fits the hypothetico-deductive model. The problem solution is predicted and when it occurs, it confirms the hypothesis that is the plan of action.

[16]Dewey says this repeatedly and in many other works. A clear statement is found in *Human Nature and Conduct*, Chapter 18. Bentham is the utilitarian Dewey talks about, seeming not to see any difference between Mill and Bentham.

I think about not hurting my mother's feelings in this set of circumstances and think about other circumstances in which lying or keeping quiet might occur. Perhaps I try the hypothesis that offering to help her cook the next birthday meal will solve the problem. I might say that I like the food but would like it better if it were cooked for a shorter time. I might say that we should talk about being more honest with each other. In these scenarios I formulate a new conditional, as was done in the nonconflict situation, but now one that replaces both of the rules that were previously used and were relevant to the situation.

If the situation repeats itself, I might formulate another and more complicated rule from the singular conditional. "If any action is one in which X is asked to tell the truth about a matter whose telling will hurt someone X loves—namely, Y—and with whom X has a special relation, then X ought to stop talking about the subject matter at hand and discuss the adoption of a policy X and Y can mutually use when one of them is concerned about hurting the other's feelings." Putting the rule this way emphasizes the pragmatist's position that no amount of thinking in one set of circumstances, no amount of cleverness in solving this problem, will allow us to solve all the future problems of this type. Circumstances change, we change, our loved ones change— everything changes. Even with respect to my mother, having achieved, we'll suppose, the end-in-view of avoiding hurt feelings and avoiding lying, the solution now changes the circumstances of future situations. New problems that we cannot now foresee will arise as a result of the solution chosen. New conflicts will occur between this new, more complicated principle and others. When this happens, we deliberate again.[17]

In the procedure just described, direct moral rules are conclusions of inquiries. We aim to improve our direct moral rules by continuing to formulate conditionals about ends to be achieved and problems to be solved. Rules are, accordingly, not constitutive of morality but are the result of another process of practical reasoning. The pragmatist has so far concentrated on one person's problem situations, but any normative ethical theory must be able to account for the phenomenon of disagreement. The intuitionist described earlier maintains that it is the singular moral judgment itself that is the basic moral unit while the pragmatist claims that it is the moral judgment as related to the relevant factual judgment that is the basic unit.

With Ma = some particular action having a particular moral predicate (e.g., saving Jim from drowning is right) and Fa = some particular action having a particular nonmoral predicate (e.g., swimming out to Jim who is drowning and towing him back to shore), the two views can be represented schematically and contrasted as follows:

Intuitionist: Ma
Pragmatist: $Fa \rightarrow Ma$

---

[17]See, for example, Dewey, *Human Nature and Conduct* 74, 75.

In the first view, there is no way to understand how factual claims could be at all relevant, or how evidence could ever be brought to bear. All one does is directly apprehend the moral "property." In such a situation, it is difficult to understand how one could argue rationally or settle disagreements reasonably. The pragmatic ethical theory holds that the basic unit of justified moral judgment is the moral judgment standing in a certain relation to the relevant factual judgment.

To arrive at the singular moral judgment unconnected with its nonmoral evidence, all you need to do is confirm the nonmoral evidence. The situation would then be as follows:

If Fa, then Ma.
Fa.
───────────
Therefore, Ma.

Moral Negotiation: A Pragmatist Method for Handling Disagreement

Disagreement is almost always traceable, according to the pragmatist, to some disagreement about F. On rare occasions there may be a psychological problem about being in a position to come to have correct singular moral judgments, or, even more rarely, to some theoretical disagreement about the nature of philosophical theories themselves. Let us start with the F's and see how such disagreement is explained. The best way to see how this kind of view works is to consider instances of moral disagreement. The pragmatist thinks the form of all such disagreements is hypothetical. In fact, if the pragmatist theorist is correct, such a conditional disagreement is more accurately called conditional agreement. Let us first show this for a somewhat artificial situation.

> *Person a:* "Slavery is morally wrong because it doesn't allow some people to develop fully as human beings, to realize all their potential."
>
> *Person b:* "Slavery is not wrong because it consists of taking care of those who really have no potential of the same sort that you and I do."
>
> *Person a:* "Can we agree that if those slaves have the same potential that you and I do, then slavery is wrong?"
>
> *Person b:* "Yes, for that is my reason for claiming that it is not wrong. However, if slaves are not really people, as you and I are, and your reason for claiming that slavery is wrong is that they are people, then you would have to admit that slavery is not wrong."
>
> *Person a:* "Yes indeed, and now the question is whether these beings have the same kinds of characteristics as you and I do."

The question of whether or not slaves have the same potential as the rest of us is not a moral question (per se). It is a question that can be answered by using established methods of the social and biological sciences. There is now moral agreement, if only conditionally.

However, you will say, what good does conditional agreement do if we are not in a position to affirm one of the two antecedents on which we have reached agreement? At least now, however, a clear and definite procedure exists that can be carried out to settle the disagreement. This enables us to work toward a settlement of our moral disagreement not only on a hypothetical level but on every level. For this reason, the method will be called *moral negotiation*.

Notice that the same problem of actual agreement or arriving unambiguously at one specific moral judgment, if it is a problem, besets the rule theorists. They begin with a rule of the form "If any x is F, then x is M," and then they must affirm the antecedent in order to generate out the justified singular moral judgment. If there is a disagreement about whether x is F (about the antecedent), then there is no way to arrive at the justified claim that x is M. Since both pragmatic and rule theories have this same problem, it cannot be an effective criticism of one of them. However, do not forget that we often do agree on the antecedent or (when these are not the same) at least can justify an antecedent.

The test of such a method, as mentioned earlier, is in practice. Let us now practice with yet another case, this one developed by students in a course. The issue before us was whether a program of affirmative action (AfA) is morally permissible/forbidden. To make the issue clear, a few preliminary clarifications are needed. In the course we had already distinguished quotas from other types of affirmative action such as recruitment, special tutoring, scholarships, Head Start, and so on. Quotas as the mainstay or only form of affirmative action were thought by almost all the students to be morally undesirable, though almost everyone admitted that in some circumstances a temporary and short-run use of quotas might be morally permitted. We had talked about what kind of society we were aiming at, and (following Richard Wasserstrom) collectively agreed that concerning race and sex, we wanted to reach the point where sex and race were no more important in securing jobs or places in educational programs than handedness or eye color is now. This was called the egalitarian ideal (EI). Finally, we distinguished between achieving equality of opportunity (EO) and equality of success (ES). ES would secure the same success rate of persons in different categories while EO would make sure that we all had the same opportunity to succeed. In order to secure ES in a slam-dunk contest between Michael Jordon and Larry Bird, we would have to strap weights to Jordon's ankles. Even though we would have confidence in the outcome, we agreed that EO was what we aimed at and not ES. In this context the following two conditionals were constructed:

1. If AfA is proposed in a context in which
   a. There is no significant difference in the potential at birth between blacks/whites or males/females that would prevent any in that group from success in the fields or programs we have discussed (educational programs and kinds of jobs), and
   b. EO will make it more likely for us to reach EI, and result in our being better off economically and culturally, and
   c. We share the EI, and
   d. AfA is the best means to achieve EO, and
   e. EO is the best way to bring about EI, and
   f. Not-(f'). Quotas, if used, will be a short-run, temporary measure.
   g. Not-(g'). Racism and sexism will diminish as we move toward EI and blacks and women occupy a variety of educational and employment niches.

   Then, we are permitted to engage in a program of AfA.

2. If AfA is proposed in a context in which
   a'. Not-(a) Because blacks are significantly less intelligent than whites (roughly one standard deviation), and
   b'. Not-(b). AfA will actually hinder the development of the potential of blacks, and
   c'. It will lower standards of performance in programs and jobs, and
   d'. It will increase and prolong racism and sexism in our country, and
   e'. It will make EO and EI less likely. (This may be the same as or part of (d'), and
   f'. It will involve indefinite (or principal) reliance on quotas to achieve the stated goals, thus increasing racism, and

   . . .

   Then we are forbidden from engaging in a program of AfA.

The ellipsis (. . .) is an invitation to add whatever additional items anyone thinks are relevant. In that class at that session no one thought of any additional items, but that does not mean you will not. If you do think of other items for the antecedents, then the method invites you to add them.

Even though all the parties, about a hundred and fifty students, agreed to the two conditionals, this does not mean they reached actual moral agreement about affirmative action. What conditional agreement did do, though, was to turn a very sensitive issue into one in which blacks and whites, and men and women could, and did, discuss the topic rationally and coolly. It turned opponents into cooperating members of a team that found conditional agreement. The likelihood of reaching agreement on the issue was thereby significantly increased, and moral outrage was not directed at those with whom one disagreed. Because the items in the antecedent are all agreed-upon values or factual claims, students had the sense that further empirical evidence would be crucial to resolving the moral dispute. This is the method of moral negotiation working in its first and, I think, most important, phase.[18]

Affirmative action is just one moral issue, and although it is a troubling one for Americans in the last decade of the twentieth century, by itself it may not be thought of as strong evidence of the success of the method. What you must do is try the method yourself.

How do we know these moral matters? What explains our ability to agree on the two conditionals. Many of you will still be puzzled by all this, no matter how successful the procedure. Here, you say, is a nonmoral characteristic or set of such characteristics F and a moral characteristic M; somehow we can get people to agree that given some specific F, some M also holds. But how are we able to make the "move" from the F to the M? In terms of knowledge or justification, how does F justify M?

The rule theorist might claim to know a rule or set of rules directly (to be justified in claiming that this is the rule or set of rules directly). At the end of the chain of justification, that which is claimed to be justified, and yet not justified by something further, is justified directly. The pragmatist, in contrast, offers the justification of successful solution to problems. Lying, for example, prevents successful interaction among humans. We attempt to solve this by adopting a policy of truth telling, which policy is formulated in a direct moral rule of the usual form: "If any action is one of lying, then it is forbidden (obligatory not to do)."

Which problems, though, are moral problems and which are other kinds of problems? In the pragmatic view, moral issues and problems are practical problems, as are economic and dietary issues. The methodology for solution is the same—the posing of and acting on hypotheses. So far, the indirect utilitarian might endorse this description of the methodology of the pragmatist. The utilitarian, however, has an indirect rule that would rationally allow the choice of a direct moral rule. The pragmatist talks about successful solutions to problems, but some successful solutions to problems might well bring about a bad situation. For example, in the summer of 1991 there was an attempted coup in the former Soviet Union. The leaders of the coup claimed they were

---

[18]After reaching conditional agreement, the facilitator would attempt to find the smallest set of items in the antecedent that would still retain agreement. Some items will turn out not to be relevant. At that point, a preliminary examination of the empirical evidence would be helpful but not final. It often happens that additional items will be proposed after reaching this point, so further discussion and elimination will be needed. The shifting of attention from disagreement to cooperation in finding conditional agreement will sometimes, just by itself, lead to a reconciliation of the moral issue. It almost always eliminates the sense of irreconcilable opposition.

attempting to solve the economic problems of the country that were threatening famine and chaos. For a few days the coup seemed to be succeeding, but then the government of Mikhail Gorbachev returned for its short stay until the USSR itself was dissolved. How would the pragmatist evaluate the proposed solution to the problems of the Soviet Union by the coup's leaders? In light of the problems following the breakup of the Soviet Union, is the coup leaders' position strengthened?

One thing the pragmatist cannot say to help explain what it is to solve a problem is that there is some likely good that is an independent measure of a correct solution. We can say that democratic mechanisms for change result in greater support among the people and that a rejection of rule by an elite was clear in events in the Soviet Union. The pragmatist can say, of course, that more good would result from restoring the Gorbachev government, but this has to be a good chosen in the same pragmatic manner as the direct moral rules. Of course, I am in no privileged position to make any of these predictions—you might well have a better analysis of the situation than I do.

What about disagreement? Rule theorists point out that if the pragmatic theorists are correct, then either there is no way to settle moral disagreements involving singular moral judgments or there are no such moral disagreements. Why this dichotomy? The first part—there is no way to settle such disagreements—is justified, say the rule theorists, because, according to pragmatists, singular moral judgments are the basic units. Thus, there can be no further evidence within the area of morality to justify the judgments and, therefore, no evidence to settle disputes. Still, say the rule theorists, the pragmatist has the other side of the dichotomy available as a choice: The pragmatist theorist might claim that moral disagreements do not occur. But this flies in the face of abundant evidence from the phenomena that there is such disagreement.

Pragmatist theorists can respond in two different ways. First, there is an unclarity, they would say, about the claim that no moral disagreements occur. Pragmatists can admit to moral disagreement, but, according to their theory, it is based on some kind of factual disagreement, some kind of ethical theory disagreement, or on the abnormality of at least one of the disputants. Disagreements of this sort can be accounted for by pragmatists. Furthermore, pragmatists use another kind of disagreement—namely, conditional disagreement—to explain many cases of what at least look like disagreements about singular moral judgments. Many cases of what start out as disagreements about singular moral judgments turn out to be instances of conditional disagreement/agreement only—not disagreements about the singular moral judgment at all.

VIRTUE ETHICS

Virtue normative ethical theories trace their written history to Aristotle (384–322 B.C.E.), so let us begin with his words:

Actions, then, are called just and temperate when they are such as the just or the temperate man would do; but it is not the man who does these that is just and temperate, but the man who also does them *as* just and temperate men do them. It is well said, then, that it is by doing just acts that the just man is produced, and by doing temperate acts the temperate man; without doing these no one would have even a prospect of becoming good.

But most people do not do these, but take refuge in theory and think they are being philosophers and will become good in this way, behaving somewhat like patients who listen attentively to their doctors, but do none of the things they are ordered to do. As the latter will not be made well by such a course of treatment, the former will not be made well in soul by such a course of philosophy.[19]

What is a *virtue*? Aristotle held, as we do today, that a virtue is a *good* (intrinsically valuable) character trait. Character traits are relatively stable tendencies or dispositions of persons to act in certain ways given certain situations. An honest person, one who possesses the virtue of honesty, has a character trait that results in returning things, telling the truth, and so on. Some people acquire the opposite disposition we call dishonesty. We can call honesty an intrinsically valuable character trait and dishonesty an intrinsically disvaluable character trait. We are inclined to think that courage is good and cowardice bad, that the former is an intrinsically good character trait and the latter intrinsically disvaluable. We think this, typically, of such pairs as kindness/viciousness, love/hate, or wisdom/foolishness. In sum, then, a virtue is an intrinsically valuable character trait. This position can be understood, as was utilitarianism and egoism, on the basis of our understanding of value from the phenomena. After we examine value theory in the next chapter, you will understand better and might wish to modify your position somewhat.

Aristotle thought that virtues are a mean between two extremes. Courage is a mean between foolhardiness and cowardice, not just the absence of fear. If someone felt no fear, we would not think that person courageous but rather cognitively or affectively defective. The courageous person feels fear at the thought of confronting a bully but acts anyway. Although we are not inclined to agree with Aristotle's view that a mean is a crucial scientific category in every science, it is nevertheless a useful category in many areas.

Aristotle's phrase 'just and temperate' actions seems to indicate the evaluation of actions. Today we call actions right or wrong, obligatory or forbidden, but this is mostly a verbal difference. The virtue ethics theorist tells us that to establish that an action is right, we need to know the character trait from which it is performed. If the character trait is a virtue, then the action

---

[19] Aristotle, *Nicomachean Ethics* (1105b5–18) in *The Basic Works of Aristotle*, ed. Richard McKeon (New York: Random House, 1941).

is right. Bernard Mayo, a contemporary philosopher, recognizes that we are interested in knowing what we ought to do in a given situation.

> Now according to the philosophy of moral character, there is another way of answering the fundamental question "What ought I to do?" Instead of quoting a rule, we quote a quality of character, a virtue; we say "Be brave," or "Be patient," or "Be lenient." We may even say "Be a man": if I am in doubt, say, whether to take a risk, and someone says "Be a man," meaning a morally sound man, in this case a man of sufficient courage. . . . Now the question "What ought I to do?" turns into the question "What ought I to be?"—as indeed, it was treated in the first place. ("Be brave.") It is answered, not by quoting a rule or a set of rules, but by describing a quality of character or a type of person. And here the ethics of character gains a practical simplicity which offsets the greater logical simplicity of the ethics of principles. We do not have to give a list of characteristics of virtues, as we might list a set of principles. We can give a unity to our answer.[20]

Neither Aristotle nor Mayo or, indeed, any virtue ethics theorist is proposing a rule to follow. Their intention is to contrast a rule-oriented theory with their own character-oriented view. The following complex passage from Alasdair MacIntyre shows this contrast and yet allows a role for rules. MacIntyre is discussing Plato's counterexample to the proposal that justice (right action) consists of returning what belongs to others. Plato, through Socrates, asks if it would be right to return a knife to someone who has since become deranged. Everyone agrees that the simple moral rule must be modified. MacIntyre thinks we must teach the youth not just moral rules but also how to modify them so they are more adequate.

> There is no objection to understanding the outcome of this process of learning in terms of the acquisition of a more and more sophisticated ability to supply a rational justification for the application of a more and more complex rule or set of rules. But it is crucial also to understand that neither the movement from a less to a more sophisticated ability to judge how the rules of justice apply and to justify those judgments nor the corresponding movement from the use of simpler versions of the [rules] . . . are themselves rule-governed forms of activity. How are they governed?
>
> The movement of learning consists in the development of at least two related sets of dispositions, two virtues, that of justice itself and that of *phronesis*, of practical intelligence.[21]

The use of rules is definitely, then, a secondary matter in terms of moral judgments. When someone who is morally mature wonders what is the right

---

[20]Bernard Mayo, *Ethics and the Moral Life* (New York: St. Martin's Press, 1958), 213.

[21]Alasdair MacIntyre, *Whose Justice? Which Rationality?* (Notre Dame, In.: University of Notre Dame Press, 1988), 114.

thing to do or what is his or her obligation, instead of quoting a rule, we might do as Mayo suggests. We might quote a virtue and say "Be brave."[22]

Aristotle, Mayo, MacIntyre, and all virtue ethics theorists deny that rule following is the basic or primary method of coming to do what one ought to do. Someone could construct a rule: "If an action would be done by a virtuous woman to fulfill her obligations, then it is obligatory to do that action."[23] Although the rule is in the familiar form, it is not what the virtue ethics theorist is proposing. A closer approximation would be:

> If a person A is virtuous (has a virtuous character), and does some action Y voluntarily, for its own sake, and from a virtuous disposition, then Y is right.

While this is a true virtue ethics description of someone doing what is right, it is not a rule to be used by others to discover the right thing to do. This is perhaps a description of what it is for an action to *be* right but not how we *find out* or *justify* that an action is right.

Once the virtues are part of one's character, right action is describable as stated. But how does one come to have the virtues? First, you must act the way a virtuous person does. To do this, you find a good person to emulate. A good person is someone known to do what ought to be done, and perhaps is known to do this for the right reasons. Parents provide this kind of model for their children.

But this raises a problem for virtue ethics theories. Few persons are completely morally wise or virtuous. Most people have many vices as well as virtues. If the primary way to discover the right thing to do is to emulate what a virtuous person does, then we need to know how to find a virtuous person. Finding a virtuous person to emulate requires recognizing the performance of right actions and wrong actions. Right and wrong actions do not come labeled "right" and "wrong," so we need to be able to reach moral judgments in specific instances. But if we can make this determination of right and wrong, there is no need to find a virtuous person to emulate. In order to find a virtuous person to emulate so we will be able, after some practice, to make justified moral judgments, we need already to be able to make such justified moral judgments.

Earlier Aristotle told us that "it is by doing just acts that the just man is produced, and by doing temperate acts the temperate man; without doing these no one would have even a prospect of becoming good." The virtue ethics theorist can remind us that people do not come to do what is right just by

---

[22]Mayo, *Ethics and the Moral Life*, 213.

[23]Virtue ethics theorists such as MacIntyre say that rules are needed to teach the young how properly to act. The young do not yet have the character traits in place from which they will act when mature. We give them, instead, rules to act from until we instill what (we hope) are virtues. Those who are adult moral actors, though, do not have rules from which to act. (See, for example, MacIntyre, *Whose Justice? Which Rationality?* 115–119.)

watching others perform right actions. To form the character trait, people need also to act in the appropriate way. The virtue ethicist maintains that this is accomplished by emulating the virtuous person. One does not become a good carpenter solely by reading manuals on carpentry. One needs also to do the kind of things that good carpenters actually do when they are engaged in carpentry. Although it is conceivable that one may become a good carpenter without having a good carpenter as a model or taking instruction from such a carpenter, the chances for success are extremely low.

We become virtuous by acting as the virtuous person does when exercising a virtue. In the real world, we learn to do this only by imitating a virtuous person. The critic would note that the basic way of finding which actions are right nevertheless cannot be the means chosen for moral education. Adults need to have a procedure to know which actions are right in order to find a virtuous person. Since some parents are not virtuous or select a nonvirtuous exemplar for their children, it is not even the basic method for all children.

A virtue ethics defender can say that children do not know what is right or wrong instinctively or by nature. Children must emulate their parents or some other person of authority. But, the critic continues, since we know there are bad models as well as some children who reject the model of their childhood, there has to be another way to arrive at justified moral judgments.

Most principle-oriented theorists recognize the importance of character training. Children are trained whether they will it or not. Adults can choose to change their own character or choose someone to help them. This is an important part of our moral lives. However, the principle-oriented theorists maintain, we can act from our own moral judgments and, *in that manner*, acquire character traits. These are moral judgments we must be able to arrive at without having the character traits that we *will* acquire as a result of acting from our judgments. The specific moral judgments are acquired by means of principle-oriented normative ethical theories.

Exercises: Basic Units of Morality

1. Write down the basic unit of morality according to the utilitarian of your choice, and next to it write the basic unit of morality according to the nonrule theories so far discussed here. Describe the differences and the similarities.

2. Show how the pragmatist (and then the existentialist) theorist either can or cannot take the utilitarian basic unit to be a summary rule. Are there counterexamples to the rule taken as a summary rule?

(continued)

(continued)

3. Find one of the constitutive rules of chess in a book of rules, and write it down. Can that rule be justified within the game of chess by additional rules? Can it be justified in some other way?
4. Choose some topic involving a moral judgment on which there is widespread disagreement. Attempt a moral negotiation—to effect a conditional agreement among those who disagree. (If you are alone on a desert island, construct various characters who disagree.)
5. Construct for a virtue ethics theorist a method for handling moral disputes. Make sure the method is consistent with the theory. Evaluate that method.

Nonrule versus Rule Theories

6. Now that you have examined the main rival normative theories of obligation, you may wish to ask yourself which of them does the best job of accounting for the moral phenomena. Turn to pages 27, 28 to refresh your memory concerning the moral phenomena discussed at the beginning of this investigation. You may wish to add some other items and should feel free to do so (as long as they are not theories that compete with the ones already examined). Present your reasons for claiming that one theory does a better job than its rivals of explaining the moral phenomena.
7. Suppose someone attempts to save a rule theory by including an "all things being equal" clause in the following way:

   If any x is an instance of F, then, all things being equal, x is M.

   When we propose a criticism in the form of a counterrexample, the person says, "Aha! This is an instance in which not all things were equal, so that case is already covered in the rule." What is wrong with this response?
8. Present the strongest reasons you can give for or against the following claim: "Whenever you offer justification for a claim within an area, there are going to be other claims within that area that are not justified."
9. Most decisions concerning travel from one point to another are made without a map, most decisions about food are made without

(continued)

> *(continued)*
> a theory of nutrition before us, and most moral decisions are made without having a normative theory of obligation before us. What are some functions for such theories? Argue either that such functions are important or that they are not.
> 10. The following quote indicates that the author holds some kind of nonrule theory. Attempt to indicate what sort it is, and if you cannot tell, indicate why.
>
>> If the exercise of moral judgment, the holding of moral views, is to be the reasonable affair which it is surely ideally supposed to be, there should not occur any simplifying, undiscriminating, rather child-like acceptance of rules; for there is nothing to make such acceptance really reasonable. Rather, there should occur the constantly repeated attempt to achieve the best judgment on the full concrete merits of each individual case. One should thus consider what there is reason to do or not do, or what view there is reason to take, rather than, less discriminatingly, what is required by some rule, or permitted or ruled out by some rule.[24]

COMPARISON OF THEORIES OF OBLIGATION: A SUMMARY

In Chapter 1, the various theories of obligation were laid out on a chart. You may now want to review that chart (see page 16) in order to see where we have been and better understand what has been done. In Chapters 2 and 3, the two main kinds of teleological theories—namely, egoism and utilitarianism—were examined. We concluded in Chapter 2 that egoism is a weak view because the psychological theory used as its main support is not itself supportable. Further, even if that psychological theory were correct, the resulting ethical theory would not cover all the moral phenomena. The version of ethical egoism that derives support from psychological egoism is the "right to" version, and one cannot, in any obvious way at least, derive actions that are right from ones that are permitted. With this view, there are problems in dealing with other people, problems with counterexamples of various types, and difficulties in accounting for moral disagreement. Kohlberg's psychologically based theory is better than egoism, but he does not seem to get legitimate support for his ethical theory from his psychological views. Utilitarianism does a better job in accounting for the moral phenomena concerning other people and disagreement. On these grounds, therefore, we concluded that some form of utilitarianism,

---

[24] G. J. Warnock, *The Object of Morality* (London: Methuen, 1971), 67.

most likely the indirect version, is the best of the teleological theories. This is not to say that that theory is free of difficulties. The primary difficulties involved various counterexamples and the problem of justice.

In Chapter 4, a variety of deontological theories of obligation were examined. We argued that a multiple categorical rule theory is most difficult to defend because of the problem of the conflict of rules. Such conflicts lead to the conclusion that we have incompatible actual obligations—an unacceptable conclusion. The two views that seemed best are the indirect single categorical rule view of Kant and the prima facie rule view. Among the nonrule views, a pragmatic view and virtue ethics appear strongest. Intuitionism has too many problems to be considered one of our finalists.

The normative ethical theories that have been most fruitful both for action and defensibility are utilitarianism, the prima facie view, kantianism, and virtue ethics. The pragmatic view is defended by many, and the position of John Dewey is enjoying a "comeback." Each of these views is subject to criticism; none is free of all problems. You must decide which of these theories does the best job in accounting for the moral phenomena—not which one is entirely free of fault. The three views that appear best among the rule theories are indirect utilitarianism, kantianism, and the prima facie rule theory. I have argued that, because of the problems facing each of these, the version of a pragmatic theory just dealt with is a better theory of obligation. The arguments for this claim are to be found primarily in this chapter; the arguments against the other theories are found in the chapters in which those theories are examined.

You may want to wait until you have examined the theories of value before you make a decision about a theory of obligation. You will recall that for the first statement of the general scheme, the teleologists replaced F with some value term (for example, "If any action of person a maximizes the greatest good for the greatest number, then person a is obliged to perform that action"). The value terms were all the most general ones—for example, 'good'—and we deliberately did not attempt to specify them further. The other half of normative ethics is a theory of value, and we shall turn to that next. It may be that a general theory with a somewhat defective theory of obligation fits best with a theory of value that is itself the best theory in that area. Given this, you would then opt for a theory of obligation that you would reject if there were no such area as theory of value. Furthermore, some theory of value may exist that will allow us to specify the value terms in teleological theories of obligation in such a way as to escape the criticisms offered so far. With all of these considerations in mind, then, let us turn to the theory of value.

RECOMMENDED READING

Dewey, John. *Human Nature and Conduct.* Edited by Jo Ann Boydston. Carbondale: Southern Illinois University Press, 1988. The text was originally published in 1922, four years after a series of lectures at Stanford on which the book is based.

Hare, R. M. *The Language of Morals.* Oxford: Clarendon Press, 1952.

MacIntyre, Alasdair. *Whose Justice? Which Rationality?* Notre Dame, In.: University of Notre Dame Press, 1988.

Prichard, H. A. *Moral Obligation.* New York: Oxford University Press, 1950. Prichard is an intuitionist who defends a theory modeled on our knowledge of mathematics.

Singer, Marcus. *Generalization in Ethics.* New York: Alfred A. Knopf, 1961. Singer argues for a rule theory via what is called the "generalization argument." This argument is not taken up directly in this chapter, though it is the subject of the next item in this bibliography.

Sobel, J. Howard. "Generalization Arguments." *Theoria* 31 (1965): 32–60. Reprinted in *Readings in Ethical Theory.* Edited by Wilfrid Sellars and John Hospers. New York: Appleton-Century-Crofts, 1970.

APPENDIX TO CHAPTER FIVE

Rule Theory General Arguments

Various criticisms of specific rule theories have been presented. We claimed, for example, that moral rules are either categorical or prima facie, and rule theories contain one or both kinds. A categorical rule, whether direct or indirect, has effective counterexamples. Kant's view continues to have the most defenders among these theories. A prima facie rule theory, whether it is Ross's, Frankena's or anyone else's, has difficulty, to say the least, in accounting for a situation in which two or more of the prima facie rules conflict. Furthermore, counterexamples exist, of the underwhelming value sort, for each of the prima facie rules. These same criticisms apply to theories that are combinations of categorical and prima facie rules. The criticisms of egoism seem effective, and, although the criticisms of utilitarianism are not as devastating, they pose serious problems for that latter view.[1] The serious difficulties faced by the rule theories give us more confidence in asserting that a nonrule theory might be what we are looking for—depending on how well such a theory can meet the criteria of acceptability of ethical theories. One thing nonrule theorists must do is respond to some general arguments rule theorists use

---

[1] The indirect version of utilitarianism (IMR) is not subject to the same criticisms as the direct version (DMR). With the IMR version, the secondary rules are DMRs whose conflict can be settled by applying the principle of utility as an IMR. The general criticism of rule theories, then, does not really apply to IMR utilitarianism. The standard criticisms of that view as presented in Chapter 4, though, do apply.

against nonrule theorists. Because these arguments are of a somewhat arcane nature, we put them into this appendix. Those interested in these complex arguments will find this a crucial section, but others might want to read through the material only casually.

THE PROBLEM OF DISAGREEMENT

One of the chief arguments of rule theorists against nonrule theorists concerns disagreement. Rule theorists point out that if intuitionism is correct, then either there is no way to settle moral disagreements involving singular moral judgments or there are no such moral disagreements. Why this dichotomy? The first part—there is no way to settle such disagreements—is justified, say the rule theorists, because, according to nonrule theorists, singular moral judgments are the basic units. So there can be no further evidence within the area of morality to justify the judgments and, thus, no evidence to settle disputes. Still, say the rule theorists, the intuitionist has the other side of the dichotomy available as a choice: that moral disagreements do not occur. But this flies in the face of abundant evidence from the phenomena that there is such disagreement.

Intuitionists may have no adequate response to this criticism, but pragmatic theorists can respond in two different ways. First, there is an unclarity, they would say, about the claim that no moral disagreements occur. There are many cases of what start out as disagreements about singular moral judgments that turn out to be instances of conditional disagreement/agreement only—not disagreements about the singular moral judgment at all.

However, someone might persist, couldn't disagreement about the singular moral judgment exist even after we have completed the process of conditional agreement? The pragmatist does not claim to be able to solve all disagreements, but if the basis of the disagreement lies in which set of factual claims is correct, then this is not a moral disagreement as such. More evidence can be brought in, as we have seen in the few sample disputes outlined earlier. This is not only compatible with the pragmatist's view, but it is the very way it is supposed to work.

It is not clear how an existentialist would account for moral disagreement, except to say it is a fact of human life. Is that so?

POSITIVE RULE THEORY ARGUMENTS

Nonrule theorists must meet an argument set forth by rule theorists that purports to show that every singular moral judgment must be justified by a rule. If this argument is successful, then some rule theory or other is correct and any nonrule theory is incorrect. We may not know which rule theory is correct, but we can be sure that some one rule theory—perhaps one not as yet known—is indeed correct. This is the argument that must be successfully countered by nonrule theorists.[2]

We begin by considering the work of R. M. Hare. Hare lists three reasons for needing principles.

> The first reason applies to anyone, even a man with complete insight into the future, who decides to choose something because it is of a certain character. The second reason applies to us because we do not in fact have complete knowledge of the future, and because such knowledge as we do have involves principles. To these reasons a third must now be added. Without principles, most kinds of teaching are impossible, for what is taught is in most cases a principle.[3]

Let us begin by examining the use of principles in teaching. Nonrule theorists can admit that what is taught in most cases is a principle, but we may need only summary principles to teach morality. One way to teach color terms to children who can count to two, for example, is to say, "Start at the top of the American flag and count the first stripe *one* and the second one *two*. Number one stripe is red and number two stripe is white." Although this rule could be used by someone who can count, the rule is not required to justify the specific judgment that this stripe is red. The child may not know that there is another way to arrive at the justified judgment that the stripe is red, but we know there is.[4]

We often use principles to teach. Most of the time, however, we use summary rules; these are not constitutive rules, rules that are required for justifying judgments. For example, when we teach American history, we can use the rule "In a nonpresidential election year, the party out of office gains power." When my daughter was about six, she was having trouble keeping the right/left distinction. I told her that her right hand was the one she writes with and the left hand is the one left over. Although this rule generally works, since most of the population is right-handed, it is not a rule that is required to justify a judgment that this is my left hand. Or, for another type of example, "If an argument has two existential premises and an existential conclusion, then it is invalid." For some subjects, such as arithmetic, we use constitutive rules to teach students how to justify judgments that fall under those rules.

---

[2]The counterarguments presented on pages 207–209 are found, in very much the same form, in Bernard Rosen, "Rules and Justified Moral Judgments," *Philosophy and Phenomenological Research* 30, no. 3 (March 1970), 436–443; and in 5, no. 1 (Winter 1970), 54–56.

[3]R. M. Hare, *The Language of Morals*, (Oxford: Clarendon Press, 1952), 60. All quotations from *The Language of Morals* that appear in this chapter are reprinted by permission of the Oxford University Press.

[4]If the children are color-blind or totally blind, there is probably no other way for them to justify color judgments than to use this rule or one like it. But the effectiveness of the rule depends on its having been established by sighted people who did not use the rule.

Since this is O.K., we cannot say that all teaching is done with summary rules (although it may be possible to get along with only such rules), and we cannot say that all teaching uses constitutive rules. What we must do, then, is determine which kind of rule is used in teaching morality.

The rules used in teaching morality appear to be such rules as, "Do not lie," "Lying is wrong," or "Never tell a lie." As we know, there are effective counterexamples to such rules. For example, if one's wife asks, "Do I look all right this evening?" one is at least permitted to lie if she looks terrible. This is sufficient to show that the general statements are not unchallengeable, and that sometimes, when they clash with specific judgments, the specific judgments are accepted. Thus, we do not always need constitutive rules for moral teaching. Furthermore, nothing has revealed a need for constitutive rules. When Hare claims that rules are required for teaching, he is right, but summary rules seem to be sufficient.[5]

Hare's first reason for the necessity of principles is that we "choose something because it is of a certain character." He gives as an example, "If I decide not to say something, because it is false, I am acting on a principle, 'Never (or never under certain conditions) say what is false', and I must know that this, which I am wondering whether to say, is false."[6]

When we decide to do something, it would seem that Hare believes our justification (and our reasoning) has the following familiar form:

1. If any x if F, then x is M.
2. This x if F.

Therefore, 3. This x is M.

For F, we can put in the appropriate nonmoral expression (such as 'is an instance of saying what is false'); and for M, we can put in the appropriate moral term (such as 'wrong'). We must obviously suppose that premise 1 is a constitutive rule. If it is a summary rule, then, as we have seen, the effective use of the rule requires that such rules are not needed to arrive at justified moral judgments.

First, counterexamples are appropriate to instances of premise 1, such as "If any action is an instance of lying, then it is wrong." It is morally permissible to lie in many circumstances—this is something we all know. From this it follows that the principle is not a constitutive principle with respect to such judgments as "John Smith's act of lying is wrong."

---

[5]Someone might say that the use of the counterexample involves a constitutive rule, and it is only because of such a rule that the individual judgment can be used as a counterexample. However, we do not seem to require a rule to justify the individual judgment that is the counterexample. Furthermore, no trouble-free constitutive rule can be found. As soon as we fix up the rule, or state a new one, it meets with the same difficulty. This is a point that will become clearer later.

[6]Hare, *The Language of Morals*, 56.

The defender of the need for constitutive principles would probably now add conditions to the principle. Such a defender would claim that the unrestricted principle is subject to counterexamples, but the restricted one (for example, "If any action is an instance of lying to a friend, then it is wrong") is not. However, we are seldom given a restricted principle or told how to construct one. Furthermore, restrict the principle as you like, and as past experience with such principles shows, counterexamples will still be found. If no counterexample-free principles are discovered, then we have good evidence that we do not need constitutive rules to arrive at justified judgments of that sort.[7]

This same sort of argument can be presented in a variety of ways, so let's examine one more instance to gain confidence.

> Moral and value judgments imply reasons, and reasons cannot apply in a particular case only. If they apply in one case, they apply in all similar cases. Moreover, in order to give a reason in a particular case, one must presuppose a general proposition. If Jones answers your question "Why?" by saying "Because you promised to" or "Because it gives pleasure," he presupposes that it is right to keep promises or that what gives pleasure is good.[8]

In this passage, William Frankena seems to be presenting another instance of the argument just examined. One new notion is introduced by Frankena—that one *presupposes* a rule or a principle when one makes a specific judgment. According to Frankena, a person a who makes a moral judgment such as "x is M" usually or always presents reasons to support that judgment. Person a justifies the judgment by saying "x is M because x is F." If there is a y that is F, then person a is committed to judge that y is M also. In short, to look back to the general scheme, if a person a asserts the third statement and gives

---

[7]One could trivialize the principle completely and make it something like "Any action of lying that is such that its conditions make it wrong to lie is wrong." Now the principle is not subject to counterexamples, but it is no longer required to justify the specific judgment. If we use it in an argument of the form presented, the second premise will be "This is an action of lying that is such that its conditions make it wrong to lie." This premise is all that is contained in the conclusion, so we do not need the first premise to arrive at the conclusion. Thus, even trivializing the principle in this way does not show that a constitutive rule is required to justify the specific judgment.

We might also restrict the rule in such a way that it uniquely describes the specific act of lying. If this were done, then we could provide no counterexamples of the sort that have been presented. Notice, though, that counterexamples could not be provided because we have described the principle so that it only applies to this one case. We did that because we knew that lying was morally permissible in this case; and if we could only restrict the application of the principle to this case, then it would be safe from counterexamples. Now, however, the knowledge that it is morally permissible to lie in this case precedes the knowledge represented by the principle. It precedes it not only temporally, but in every other sense. If the knowledge that lying in this case is morally permissible is prior to the knowledge of the principle, then the knowledge of the principle is not required to justify the specific judgment, and the principle is not, with respect to that judgment, a constitutive rule.

[8]William K. Frankena, *Ethics*, 2d ed. (Englewood Cliffs, N.J.: Prentice-Hall, 1973), 25.

the second as the reason, then the first is presupposed. No one can deny the first and consistently give the second as the reason for the conclusion. Once statement 1 is accepted, then person *a* has accepted a moral principle. Therefore, Frankena concludes, any specific judgment presupposes a principle.

The preceding line of reasoning may be perfectly acceptable, but it does not establish that constitutive rules are required to justify singular moral judgments. This can be shown by presenting another argument of the same form that fails to establish anything about constitutive rules. Suppose person *a* gives as her reason for the claim that a stripe of the American flag is red that it is the top stripe. She says "x is red" (third statement) and gives as her reason "x is the top stripe of the American flag" (second statement). If person *a* denies that any similar stripe is red, she is, assume for the moment, being inconsistent. She cannot give statement 2 as the reason for the conclusion and yet deny statement 1—namely, "Any top stripe of the American flag is red."

If the ethical argument Frankena presents allows us to conclude that principles are required to justify individual moral judgments, then we can equally conclude that principles are required to justify individual color judgments. Since the latter claim is apparently false, the former is not established by the argument presented.

In an attempt to show a difference between the two arguments, someone might be tempted to claim that any principle concerning colors, such as "If any x is the top stripe of the American flag, then x is red," is false, and so the two kinds of argument cannot be compared. However, any unqualified moral principle of the form "If any x is F, then x is M" is just as unacceptable. We say the color principle is false because the top stripe of flags is sometimes dyed, or factories make mistakes, or something else happens. We have seen the various difficulties that different kinds of moral principles fall prey to.

Others might be tempted to say that we do not require color principles because we have other ways of determining the color of objects, but we do require moral principles to justify our specific moral judgments. This claim, however, begs the question. Nonrule theorists claim that moral principles are not required to justify singular moral judgments, so the contrary assumption is not at this point allowable. It is a claim that must be argued for.

We can all admit that perhaps there is some relation of *presupposition* between making a specific judgment and a general principle. However, as has just been shown, the relation of presupposition does not demonstrate that constitutive rules are required to justify specific moral judgments.

RULES AS NEEDED FOR KNOWLEDGE

Variations of Hare's first reason for the necessity of principles seem not to be successful, so we conclude that none of them show that constitutive rules are needed to justify singular moral judgments. Let us consider Hare's last reason,

"We do not in fact have complete knowledge of the future, and because such knowledge as we do have involves principles." Hare elaborates on this:

> The kind of knowledge that we have of the future—unless we are clairvoyant—is based upon principles of prediction which we are taught, or form for ourselves. Principles of prediction are one kind of principle of action; for to predict is to act in a certain way. Thus, although there is nothing logically to prevent someone doing entirely without principles, and making all his choices in the arbitrary manner exhibited in the first kind of answer, this never in fact occurs. Moreover, our knowledge of the future is fragmentary and only probable; and therefore in many cases the principles which we are taught or form for ourselves say, not 'Choose this kind of effect rather than that,' but 'You do not know for certain what will be the effects; but do this rather than that, and the effects are most likely to be such as you would have chosen, if you had known them'. It is important to remember, in this connexion, that 'likely' and 'probable' are value-words; in many contexts 'It is probable (or likely) that P' is adequately rendered by 'There is *good* reason (or evidence) for holding that P'.[9]

To what sort of principles of prediction can Hare be referring? The most likely candidates are principles such as "Do not lie to a student who has failed your course, even though lying will at the time cause less pain, because in the long run it will bring about a worse situation." It is not necessary to go through the complete critical procedure again, but we should point out that the principle is open to effective counterexamples. Furthermore, in this instance, the principle seems to be a summary based on past happenings. If this is so, then the principle requires that we have garnered individual justified judgments of that sort via some means other than that rule; thus it is not a constitutive rule.

In the preceding quote, Hare points out that our knowledge of the future is fragmentary and only probable. This is true, and it is precisely why we do well to rely on summary rules or hypotheses firmly grounded in our past experience. Summary rules seem to fulfill our need for principles. Furthermore, we often abandon the general principle when the evidence of the specific situation seems to warrant it. The fact that we are sometimes justified in doing this is good evidence that the principle used is not a constitutive rule.

Finally, we can admit that "It is probable that P," in most contexts is to be rendered as "There is good reason for holding that P." One can say the good reason for holding the P that is a moral principle is past success in acting on it—that it is a fruitful hypothesis to adopt. This is just what the pragmatist says! Now that we have come this far, this last bold claim is not to be taken as simply a claim, but as being supported by the failure of the rule theory arguments and the apparent fact that all the moral phenomena

---

[9]Hare, *The Language of Morals*, 59–60.

that involve rules can be accounted for by the use of summary rules taken as hypotheses for successful action.

If the preceding distinctions are acceptable, and there are no other *kinds* of arguments to examine, then there are no good reasons to suppose that constitutive rules are required to justify singular moral judgments. Because we have reason to suppose that such rules are not needed,[10] and the need for rules seems to be fulfilled by summary rules, we can conclude that rules do not play a constitutive role in justifying singular moral judgments.

PROMULGATION

One part of the preceding argument in favor of rule theories deserves additional attention. When the rule theorist claims that rules are required to justify singular moral judgments and that singular moral judgments presuppose moral rules promulgated by a rational judge, we should ask the sense in which the rule is promulgated.

In the clearest sense, a rule is that which someone lays down—that such and such is to be the case or is to be done. Many people suppose that in a like manner someone laid down the moral law. God has been the most popular candidate for the role of lawmaker. But some philosophers have supposed that human beings collectively legislate (Rousseau); and some supposed that individual people legislate for all people (Hegel). What is relevant here is that some people suppose that when a person wills for himself, he is somehow, by virtue of some principles of logic or reasoning, willing for everyone (this is something like the view of Kant and Hare).

The traditional problems with God as a promulgator are sufficiently difficult that we need not add them to the discussion. At this time, neither the metaphysics of Hegel nor Rousseau's notion of the *general will* requires close attention. Many philosophers, though, endorse what is called the "generalization argument." Sometimes this seems to be a kind of promulgator view and sometimes it doesn't. Let us consider it as a promulgator view to determine if it fares better in that guise.

The generalization argument, in this interpretation, is an attempt to support the claim that each person is a promulgator for all people. The authority for the promulgation is, in some sense, reason or logic. However, we run into a problem right away, for examples of such general moral statements are not of the form of statement 1 of the general scheme. They do not connect nonmoral and moral characteristics or terms.

---

[10]As indicated by the success of the nonrule theorists' methods earlier.

(U4) If A is good, then anything similar in all non-moral but morally relevant respects is also good.[11]

It is true that the generalization argument involves an inference from "not everyone has the right" to "no one has the right," from "it would not be right for everyone" to "it would not be right for anyone." This inference, however, is mediated, and therefore qualified by the principle that what is right (or wrong) for one person must be right (or wrong) for any similar person in similar circumstances. For obvious reasons I shall refer to this principle as "the generalization principle," even though it has traditionally been known as the principle of fairness or justice or impartiality.[12]

The fact is that when one makes a moral judgment in a particular situation, one implicitly commits oneself to making the same judgment in any similar situation, even if the second situation occurs at a different time or place, or involves another agent. Moral and value predicates are such that if they belong to an action or object, they also belong to any other action or object which has the same properties. If I say I ought to serve my country I imply that everyone ought to serve his country.[13]

If I call a thing red, I am committed to calling anything else like it red. And if I call a thing a good X, I am committed to calling any X like it good.[14]

These are representative interpretations of the claim that all moral judgments somehow presuppose a general statement. However, they clearly are not instances of statement 1 of the general scheme. They cannot, in conjunction with a corresponding statement 2, allow the derivation of a singular moral judgment. Here is the general scheme that results when we replace statement 1 with a general statement like those described by the quoted authors:

1'. If any x is M, then any y that is like x in respect R is M.
2'. This x is M.

Therefore, 3'. Any y that is like x in respect R is M.

Note that statement 3' is not a singular moral judgment but is another general statement—perhaps a kind of moral rule. Thus, statement 1' allows only a general statement to be derived, whereas statement 1 allows a particular statement (the singular moral judgment that this x is M) to be derived. Therefore, this scheme cannot by itself support a statement of the form 'y is M'. However,

---

[11] Andrew Oldenquist, "Universalizability and Nondescriptivism," *The Journal of Philosophy* 65, no. 3 (1968), 59.
[12] Marcus G. Singer, *Generalization in Ethics*, (New York: Alfred A. Knopf, 1961), 5.
[13] Frankena, *Ethics*, 25.
[14] R. M. Hare, *Freedom and Reason*, (New York: Oxford University Press, 1956), 15.

since statement 3' is an instance of premise 1, the rule theorist might suggest it can be rewritten to derive 'y is M':

3'. [Rewritten] If any y is like x in respect R, then y is M.
4. This y is like x in respect R.

Therefore 5. This y is M.

Here, says the rule theorist, is an instance of statement 3 of the original scheme derived by making use of a general statement that is, we shall assume, promulgated by an individual.

However, the picture is clouded by the fact that statement 2' ('This x is M') is required to get statement 3'. Statement 2' is also an instance of statement 3 of the general scheme (a singular moral judgment); and if we can arrive at statement 2' without using statements 3' and 4, then statements 3' and 4 are not required to arrive at instances of statement 3. In other words, this kind of scheme presupposes that we are able to arrive at singular moral judgments without moral rules. Regardless of the correctness of the generalization argument as interpreted here, it can apparently shed no light on the original general scheme and the justification of singular moral judgments. It is certainly of no help to the rule theorist.

Furthermore, there is a problem with statement 1' ('If any x is M, then any y that is like x in respect R is M'). Either x and y have *some* similar nonmoral characteristics or they are alike in *all* such respects. An example of the former is when both x and y are instances of truth-telling, although they differ in other respects. "If any action x is right, then any action y that is like x in being an instance of truth-telling is right" is the general statement. This interpretation, however, runs afoul of effective counterexamples. No matter what characteristic or group of characteristics you suggest, there are instances of things having those characteristics that are not M. It would seem that there are many instances of truth-telling that are not right (as well as instances of lying that are right). You are not likely to have difficulty in finding such cases, for they are abundant.[15]

It might be claimed that the general statement is true only when x and y have all their nonmoral characteristics in common. The statement would then look something like the following: "If any action x is right, then any action y that has all its nonmoral properties in common with x is right." Notice, though, that we now need to say nothing about truth-telling and have arrived at something very much like Oldenquist's statement (U4). If we add that the

---

[15]When someone asks whether the water is safe to drink, in most circumstances telling the truth is the right thing. However, if someone performs the like action of telling the truth to our familiar maniac when he asks if his intended victim is hiding under the bed (when that is indeed where the victim is), then that person is not doing the right thing.

rightness of an action is a function of other characteristics, then this statement is quite safe; it is necessarily true.[16] Unfortunately, the use to which such a statement can be put is limited. It cannot, as has been argued, shed any light on the general scheme with which we began since its use requires the very statement we wish to derive. However, enough of such speculation—those who believe that it has an important role should tell us what that role is.

MORAL EDUCATION AND MORAL MATURITY

One further purported reason in support of rule theories concerns moral education and moral maturity. Parents teach their children moral rules, as was noted earlier, and the children usually take these rules to be constitutive. When a parent teaches a child not to lie because it is wrong, the child does not distinguish between the rule as summary and the rule as constitutive. The parents, however, if asked, would certainly say one should lie if a maniac asks where his enemy is hiding. If the enemy asks where your family is hiding, you are permitted to lie. The parents know this, and insofar as they do, they know that the moral rules are not constitutive. Of course, the parents probably don't know the fancy terms 'constitutive' and 'summary', and most would be hard-pressed to follow the complicated discussions in this work. However, in their actions and in their responses it is not difficult to elicit the belief that the rules are summaries. Thus, moral education, as given by the parents, indicates that summary rules are taught, even though the children take them to be constitutive. (What would Kohlbergians say about this?)

[16]This may seem like an extraordinarily complicated claim, but in actuality it is not all that complicated. Suppose that figure *a* is a *triangle* by virtue of being a three-sided (*F*) plane figure (*G*) that is enclosed (*H*) by straight lines (*I*). All and only those four properties determine that a figure is a triangle. Suppose this is true, and suppose we find that figure *b* has all the properties that figure *a* has that are relevant to something's being a triangle. It would be necessarily true to assert, "If figure *a* is a triangle solely by virtue of having *F, G, H*, and *I*, and if these are all and the only properties determining triangularity, and if figure *b* has *F, G, H*, and *I*, then figure *b* is a triangle." It would be a contradiction to assert that figure *a* is a triangle solely by virtue of having *F, G, H*, and *I*, that these are all and the only properties determining a triangle, that figure *b* has *F, G, H*, and *I*, and that figure *b* is not a triangle.

The problem is that this statement, which is necessarily true and whose negation is a contradiction, does not offer any help in finding new instances of triangles until we establish that all parts of it are true. Is it true, we would ask in this instance, that something is a triangle on all and only those occasions in which it has those four properties? If the answer is yes, then we have found a rule—no doubt a constitutive rule—of geometry. Now the similar question in morality is whether there is some set of *F*'s (plus *G*'s, *H*'s, and so on) that result in a similarly true or correct statement. The fact that we have found counterexamples to all the proposed statements of this type, and that there are other kinds of troubles as described in Chapter 4 and in this chapter, indicates that there is no such set of *F*'s.

Once again, then, the argument that was to establish that there is such a set of *F*'s, and thus that there is some constitutive moral rule, fails.

Interestingly enough, though, at a certain age children do recognize that moral rules are not constitutive. Without proposing a study now as to when that time comes, it does nevertheless come. Instead of applying rules as if they were constitutive, they come to understand that moral rules may sometimes be broken. Not only do we break them when we are not acting morally or in the proper way, but we may also break them occasionally *in order to* act in the morally proper way. When a person knows how to do this with sensitivity and insight, we say the person is wise. The ability to know when to abandon a rule and to act in some other manner is something that almost all human beings come to have—it signals the onset of moral maturity.

This ends the long section presenting reasons in favor of nonrule theories. The arguments are by far the most complicated we have examined, and the discussion has opened up yet new problems. However, if you review the arguments, your efforts will be rewarded with greater understanding. Philosophy is not easy, and the area you are now in is not an easy area in philosophy, but it is one that has practical importance for every human being.

CHAPTER SIX

Value

Normative ethics includes theories of obligation and theories of value. We have examined the main theories of obligation in Chapters 2 through 5 and presented the main tools required to evaluate those theories. Using the familiar if-then statement, we can exhibit the general form of a statement of obligation by allowing 'MO' to stand for any term of moral obligation such as 'right' or 'obligation'.

If any person *a* performs an action that is F, then that action is MO.

The statement tells us that if someone does something of a certain sort, then it is obligatory, right, or something similar. 'F', recall, stands for the appropriate nonobligation predicate. One of the substitution instances of F, especially for teleological theories of obligation, is a value predicate. The utilitarians, for example, specify F as 'increases the amount of benefit or value for the greatest number'. In the discussion of utilitarianism—and all the other theories of obligation—when a value term was used, we said that no specific theory of value was presupposed because we had yet to examine such theories. We further claimed that some people believe pleasure alone is of value, while others believe pleasure plus love, friendship, knowledge, and many other things are of value. Well, now it is time to investigate those theories of value. Having already examined theories of obligation, we know better how to evaluate ethical theories and so our task is made easier. Furthermore, most of the tools and arguments we shall use in this chapter have been introduced before.

INTRINSIC VALUE

The key notion in this chapter is *intrinsic value*. Although the following definition tells us what intrinsic value is, it requires further explanation:

x has intrinsic value = df
1. x has value.
2. The value of x is not exhausted by the value of what it leads to.

In this definition, we find the term 'value', which is another value term. So if you thought the definition was going to define 'intrinsic value' via nonvalue notions, you are no doubt disappointed. However, in every area, some term is taken to be basic and is assumed to be understood without definition in that area. This was done in theory of obligation, and there seemed to be no difficulty. The notions in theory of obligation were more closely specified by the individual theories of obligation, and, in the same way, the notion of value will be more closely specified by theories of value. However, some further explanation of the notion of value is possible.

There is a close connection between what we take to be valuable and the goals we voluntarily pursue. If my brother chooses to go to the Pumpkin Festival in Circleville, Ohio, then this is at least partially explained by showing that there is something there he values. Perhaps he likes pumpkins or is fond of small towns or enjoys a ride in the country. These are all goals or ends my brother may be seeking, and we suppose they are goals he finds valuable. We can say, generally, that people seek ends voluntarily because they believe the ends have value.

The goals we seek are almost never isolated from other goals. For example, if you choose voluntarily to go to college, this leads to the goals of a degree, greater knowledge, and increased mobility. This set of goals, when achieved, in turn leads to such goals as having friends of a certain sort, obtaining a job of a certain type, living in a certain city, and so on. Some of these goals are thought valuable only because they lead to other goals, and some are not. For example, you may not ever choose pain for itself, but you do choose voluntarily to go to the dentist and subject yourself to considerable pain. This is chosen, though, to secure health and perhaps freedom from other pain. You choose to suffer pain, then, not for its own value, but only for the value for which it is an instrument. Freedom from pain, in contrast, is likely to be chosen not only because it leads to other things of value, but because it has some value in addition to, or independent of, the value to which it leads. For example, the freedom from pain may lead to enjoying an evening with friends that otherwise would not have been possible. However, even if that evening had not come about, the freedom from pain would still have had some value. This is not so of the suffering in the dentist's chair. Had the dentist been a poor one, so that at the end of the suffering the original problem remained or even became worse, we would say the experience of being in the dentist's chair was of no value at all. When an experience (or relation, or institution, or character trait, or any other large number of things) has value, and its value is not totally exhausted by the value of other things to which it leads, then it has *intrinsic* value. It is for this reason that people often say that things of intrinsic value are *good in themselves*.

In the sense used here, something not only can have intrinsic value but can lead to other things of intrinsic value. Something might have a small amount of intrinsic value and be very valuable because it leads to other things with great intrinsic value. This can be made clearer if we contrast the notion of intrinsic value with that of *extrinsic* value.

x has extrinsic value = df
1. x has value.
2. x leads to an intrinsically valuable y.

The painful experience was extrinsically valuable for the absence from pain; its value results only from the fact that it leads to something else. However, something can be both extrinsically and intrinsically valuable. The absence of pain is apparently valuable whether it leads to anything else of value or not. When it leads to enjoying an evening with friends, which is assumed to have some intrinsic value, the freedom from pain is also extrinsically valuable. In fact, given the interconnections among our experiences, only very rarely would something be intrinsically valuable and not also extrinsically valuable. In contrast, however, many things—foremost among them, pain—are sometimes of extrinsic value but never of intrinsic value. We could make up a special term for things that are extrinsically valuable but not intrinsically valuable, but that doesn't really seem necessary. We can say of such a thing that it is extrinsically valuable only, or that it has only extrinsic value.

It has been held by some philosophers, most notably G. E. Moore, that the notion of intrinsic value is best explained via the notion of isolation. That is, Moore defines intrinsic value in terms of its continued value even if it should be the only thing in existence. Dewey and other philosophers deny there is anything that would be intrinsically valuable *even if nothing else existed*. Philosophers who think that things are interconnected with other things—that nothing could exist in the kind of isolation Moore requires us to suppose— would say there is no such thing as intrinsic value in Moore's sense.[1] But, the sense of 'intrinsic value' used here does not presuppose or use the isolation test. So, we can agree with Dewey that there is nothing of intrinsic value in Moore's sense, but still claim that in the sense introduced here there are many sources of intrinsic value.

---

[1] Dewey also denied there is a hard and fast distinction between means and ends. The means we use become part of the history of the end as reached. It is just this end, having just those means. So, even supposing that Stalin reached the goal of industrialization, he did so by means of killing more than eight million peasant farmers. The object of our valuation is the achieving of industrialization at the cost of killing eight million people, not the industrialization alone.

Intrinsic Disvalue

We shall have some small need for a notion of intrinsic disvalue as well. There is certainly a difference between an absence of intrinsic value and the presence of something that makes itself felt as disvaluable. A drink of water when thirsty results in a pleasurable experience. Further drinks might result in an experience neutral with respect to value. But continued drinks would result in a positively disvaluable experience. The pain that is experienced is something whose disvalue is not exhausted by the disvalue it leads to—it is disvaluable in itself. We can construct formal definitions of disvalue notions on the model of the definitions of the value notions.

x has intrinsic disvalue = df
1. x has disvalue.
2. The disvalue of x is not exhausted by the disvalue x leads to.

x has extrinsic disvalue = df
1. x has disvalue.
2. x leads to an intrinsically disvaluable y.

Pain is a clear instance of something that has intrinsic disvalue. It has been proposed that slavery is another instance, but that perhaps is a clearer instance of something with extrinsic disvalue. Slavery leads to pain, ignorance, loss of dignity, and many other things that appear to have intrinsic disvalue.

Some things have only extrinsic disvalue—for example, having put the wrong answer down on a test. These are not intrinsically disvaluable things, but they lead, more often than not, to things that are intrinsically disvaluable—for example, pain and humiliation.

In some discussions, it will be useful to have the notion of intrinsic disvalue, and so we add it to our arsenal.

The Notion of 'Leads To'

Having added to our supply of terms, we can now explain the rest of the key notions in the definition of *intrinsic value* (as well in *intrinsic disvalue*). The term 'leads to' is deliberately vague because it is intended to include a variety of different relations. For example, one kind of 'leading to' is a kind of causal relation, as when breathing deeply causes the smell of fresh air to be conveyed to us. There are other kinds of causal relations, as when we study all night to pass an examination. The studying is not as good a guarantee of passing as breathing deeply is of smelling the fresh air, but they are both kinds of causal relations. Sometimes, the relation is part to whole, as when there is a total experience (for example, enjoying the outdoors) and one part of it (say, smelling) is necessary for the total experience. It may well be that the smelling, by itself, would have little or no intrinsic value without the activation of the other senses. Suppose, for a moment, that a certain melody has intrinsic value. One note that is essential to the melody does not seem to have any intrinsic value, but it, along with many others in a relation, comprise the melody.

Moral and Nonmoral Value

The justification for making *extrinsic value* so broad is that it allows us to use few key terms and so examine many theories with a minimum of verbiage. However, a bit more clarification is necessary.

Philosophers sometimes distinguish between moral and nonmoral senses of 'value' on the same model they use to distinguish moral and nonmoral senses of, say, 'right'. In the expression 'The right way to build a house is to start with the basement', the term 'right' is used in a nonmoral sense. There are legal obligations that are seldom confused with moral obligations, and there are legal rights that are not the same as moral rights. Are there moral and nonmoral senses of 'value', 'intrinsic value', and the other terms of value? Something very much like that exists, which we shall call the distinction between the efficiency and the value sense of value terms.

When we say that this is a good knife or a good car, or that a person does something well, it is usually a statement about efficiency in carrying out a task. A knife cuts meat without great difficulty, a car carries passengers without discomfort and at a reasonable cost, or a runner can run at a certain pace for a certain distance. There is usually an implicit comparison with others of the same kind, so that the standard of what is efficiently good may, over time, gradually change. The surgical tool that is now a good scalpel must meet a higher standard than scalpels of a hundred years ago. Many of the items in the list of efficiently good things can equally well be called instrumentally valuable, or valuable for carrying out a certain purpose. The knife is good for cutting, and the car for transportation. However, the notion of *efficient value* seems broader and appears to include the notion of *instrumental value*. When we discuss *intrinsic value* and *value*, it is not in either of these senses. It is important to distinguish these other senses only to make clear that they are not the concern of this chapter. They cannot explain why we carry out tasks and seek certain ends. If we ask the murderer why he carried out his deed, it is not acceptable for him to say he had a knife and everyone knows that a knife is good for cutting throats. So remember, when we talk about value, we are concerned about the value sense and not the efficiency sense.

The Value Sense of 'Value'

The value sense can be made somewhat clearer when we understand that it applies primarily to people and to things true of people. Consider, for example, this list of kinds of things, some instances of which most people hold are intrinsically valuable:

1. People ("Socrates was a good man.")
2. Character traits of people ("His most valuable assets were his courage and integrity.")
3. Relations among people ("Friendship is valuable." "Slavery is evil.")
4. Experiences ("Pleasure is good, pain is not.")
5. Institutions ("Slavery is evil." "The best government is a democracy.")

It would help us if we could relate some of these things to each other to reduce them to a more manageable number. For example, people are good or not depending on the character traits they have. If the character traits turn out to be good ones, such as honesty, intelligence, loyalty, wisdom, and the like, then the person is a good person. Institutions too are apparently good if they foster certain character traits in people and allow for certain experiences. We may be able, then, to cut the list down to the middle three things. Whether we can pare the list down to fewer basic things of value or not will be seen shortly.

The question of whether there is actually anything of intrinsic value can be settled only after we have chosen the best theory of value, given the evidence available. However, given the value phenomena, we can argue that there are things of intrinsic value. It was part of the phenomena of theories of obligation that some actions are obligatory and some are not. In theory of obligation, no one term was taken as basic and the rest defined via that term, so the tendency was to appeal to the phenomena directly when discussing such different notions as *obligation* and *right action*. In theory of value, though, one notion (*value*) has been taken as basic, and others are defined via that term. So if we are to say that something is intrinsically valuable, since it is a defined notion and is not found in ordinary discourse in the clear sense presented here, we must provide some additional evidence for this claim. The following evidence will come from the phenomena, but in an indirect manner.

Even though the notion of *intrinsic value* is not an ordinary notion, it is not difficult to show people that they use it, or something very close to it, in ordinary situations. The primary way to show that someone accepts something as having intrinsic value is via the notion of rational choice. Suppose someone chooses to do something, almost anything, rather than do nothing or not make a choice. For example, suppose someone reading this book decides—rationally and consciously—to turn the page and read the next page. We can ask the person why she continues to read on rather than stop (and perhaps do something else). A common answer would be that the person wants to see how the paragraph ends, or, more likely, that it is a part of an assignment. However, we can reasonably ask why she chooses to fulfill the assignment. If the person is patient and continues, we shall perhaps learn that she made a decision to try to pass the course. When we pursue the question *why*, we may find a sequence of answers such as the following: I choose to pass the course so as to get credit; the credit is needed to secure a degree; the degree is required to get a certain kind of job; the job is sought because it brings other things. At this point, the answers would become more diverse; some readers would answer that they want a certain job because it is interesting or it brings security, fulfillment, freedom from worry, prestige, and so on. These are all ends that, even though they may lead to other things that have value, seem not to have their value exhausted by the value to which they lead. In the preceding dialogue with the reader, we seem to have reached something that person supposes is of intrinsic value; and having reached this kind of goal, we can for the time rest satisfied.[2] We shall probe further and inquire as to whether the belief that there are things of intrinsic value is justified. This is part of the subject matter of theories of value.

Contrast that dialogue with the following:

"Why did you go to the dentist?"
"To have holes drilled in my teeth."
"Why did you want to have holes drilled in your teeth?"
"So they could be filled with a plastic compound."
"Why would you want to do that, though?"
"Because of the pain and discomfort one gets from such visits and operations."

If the person does not value pain independently of what it leads to, as most of us do not, this kind of dialogue is very difficult to understand. Unless some recognizable goal is being sought that contains something that person or we would call intrinsically valuable, it is difficult to understand why the visit to the dentist occurred. The person could say he wanted to have healthy teeth, or avoid the pain of tooth decay, or have an attractive smile. However, without some such answer, we would begin to suspect the person had not acted rationally. It appears that we understand rational choice among goals in terms of what things a person finds intrinsically valuable; the person has given a justification of working to attain a goal when the goal (or something it leads to in fairly short order) represents something of intrinsic value. Unless there is something a person takes to be of intrinsic value, it is difficult to explain rational action. Thus, the occurrence of rational choice among alternatives of action is evidence a person takes something to be of intrinsic value.

The limiting case of this kind of reasoning concerns death. Each of you reading this now has decided to continue to live or at least did not decide not to live. The explanation of why someone would do something rather than either do nothing or commit suicide almost always has to do with weighing the positive and negative values of the alternatives. Most people have thought

---

[2]People understand the notion of *intrinsic value* and can use it to describe phenomena concerning themselves and others, even though they would not have been able to construct the notion themselves and may require help in its application. The application to situations, people, institutions, character traits, and such generates the phenomena for our investigation.

about committing suicide and have decided not to do so. In terms of this model, the explanation is a decision that there is more of intrinsic value to be realized by staying alive than not. (This is not to say that living, or life itself, is intrinsically valuable, only that there is something or some group of things of intrinsic value that can be had only in life.) You may not understand what intrinsically valuable things are gained only in life, and it is not part of the claim here that you do. However, the reasoning shows that the best explanation of your decision (or lack of decision) concerning life and death is that you accept something as having intrinsic value. This, then, is the second piece of evidence of the existence of something intrinsically valuable in the phenomena. Again, one of the main purposes of a theory of value is to help us find those things that are of intrinsic value, if anything is.

There is a third way to establish that things of intrinsic value are in the phenomena. Consider the distinctions drawn so far: the notion of *value* as undefined and the defined notions of *intrinsic value* and *extrinsic value*. If we admit that something has intrinsic value, then we have accepted as part of the phenomena that something or other has intrinsic value. This is also true if a person admits that something has extrinsic value, for it leads to something that has intrinsic value. It could not lead to something of intrinsic value if that thing of intrinsic value did not exist. (This is true in all the uses of 'leads to'—the causal sense and the part/whole sense.) The other sense of *value* discussed—the sense in which things merely have utility—was seen as not relevant to the theory of value and its questions. *Value* itself is a notion that appears to require further specification in terms of *intrinsic* or *extrinsic* and, at any rate, cannot alone bear the burden of explaining the topics just discussed. So it would seem, once again, that when we begin with these value phenomena, the best explanation of them involves something of intrinsic value. However, this is not to assume that this or that theory of value is correct; it may turn out that nothing at all is actually of intrinsic value.

Value and Obligation

As a last topic in this first section, let's contrast the views of those who think that value predicates are explained in some way by, or are reduced to, obligation predicates with the views of those who think it goes the other way. This topic will be discussed in Chapter 7, but simply consider, so that you can see what such people have in mind, the following definitions:[3]

---

[3] I do not present these definitions as my own. They are only contrasting specimen views. One character trait that is apparently valuable is the tendency to fulfill obligations. Some people may be called good simply because they do almost always, in spite of temptations and difficulties, fulfill their obligations. In this case, this valuable character trait requires a theory of obligation for a complete understanding of what it is. But this is not necessarily a bad thing.

x is intrinsically valuable	= df	Any person a in a position to bring x into existence has an obligation to do so.
a has an obligation to do B	= df	B brings more intrinsic value into existence than any other available action.

Although both definitions are probably compatible with the definition of intrinsic value (since the latter is an analysis of the notion itself as contrasted with what it depends upon or is reduced to), they represent opposite and conflicting positions about what is the basic notion within morality. The discussion of theory of value will not attempt to settle that question, but will instead concern itself with an examination of different theories of value—just as we concerned ourselves with different theories of obligation without concern for theories of value.

Exercises: The Various Value Notions

1. Now that you have a better understanding of the notion of *intrinsic value*, but before you have examined particular theories of value, examine the value questionnaire you filled out at the beginning of the book. Make any changes that now occur to you in light of your understanding of intrinsic value. Describe what kinds of changes, if any, you made, and explain why you made them.
2. Give examples of things that are:
   a. intrinsically valuable and extrinsically valuable
   b. intrinsically valuable and extrinsically disvaluable
   c. extrinsically valuable and extrinsically disvaluable
   d. intrinsically disvaluable and extrinsically valuable
   e. intrinsically disvaluable and extrinsically disvaluable
3. List two or three kinds of things (experiences, institutions, character traits, or whatever) that you think a friend of yours supposes are intrinsically valuable. What led you to think your friend supposed those items to have intrinsic value? Now do the same thing for two or three kinds of things a friend of yours supposes are intrinsically disvaluable.

AN OUTLINE OF THEORIES OF VALUE

The general scheme used to explain the common and different elements in theory of obligation can be used in a similar way in theory of value.

If any x has F, then x is IV.[4]

F will be replaced by some appropriate nonvalue notion such as *pleasure, friendship, democracy*, or whatever. We will place the appropriate value term or phrase, usually 'intrinsic value' in the consequent. The method of distinguishing theories of value will be the same as that used for theories of obligation; theories are either rule theories or nonrule theories. If they are rule theories, they are categorical or prima facie rules. If they are categorical rule theories, they are either of the direct or the indirect variety. Within a categorical rule theory, there is either one or more than one such rule. Among the single categorical rule theories we shall examine are hedonism (the sole replacement for F is pleasure), happiness theories, and value relativism. We shall examine Ross's prima facie rule theory of value and attempt to apply the results there to any prima facie rule theory. Finally, we will examine the theory that is the value correlative to a pragmatic theory of obligation. We shall begin with the categorical rule theories.

CATEGORICAL DIRECT RULE THEORIES

In Chapter 4 we showed that a multiple categorical rule theory (one that maintains the existence of many categorical rules of obligation or value) has insuperable difficulties. One of these problems is the inconsistency that results when two of the rules apply and give different results. So such a theory will not be examined here. All the categorical rule theories propose only one rule, whether the rule is direct—that is, applies directly to the things—or indirect—that is, picks out the rules of intrinsic value that apply directly to the things.

Hedonism

The first view to be examined will be *hedonism*, whose single categorical rule is as follows:

If any x is an instance of pleasure, then it is IV (intrinsically valuable).

The hedonist will want to account for intrinsic disvalue, just as the egoist will want to account for wrong actions as well as right actions. We will assume that for each of these theories of value there is an obvious way to generate out the rule concerning intrinsic disvalue—that is, by making use of the polar opposite characteristic of the one connected to intrinsic value.

---

[4]IV, of course, is translated as 'intrinsic value'. 'Thing' is to be taken in a wide enough sense to include experiences, character traits, relations, and the other items on the list in the preceding section. IDV is 'intrinsically disvaluable'; EV, 'extrinsically valuable'; and EDV, 'extrinsically disvaluable'.

If any *x* is an instance of pain, then it is IDV (intrinsically disvaluable).

Negative hedonism can be taken as the claim that although pain is intrinsically disvaluable, it is only the absence of pain that is intrinsically valuable. The pleasures we have are either not really intrinsically valuable or, because they always lead to more pain than pleasure, not worth pursuing. However, we shall suppose that this is not always so and will consider the version of hedonism that maintains that pleasure, and not just the absence of pain, has intrinsic value.

Recall what a categorical rule is: one that holds no matter what else is true of the thing to which it applies.[5] The rule works to get out singular value judgments by adding a statement that affirms the antecedent, thus allowing us to derive the singular judgment that this particular *x* is intrinsically valuable. The first and second statements, along with the singular value judgment, are as follows.

If any *x* is an instance of pleasure, then it is IV.

This *x* is an instance of pleasure.

Therefore, this *x* is IV.

The notion of *pleasure* is thought by most to be clear, but some people have doubts about it. At the very least we must distinguish *pleasure* from *happiness*, the former being a short-run experience and the latter being a relatively long-run state. For example, suppose you hike the whole of a hot afternoon under a fierce sun on a dusty plain. At the end of that time you are very thirsty, and when you come to the waters of a stream just down from the mountains, you take a drink. Imagine the feeling you have when you drink the water—*that* is a pleasurable experience. Suppose again, that you like to have your back massaged, as most of us do, and now someone is expertly doing it. You are having an experience that is pleasurable. It is hard to imagine a human being who does not know what we are talking about when we speak of pleasurable experiences.[6]

Contrast the experience of drinking cool water when you are thirsty with being happy with your job. The former is something that occurs within a short time span; you have the pleasure and then, a short time later, it is gone. You

---

[5]See pages 16 and 17.

[6]There are those (for example, G. Ryle in *The Concept of Mind* and elsewhere) who insist that pleasure is not an experience of the sort pain is. There are pleasurable experiences, they insist, but no experience of pleasure. I think the former is probably all the hedonist needs, but I also think there are not only pleasurable experiences but something identifiable in those experiences that is itself an experience of pleasure. For example, drinking water is an experience that causes or includes a pleasurable experience (under certain circumstances). However, you should decide for yourself.

can have it again with another drink, but you may have to wait a bit. In contrast, being happy with your job is not an experience you have one day while working; it is something true of you over a fairly long span of time. It may come to you suddenly while at work or on your way home that you are happy with your job, but the happiness itself is not something that occurs on the way home or while working. Other terms that have a weaker force than 'happiness' but are of the same type are 'satisfaction', 'contentment', and 'fulfillment'. The hedonist claims that pleasure is the only thing of intrinsic value, not that happiness, in the sense described, is the only thing of intrinsic value.[7]

To the suggestion that some other thing also has value, the hedonist's response is that the thing has only extrinsic value—no intrinsic value—unless it too is an instance of pleasure. If someone claims, for example, that love has intrinsic value, the hedonist will respond, whether correctly or not remains to be seen, that love has value only because it gives the people involved some pleasure. That is, the value of love is just its extrinsic value in leading to pleasure. The same claim will be made by the hedonist whenever any other proposed intrinsically valuable thing is mentioned. Is this, though, a correct claim? This claim is similar to the one made by the utilitarian, for example, when we propose sources of obligation other than those involving the maximization of happiness for the greatest number. The utilitarian will attempt to show that such other actions are obligatory only because they do maximize the happiness of the greatest number. As you will recall, though, the mere claim that this is the sole source of obligation is not enough; there must be some plausibility to the claim stemming from some positive reasons. If these conditions are not met, and if another theory can do a better job of explaining obligation, one that can respond to objections without employing ad hoc devices and has some other reasons in its favor independently of the statement of the theory, then that theory is preferable to utilitarianism. Similarly, we must now examine hedonism to determine its acceptability.[8]

Hedonism as a Theory of Motivation: An Evaluation   As was true of ethical egoism, the most commonly found support of hedonism is a psychological theory of motivation. Fortunately, we have already examined that theory in its most general form and so will not have to spend much time on one specific instance of it. In its general form, which we called psychological egoism, it looked like this:

> If any person *a* performs a voluntary action, then person *a*'s sole motive for performing that action is self-benefit.

In the specific version we are now considering, psychological hedonism, the term 'benefit' is replaced with 'pleasure':

---

[7]Some hedonists, recall, have identified pleasure with the absence of pain, but this will not be the main view considered here.

[8]You may wish to review the criteria of acceptability discussed on pages 24–26.

> If any person *a* performs a voluntary action, then person *a*'s sole motive for performing that action is to increase *a*'s pleasure.

If the criticisms of the general theory of psychological egoism in Chapter 2 are effective, then they are effective against psychological hedonism. Please review those arguments, simply replacing 'benefit' with 'pleasure' throughout.

We will suppose that those arguments against the general position are effective whether we are considering the view as a more strictly scientific theory of motivation or as a commonsense theory of motivation. The very same evidence cited to show that psychological egoism is not acceptable as a more strictly scientific theory of motivation shows that psychological hedonism, taken in the same way, is also not an acceptable theory of motivation. We need to say a bit more about the theory when taken as a commonsense view of motivation.

You will recall that we constructed a theory called *psychological altruism* that contended that our only motive was to bring about good for others. We argued that psychological altruism was very low on the scale of acceptability of theories, and that since it and psychological egosim were equally acceptable, then psychological egoism was also low on the scale of acceptability of such theories. We can apply the same argument to psychological hedonism, but just as we specified *benefit* or *good* as pleasure in this last theory, we now must specify it this way for psychological altruism. Briefly, then, the more specific version of psychological altruism holds that our only motive is to bring about pleasure for others. In the more familiar form,

> If any person *a* performs a voluntary action, then *a*'s sole motive for performing that action is to increase others' pleasure.

In response to purported counterexamples, on the commonsense level, the defender of psychological altruism uses ad hoc devices to "explain" why the counterexamples are not acceptable. Suppose the purported counterexample is drinking a glass of water when I am thirsty for, as I think, the pleasure I get when I take the drink. The psychological altruist might suggest that if I did not drink the water, then I would become irritable, thus disturbing others, and finally becoming ineffective in securing the pleasure of others. The psychological altruist concludes (mistakenly) that the motive in drinking the water was to increase the pleasure of others. This kind of explanation is not very good, as we all recognize, yet it is apparently the same kind of explanation psychological hedonists give when they "defend" their view. If this is the only kind of defense for that view, then we would be justified in ranking hedonistic psychological altruism and psychological hedonism at about the same level on the scale of acceptability of theories—in a very low place.

Given the examination of psychological egoism in Chapter 2 and the apparent effectiveness of the criticisms of that view against psychological hedonism (which is merely a specific version of the former), we are justified in rejecting psychological hedonism.

In Chapter 2 we looked at an argument that explains how one could support a "right to" version of ethical egoism on the basis of psychological egoism. (We then argued that this did the ethical egoist little good because psychological egoism is indefensible.) However, no similar argument can be used to support hedonism with psychological hedonism. Keeping in mind that a separate argument has been presented to support the claim that the conclusions are not just unsupported but are false, the situation can be represented in the following way:

Ethical Egoism
True   If PE, then EE.[9]
False   PE.
                ―――――――――
Unsupported   EE.

Hedonism
Not true   If PH, then H.
False   PH.
                ―――――――――
Unsupported   H.

Arguments have been presented to show that the second premise in each argument, the psychological theory of motivation, is not true. In addition, there is apparently no way in which the antecedent of the first premise of the second argument supports its consequent. This is because humans often fail to value what is valuable. So, from the supposition that people can value only pleasure, it would not yet follow that only pleasure is valuable. We might be able to conclude that people are permitted to value only pleasure, but that is not the claim of hedonism. Hedonism holds that only pleasure is (intrinsically) valuable. Because there is no argument to establish the absence of a connection between psychological hedonism and hedonism, it is premature to say that the premise is false—but we can conclude that there is no evidence to suppose that it is true.

The conclusions of the two arguments, which represent the theory of obligation and theory of value, respectively, must find some support other than the previously presented arguments. It was argued in Chapter 2 that ethical egoism was not a very good theory; competitors such as utilitarianism do a better job as theories of obligation. It is now time to examine hedonism as a theory of value.

There seems to be little question that pleasure is *one* goal that humans seek not just for what it leads to. We often do things—drink certain wines,

―――――――――

[9]This is true only when we resrict the ethical theory to notions of *permission*.

sing certain songs, and carry on with members of the opposite sex—not only for the more remote goals (euphoria, stardom, parenthood) those activities bring into existence but also for the pleasure. To the question "Why did you put yourself in that state?" a sufficient answer often is "Because I find being in that state pleasurable." So, as J. S. Mill points out, it is some evidence that pleasure is the only thing of intrinsic value that it is at least one of the things of intrinsic value. We shall take it to be a part of the phenomena that pleasure is one of the things of intrinsic value. Our final decision may be that pleasure has no intrinsic value at all, but that is a conclusion we should reach only after we have completed our inquiry into theory of value.

Hedonism as a Theory of Value: An Evaluation It is much more difficult to establish that pleasure is the only thing of intrinsic value, but the hedonist makes that strong claim. We shall examine a few (apparently ineffective) arguments that have been used to attempt to establish just that claim. There are two main types of criticisms of single categorical rule theories of value, hereafter called *monist* views for short. First, there are counterexamples—instances of pleasure, for example, that are not intrinsically valuable. Second, there are additional kinds of things that are of intrinsic value. The first type is easier to consider, so let's start there.

Some philosophers indicate that there are instances of pleasure that have intrinsic disvalue. For example, the pleasure that a sadist experiences when torturing a victim is thought by some to be positively disvaluable. However, it does seem that the hedonist can reasonably claim that the pleasure of the torturer is intrinsically valuable, but the pain of the victim is intrinsically disvaluable. We may all admit that the total situation consisting of the pain of the victim plus the pleasure of the torturer contains more pain than pleasure, and thus the total experience is one that does not have positive intrinsic value $[IVa + IDVb \rightarrow IDV(a + b)]$. However, this is compatible with the pleasure of the torturer having intrinsic value. This is not the clearest kind of case, and if we can find more clear-cut examples, then we are well advised to do so.

You will recall that in the discussions of counterexamples to egoism and utilitarianism, we used some counterexamples of the "underwhelming" value type. An action was described that would increase a person's good or the good of the greatest number, but the amount of good was so small that it did not impart an obligation to realize it. It may be that scratching an itch, a very mild itch, brings some benefit for oneself, but the act does not seem thereby to be obligatory. Similar considerations were raised with respect to utilitarianism.[10] The notion of benefit in those examples was usually instanced by pleasure, so they can be used as counterexamples to the claim that if anything is an instance of pleasure, then it is intrinsically valuable. For example, that

---
[10]See pages 85 and 116.

very same small sensation of pleasure we get from scratching an itch is an instance of pleasure, but it does not appear to have any intrinsic value. We may indeed reap great pleasure from drinking a glass of water when we are quite thirsty, but suppose we take a drink when we are not thirsty at all. The successive sensations of pleasure that we derive from drinking successive drinks of water decrease until there is no pleasure at all, and finally pain results. Consider the smallest discernible amount of pleasure one would get from drinking water; it is an instance of pleasure, but many insist it is not something of intrinsic value.

We draw all examples of this type, as well as all counterexamples, from the phenomena with which we began. It is open to any theorist to show that something appearing to be a counterexample is not actually a counterexample at all. Furthermore, the underwhelming value counterexamples are not nearly as strong a criticism as the forcing of additional sources of intrinsic value. However, some kind of response must be given by the monist or even by those who hold to a belief in a multiplicity of intrinsic values.

The main type of criticism leveled against hedonism, and against all monist (single-rule) theories, is that additional things of intrinsic value do exist. The argument to establish this is called the *Addition Test*. According to this test, if we show that a thing—say, pleasure—has intrinsic value and also show that adding an instance of another thing—say, happiness—to pleasure results in a total amount of intrinsic value greater than the intrinsic value of the pleasure alone, then we can conclude that the happiness also has intrinsic value. Schematically, this appears as follows:

1. IVx.
2. IV$(x + y)$ > IVx.

Therefore, 3. IVy.

The first premise says that something, x, has intrinsic value. It might be the claim that an instance of pleasure has intrinsic value. The second premise says that when we add some y—say, an instance of happiness or love—to the pleasure, the resulting whole has more intrinsic value than the pleasure alone. This entitles us to conclude that the thing added has some amount of intrinsic value itself.

This argument does not commit us to the view that value is quantifiable in a strict sense. It will be supposed that values can be compared in quantity and added, but only in a rough sense. If hedonism were correct, perhaps some strictly quantifiable manner of talking about intrinsic value would be possible, but whether hedonism is correct or not remains to be seen.

The "addition principle" is widely accepted by philosophers, though there is another widely accepted principle that we shall show is inconsistent with it. The "principle of *organic unities*" tells us that in some contexts intrinsic value is not additive. Assuming that pleasure has intrinsic value and that humiliation and embarrassment have intrinsic disvalue, it does seem that the humiliation and embarrassment of tripping as you mount the podium to receive your diploma added to the pleasure that your archenemy has in witnessing it has more intrinsic disvalue than the humiliation and embarrassment alone. This would not be the case if we used the Addition Test, for then we would subtract the intrinsic value of the pleasure from the intrinsic disvalue of the displeasure to arrive at the total of intrinsic value (or disvalue) of the situation.

To see the point of the defender of organic unities, let us look at the example schematically.

h = humiliation and embarrassment of the speaker

p = pleasure of your enemy

$IDV(h + p) > IDVh$

This is so even though IVp! If the Addition Test were correct, we would not get this result, for the intrinsic value of the pleasure would decrease the amount of intrinsic disvalue of the whole. For this situation we can say, in defense of the Addition Test, that the intrinsic disvalue increased because human beings usually feel more humiliation when they are in such a predicament *and* it is noticed by their enemies. This is not an effective response, though, for even adding in the extrinsic disvalue of the pleasure of the rival does not stop the kind of example. Suppose all your enemies have been invited to witness your humiliation and embarrassment, so we have many people gleefully watching you trip. We might even add that they planned your "accident" by painting a sticky substance on one of your shoes and on the top step so you would be likely to trip. Suppose the room contains only your enemies, wouldn't the total amount of intrinsic disvalue be even greater even though the pleasure is greatly increased?

A way to defend the Addition Test is to reveal another intrinsic disvalue, not try to argue for the extrinsic disvalue of your humiliation and embarrassment being noticed. What is a plausible intrinsic disvalue that is not just some ad hoc insertion? One source is from character traits—virtues and vices. A vice, recall, is an intrinsically disvaluable character trait such as cowardice. Those who take pleasure at the discomfort of others, especially those who do not deserve the discomfort, are unkind. If they have this trait to an extreme degree they are called sadists. (We are not talking here about those who have a personality disorder, for they otherwise function adequately and treat people in acceptable ways.) Unkindness and sadism are sources of intrinsic disvalue that would account for the result the defender of organic unities uses to support that view. Is this defense of the Addition Test a good one? Think about it some more.

Although the defenders of organic unities might not be satisfied with the defense of the Addition Test, we shall have to leave that dispute.[11] We now return to the use of the test against hedonism taken as a monist theory of value. Most critics question the truth of the second premise, for there is little question that the argument form is valid; what we must show is that there actually are such *y*'s that when added to pleasure give us more intrinsic value.

Let us consider first *happiness* and *pleasure*. *Happiness* is, recall, a relatively long-run state, and *pleasure* is a relatively short-run state. There appear to be many times in each of our lives in which we have an adequate amount of pleasure but are short on happiness. Films, such as *La Dolce Vita*, are made about this state. However, we do not have to take the most dramatic cases since many moments in each of our lives appear to contain the same ingredients. Consider such moments in your own life, and if there are such moments, then you admit thereby that happiness has some intrinsic value.

The same kind of reasoning can be applied to *love* and *pleasure*. Which is more valuable: a life that contains only pleasure or one that contains both pleasure and love? If it is the latter, then you have thereby admitted that love has some intrinsic value. If you feel more comfortable considering *freedom, security, friendship, motherhood*, or any other number of candidates, then, of course, feel free to use those things.

When the Addition Test is used, the monist attempts to show that any additional intrinsic value results from just more of whatever is the supposedly only thing of intrinsic value. For example, the hedonist will claim the explanation of why the addition of happiness or love makes pleasure more valuable is that each of those leads to more pleasure; that is, they are valuable only because they are extrinsically valuable. How are such claims evaluated?

First, it would be an error to conclude that whatever some experience, relation, state of affairs, or whatever leads to is the *value* explanation of why that thing is sought. If someone seeks happiness in addition to pleasure, hedonists claim that the happiness is sought only for the pleasure it leads to. Their evidence, if any evidence is presented, is that pleasure results from happiness. However, this argument is "too strong," as philosophers are fond of saying. If this were a good argument, we could establish, contrary to the claim of hedonists, that pleasure is not intrinsically valuable at all. Almost all pleasure leads to a loss of energy, and sometimes to a state of pain. This is certainly true of such pleasures as sex and food. Shall we say that the thing of value sought from sexual relations is fatigue? Shall we say, finally, that what we seek from

[11] The principle of organic unities is stated clearly by G. E. Moore: "It is certain that two bad things or a bad thing and an indifferent thing may form a whole much worse than the sum of badness of its parts. . . . *The value of a whole must not be assumed to be the same as the sum of values of ts parts*" [G. E. Moor, *Principia Ethica* (London: Cambridge University Press, 1959), 28]. *Principia Ethica* was published in 1903, when the principle of organic unities was widely accepted. Whether it is now I cannot say.

everything we do is death? After all, in the course of our experiences, sooner or later we all die.

Eating food leads to defecation. It would be a mistake, though, to conclude that the purpose of eating is to defecate and the end we seek when we eat is to increase the amount of fecal matter in the universe. None of us accepts this defense of fecal monism as plausible, and yet it appears to be as good as the hedonist's defense of his view. So, this kind of defense, by itself, cannot be used to support hedonism.

Even if happiness did lead to pleasure, we could not conclude that happiness was only extrinsically valuable. Furthermore, there are times when happiness, apparently, does not lead to more pleasure but is nevertheless apparently intrinsically valuable. This is the claim J. S. Mill makes when he suggests that it is better to be a Socrates dissatisfied than a pig satisfied. All of us have completed tasks such as building a model airplane when not finishing it would have resulted in more pleasure. However, we do such things for something we can call satisfaction or happiness. Again, a person may pass up sexual pleasure to achieve other goals, such as fidelity or happiness.

It is open for the hedonist to claim that the person actually pursues pleasure, but then again, it is open for anyone to say anything. When we question people, and here it is best if I talk about myself, it seems that on many occasions the goal sought is not pleasure but something else. Sometimes, the other additional goal sought is happiness. When we asked earlier how to evaluate the claim that pleasure is always sought when we seem to seek other things, surely one part of an answer is to discover what the person who is pursuing the goals believes. If that person supposes that it is some goal other than pleasure that is sought, we then have some evidence of goals other than pleasure that have intrinsic value. Of course, the person could turn out to be mistaken because not all the things we suppose have intrinsic value do indeed have intrinsic value. However, when hedonists make the claim that it is a mistake to think that happiness has intrinsic value, they must present some reasons.

Anyone can maintain that y, whatever it is, is the only intrinsically valuable thing, and then provide us with ad hoc explanations of why, even though other things seem to have intrinsic value, they do not. For example, someone could maintain that only knowledge has intrinsic value. Suppose we say that pleasure in addition to knowledge has intrinsic value and use the Addition Test for our evidence. An instance of knowledge plus an instance of pleasure has more intrinsic value than the instance of knowledge by itself. The person can always say that the pleasure is just extrinsically valuable for more knowledge. After all, we do know that pleasure is one of the elements that leads to knowledge—as in conditioning models of learning. The same kind of "defense" can be provided for any theory. If this defense were any good, all the competing and inconsistent theories would be the best theory. This is obviously not possible, for it is not possible that pleasure, knowledge, freedom, love, and so on are each the only intrinsically valuable thing. This is a situation exactly similar to the kinds of suggestions in Chapter 2 when we discussed psychological and ethical egoism. You may want to look again at that discussion to refresh your memory.

Summary of Hedonism To summarize this section, there is apparently no way to establish the correctness of hedonism as a theory of value on the basis of psychological hedonism. That is, 'If PH, then H' appears not to be true. In addition, PH is not true—for all the evidence adduced against psychological egoism applies against it. Finally, when we consider hedonism as a theory of value, it appears not to fare very well. There may be counterexamples of the underwhelming value sort, and, more importantly, the Addition Test seems to show that once we establish that at least one thing of value exists, we can show that others exist. As usual, though, no one should make a final decision to reject hedonism until we compare it with other theories.

A Theory of Happiness

In this section we are examining monistic theories of value—those which maintain that one and only one kind of thing has intrinsic value. The most popular candidate among nonphilosophers for that one thing is pleasure, but among philosophers happiness probably ranks first. In distinguishing *pleasure* from *happiness* for the discussion of hedonism, we also described *happiness* sufficiently for our purposes here. It is a relatively long-run state in contrast with the relatively short-run state of pleasure. It goes under other names, such as 'satisfaction', 'fulfillment', and 'contentment', but we all understand fairly well what it is. Presented as a single categorical rule of intrinsic value, the view appears as follows:

If anything is an instance of happiness, then it is IV. ($Hx \rightarrow IVx$)

This statement works, as do all the others, with an appropriate second statement to the effect that a particular thing is an instance of happiness, to derive the judgment that this particular thing has intrinsic value.[12] If the rule is the only one, then the claim is that it and only it is required to justify singular intrinsic value judgments.

The evidence in favor of happiness theories is of the same type as the evidence presented by the hedonist in favor of that theory. There is some evidence that happiness is intrinsically valuable; we can conclude this from an examination of the phenomena and the use of the Addition Test. Furthermore, on at least some occasions, other things are extrinsically valuable for happiness. For example, we might take a lower paying job not for lower earning power but because of the happiness we suppose we shall get. We abstain

---

[12]More clearly, when we talk about happiness, we are concerned with states of people, and not character traits or relations between people.

from certain sexual relations with, for example, sheep and seek relations with human beings not because we suppose human beings are intrinsically better than sheep or (we'll suppose) because there is more pleasure, but because there is usually more satisfaction from sexual relations with other human beings.

In addition to this kind of evidence, some have presented a happiness version of psychological egoism—namely, that the only motive one has is to increase one's own happiness. This is suggested most notably by J. S. Mill.

> There is in reality nothing desired except happiness. Whatever is desired otherwise than as a means to some end beyond itself, and ultimately to happiness, is desired as itself a part of happiness, and is not desired for itself until it has become so.[13]

Since this view in various forms was examined at great length in Chapter 2 and in the immediately preceding sections, there is little reason to discuss it once again. Recall, though, that there is apparently no way to go from this kind of psychological theory of motivation, even if it were true, to the corresponding theory of value.[14] However, this fact is less important than the fact that the psychological theory is apparently mistaken.

Evaluation of the happiness theory is made easier because much of what was said about pleasure applies to happiness. For example, if we suppose that contentment is one part of happiness (or another name for it), we may note that some degrees of contentment are so slight that they seem not to have any intrinsic value at all. One may get happiness from a job well done, but the happiness one gets from properly drying a plate does not usually appear to have any intrinsic value. Again, self-improvement may be a part of happiness, but improving your vocabulary by one word does not appear to be intrinsically valuable. The Addition Test criticism, it should be noted, is more important than this type of counterexample.

The Addition Test against hedonism made use of happiness and love as the two proposed additional items of intrinsic value. We can use the same trio to examine the happiness theory. Imagine a life that has a certain degree of happiness, and add to it a degree of pleasure. If the resulting complex of happiness and pleasure has a greater amount of intrinsic value than does happiness alone, then there is something—namely, pleasure—in addition to happiness that has intrinsic value $\{[IV(h + p) > IVh] \rightarrow IVp\}$. This application of the Addition Test is not problematic, for it seems that all of us are

---

[13] John Stuart Mill, *Utilitarianism. (with Critical Essays)*, ed. Samuel Gorovitz (Indianapolis, In.: Bobbs-Merrill, 1971), 38. Mill goes on to allow many other intrinsic values, such as friendship. We now do desire this friendship for itself, though originally it was desired because of its connection to happiness. Utilitarianism "maintains not only that virtue is to be desired, but that it is to be desired . . . for itself. . . . [Utilitarians] also recognize as a psychological fact the possibility of its being, to the individual, a good in itself. . . ." (38).

[14] You can find in Chapter 4 of *Utilitarianism*, Mill's attempt to do just that.

familiar with both happiness and pleasure. The specifics of any example, though, will be left to you. (Having gotten this far, you realize by now that you must take an active part in this enterprise.)

The same type of countermoves are open to the happiness theorist as were open to the hedonist, but the same type of counter-countermoves are also available. It could be claimed, for example, that the pleasure is only extrinsically valuable; that is, it is only valuable insofar as it leads to more happiness. However, the evidence from the phenomena does not indicate this. All the remarks made concerning pleasure can now be carried into this discussion with only a substitution of 'happiness' for 'pleasure'.

Other Candidates

The presentation of counterexamples of the underwhelming value type, and the use of the Addition Test lead to the conclusion that there are serious difficulties with the happiness view. These difficulties are of the same type as those faced by hedonism; furthermore, we find the same difficulties with all single categorical rule theories. Given this, it is unnecessary to examine each such view at length. Following you will find a list of monistic views—candidates thought by some to be the only source of intrinsic value. At the end of the chapter you will find a bibliographic entry for each one so that you may investigate further any interest you have.

1. If anything is an instance of love, then it is IV. (value agapism)
2. If anything is an instance of freedom, then it is IV. (moksaism)
3. If anything is an instance of (having or exercising) power, then it is IV. (nietzscheanism)
4. If anything is an instance of health, then it is IV. (vitaminism)
5. If anything is God, then it is IV. (theologism)
6. If anything is an instance of a good will, then it is IV. (kantianism)

THE PROBLEM WITH MONISTIC VALUE THEORIES: A SUMMARY

Since a large amount of material has been presented in this chapter in a very short space, a review of what has been done is in order before we go on. The key notions, *intrinsic value* and *extrinsic value*, were explained. Then it was argued that if someone made conscious, rational, voluntary choices, this was evidence that something was taken to be of value. Furthermore, if someone supposes that something has value, the best explanation of this includes the supposition that something does indeed have intrinsic value. Finally, the Addition Test shows that if you admit that one thing has intrinsic value, then we can show you that you admit that at least two things have intrinsic value. In list form we have argued the following:

1. Something x has value.
2. If something x has value, then something y (x and y may be the same or different) has intrinsic value.
3. If one thing x has IV, then another thing y in addition to x has IV.[15]

What we are showing, then, is that monistic value theories are not correct. Let us briefly look at one indirect rule value theory before we turn to the pluralistic or multiple-rule theory views.

Exercises: Problems of Intrinsic Value

1. The Addition Test and the principle of organic unities can be compared directly if we put each in the form of a principle. One difficulty is that the Addition Test makes universal claims about all things and the organic unities principle deals with specific things. This is solved, in what follows, by using logic quantifiers. (These versions are just one of many statements of the view that can be set out.)

    Addition

    $(x)\ (y)\ \{[IDVx < IDV(x + y)] \rightarrow IDVy]\}$

    Organic Unities

    $(Ex)\ (Ey)\ \{[IDVx\ \&\ IVy]\ \&\ [IDV(x + y) > IDVx]\}$

    In English, the first statement, one of the variations of the Addition Test, claims that if the intrinsic disvalue of any thing is less than the intrinsic disvalue of that thing plus another thing, then the second thing has intrinsic disvalue. The second statement, one of the variations of the organic unities principle, says that there are some things such that one of them has intrinsic disvalue, the other intrinsic value; and yet, when you add the two things together, you get a whole that has more intrinsic disvalue than the intrinsic disvalue of the only one that has intrinsic disvalue. Present considerations, perhaps in the form of an example not given in the text,

    (continued)

---

[15] This is not an unqualified statement that can be used to generate an infinite number of intrinsically valuable things. It works for monist views and does appear to increase the kinds of intrinsically valuable things to a large, perhaps indefinitely large, number.

> *(continued)*
>
> in which the two principles give different results. Argue in favor of one of the principles and against the other—at least in this context. Can your argument be made general?
>
> 2. Obviously, we cannot say that whenever something x leads to something y, that y is what a person who pursued x actually wanted or sought. For example, taking one more picture of the Grand Canyon leads to your missing the tour bus, but you didn't take the picture so as to miss the bus. On the other hand, sometimes we seek x only because of its extrinsic value. Try to give some guidelines as to when we are justified in making the "leads to" claim and when we are not.
>
> 3. Suppose the form of hedonism presented claims that pain is the only intrinsically disvaluable thing and the absence of pain is the only intrinsically valuable thing. Critically evaluate that view, making clear which of the criticisms offered so far apply and which do not. Does this version of hedonism fare better than the one that assumes pleasure is the positive value?

A SINGLE INDIRECT RULE THEORY: RELATIVISM

Value relativism is the value-theory analogue of the relativism discussed in Chapter 4 as a theory of obligation. It is a single rule that does not itself select what is intrinsically valuable but chooses the rules that then directly select the things of value. The statement of the single rule is as follows:

> If any proposed direct value rule R is accepted by the majority of people in culture C as a direct value rule, then R is a direct value rule (in culture C).

A *direct value rule* is the kind represented by hedonism or value agapism. It is a rule that, in conjunction with an appropriate second premise, allows the derivation of singular value judgments. For example, one instance of R might be "If anything is an instance of freedom, then it is intrinsically valuable." This rule, along with the fact that not being owned by anyone is an exercise of freedom, would allow us to conclude that not being owned by anyone is intrinsically valuable. In addition, though, there may be many other rules that are believed by the majority of persons in culture C to be direct value rules. They might suppose that satisfying the gods and bathing once a month are intrinsically valuable also.

We often hear people say that in our society success is valued, whereas in other societies it is not. The same sort of thing is said about aggressiveness and security. One can see how this kind of observation fits in with value relativism and might lead people to hold that view.

Carryover from Obligation Relativism

The same distinctions and problems we found with ethical relativism as a theory of obligation arise with value relativism. You will recall from Chapter 4 that cultural relativism is the view that in different cultures different actions are thought obligatory and the cause of that, in part at least, is that the people involved are from different cultures (see the section on cultural and ethical relativism, pages 158–167, for a fuller discussion of those views). This position can be extended to judgments of intrinsic value without any difficulty. The explanation, or part of the explanation, as to why freedom is more highly valued by people in India than it is by people in the United States is that the people live in different cultures.

Assuming that CR stands for cultural relativism, ER for ethical relativism (the view discussed in Chapter 4), and VR for value relativism (the value theory just described), we can set out the relation among the theories in the following manner:

Ethical Relativism

If CR, then ER.

CR.

Therefore, ER.

Value Relativism

If CR, then VR.

CR.

Therefore, VR.

In Chapter 4 we pointed out that no argument is available to establish the truth of the first premise of the scheme representing ethical relativism. We admitted that the second premise, the thesis of cultural relativism, is correct, but that without the truth of the first premise, the truth of that second premise is not enough to establish ethical relativism. We then examined the latter view, as we did other theories of obligation, and found it wanting.

The two main arguments that purport to establish ER on the basis of CR were deficient for reasons that had nothing to do with the subject matter. In one case the argument was invalid, and in the other the inductive argument required the assumption of ER, the very view the argument was going to establish.[16] This is not to say, though, that values are the same all over the world. People in one culture value deceit and in another think it disvaluable. Just as in different cultures different actions are evaluated differently, the same is true of value. However, it does not follow that the best value theory to explain these differences is value relativism. Ethical relativism was not the best theory of obligation to explain cross-cultural differences between, say, Eskimos and Americans. Similarly, value relativism is not the best value theory to explain cross-cultural value differences. This should become clear when we have examined the rival value theories.

Are there any additional arguments that can be used to show that CR can support VR? There are none that I know of; usually the very same bad arguments are put forth. It is a mistake in logic to attempt to conclude that something is intrinsically valuable in one culture and not in another merely from the fact that the thing is valued differently in the two cultures. The defective argument would appear as follows:

In culture C1, x is believed to be F.
In culture C2, x is not believed to be F.

Therefore, x is F in C1 and x is not F in C2.

This argument can be shown to be an unacceptable deductive argument on the grounds that it is invalid. Validity, as you will recall, has nothing to do with the content of the arguments, but only with the form. If other instances of the argument form go from clearly true premises to clearly false conclusions, then the argument is invalid. As was shown in Chapter 4, this is quite easy to do with the preceding argument. The form of the argument is:

In culture C1, x is believed to be IV.
In culture C2, x is not believed to be IV.

Therefore, x is IV in C1 and x is not IV in C2.

A clear argument of this form that goes from true premises to a false conclusion is as follows:

In the United States, disease (x)(of a certain type, say, measles) is believed to be caused by germs (F).

In some parts of New Guinea, disease (x) is believed not to be caused by germs (but by evil spirits).

Therefore, disease is caused by germs in the United States and disease is not caused by germs in certain parts of New Guinea.

---

[16]Look again at these arguments on pages 164–166.

This argument form is clearly invalid. If you are tempted to say that judgments of value are not like judgments about disease, then you should turn back to Chapter 4 and go over all those moves. Recall that the subject matter in the arguments is not being compared at all—only the argument form is under consideration.

It does not seem necessary to go through the arguments concerning value relativism, for they would be exactly the same as those presented about ethical relativism. You can, as an exercise, go through the arguments presented with respect to ethical relativism and translate them into the appropriate language concerning value. The outcome will be the same in each case since we concluded that the arguments to establish ethical relativism on the basis of cultural relativism fail. If they do, then so do the arguments to establish value relativism on the basis of cultural relativism. Thus, we must examine value relativism as a theory of value without any support from cultural relativism.

Value Relativism Evaluated

Just as there were several problems with ethical relativism, there are several with value relativism. There are counterexamples and there are the problems of disagreement and change of opinion within a culture. The Assyrians, more than 3000 years ago, valued heartlessness toward enemies and tortured them cruelly. In Nazi Germany, loyalty as a character trait was held to be extremely valuable—certainly among the highest of all the intrinsic values. Even if we suppose that loyalty is intrinsically valuable, we do not suppose it is at the level the Nazis thought. These are apparently instances in which something was valued in a culture and yet is not valuable or not valuable to the degree they supposed. These elements from the phenomena represent counterexamples to value relativism.

The standard moves are open to the value relativist, but you must recall your philosophical obligations. It does no good to say that on the *supposition* that value relativism is correct, the purported counterexamples are not actually counterexamples. That is true of any theory and any set of purported counterexamples. If we assume the theory to be correct, then the purported counterexamples are never actually counterexamples. However, since the counterexamples are drawn from the phenomena, we must be given some reason for supposing that they are not actual counterexamples. Failing that, we are justified in treating them as effective until we can be shown otherwise.

In addition to counterexamples as a kind of problem, the value relativist has difficulty in explaining the change of mind of a person and the change of mind, so to speak, of a culture. Until about the nineteenth century, the majority of people in the United States thought that slavery as an institution was a good thing. To present this first as a counterexample, we shall say that anyone who asserted that slavery was a good institution was mistaken—regardless of what the majority of people in that culture said. However, the explanation, or at least part of the explanation, of why people changed their minds was that they came to believe that slavery was not a good institution and that slavery was not intrinsically valuable—perhaps extrinsically disvaluable or intrinsically disvaluable. We say this change was based on considerations other than what the majority supposed was correct, or else the change could not have come about. The fact that such changes occur[17] within every cultural group and subgroup is something that weighs against value relativism.

The same kind of consideration can be put dramatically, as we did in Chapter 4, by discussing an instance of change. When Harriet Beecher Stowe claimed that slavery as an institution was evil, intrinsically disvaluable, she could not be refuted, even in Mississippi, by being shown that a majority of people accepted it as being intrinsically valuable (or not intrinsically disvaluable).[18]

When you as an individual change your mind about the value of something, only very rarely do you do it on the basis of what the majority of people in your culture accept. This may be what is going on all the time; but if so, it is strange that we are not aware of it. This indicates that the phenomenon of changing opinions—both opinions of individuals and those of cultures—is not something that value relativism adequately explains. If other theories of value do not have these problems or do a better job of accounting for the phenomena, then we shall not, of course, adopt value relativism as our theory of value.

Recall, however, that the rejection of value relativism and the adoption of another view, whatever it is, does not commit us to a doctrine of "absolutes." Hedonists and happiness theorists can account for many, if not all, of the phenomena in this area that can be accounted for by the value relativists. Certainly, what gives one person pleasure or leads another to be happy is not always what gives someone else pleasure or leads still another to be happy. In various cultures, for whatever reason, certain kinds of experiences are chosen for pleasure and other kinds are chosen to reach happiness. These are claims that these two theories, and many others, can accept. So, if you wish to maintain the "subjectivity" of value judgments, you need not think that you must adopt value relativism, for this is not true. We shall see why this is so in the next chapter.

---

[17] This is a purported fact, an empirical claim. The problem with ethical relativism was put in terms of new moral problems; ethical relativism cannot handle new moral problems. Similarly, value relativism cannot account for new or additional values. Only when human beings had sufficient leisure based on sufficient wealth could they create literature, philosophy, biology, and physics. If value is only what is believed by the majority to have value, then anything new brought into existence could not be believed to have value since no one yet has any beliefs about it. It does happen, though, that new kinds of value are created by humans.

[18] This should be cast in the indirect rule framework, but it is less obvious when so cast. It can be done, though. Mrs. Stowe claimed that a direct rule of value was "If anything is an instance of the institution of slavery, then it is intrinsically disvaluable." Her opponents made use of the indirect rule to show that it is not a direct rule in Mississippi because a majority of people in that subculture did not accept it as such.

> *Exercises: Value Relativism*
>
> 1. Critically evaluate the following claim: "No one can make something valuable for someone else; anything that a person thinks is valuable is valuable for that person. No one can impose values on someone else. Each society has its own values, and this is what value relativism claims. In order to deny this, you must suppose that there are some things that all cultures suppose are valuable, but this is just what cultural relativism shows is not so."
> 2. Give an explanation consistent with value relativism for the phenomenon of people changing their minds and of whole societies doing the same thing. (Remember, any theory can be made consistent with any set of phenomena, although this is not to say that the theory thereby does a good job in explaining the phenomena.) Now offer a critical analysis of your explanation. Compare the explanation you have given with a happiness value theory.
> 3. Relativism has two versions: a theory of value and a theory of obligation. If you think that one of these views is better—is a better theory in its area than the other—explain why you maintain that view.

PLURALISM: MULTIPLE-RULE THEORIES— PRIMA FACIE AND CATEGORICAL

There is a difference between theories of obligation and theories of value concerning multiple categorical rules. The difficulty with the Ten Commandments taken as a categorical rule theory of obligation, recall, was that we could wind up with incompatible obligations (for example, to visit a parent and not to visit a parent). This problem was solved by interpreting each obligation as a prima facie obligation, so that although we had two different and conflicting prima facie obligations, we did not have two conflicting and incompatible actual obligations. One of the prima facie obligations was said to override the other, and thus the conflict did not arise on the level of actual obligations. This same kind of problem cannot arise in theory of value as it is set up because of the way the notion *intrinsic value* is defined. A person can hold that happiness is always intrinsically valuable and also hold that pleasure in all of its instances is intrinsically valuable, as well as hold that there are times when you have to choose between the two of them in a given set of circumstances. For example, you may find that a night (or a week) spent visiting close relatives will contain little pleasure but a great deal of happiness. Suppose you must choose between the two for a given period of time. There is no incompatibility of values as such, only the fact that one person cannot realize the two situations within the same time period. It was the very action of traveling to see your parents that violated the commandment to honor the Sabbath and fulfilled the one to honor your parents. This was a moral conflict, and there was no way to choose without violating an actual obligation. In the value case, you have a way to choose, even if you hold both rules to be categorical rules of intrinsic value. Choose the one that has the most intrinsic value. This phrase is almost the same as the one involving prima facie obligations—namely, choose the one that is strongest with respect to obligation. So it seems the very notion we have used as our basic working notion has the idea of prima facie built into it.[19]

Thus, multiple-rule theories in theory of value, in contrast with theories of obligation, will be of one type only. We shall interpret such theories as claiming that there are at least two rules of intrinsic value that pick out at least two different kinds of things of intrinsic value. The use of the Addition Test indicates that perhaps once we begin adding kinds of things as intrinsically valuable, we are not justified until we have added a large number. Certainly, all the rules, and thus the kinds of things, listed at the end of the section on categorical direct rule theories seem to be good candidates. So, although it will seem like a rather vague way to state a theory, this manner of saying what is meant by a multiple-rule theory of value appears to be adequate.

The Counterexample Problem

What are the problems with such a theory? The problems are the same ones that beset prima facie rule theories of obligation: If the criticisms are effective, we have the counterexamples of the underwhelming value sort and the problem of a decision procedure when more than one value is available and we must choose between them. Let us begin with a mention of the counterexample problem.

In the examination of the monistic views, underwhelming type counterexamples were presented—for example, an amount of happiness that is so slight as not apparently to warrant a judgment of intrinsic value. Such counterexamples are apparently available for each kind of thing claimed by our pluralist to have intrinsic value. The existence of counterexamples would constitute a criticism of such a theory, though not one of great force. In addition, some claim there are instances of the kind mentioned in the rule (say, pleasure) that are intrinsically disvaluable. As was mentioned, some philosophers think that an experience

---

[19]Some people may say that this is not a good thing because it destroys the parallel between theory of obligation and theory of value. There is some force to this complaint, but I think this points out the difference between the "action" orientation of theory of obligation and the "state of affairs" orientation of theory of value. This is, I think, a difference in the subject matter. If the subject matters were the same in every respect, we could treat them the same—but then we wouldn't have two subject matters, but only one.

of pleasure derived from sadistic torture, say, is such an example. Although it does not strike me that this kind of criticism is effective, you should form your own opinion. My own view is that taking pleasure at the suffering of others is to exhibit a vice, a character trait that is intrinsically disvaluable. So, although the pleasure is still intrinsically valuable, it is part of a whole that has more intrinsic disvalue than intrinsic value.

The Decision-Procedure Problem

The most serious problem, though, facing multiple-rule theories of value is the decision-procedure problem, when we have to choose between two complexes made up of a different mix of the intrinsic values. A situation can be brought into existence that is high in pleasure, say, and low in happiness. Consider the situation of consuming a gourmet dinner, where the food consumed is part of what is required for adequate nutrition of another group of persons. Perhaps you can create a society in which 90 percent are happy but 10 percent are unhappy because they are the slaves of the majority. Construct for yourself a situation in which two of the things you suppose have intrinsic value seem to conflict, a situation in which one thing has a positive instance and the other a negative instance. In this situation, the two rules conflict; that is, if each were the only one that applied, the total situation would be intrinsically valuable and intrinsically disvaluable, respectively. The problem is to decide whether the total situation has a surplus of intrinsic value over intrinsic disvalue, or the other way around. Another way to state this is to ask if the total situation is one that is intrinsically valuable or one that is intrinsically disvaluable. This problem shows the need to have some epistemic mechanism in addition to the multiplicity of value sources. The prima facie theory of value no more supplies this than the prima facie theory of obligation.

One could be an existentialist about this situation and say we just choose which complex is more valuable, but that is hardly a rational approach. Similarly, one could say that one just intuits which complex has more intrinsic value. But intuitions have been known to clash, and there would be no way to adjudicate such a disagreement. All the criticisms of existentialism and intuitionism presented in Chapter 5 apply again in theory of value.

The pragmatic view claims that the value predicates are a *resultant* characteristic; that is, they are dependent on the other characteristics of the "thing." The intuitionist views of the Plato/Moore type hold that value predicates are *nonresultant* characteristics. According to the resultant theory, the basic unit of morality within each area is a conditional—a singular moral judgment related to its appropriate nonobligation or nonvalue term. You will recall from the last chapter that every theory proposes some units within an area that are not justified within that theory. This is true of rule theories such as utilitarianism as well as nonrule theories. The two theories disagree, of course, on what the basic unit is. The examination of theories is in large part an attempt to determine which purported basic unit is best taken as the basic unit within the area of morality. Over the last four chapters, we argued that a pragmatic theory of obligation is the best of the lot. We have deferred until Chapter 7 the question of whether the basic unit within the area of morality is basic to all areas. We are getting close to that question now. However, first we are engaged in this one last task of normative ethics—a comparison of theories of value.

The nonresultant model of the intuitionists cannot explain why the presence or absence of other characteristics is relevant, and it does a very poor job of explaining how reasons can be relevant if all we need to do is be aware of the value property itself. However, this does not show us in any concrete way how a pragmatic theory of value works to arrive at justified singular moral judgments.

The key element in adjudicating disputes, you will recall, was the method of conditional agreement. However, we shall be working with a different framework in theory of value than in theory of obligation, for the basic notion chosen within the area of value, *intrinsic value*, has built into it, as it were, the notion of prima facie—or something equivalent to it. The disagreements will not be whether or not something has intrinsic value, but which of two or more things has greater intrinsic value. Let us try some examples, and then explain this further.

In the last chapter, we examined a constructed conversation concerning slavery. The dispute was whether or not a person was doing something wrong if he or she kept slaves. The dispute can also be seen as a disagreement concerning the relative values of two different societies—a free society versus a slave society.

Person a: "When we agreed that slavery's interference with the development of a person's potential would be a reason for claiming that slavery is wrong, we seemed to be agreeing also that the development of human potential is intrinsically valuable. To take this stand would help us solve many more problems, both economic and social, than we now can because we would have more intelligence available to us."

Person b: "Yes, but we should say *if* slaves have human potential, *then* there is a reason for saying that slavery is wrong. However, there does seem to be agreement that developing the potential of certain kinds of creatures, of which I am a good example but blacks are not, results in the creation of something intrinsically valuable. You, though, must agree that if blacks do not have the same potential and must be taken care of in order to prevent them from harming themselves, then we create the intrinsic value by taking care of such people. It is by preventing them going off on their own to try to develop a potential they do not actually have that prevents social and economic problems. It would perhaps even be intrinsically *dis*valuable to allow such creatures to attempt this kind of development. The institution of slavery has the characteristic of protecting limited humans, and it does not have the characteristic of preventing human development of the clearly valuable type."

Person a: "I can agree that the protection of those who are not capable of taking care of themselves is valuable, and can even admit that it is intrinsically valuable, although that is not a very clear case. You, I assume, will agree that the development of human potential is intrinsically valuable. Now we must determine the factual question about the potential of blacks, for that is all that remains in dispute."

Here we have a highly simplified disagreement (soon to be complicated) in which the two parties are disputing about only the presence or absence of intrinsic value. Intrinsic value, in the pragmatic position, is (originally) a hypothesis that if we aim at and secure a certain end then we will solve problems. We are supposing that inquiry is finished but there is disagreement about a specific proposed instance of that goal and about the compatibility of two values we have already established. In the following, let $Fx = x$ consists of the protection of those who are not capable of taking care of themselves and $Gx = x$ consists of preventing those who are capable of developing as humans from doing so. Then we can represent the dispute concerning slavery (in the United States in the eighteenth century, say) x, as follows:

Person a: If Gx and not-Fx, then not-IVx.

Person b: If Fx and not-Gx, then IVx.

This situation is too simple, for usually there is competition among recognized intrinsic values, and, acompanying the conditional agreement, there is disagreement about value. A more realistic dialogue would appear as follows:

Person c: "Blacks are more like whites than they are like cats or dogs—that is, they are a kind of human being. However, they are human beings with much less potential than whites. They are much less capable of taking care of themselves, of being creative, and so on. So, although some intrinsic disvalue is brought into existence as a result of the institution of slavery (for, being enslaved, they are deprived of some dignity, control over their own affairs, and so on), the amount of intrinsic value brought into existence is greater. The resulting whole situation that contains slavery and not the negative intrinsic value of people being taken advantage of by businesspeople, of people receiving improper health care, and the like has more intrinsic value than a whole situation that does not have slavery but has all those other things. This is the argument in favor of slavery."

Person d: "The argument is somewhat more complex than the previous one, but it is still essentially the same. You suppose that blacks lack the degree of potential that whites have, and it is this lack that justifies you in thinking that slavery is right. If the potential of the races was the same, or very nearly the same—for after all, this is not a matter of exactness—then you would admit that your on-the-whole argument does not work."

If we are to represent this kind of argument as we did the first, we must have more complicated predicates. Those predicates might appear as follows: $Fx = x$ (blacks) have significantly less potential than whites (for such things as taking care of their own affairs, education, culture, and so on); $Gy = y$ is a situation in which human beings are deprived (of a significant part) of the opportunity to live with dignity and to realize their own potential; and $Hz = z$ is a situation in which human beings are allowed to live freely (that is, to develop their own potential). Suppose that s equals 'institution of slavery', and b equals 'blacks'.

Person c: If not-Hs & Gs & not Fb, then not-IVs (or IDVs).

Person d: If Fb & not-Gs & not-Hs, then IVs.

Person d might even agree that slavery in the United States in the eighteenth century deprived human beings of a significant part of the opportunity to live with dignity and to realize their own potential. However, he would add, this is not so significant a deprivation as to create more intrinsic disvalue than the value created by slavery and the disvalue created if blacks attempt to run their own affairs when they are not capable of doing so.

Even this more complicated statement is not yet elaborate enough to say all that should be said, and does not allow us to capture what is perhaps the most important kind of value claim we make—namely, a comparative value claim. If in the preceding instance we wanted to replace the IVs and not-IVs predicates with comparative predicates, the statements of persons c and d would become:

Statement c': If not-Hs & Gs and not-Fb, then not-IVs > IVs.

Statement d': If Fb & not-Gs & not-Hs, then IVs > not-IVs.

The consequent in statement c' says that the intrinsic value of not having slavery is greater than the intrinsic value of slavery. The consequent in statement d' claims the opposite—that the intrinsic value of slavery is greater than the intrinsic value of not having slavery. This statement, the capturing of the dispute in two conditionals that have comparative value judgments in the consequent, reveals much better the nature of value disputes.

One thing remains constant in the restatement of the conditionals: the normative disagreement appears to revolve around the factual questions of the potential of blacks. This question, although a socially sensitive one, is capable of being settled. Even if we accept as accurate the studies that show a slight difference in IQ between the races, this is not the kind of difference we need to establish in order to support slavery. In addition, as is well known, the measurement of IQ is just one way to measure the complex concept of intelligence. There is reason to suppose that IQ scores reflect quality of education both in school and at home. The overwhelming number of blacks, having suffered from racism, are at an educational disadvantage that explains most of the test score difference. Furthermore, even if IQ level and intelligence were the same and there were no educational bias, we still aim to develop human potential at all levels, not just the genius level. It is this potential that is being shut off, and it is to this area that we trace most of the intrinsic disvalue.

Most of the disputes concerning intrinsic value, especially those concerning what course of action we should take to secure something of value, are about the comparative value of different "bundles" of what we already take to be of intrinsic (and extrinsic) value. So let us consider one case of that sort. Suppose someone is considering whether to pursue a career as a dentist or as an auto mechanic. With the following defined predicates and constants, we can represent one way of deciding schematically:

d = career as a dentist

m = career as an auto mechanic

Mxy = x will result in more money than y

Pxy = x will gain more prestige than y

Txy = x will result in more tension than y

Hxy = x will contain more happiness than y

If (Mdm & Pdm & Tdm & Hdm), then ($IVd > IVm$).

If (Mmd & Pdm & Tdm & Hmd), then ($IVm > IVd$).

In English, the first statement says that if a career as a dentist results in more money than a career as a mechanic and also brings more prestige and happiness, and even granted that being a dentist will bring more tension than being a mechanic, it is better to be a dentist than a mechanic. The second statement claims that if the money earned as a mechanic is greater than that earned as a dentist (or perhaps about the same) and granting that there is more prestige as a dentist than as a mechanic, but holding fast to the view that dentistry carries more tension and that being a mechanic will result in greater happiness, then being a mechanic is better than being a dentist.

If this were a self-dialogue, the person would have to find out the facts about himself or herself in order to determine which of the two antecedents was more likely to be true. It would be very difficult to make the decision, for evidence about such matters is difficult to come by. However, once again, the truth of the matter is something that is not, as such, a value concern. Later in life, after you have made your decision, you may decide that you made a mistake. This makes clear that when a value judgment is made, it is justified in large part by what happens in the future. When a decision is far-reaching and people must decide without the best evidence, we have anxiety about making a mistake. This method will not make the evidence any clearer, but it will enable you to see more clearly what kind of evidence is needed and where it applies.

A dispute between two people would have the same form as the preceding one, which is conceived as a self-dialogue. There is no way really to understand how this method is to work without trying it. You will find, I think, that when you try to use it, it is much easier than the abstract description might lead you to think.

The final question concerns how the values that are being compared are first established as values. Here, the pragmatic method involving solutions to problems fits nicely. "Good consists in the meaning that is experienced to belong to an activity when conflict and entanglement of various incompatible impulses and habits terminate in a unified orderly release in action."[20] We can apply this abstract claim to the following constructed problem.

Huckleberry Finn and the escaped slave Jim are on a raft in the Mississippi when Huck realizes that one of his values plus a complex of rules involving it require that he turn in Jim as a runaway slave. This is what is morally required if Huck is to escape the torments of Hell, as he so believes. However, Huck comes to regard Jim as a fellow human being, someone toward whom he feels friendship. To turn a friend in to the authorities would be a betrayal of friendship. Here we have a conflict of two values, where not both of them can be acted from. At this point Huck is involved in a problem situation. He does not consciously resolve the problem, but one way to explain the text is that he creates the value of loyalty to friends in the face of personal loss. This judgment may be only a short-sighted one, for though Huck is now enabled to proceed down the river and to keep his friendship with Jim intact, should he wind up in Hell he may decide after a few centuries of torture that he made a mistake. The short-run decision would turn out to be a long-run mistake. However, Huck decides that the theological force is not as clear as the friendship issues. Most of us would side with him on this, and Mark Twain knows we will. This example involves a conflict of values and an indication via the methodology of the pragmatist as to how it might be resolved by the invention or discovery (if you are not a pragmatist) of a new value.

Obligation versus Value in a Pragmatic Theory

We are now in a position to compare the basic units in theory of obligation with the basic units in theory of value. We shall consider only resultant theories of obligation and value.

Obligation
$(Fa \ \& \ \text{not-}Ga) \rightarrow MOa$
$(\text{not-}Fa \ \& \ Ga) \rightarrow \text{not-}MOa$

---

[20]John Dewey, *Human Nature and Conduct*, ed. Jo Ann Boydston (Carbondale: Southern Illinois University Press, 1988), 146.

Value (noncomparative)
$(Fa \ \& \ \text{not-}Ga) \to IVa$
$(\text{not-}Fa \ \& \ Ga) \to \text{not-}IVa$

Value (comparative)
$(Fa \ \& \ \text{not-}Gb) \to (IVa > IVb)$
$(\text{not-}Fa \ \& \ Gb) \to (IVb > IVa)$

In the value area, the first two pairs of conditionals represent the conditional agreement concerning the intrinsic value or the lack of intrinsic value of one thing. This is labeled the noncomparative value conditionals. The second pair of conditionals represent the comparative value judgments. In those two conditionals, we compare two different things, a and b, and find that if one set of "facts" is so, then the intrinsic value of a is greater than that of b, and if the second set is so, then the intrinsic value of b is greater than that of a.

In the consequents of the comparative pair and the noncomparative pair, the denial that any given thing has intrinsic value may be the result of the thing's having intrinsic disvalue. So, if a has intrinsic disvalue (IDVa), then it is at least true that it does not have intrinsic value (not-IVa). Thus, you might want to claim that slavery has not just a lack of intrinsic value but also has some intrinsic disvalue.

Working with a Pragmatic Theory

With this last piece of theoretical explanation, we might say that we have the complete theoretical apparatus of pragmatic theories before us. However, it is one thing to understand in a theoretical manner solely how the method of conditional agreement is supposed to work and another to acquire some facility in using it. The comparative judgments are somewhat more difficult to work with, but they too are easy to master with practice.

Even for those of you who are able to use the method of conditional agreement, the usual kinds of questions arise. "Suppose that people do not agree with the hypotheticals?" The claim made is that for any two (or more) people, and for any dispute of value, we shall be able to discover the relevant and appropriate pair of conditional statements on which there is agreement. It is quite possible, of course, that there will never be agreement on the antecedents, that we will not be able to arrange for factual or nonvalue agreement—but that is another matter. If it should turn out that we do not find the pairs of conditional statements, this is evidence that this pragmatic theory is mistaken. The evidence presented in favor of the claim that such pairs are available is the past success in finding them. This theory of value is not thought to be immune from the evidence of our experience; it is, instead, based on what we do experience.

"Can't other theories do as good a job as the kind of pragmatic theory you defend?" This is a question for the reader to answer. I have claimed the pragmatic theory is the best one, especially given the difficulties of the other theories we have revealed. Undoubtedly, however, any of the theories can explain the phenomena. That is not the primary concern of a theory of value; rather it is a concern with which theory does the *best job* in explaining the phenomena. Monistic theories have a much more difficult time, so it has been argued, in explaining the phenomena. By this time, you have followed many arguments and have examined many theories. It should be clear that the task before us is to find the best theory, not just to find some theory or other that can do some kind of job in explaining the phenomena.

Suppose that someone wants to claim that value judgments are a disguised expression of emotion or feeling? Nothing so far said would prevent that theory from being defended. The issue represented by this question will be taken up in the next chapter, however.

It has been said that within the area of theory of value the basic operative notion is *intrinsic value*, with the notion of *value* being the basic undefined unit in that area. Within the area of theory of obligation it seems we need *obligation* and *right* as two separate notions, notions not reducible to each other. What about the relationship between *value* notions and *obligation* notions? Perhaps one of these notions is more basic than the other? This question essentially asks what the basic units and notions are within the area of morality. This too is a question that is addressed in the next chapter. For now, we can say that we have worked out theories of value and obligation that use notions that may or may not turn out to be independent. If they are independent, we don't have to worry, for the theories have been worked out independently. If they are reducible one to the other, then we shall see a relationship between the two areas that we have not seen before. However, that would not really affect the normative theories worked out.

TAKING A STAND; LOOKING AHEAD

In the preceding chapters we have examined the major theories of obligation and value. More importantly, we have presented the tools whereby one evaluates such theories. You are now in a position to select from the available theories the one best supported by the available evidence. I have, as promised, argued for one of the theories in each area. However, this is not very important. People find themselves taking stands on all manner of issues; philosophical issues are just one kind in which theories are examined. Of course, I assume my theory is correct; after all, people do not defend a theory they assume is incorrect. Many of you reading this book will disagree with me, but this is to be expected.

In the next chapter we shall take up the questions that have not yet been treated adequately. We have indicated that we shall examine the cognitive status of normative judgments as well as basic units in the area of morality and their relation to other areas. In addition, we shall examine some problems of meaning and inquire briefly into the nature of moral predicates.

Exercises: Evaluating Value Theories

1. Describe a disagreement that you are aware of from your own experience. Apply the theory of value you think best to that disagreement in order to explain what was happening. Now apply what you take to be the second best theory of value. Now try to show that the theory you think is best has done a better job than its competitor.

2. Many religious traditions posit an evil being. Shall we describe such a being as one who pursues what it accepts as intrinsically disvaluable? Do your best to present a picture of what such a being would have to accept in the way of a theory of value.

3. Utilitarians—some being monists and others being pluralists—have disagreed about which theory of value to adopt. Even the monists have not agreed, some being hedonists and others not. Choose one theory of value that you take to go best with your favorite form of utilitarianism and defend your choice.

4. Perform the same task for your favorite ethical egoist position that you performed for your utilitarian position in exercise 3.

5. Look back at the descriptive ethics questionnaire and the values questionnaire that you filled out (if you did so) at the beginning of this book. What theory of obligation and value best accounts for the answers you gave at that time? What changes did you have to make in your answers to achieve a consistent view? What changes would you now make in your answers to achieve a consistent view? What changes would you now make in your answers to the questionnaires? What position do you now find yourself taking in theory of obligation and value?

6. The comparative form of judgments of intrinsic value was presented earlier, but no comparable kind of comparative judgment of obligation was presented in Chapter 5. According to the model of comparative judgments of intrinsic value presented on page 247, construct a model of comparative judgments of obligation. Argue that such judgments are or are not significant for normative ethics.

RECOMMENDED READING

Aristotle. *Nichomachean Ethics.* In *The Basic Works of Aristotle,* edited by Richard McKeon. New York: Random House, 1941. In books 1 and 10 you will find what is likely the first happiness theory.

Dewey, John. *Theory of Valuation.* Chicago: University of Chicago Press, 1939. Dewey is concerned with denying that anything has intrinsic value, but I don't think he would deny the intrinsic value of things in the sense used in this chapter.

Ellis, Albert. *Reason and Emotion in Psychotherapy.* New York: Lyle Stuart, 1962. The author presents a psychotherapeutic theory that fits in well with the views expressed in the appendix to this chapter.

Fletcher, Joseph. *Situation Ethics: The New Morality.* Philadelphia: Westminster Press, 1966. Agapism, as it is laid out in this chapter, is discussed.

Kant, Immanuel. *Groundwork of the Metaphysics of Morals.* Translated by H. J. Paton. London: Hutchinson University Library, 1948. Kant seems to argue that only a good will is intrinsically valuable.

Moore, G. E. *Ethics.* London: Oxford University Press, 1965. The author presents a view of intrinsic value, primarily in Chapter 7, that is quite different from the one presented in this chapter.

Nietzsche, Friedrich. *Beyond Good and Evil.* Translated by Walter Kaufmann. New York: Vintage Books, 1966.

Plato. *Philebus.* In *The Dialogues of Plato,* translated by B. Jowett. New York: Random House, 1937. A rejection of hedonism from the philosopher who first stated most of the antihedonist arguments.

Potter, Karl H. *Presuppositions of India's Philosophies.* Englewood Cliffs, N.J.: Prentice-Hall, 1963. The author claims that freedom, or *moksa,* is the one goal thought to be intrinsically valuable by a variety of different philosophical movements that began in India.

APPENDIX TO CHAPTER SIX

Meaninglessness and Futility: An Application of the Tools of Moral Philosophy to a Traditional Problem

One of the traditional roles of philosophy is to help people solve perplexing problems and personal dilemmas. Philosophy has done little recently to keep up this role, although we have seen more of this type of help in the last decade of the twentieth century than in preceding decades. Part of the reluctance of philosophers to discuss problems stems from the absence of reward for those who do. In addition, philosophers mostly work on problems that have grown distant from the more "applied" concerns. In this appendix a problem that has traditionally been in the province of philosophy but has not recently received much attention from philosophers will be treated: the problem of "the meaning of life." I shall attempt to show that this problem can be handled with the tools and techniques outlined thus far, and then will indicate what steps individual people will have to take to solve their own problems. Some of you will be relieved to know that I will not attempt to explain the meaning of life on the "life is a fountain" model.

INFORMAL STATEMENT

Sooner or later everyone asks, "What is this all about?" "Why am I doing anything rather than nothing?" "After I have done all these things, what does it amount to?" "Is any of this worthwhile?" or equivalent questions. These questions begin at a relatively early age, as soon as a child or adult begins to wonder what will be done with the rest of his or her life, for then the value of alternatives must be weighed. This questioning, in turn, gives rise to serious and often nagging doubt: If we make a mistake, we might live a life that is not worthwhile. If we answer any of the other questions incorrectly, then the rest of our life could turn out to be pointless, based on a mistaken conception of what life is about or why anyone should do something. We don't feel we have more than one "time around,"—although in some cultures reincarnation is a widely held view—so we attach great importance to these questions and our answers to them.

Any help we can get in answering these questions is appreciated, so it is no wonder that philosophers as well as theologians, sociologists, economists, political scientists, movie stars, and football coaches have been listened to with interest and respect. The help offered here is in the form of a do-it-yourself kit, not a finished product. The aim is to allow each of you to have a greater understanding of the nature of the questions and the kinds of answers available so that you can arrive at an answer. There does not seem to be one correct answer to any of the questions, for answers depend on the character and talents of each person.

A QUESTION OF VALUE

It is not accidental that discussion of the meaning of life inevitably involves questions of value. The usual way of answering any question about why an action is performed is to say something about the value of the action or the value of what the action achieves.

"Why did you go to that restaurant rather than another?"

"Because the food at the first is better than the food at the second."

Usually people do not use 'value' or one of its synonyms in their first or second response to questions about *why*, but the term (or one of its synonyms or species) naturally and invariably comes out. For example:

"Why do you attend this class?"

"To get a degree."

"Why do you want a degree?"

"To get a high-paying and interesting job."

"Why those things?"

"That is the kind of life I choose to live."

"Why that kind of life?"

"That is the one I think is good."

There are various kinds of stopping places to the question of why something is done. Some of them are the result of fatigue, some the result of impatience, and some the result of finding a natural stopping place. We can describe a natural stopping place by means of the notion *intrinsic value*. Something is believed by a person to have intrinsic value when he or she supposes its value does not depend on its leading to something else that has value. The thing may, of course, lead to something else that does have value, but regardless of whether it does or not, it still has value. When someone catalogues all the things in life that she or he believes have intrinsic value, then we have an answer to the question "What makes my life worth living?" and "What is the meaning of my life?" If we can find the list, then we have the meaning of that person's life.[1] If the items on the list are believed by the person to be valuable enough to justify his or her existence, then to that person life is worth living. Or, on the contrary, a person may say, "This is the meaning of my life, and it doesn't come to much. These are the intrinsically valuable things, but they do not compare favorably with the suffering or with what I could or should have obtained."

The usual questions about goals require some answers about value. To the question "Why should I study?" we can answer "Because it will enable you to achieve the goal of passing the course." If someone asks whether this goal is worthwhile, we can answer by saying that it leads to getting a degree. This, in turn, will enable a person to get a certain kind of job, which leads to a certain type of life. It is language such as this that we use to answer questions about the justification of goals by saying something about the value of the goal. A satisfying stopping place of such a sequence of questions and answers is when we reach something(s) of intrinsic value that we think is (are) enough to justify all the other intermediate goals. We may say that we do everything for pleasure, and only pleasure is pursued for its own sake. Others may say that pleasure, even if intrinsically valuable, is not enough to justify all the other goal achieving (and striving); it is not sufficient to carry the weight of all that we do.

When we list all the intrinsic goods that justify the achieving and striving for goals—all the doings of our life—then we have rationally explained why we live rather than die and why we live a certain way rather than another. To find the meaning of life, we must then find what things are intrinsically valuable and, if there is more than one, place them on at least a rough scale of relative value. In this way we translate the question concerning the meaning of life into a question about intrinsic value.

Now we shall consider a move that is easy to see but difficult to justify in an informal way.[2] This is the assumption that unless something has intrinsic

---

[1] I think there is a difference between what a person *believes* has intrinsic value and what *does* have intrinsic value. For the purpose of this discussion, though, this distinction need not be made; we can stick with what a person believes has intrinsic value and, accordingly, with what a person believes is the meaning of his life. This is, after all, what is important when you are talking with a person. For the objective sense, we could substitute 'is justified in believing has intrinsic value'.

[2] See pages 216–218.

value, then nothing has value at all. Given the senses of 'value' and 'intrinsic' used, this seems to be a trivial enough truth, but there seems to be no neat way to show that it is true.

If we wish to find out what things are intrinsically good, we can use a test that is of extrinsic value. The Addition Test is a partial test to determine whether something should be added to the list of intrinsic values.[3] Suppose a friend of yours claims that only happiness is intrinsically good, that the only value for F is happiness when the value of M is intrinsic value. We can show your friend that she herself does not hold this if we can show she believes that a life (or situation) that has happiness and freedom is of more value than one that has only happiness. If the reasoning or the principle in the preceding is acceptable, then we must conclude that freedom, or something that freedom leads to, has intrinsic value in addition to happiness. One can claim that freedom is valuable only because it leads to happiness, but then again, one can claim anything. One can claim that happiness is valuable only because it leads to freedom. The difficulty is to justify claims, not simply to make them.[4]

People have thought many other goals to be of intrinsic value: love, friendship, power, pleasure, absence of pain, freedom, peace of mind, and peace in the world, to name a few.

A LIFE, HUMAN LIFE, AND SENTIENT LIFE
Finer Distinctions

The translation of these concepts into more technical language, although a necessary first step, has not taken into account the finer distinctions we can make at this point.

> The life of person a has meaning: There is, in person a's life, enough positive IV to outweigh the IDV.[5]
>
> Human life has meaning: There is, taking all human life together, enough positive IV to outweigh the IDV.
>
> Sentient life has meaning: There is, taking all sentient life together, enough positive IV to outweigh the IDV.

Obviously, there are going to be occasions and some lives where all these differ. Someone may very well live a life that contains practically nothing of value, while the lives of most other human beings contain a great surplus of intrinsic value. On the one hand, there are always those among us who live

---

[3] See pages 226–230.
[4] These moves are covered at greater length on pages 228–230.
[5] IV stands for intrinsic value and IDV for intrinsic disvalue. See pages 212–218 for fuller explanations of these terms.

a life that is not worth very much at all, while on the other hand there are those whose lives are full of great value in the midst of an otherwise bleak period of human existence. If we shift the scale to all sentient creatures, the same kinds of distinctions can be made. Human existence may be a happy accident in the midst of an otherwise unhappy universe, or vice versa. These are often the questions we ponder without reaching any conclusion. These distinctions do not, by themselves, of course, provide an answer, but they do provide us with a means of asking a clear question. Any answers will have to be provided by some means, but the means are available. Each individual is capable of determining the value and the likely value of his or her own existence, even if the determination requires some pain and great difficulty. Each person might want some help in doing that—help from friends, therapists, or whomever—but it can be done. Furthermore, it may well be that this is the most important question of this type that we as human beings ask ourselves. People hold some views that interfere with our ability to determine the value of our life, or life in general. On this problem the philosopher can be of great help.

Calculus of Intrinsic Value

I am not claiming we can calculate in some precise way the intrinsic value, both positive and negative, in our life. However, it is possible to tell roughly what value there is and, in all except a very few instances, this is sufficient for our needs. The value scale talked about is a qualitative one, but since we are all pretty much able to construct and read such scales, this is no great handicap.

Futility

What we as individual human beings ask is not only about whether our own life has meaning, in the sense described, but whether it has enough meaning, enough intrinsic value to make it reasonable to continue to live. We can ask that in a variety of situations. First, our future may clearly hold little of value and may clearly be filled with a surplus of intrinsic disvalue. For example, if you were told you had exactly one year to live and after one month your entire existence would be colored by intense pain, that would be a clear instance of such a case. It is tempting to say that such a life is not worth living any more. Notice, though, that this does not justify the claim that your whole life, even if you should live that last pain-filled year, would not have been worth living and would not have had a significant surplus of intrinsic value. More on this shortly.

A different kind of situation is one in which your past life seems not to contain enough intrinsic value to make it worthwhile and the future seems to hold no promise except more of the same. In both these cases it might be appropriate to say that living was futile. There are undoubtedly other kinds of cases, but not as many as some think.

Journey View

One view of human life that leads some to think (mistakenly, as will be argued) that their life is meaningless and futile is the view that the value of anything is just what it spatially or, more usually, temporally leads to. Since life leads to death or to pain and misery in old age, then, according to this view, no life is worth living. As the first step in philosophical therapy we can say that the notion of *intrinsic value* or its appreciation does not include the occurrence of intrinsic value at any given time.

Some activities are clearly never done with any temporal or teleological end in view. Contrast dancing for a half hour and walking to the post office (which also takes a half hour). Each of these activities takes a half hour, but in the first there is no place to get to, no spatial or temporal end to the activity that constitutes its purpose. There is a goal, of course, but the goal is the activity, not something the activity leads to. The activity no doubt leads to all manner of things—increased heartbeat, relaxation, mild fatigue, and so on. However, these are not the goals sought in the activity, and they are not the goals that make it worthwhile. The goals are other things gained in the activity, such as a kind of communion with your partner, esthetic satisfaction, or whatever. (This is not to deny that you may have some ends that are clearly of the teleological type, such as winning a prize for dancing, making a social contact, and so on.)

Some activities lead to a goal at the end of a temporal sequence, which goal justifies the activity; other activities apparently do not require such a goal to justify them. Freedom is apparently valuable not because it leads to something else at a later time, but because of something it gives people at the present moment. It is usually true, of course, that freedom does lead to other things at a later time—things such as dignity, achievements that without freedom would not be possible, and so on.

A human life is apparently not to be judged worthwhile or not worthwhile on the basis of a goal achieved at the end of a temporal sequence. One clear temporal end is death, but we would all judge that death is not something of value that justifies the activity of living. It is this kind of thinking that leads some people to postulate a goal that is (temporally) beyond what we find in life. For given this kind of view about the nature of ends and values, people think there must be such an end or all we do now is worthless and meaningless. Such people reason that since death is not that goal, there must be something else "beyond" death that justifies the activity of living. Some ends so chosen are communion with God, another activity of living that is of a higher quality than the one carried on now, and a merging with some greater being. It may be that when death comes we really do move on to something else. Nothing said so far denies there is another kind of world and another kind of life. We are claiming rather that this need not be assumed in order to make sense of our lives.

What is required for a meaningful life is that during the course of that life a certain kind and amount of intrinsic value be created. If there is such value, then this life has meaning and perhaps enough meaning; and if not, then it doesn't. This consideration doesn't prove that your life or the life of any given person has meaning; it does show, though, that whether your life has meaning does not have anything to do with a goal to be achieved at the end of a temporal sequence.

Nonjourney Teleological View

Some people suppose not that there is some temporal last goal toward which we are striving, but that there is some goal or set of goals that we must achieve during our lives to make living worthwhile. Furthermore, these goals have to be set by some being other than a human being. The last clause has to be added, for otherwise the view could be made perfectly compatible with what has been said here so far. A general end we are all searching after is a meaningful life; and if that is taken as the goal, then certainly the attainment of it makes life worth living and failure to attain it renders life meaningless. However, that goal is not a specific goal, and it is likely that the people who hold this kind of view think that we must have a specific goal, such as serving God or serving God to accomplish a specific end.

GOD-GIVEN KNOWLEDGE OF WHAT IS INTRINSICALLY VALUABLE

One way to interpret the introduction of God is that He is a moral expert. This is perfectly compatible with what has so far been claimed, but it is not the type of view now being considered. Suppose someone claims that unless God communicates with you, you won't *know* which goals are valuable and you won't succeed in living a meaningful life. This requires there to be some activities that will result in a meaningful life and others that won't, independently of God informing you.[6] God is all knowing with respect to all things and is thus all knowing with respect to values. Such a being is clearly the best consultant there can be. However, there seems to be a problem of coming to know which goals are valuable.

There is an additional problem that is best brought out by the numerous examples we are all aware of from the newspapers, about people carrying out what they take to be God's commands. If someone kills all his neighbors because, as he says, God told him to, we think the person was deluded. In a newspaper

---

[6]The activities and goals are not ones that God *makes* valuable; they are ones He *knows* about and tells you about so that you too will know.

story it was reported that a passenger on a bus killed a fellow passenger because he thought the person was the devil and his Lord, Jesus Christ, had told him to kill the devil. Very few of us would say that Jesus Christ did indeed tell the person to murder a fellow passenger. (Suppose for a moment that Christ, in contrast with Jesus, is indeed God.) We suppose God would not tell us to do things of that sort—the sort of thing that is morally wrong. We believe this also of things of value; God would not have us pursue something if it was not, finally, of some intrinsic value. If someone whispers in your ear, or speaks through a burning bush, or communicates in some way that the sole intrinsically valuable end is counting the number of hairs on your body, you take this to be very good evidence that it isn't God who is speaking.

Human beings, especially those who are most religious, use a value test for whether information given is from God or not. If the information is *not* in accord with what we know, independently, to be acceptable moral advice, then it is not from God. If this is so, as the simple inspection of the kind of case just mentioned seems to show, then we cannot rely on God to tell us everything, or even all the important things with respect to value. We have to know such things already in order to make use of God as a moral expert.

Whether God exists or not, and whether He gives moral advice or not, it is not prudent to depend on hearing from Him. Life continues, and if God can know, there is some chance that you can know, however imperfectly, what He would have told you. Others seem to have discovered activities that are worthwhile, and that is some evidence, again, that you can too.

GOD AND WHAT IS OF INTRINSIC VALUE

A stronger claim can be made that requires God's existence for anything to *have* value, not just for knowledge about it. In response, we can point out that nothing about the nature of intrinsic value and its application to goals seems to require that they be set by some external being. The claim that such a being must set the goals in order for them to be valuable requires some support for our acceptance; and failing such support, there is no reason to accept the claim. Because there is some reason to suppose we understand the nature of goals, and that they have value without the aid of such a being setting them, we would be justified in rejecting such a view. Finally, if it is a general truth that in order for a goal or an activity to have worth there must be some being external to the being reaching the goal or carrying on the activity who sets it, then this requirement also applies to God. He has, so it is supposed, the goal of setting goals for human beings. This, plus the general principle just stated, would require a being that sets the goals for God, otherwise His goals, and thus, I assume, our goals, would have no meaning. And so on, *ad infinitum*. Thus, the postulating of a being would not solve the problem but only replace it with one that we know can't be solved—namely, escaping a vicious infinite regress.

Suppose, as the last view of this type, we consider the view that it is God's existence or His activities alone that have intrinsic value; everything else has only extrinsic value insofar as they lead to those. First, it is not God's existence alone that could render some meaning to our lives, for nothing we can do or fail to do can have any effect on God's existence. It does not seem that the mere existence of anything has value; value arises either from some action or some character trait the thing has. Character traits, in turn, are explained in large part by the actions that follow from them. For example, we understand the character trait of honesty in terms of the kinds of actions an honest person performs.[7] If God has character traits of this type, then, once again, our understanding of His nature requires some kind of action. There may be some other kind of character trait, or God may have no character traits, but then either the person making the claim about the necessity of God's existence for value is speaking without knowledge or understanding, or we are told that a being with no character traits has value. In either case, the claim is very difficult to understand or make sense of.

Let us consider the second possibility: that God's activities (and the goals reached through them) alone have intrinsic value, and that without these, our activities would not have any value. Those who hold this view suppose that God brings us into existence in some way or other. (This need not be supposed, of course, but let us consider the view commonly held by people and not consider every possible view that could have been held.) The crux of the counterargument is that God's action of creating human beings is sufficient evidence that the activities of human beings and at least some of the goals reached through them do have intrinsic value independent of God's activity, except, trivially, the action of creation.[8]

We must admit, first, that God does not do anything that is purposeless; He is not a capricious God. The Addition Test shows us that a universe with human beings must have more value than a universe without human beings, for otherwise God would not have created a universe in which there are human beings.[9] No being who is all good, all knowing, and all powerful will create a universe that is less valuable than another possible one. (Is this really the best of all possible worlds?) Thus, it must be that human beings, either in their activities or what they bring about through their activities, increase the intrinsic value in the universe. This can only be done if those activities or ends do have some positive intrinsic value. So if God exists, then, contrary to the claim being

---

[7] See pages 192–194 for a fuller discussion of this point.

[8] However, your parents are the cause of your existence, but the value of what you produce is not dependent on the value of the creation, birth, conception, or anything of that sort.

[9] Remember, this is a particular God being discussed, and so do not, in answering this argument, talk about another God. If you seriously hold that another kind of God works in the universe, then such a position will have to be worked out separately; each position deserves and requires separate attention.

considered, some of what human beings bring into existence has intrinsic value independent of the value of what God brings into existence with His actions. If God does not exist, then of course the argument that begins with the assumption of His existence does not get started.

This argument notwithstanding, you may be uncertain about the amount of intrinsic value in your life, but that is another matter. All the argument is intended to show is that the intrinsic value of God's goals and actions plus the intrinsic value of the actions and goals of human beings is greater than the intrinsic value of God's actions and goals alone. This, as a simple application of the Addition Test, shows that at least some actions and goals of human beings have intrinsic value. The value of the goals we now have and the actions we carry out do not depend on the value of the goals that God has and the actions that He carries out.

ADDITIONAL TOPICS

Here now, in brief form, are some other topics that you may want to discuss at greater length.

Intrinsic Value and Transience

From the fact that something passes away, say, a certain state, it does not follow that it did not, during the time it did exist, have value. Human life and especially individual humans come into existence and go out of existence, but this does not show that a human life did not have value and, indeed, a great deal of value. Sometimes, the value of something depends on its passing out of existence. This is clearly true of food; perhaps youth is another instance—although it is certainly more controversial.

Intrinsic Value and Regret

It might be regretted that something passes away—say, the life of a friend or your own life—but it is one thing to regret the passing away of something and another to claim that because it passes away it does not have value now. The fact that it will not exist at some future time does not show it to be valueless now.

Intrinsic Value and Finiteness

Some people claim that finite beings do not know enough to set their own goals and only an infinite being can know what is valuable. We have talked about many goals and activities that appear to have intrinsic value, as well as lives that appear worth living, so there seems no reason to accept this claim.[10]

Intrinsic Value and Pessimism

Skepticism is very debilitating and occurs frequently. Individuals may very well accept all that is said here and yet be pessimistic with respect to their own life. This pessimism often takes the form of great despair as a result of what seems to be the futility of doing anything. I suggest that this sense of futility results primarily from a lack of knowledge about what is available, or a mistaken theory about what is valuable or what value is. There are steps that can be taken even for such a person.

PHILOSOPHICAL THERAPY AND FUTILITY

According to the view presented here, even though you may receive comfort from others, including God, the meaning of your own life is determined by what you do. The meaning of your life is determined by factors primarily internal to you, not external. However, as indicated, a chance exists that any given person will have lived a life with little meaning or significance. All of us suspect, on some occasions, that our own life is one of those. There are various things that one can do to overcome this suspicion and the feeling of futility that often accompanies it:

1. Talk with others who have had the same kinds of problems and who share the same kind of outlook as you do.
2. Calculate, from the opportunities available, what you can do with the rest of your life. It is the rare person who cannot, living within her or his abilities, live a life worth living—one with enough intrinsic value to make it worthwhile. There is the friendship of many, the love of a few, the satisfaction of a job well done, the experiences of the senses, and many other things.
3. Consider the philosophical positions you may have adopted that have led you to consider that life is futile and meaningless. Presented here are some tools that can be used to combat positions leading to conclusions that make futility a perfectly understandable and justifiable position. If you can show yourself that the philosophical positions that support the claims of meaninglessness are not justified, then you can often dispel the feeling of futility. This kind of activity can, without obscurity, be called philosophical therapy.

---

[10]Furthermore, the preceding examination of theories of value does not justify this pessimism.

4. There are those, however, who know all the philosophical "moves" and yet find that they cannot apportion their emotional responses to fit what their reason tells them. This is not a philosophical problem, but a psychotherapeutic problem. Since the whole tone of this book has been rationalistic, I should point out that this is no cause for despair, for there are methods of psychotherapy that do not depart from this rationalistic mode.

CHAPTER SEVEN

Metaethics

In the first six chapters, various normative ethical theories were examined. Such theories aim at providing us with singular moral judgments of obligation or value, whether the mechanism for arriving at such judgments essentially involves a rule or not. Rules may be direct—ones that allow the direct derivation of singular moral judgments—or indirect—those that pick out direct rules. I have opted for a particular theory of obligation and value. Your obligation (intellectual) has been to enter into the activity of evaluating competing theories, not to adopt my views.

The activity of choosing from among the competing normative ethical theories required discussing many problems that may not seem closely related to this primary task. The discussion of psychological theories in Chapter 2 is a clear example. There are, though, a number of problems in moral philosophy that are, as it were, left over. These are problems that have yet to be discussed, or, at least, discussed fully. In this chapter we shall briefly discuss a number of these problems and indicate, for most, the kind of solution that seems best. In the following sections, those on basicness, *M*, and the moral connection are related in a more important way than any of the others—both to each other and to the other sections.

THE NATURE OF NORMATIVE ETHICS: A REVIEW

We have maintained that normative ethical theories are used primarily to arrive at justified singular moral judgments. Human beings find this task important, we suggested, because they act in part on the basis of judgments of value and obligation. Thus, securing such judgments has significant practical importance, not just theoretical importance. This is not to say that all or even most people typically use these theories consciously. When we face difficult moral problems, though, we can use help from our normative ethical theory.

We made a minimal number of assumptions in our examination of various normative ethical theories. We assumed that moral phenomena are the items we accept at the beginning of our investigation and not the ones that represent facts or undeniable conclusions. We assumed, also, that we could distinguish the better from the worse among competing theories. The criteria of acceptability, though, were not thought to be peculiar to moral philosophy, but are the kind of tests used in every area. Armed with the criteria, and using the phenomena as the ammunition, we evaluated the main kinds of theories of obligation and value. Your primary task was to acquire the skills to do a bit of philosophical hunting. I suppose I have, to continue the metaphor for a moment, hit the target, but you are fellow hunters.

Other conceptions of what normative ethics should be follow from certain other positions philosophers have taken. Some of these alternative conceptions will be mentioned and briefly discussed shortly. None of them will show that if we had accepted them we would have been wasting our time doing what was done in the past six chapters.

BASICNESS

In Chapter 5, the notion of what is basic arose explicitly for the first time. Now, after the survey of normative ethics is complete, we can restate that concern in a more general way. Since the pragmatic normative ethical theory is the one I have chosen, I feel constrained not to present a pragmatic metatheory as the framework of this section. The pragmatic metaphilosophical view holds that all claims are theoretical claims, and that such claims are justified by the outcomes of acting on them. We are justified in holding the germ theory of disease, for example, because of the success of disease treatment when we assume it.[1] There is nothing about the germ theory itself, or about our mental state in considering it, that justifies it. In contrast to this metaphilosophical method is the method of analysis. Those who practice this method practice it as if there is something about notions themselves, independent of the empirical inquiry of theories that use them, that allows us to say of them that they are the best. This position may or may not be so, but we shall try to present the

---

[1] The germ theory is the best because it does a comparatively good job in explaining the disease phenomena. This discussion does not "go back" on this approach. I am here attempting to compare the pragmatic metaphilosophical theory with a standard analytic philosophy metaphilosophical theory without begging the question against the latter.

concerns of analytic philosophy about basicness, and then contrast this view with that of pragmatism as conceived in this work. One other kind of view will not be discussed in this section—that is, virtue ethics. The virtue ethics theory would deny that reasoning is the heart of normative ethical theory. In this sense, there is no basic unit, though what is basic about normative ethics is the set of virtues and vices. The discussion in Chapter 5 will have to suffice for such theories.

In what follows, three separate concerns about what is basic will be examined: (1) which *notions* are basic within the area of ethics, (2) which "units" of justified judgment are basic within the area of ethics, and (3) whether the notions and units that are basic to ethics are basic to all areas. The task of explaining these questions and describing some of the important alternatives starts, once again, with our familiar general scheme:

Rule Theories

$(x)(Fx \rightarrow Mx)$

Pragmatic Theories

$Fa \rightarrow Ma$

The rule theorist directs us to find the appropriate covering rule—that is, something of the form shown—if we wish to justify a singular moral judgment. Once we have found that, it is a straightforward matter to determine the facts—that is, Fa—and thus to arrive at Ma as the justified singular moral judgment. Pragmatic theories, in contrast, attempt to find the appropriate covering unquantified or singular conditional. With that conditional in hand, the justification would proceed in the same manner as the rule theorist's. When we arrive at Ma, we suppose we have a justified judgment. Without attempting to be very precise about it, we can say that since the singular moral judgment, Ma, requires the conditional moral judgment (either as a rule or as a singular conditional) for its justification, that singular moral judgment is not a basic justified unit within the area of morality. When we have reached the unit within an area that is required by some other unit within that area for justification but that itself does not require justification in that area,[2] then we have reached a basic justified unit within that area.

To claim that a unit is a basic justified unit within an area is not to claim that it is necessarily true, that it is undeniable, or that we have arrived at it by some particular faculty. It is only to say that within every area some statements or judgments are accepted or acceptable without further justification in that area. Different areas have different characteristics, so the characteristics of a formal axiom system are quite different from those of common sense. It is not necessary to discuss whether the axioms of a formal system

---

[2] It may also be that it is not possible for us to find justification for the unit within the area, but this is a much stronger claim, one that we do not have to make now.

are "arbitrary" or descriptive of necessary truths of the world we live in in order to say what has been said so far. At the end of this discussion, a pragmatic defense of the basic units within an area will be presented. In what follows, this defense will not be presupposed and alternatives will be discussed. The metaphilosophical defense of a normative ethical theory need not be of the same type as the mechanism within the normative ethical theory. For example, one might be an intuitionist concerning obligation, but defend that theory pragmatically.

Some clear examples of what we take to be basic will help to fix the subject matter in mind. Most people learn plane geometry axiomatically; they study some variation of Euclid's system devised more than 2000 years ago. One of those axioms says, roughly, that when equals are added to equals, the results are equal. On the basis of this claim and some others, as well as on the various rules of inference, we can deduce the theorems of plane geometry.

When we practice the science or art of sociology, we assume we can know when a person is alive and when that person is dead, that person a is the father of person b, that person a learns from person b, and so on. The claim that person a is the father of person b does not require any sociological evidence. If someone challenges the claim, we would provide evidence, but it would not be evidence that is peculiarly sociological.

The claim that someone's aortic valve is defective and requires replacement is a medical judgment that needs to be justified. The justification consists of presenting the evidence of certain tests, X rays of the heart, internal measurements of the flow of blood through the aortic valve, and other such evidence. This evidence supports the claim that the valve is deficient and has to be replaced if death is not to occur in a short time. Since other support is required for it within the area of medicine, the defective valve claim is not basic within the area of medicine.

Some supporting evidence about the valve is further justifiable and sometimes requires justification, even though some of it cannot be justified within the area of medicine. The reliability of X rays is supported by evidence provided by physicists or gathered at autopsies or from open-heart surgery. Suppose, for example, the diagnosis is that the aortic valve is deficient because calcium deposits have built up around a congenitally defective valve. When the chest is opened, the surgeon observes that calcium is deposited and the valve is defective in the ways predicted. This confirms the claims made on the basis of the X rays and shows that such claims can be relied on in the future. Of course, there is more support from knowing the nature of X rays as a result of studies in physics. These two methods of providing evidence for the claim that X rays show how the heart is working are methods from other areas; one is from physics and the other, as we might say, is from common sense. What, though, is common sense?

The surgeon has all manner of medical knowledge that enables her to recognize calcium deposits and defective valves in the exposed heart. There is no denying that. However, the method used to establish the claim that there is calcium and that the valve is defective is *looking*.[3] This is a method that is not part of the area of medicine although those who practice medicine use it all the time. It is a method used by those who practice physics also; philosophers use this method, as does almost everyone else who does anything. We all adhere to some form of "seeing is believing." This is not to say that we cannot distinguish between trustworthy and untrustworthy perceptions. However, even though no analysis of this has been given, we do use visual perception as a means of gathering reliable information and base many of the claims we make about the world on such information.

Within the area of medicine are some claims that are supported by evidence that is within the area of medicine (for example, that the heart valve is defective) and others that are not (for example, that this substance around the valve is calcium). Claims requiring support from claims in other areas are *derived*. If the surgeon has doubts about the nature of the substance in the valve, she will send it to a chemist who will, exercising expertise as a chemist, determine that it is calcium. In this instance, the claim that x is calcium is supported not within the area of medicine but within the area of chemistry. So the claim may be said to be basic within the area of medicine[4] but derived within the area of chemistry. A claim that is basic in an area that sometimes requires support from another area is one that is basic within the first but not basic among all areas. A claim is basic among all areas when it is justified but there is no area in which there is evidence that supports it *and* that is required to support it. Are the basic claims in the area of morality basic in all areas?

Nothing in the previous discussion should be taken to suppose there are *natural kinds* or categories that are fixed in the nature of things. An assumption of natural kinds supposes that what is in an area is fixed. The pragmatic assumption that kinds are changeable depending on what will facilitate inquiry and solve problems is compatible with the preceding discussion. The categories or kinds we use in philosophy are, in the pragmatic view, no more fixed than are the species of living things. In biology we used to employ many teleological categories in our explanations. "Eyes are designed to see and ears to hear." Today we say this only metaphorically or as a linguistic remnant of now abandoned theories. We no longer say "Zeus rains," but we do say "It is raining." We don't think there is any being that is doing the raining but that rain as a phenomenon has a purely nonteleological explanation.

---

[3]It is not part of the view being expressed that one sees calcium without knowing what calcium is. To know this requires sophisticated theoretical knowledge just as, in my view, to see anything in a way that results in knowledge requires some theory that you have and use. We are here interested in the method of gaining knowledge and not in what additional knowledge we would need to make the method work.

[4]Some claims that are basic within an area occur in other areas, and others do not. The claim 'x is red' does not occur within the area of arithmetic.

The preceding account of what it is for a claim to be basic among all areas may be correct, you may say, but what are those claims in our ordinary experience? They are likely to be of the sort called common sense.[5] The claim that an object is red or square is usually justified but does not require some area in which it is justified. Suppose you look at any object and make the claim that it is red. Isn't there a great deal you can do to support this claim? Yes, of course there is. You can ask someone else what the color is, or you can determine which wavelengths of light the object reflects and check on a chart to see which color that is correlated with. You can look again, you can take a picture, and so on. All this would supply additional evidence for the redness of the object. Similar moves would be made with the claim that an object is square. You can measure the sides and angles to determine if they approximate the relations that hold when something is a square. You can ask others, look again, and so on.

In the analytic tradition, it would be said that checking a chart after getting a reading from a machine, requires a number of prior justified judgments that some objects are red. Whoever made the first correlations had to do so without the aid of such a chart; that is, the person knew that things were red without using a chart. If there were not such a person, then no chart would have been constructed. So for at least some ways of supporting a claim, those ways presuppose some method of supporting the claim other than the ones used. In addition, even when there are other ways of supporting a claim that is, as we want to say, basic among all areas, none of them is *required* to support the claim. We can tell the color and shape of an object, as we say informally, without using such methods.

These kinds of claims are apparently justified, and there is no requirement of support for these claims from another area. We might call these the five (or seven) senses claims. There may be additional claims of this sort, for there is no reason to limit the kinds of claims to one type. In contrast to this kind of explanation is the pragmatic view that the justification of claims of an entire area (what is here called common sense) is itself justified by the success we have in solving problems when we use judgments within that area. This is true of shape and color judgments as categories and also of the criteria we use within those areas to justify particular judgments. When we engage in social activities such as hunting and fishing, communication is important to our success. Success in communicating what kind of vine to collect to make nets or what kind of seed to collect to grow crops is instrumental to our survival. We are justified in using a category and a given test for its effective application when we have success of this sort. This is a *forward-looking*, in contrast to a *static* or *backward-looking*, justification. This contrast with types of

---

[5]Recall, though, that these will not turn out to be undeniable claims. Commonsense claims are, in some sense, based on phenomena, as are other kinds of claims. They are consequently correctable, just as any claim based on the phenomena is correctable.

justification of units that are basic within an area sets the stage for the more important claims in metaethics.

Is morality a kind of inquiry that is basic among all kinds? A yes answer does not depend on the kind of normative ethical theory one holds, for any two theorists might agree that the basic unit within the area of morality is basic among all areas and yet disagree about which unit is basic within the area of ethics. The competing normative ethical theories disagree on what is the basic unit within the area of morality.

Ethical relativism is a normative ethical theory that appears to hold that the basic unit within the area of ethics is not basic among all areas. One way of understanding such theories is through their claim that moral rules, whether direct or indirect, are justified because they stand in a certain relation to the mores of a society. In this instance, the moral rules can be said to be the same thing as the mores, or, to add the proper flavor to the claim, moral rules are nothing but mores. Mores, as an object of study, are completely within the area of sociology-anthropology, or sociobiology, according to some social scientists. Thus, according to this interpretation, mores are more basic than moral rules within the area of sociology.[6] Is this true? Well, in part we can determine the acceptability of this particular claim by determining the acceptability of ethical relativism. This task was attempted in Chapter 4 (pages 158–167) and Chapter 6 (pages 234–238).

We can maintain that support of moral rules in the form of, say, the mores of a society, requires further evidence. This position, as we saw, is difficult to support, but it is clear. One way in which a claim of nonbasicness can be supported, then, is via one's normative ethical theory. The fact that the only instance we saw of this appears to fail does not detract from this view—nor would the failure of all such attempts, for we are interested in ways in which such claims might be supported, not just in the ways that succeed.

An attempt has been made to make clear the notion of a basic unit within an area and to contrast that with basicness among all areas. If we ask the question, "Which units are basic within the area of ethics?" the answer supplied by the rule theorist will be different from the one supplied by the pragmatist or virtue ethics defender. The first will say one or more rules, and the pragmatist will tell us that singular conditionals are the basic units within the area of ethics. Those who defend virtue ethics will posit a set of basic virtues. The rule theorists will continue the discussion among themselves as to whether there is one rule or many and whether the rule(s) is (are) direct or indirect. Having answered

---

[6]Suppose that two people each claim that *their* area is more basic than the other and that the basic unit within the other area is reducible to something in theirs. In other words, each claims the basic unit within the other area requires support from their own area. Given what has been said, they are not both correct, even though they both suppose they are correct. The way we would determine which of them was correct is the way we determine the correctness of any theory of that type. More will be said about this shortly.

the question of which unit is basic within the area of ethics, though, we may go on and ask if it is basic among all areas. This question, however important, is different from the first.

Another question concerns not the basic unit of justified judgment, but the basic notions or terms within the area of ethics.[7] At the end of this section you will find some representative statements of various positions. You can examine those and see how philosophers have stated actual views of the different sorts mentioned earlier. In addition to the normative theories, which sometimes commit one to a view that *good*, say, is the basic notion within the area of ethics, there are theories that appear to have other considerations.

> What we ought to do, in fact, is limited by our powers and opportunities, whereas the good is subject to no such limitation. And our knowledge of goods is confined to the things we have experienced or can imagine; but presumably there are many goods of which we human beings have absolutely no knowledge, because they do not come within the very restricted range of our thoughts and feelings. Such goods are still goods, although human conduct can have no reference to them. Thus the notion of good is wider and more fundamental than any notion concerned with conduct; we use the notion of good in explaining what right conduct is, but we do not understand the notion of right conduct in explaining what good is.[8]

[7] We say, for example, in Chapter 2, that we can interdefine *right to* or *permission* and *obligation*, but that neither of these notions can be used to define *right*. Given the theory of definitions presented in Chapter 1, when we offer a definition we are not simply proposing a verbal equivalence but are offering at least part of a theory. If we accept the definition, we are no doubt accepting a lot more than a formula of the form $p = df\ q$. One way to find the basic notions within an area is to find the basic units of justified judgment in that area and then see which notions in that area occur in them. For example, if utilitarianism (direct) is correct, then the basic unit within the area of obligation is something to the effect that "If any action maximizes good for the greatest number, then that action is right." We might also find a rule concerning *obligation* that is separate from and not reducible to the rule concerning right (see Chapter 3, page 100, for the discussion on this). We also know, given this normative ethical theory, that some value notion such as *good* is more basic within the area of ethics than notions in theory of obligation, for obligations and right actions are a function of value brought into existence. In this way we would have made a choice as to which notion in the area of ethics is most basic, and we would have determined this by finding out which unit of justified judgment is most basic within that area. If this approach is used, though, we have to finish, as it were, our normative ethical theory in order to determine which notion or notions are the ones basic within the area of ethics. If one holds to the kind of normative ethical theories covered in this work, one may then suppose that there are at least two kinds of notions in ethics: value notions and obligation notions. In addition, there may be at least two kinds of obligation notions that are equally basic within theory of obligation. In general, the suggestion is that to find which notion is basic, or which notions are basic, find the basic units. To do the latter task, though, you must critically evaluate competing normative ethical theories. Since we have done that, though, this is not a setback in our investigation.

[8] Bertrand Russell, "The Elements of Ethics," in *Philosophical Essays* (New York: Simon and Schuster, 1910); reprinted in *Readings in Ethical Theory*, eds. W. Sellars and J. Hospers (New York: Appleton-Century-Crofts, 1970), 5.

These are the words of Bertrand Russell, who was at the time following Moore. This kind of view is in sharp contrast with Ewing's position.

> We might define "intrinsically good" as "worth choosing or producing for its own sake." However, even though this definition will mostly serve, there may be cases where it cannot well be applied, and it is difficult to find a single form of words which is always applicable. But we might adopt a technical term and define "good" as what ought to be the object of a pro attitude (to use Ross's word). "Pro attitude" is intended to cover any favourable attitude to something. It covers, for instance, choice, desire, liking, pursuit, approval, admiration . . . . When something is intrinsically good, it is (other things being equal) something that on its own account we ought to welcome, rejoice in if it exists, seek to produce if it does not exist. We ought to approve its attainment, count its loss a deprivation, hope for and not dread its coming if this is likely, avoid what hinders its production, etc.[9]

A more recent version of Ewing's position is stated by Allan Gibbard.

> What a person does is *morally wrong* if and only if it is rational for him to feel guilty for having done it, and for others to be angry at him for having done it.[10]

These are but two different positions; there are many who line up on one side and many on the other. Given the difficulty of the task and the necessity of a long discussion, in this instance I shall not take a stand on the issue. Almost any theory could maintain either that *good* is the basic notion or that *obligation* is, or that they are equally basic. Since this is so, I shall not try to decide the issue.

There is a distinction, then, among the claim that a notion is basic within an area, the claim that a unit of judgment is basic within an area, and the claim that the notion or unit that is basic within an area is (or is not) basic among all areas. These are issues philosophers have argued over and continue to be concerned with, as the quotes show. However, this discussion should be enough to make you at least aware of the kinds of issue.

M AND MORAL REALISM

In the general scheme we used the letter M as the replacement for the most general moral notion, as in $[(x)(Fx \rightarrow Mx)]$ or All F are M. Let M stand for whatever moral predicate or moral predicates you suppose are, or represent,

---

[9]A. C. Ewing, *The Definition of Good* (London: Routledge, 1948), 148–149.
[10]Allan Gibbard, *Wise Choices, Apt Feelings* (Cambridge, Mass.: Harvard University Press, 1990), 42.

the basic notion(s) within the area of ethics. There are a variety of questions we have to ask about this predicate:

1. How many places does the predicate have?
2. To what kind of "thing" does M answer? (Is it a property, such as 'square'; a relation, such as 'to the left of'; or what?) Do moral predicates "answer to" something "real" or "really in the world?"
3. What is the meaning of 'moral predicates'? (This may be the same as question 2, depending on what your answer is there.)

How Many Places Does the Predicate Have?

The answer to this question will depend on whether you are concerned with value predicates or with obligation predicates. You may recall that obligation predicates usually have at least three terms and perhaps five or more. For example, suppose we translate the following judgment into an entirely unambiguous set of symbols: "Peter is obligated to pay Paul $10 for the chair he bought at Paul's garage sale." We let p = Peter, l = Paul, $ = $10, c = chair, and C = circumstances in which Peter bought a chair from Paul at this garage sale. With these symbols, we can offer up a complicated obligation statement (O = obligation): $Opl\$scC$. This obligation statement has five terms; five different symbols follow O, all of which are required for the translation. In this text most examples were simplified for discussion, so we often translated such judgments as Ox. However, when we are concerned with being more precise, we must provide a fuller translation.

In contrast with obligation predicates, value predicates are more difficult to capture because of the different uses to which such predicates are put. We used IV to stand for 'intrinsic value' and then translated statements such as "Pleasure is intrinsically valuable" as IVp. We did not include any person variable in the statement, but it is obvious that pleasure is always an experience of a person or other sentient creature. So a more precise statement would include reference to at least one person—perhaps to any people or all people. We might then translate the hedonist's claim that pleasure is the only intrinsically valuable thing as "For any person, the only thing of IV is pleasure." When we discuss such proposed intrinsically valuable things as freedom and love, the situation becomes more complex. Freedom, taken for a moment in contrast with slavery, involves a reference to at least two people. We have to say that person a loves person b, and that person a is free within a given political system of government (which is a legal person). So when we translate a claim about love, we have $IVLab$, which we can read as the claim that the love between person a and person b is intrinsically valuable. Just as we did for obligation, though, we may want to add some information about the context. When such things have been pointed out, then we are more fully aware of the nature of the predicate *M*. This will help us avoid certain mistakes that result from an oversimplification of moral predicates.

A more difficult issue is what kind of being can be involved in a value or obligation relation. Can we have an obligation to the environment (not to pollute or destroy)? Some think that we can have obligations only to persons, while others think we can have obligations directly to forests, nonhuman animals, rivers, and so on. Do animals have rights? How about rivers or forests? These are important issues in fields such as environmental ethics.

To What Kind of "Thing" Does M Answer? Realism and Antirealism

It would be nice to be able to say that everyone agrees on what it is for morality to be objective or what a realist value view is, but it is not that simple. To get the discussion started, let's begin with what seems to be a common specification of moral realism—that is, that attribution of justification or truth in morality is of the same type as that used in science.[11] Those who deny the objectivity of morality typically talk about what moral predicates *refer* to. They have Moore in mind as the paradigm of a philosopher who posits the kind of objective property whose existence they wish to deny. For example, Wong tells us:

> Today, few moral philosophers would subscribe to Moore's theory of moral language. Yet he presents the clearest, most straightforward, and detailed theory of how moral terms refer to irreducible moral properties, and *all philosophers who find such a general view appealing must find a way of incorporating these virtues of Moore's theory while avoiding its problems.*
>
> The core of his theory is the notion of intrinsic goodness. That which is intrinsically good possesses a property that is simple in the sense that it cannot be analyzed into component parts, and it cannot be identified with any other simple property.[12]

One thing that is wrong with Moore's view, in Mackie's (and Wong's, and Blackburn's and many others') interpretation (which is typical of contemporary philosophers) is that it requires that 'good' function as an attributive adjective while it actually functions as a predicative adjective. When 'good' is used as a predicative adjective, statements are of the form "*x* is a good *y*."

---

[11]Richard Boyd describes moral realism in terms of three claims, the first of which is, "Moral statements are the sorts of statements which are . . . true or false (or approximately true, largely false, etc,) . . ." in "How to be a Moral Realist," in *Essays on Moral Realism*, ed. Geoffrey Sayre-McCord, (Ithaca, N.Y.: Cornell University Press, 1988), 182. Boyd does a splendid job in comparing scientific realism with moral realism. Boyd is not a pragmatist, as I count myself to be, though I agree with most of his negative criticisms of the antirealists.

[12]David B. Wong, *Ethical Relativiy* (Berkeley: University of California Press, 1984), 100. Emphasis added. I shall return to the claim of irreducibleness in a short time, for it is behind another concern clearly expressed by Blackburn.

For example, "M. L. King, Jr., is a good man" and "Democracy is a good form of government." When 'good' is used as an attributive adjective, it has the form "x is good." Clear examples of this kind of claim would be, "Courage is good," and "Friendship is good." This makes it seem plausible, says Wong, that 'good' is a property of courage or friendship in the same way in which, say, round is a property of a ball. Though there are variations of Moore's view, says Wong, all such views must fail because "'Good' behaves like an attributive rather than a predicative adjective."[13]

In short, this criticism says that moral objectivity requires that good be a special kind of property in a special realm, a property that would have to be known in a special way. But, there is no such special property or special realm, and there is no special way of knowing, as this view requires. So, moral objectivity and moral realism are mistaken. Although I find Mackie's and Wong's negative claims about Moore congenial, in this work I have set out different reasons for the claim of objectivity than special realms and special ways of knowing.

Mackie makes empirical claims that are not obvious. He claims, for example, that ordinary morality requires acceptance of categorical obligations to do particular actions.[14] For years I have been giving students a survey containing a choice between such a view and a view involving variable-weight first-order moral rules. (See the survey in Chapter 1.) The vast majority reject the absolutist view and choose a prima facie account of moral rules. This is not a great deal of empirical evidence, but it is considerably more than Mackie presents. In a similar vein, Mackie tells us, "Disagreement about moral codes seems to reflect people's adherence to and participation in different ways of life."[15] Not being partial to a Wittgensteinian outlook, this disagreement doesn't seem to me to reflect at all what Mackie says it does. The only objection to the kind of explanation given by Mill—that is, that in different locations different means are best used to reach happiness—is rejected because our specific moral judgments would be "objectively true, but only derivatively and contingently—if things had been otherwise, quite different sorts of actions would have been right."[16] Again, Mackie has imposed a requirement that does not belong. Unless objectivism results in objectively true specific moral judgments in a certain direct manner, and not via rules that are objectively true, it is not really objectivism. Where did this requirement come from? The only reason to include it is the supposition that a very strong certainty component must be part of objectivism. Mill and Dewey are "objectivists" who reject a

---

[13] Ibid., 101.

[14] J. L. Mackie, *Ethics: Inventing Right and Wrong* (New York: Penguin Books, 1977), 27–30. In these pages, Mackie is continuing the specification of what objectivity requires or is explained as. This is the view of what he calls "ordinary morality."

[15] Ibid., 36.

[16] Ibid., 37.

certainty component. No reasons are given why any such requirement is needed, and to include a certainty requirement that is stronger even than Descartes's is surely to construct a straw man position.

Does moral objectivity require the kind of metaphysical view that Moore held? Let us first note that Wong and the other subjectivists concentrate on value and not on right and wrong—on theory of value and not on theory of obligation. Theory of value is concerned with nonaction items, whereas theory of obligation is concerned with the evaluation of actions of persons. In both instances, the contemporary subjectivist attempts to point out the absence of a common standard that will prevent ultimate disagreements. This is sometimes put in terms of relativism because of the claim that within a culture there are standards that allow the resolution of disagreement. However, when we have different standards in different cultures, the ultimate disagreement is much clearer.[17] The response to the ultimate disagreement move and to disagreement across cultures claim is the same; as an empirical fact, no such disagreement is found. Certainly, Wong does not present any such evidence. Evidence of agreement can be based on claims such as those of John Ladd, a philosopher, or in terms of empirical studies by psychologists such as Lawrence Kohlberg.[18] The setting out of the claims in the conditionals noted in Chapter 5, though, was always done in terms of obligation or right, not in terms of value. Is value different in ways that establish the subjectivity of morality in this half of morality even if not in the action evaluation half? Let us see.

Moore thought that the meaning of 'good' was the unique property to which it referred. Let us grant that the meaning of moral terms is not reference to unique entities in the moral sphere. Are there other areas concerning which the meaning of the terms is not some object to which the term refers and yet the judgments that result are objectively true or false? The answer is clearly yes. Consider, for example, the relations *larger than* and *next to*. When I claim that *b* is higher than *a* in *that*, this is an objectively true assertion. We do not throw this into doubt by saying there is no *object* that is (the meaning of) *larger than*. The metaphysical status of relations is not very clear, though most agree the relation itself does not exist independently of things that are in the relation—there is no object that is the relation. From our unclarity concerning the metaphysical status of relations, though, it does not follow that the judgment that an object is larger than another or next to another is subjective or relative to a standard that exists within a culture. What we have, first, is an account of how to justify judgments of larger than. Following this, we need

---

[17]See Alasdair MacIntyre, *Whose Justice? Which Rationality?* (Notre Dame, In.: University of Notre Dame Press, 1988), ch. 1., for a very good discussion of this point.

[18]John Ladd, *The Structure of a Moral Code* (Cambridge: Harvard University Press, 1957); Lawrence Kohlberg, *The Psychology of Moral Development*, vol. 2 of *Essays on Moral Development* (New York: Harper and Row, 1984). See also the discussion in Chapter 2.

to find some metaphysical view of the status of the relation. We are not justified in rejecting some mistaken account of the metaphysical status and then concluding that the relation is subjective. If we do not now have an acceptable metaphysical theory of the nature of relations, let us keep looking.

Do we have an acceptable theory about how to justify judgments involving 'good'? That is, do we have an acceptable theory of value? We do if the theory defended by Mill, or Dewey, or Kant, or Aristotle, or MacIntyre, or . . . is the best one. Mackie and Wong seem to forget we are looking for the best view that accounts for the moral phenomena. They assert their own views as correct because one other view fails. Instead of this simplistic procedure, we need to look at the arguments the various authors present, and look at the complete theory—both the normative ethical theory and the metaethical theory. Present better views if you have them.

What is the correct metaphysical account of the status of intrinsic value? That is so far a secondary issue to the one discussed here, but a congenial theory is the pragmatic view expressed by C. S. Peirce and John Dewey that the metaphysical status is akin to that of *solution to problem*.[19] John Dewey likens a solution to a key that fits a lock. The key allows us to open the door, to get to where we aim to go. Is the relation of being a solution to a problem an object, either in this world or in another? Clearly not! Can we say that there are some objectively true or correct solutions to problems? It would seem so. What is the metaphysical status of something being a solution? It is not something that exists in a special realm, and it is not something that we introspect or directly know. A proposed solution is another kind of hypothesis or theory. We are justified in saying that something is a correct solution depending on the outcome of acting on it. The truth of the hypothesis is determined by the outcome. One way to contrast the pragmatic view with those of most rivals is to note that pragmatism offers "forward-looking" accounts while most rivals offer "backward-looking" accounts. There is not now something present that is the value—something to which we compare our value candidate to determine if it is valuable. Depending on the (future) outcome of an action, we are justified or not in making a value claim.

You may not accept the pragmatic account of the metaphysical status of value predicates. You may have another view in mind. You might prefer the kind of realist view that Richard Boyd posits or the quasi-realist view of Hillary Putnam.[20] Whatever the best account, though, of the metaphysical status

---

[19] The best statement of this kind of view is found in John Dewey, "The Logic of Judgments of Practise," *The Journal of Philosophy* 12, no. 19 (September 16, 1915). Reprinted in *Dewey and His Critics*, ed. S. Morgenbesser (Lancaster, Pa.: Lancaster Press, 1977), 567–585. See also Dewey, *Human Nature and Conduct*.

[20] See Boyd, "How to Be a Moral Realist" and Hillary Putnam, *The Many Faces of Realism* (LaSalle, Ill.: Open Court, 1987).

of value, we cannot establish its subjective or relativistic status by rejecting the view of G. E. Moore. Such a procedure is not legitimate because there are other options. One cannot establish relativism by rejecting absolutism, and one cannot establish the metaphysical subjectivism or projectivism of value by rejecting Moorean objectivism as the only realism. It is the same mistake. Much more needs to be said about the metaphysical status of value—philosophers need to engage in the theorizing needed to come up with a good solution to the problem of that status. However, failure to present a completely problem-free account no more shows that subjectivism is correct than the claim of the creationists that their own six days of creation view is true because of their correct observation that there are problems with the doctrine of biological evolution.

THE MORAL CONNECTION

The moral simples view of Moore would not, of course, have a problem concerning the nature of the connection between nonmoral and moral predicates, for those views suppose, at most, only an accidental connection. If you suppose only an accidental connection between a tennis ball and its color, you suppose that a tennis ball can be any color and that any relation between a tennis ball and its color is accidental; one that could easily be otherwise. It might be true at some time that all tennis balls were orange; then we could claim that all tennis balls *were* orange. However, we know that any color could be used for tennis balls. If we ask what is the connection between the predicates '*x* is a tennis ball' and '*x* is orange', we can say there is really no lawlike connection, no causal connection, no "metaphysical" connection, but only an accidental connection. According to the nonresultant model, the connection between any nonmoral property and any moral property is merely accidental.

Since the nonresultant theories have no concern with a connection between nonmoral and moral predicates, we shall not be concerned any further with such views. This leaves us, though, with the vast majority of ethical theories, for they do suppose moral predicates are resultant. What are some of the options before us?

1. Logical connection
2. Nonlogical necessary connection
3. Causal connection
4. Noncognitive connection
5. Moral connection

Logical Connection

Logical relations are clear instances of a connection between one set of predicates and another. This connection is seen most clearly in argument forms such as affirming-the-antecedent. If we establish that 'if p then q' and 'p', then 'q' follows. The connection between the first two claims and the third is logical. We can say that the first two are logically sufficient for the third, or that the nature of the connection is logical. When we have a logical connection, the denial of the part that is said to follow from the first in conjunction with the first results in a contradiction. If we assert 'If p, then q and p', and then deny 'q' by asserting 'not-q', we can derive the contradiction of 'q and not-q'.

Does the nonmoral claim provide a logical support for the moral part of the resultant theorist's basic unit? We are asking this of any theorist: whether the basic unit is $Fa \rightarrow Ma$ or $(x)(Fx \rightarrow Mx)$, and whether the rule is direct or indirect. It would seem that no matter what the unit, we cannot derive a contradiction from the assertion of the nonmoral part and the denial of the moral part. To see what the problem is, let us choose some theory, such as utilitarianism. A simple direct rule theory version of utilitarianism would maintain the rule "If any action maximizes the greatest good for the greatest number, then that action is obligatory." The F is the antecedent part, which is about maximizing the greatest good for the greatest number, and the M part concerns *obligation*. If we consider the negation of this rule—an instance in which the antecedent is true and the consequent false—the resulting statement "Some actions maximize the greatest good for the greatest number and they are not obligatory" does not seem to be self-contradictory. It is, of course, inconsistent with the original rule of which it is the contradiction, but it is not self-inconsistent. This constitutes evidence, concerning this one rule, that the relation is not one of logical sufficiency. It also would appear the same way if we were to consider any other rule and its negation, and any particular $Fa \rightarrow Ma$. If this latter were to be so, then we would have a good deal of evidence that the relation, no matter what ethical theory should turn out to be correct, is not one of logical sufficiency.

At this point you must guard against a tempting move. You might think that this argument against the moral connection's being logically sufficient works only against discredited theories and, if you chose a correct theory, the argument would not work. This response, though, confuses a self-contradiction with an inconsistency between two statements. Choose any claim whatsoever—for example, "The earth is a sphere"—and this statement and its negation when conjoined result in a contradiction. This does not show that the original statement is logically necessary. In a similar manner, choose any true if-then statement—for example, "If you eat ten hot dogs at one sitting, then you will have a stomachache"—and if you conjoin it with its negation, you will have an inconsistency, and a contradiction will be easy to come by. This does not, of course, show that eating ten hot dogs is logically sufficient for a stomachache, for it clearly is not.

Nonlogical Necessary Connection

There are kinds of sufficiency short of logical sufficiency that we must look at. One such purported relation involves some kind of necessary connection between properties or predicates, but not a logical one. Such claims as "If something is red, then it is colored" and "If anything is an event in the physical world, then it has a cause" are examples of such statements. It has turned out, most would agree, not to be possible to derive a contradiction from the negation of such claims, but they are somehow necessarily true. Perhaps the claim should be that the basic moral units are necessarily true and the connection between the *F*'s and the *M*'s is a necessary connection. This is an appealing view to people who hold a kantian position, for they are inclined to think that the categorical imperative, here interpreted as an indirect moral rule, is in this sense necessarily true. Kant indicates this position in the following passage:

> If then there is to be a supreme practical principle and—so far as the human will is concerned—a categorical imperative, it must be such that from the idea of something which is necessarily an end for every one because it is an *end in itself* it forms an *objective* principle of the will and consequently can serve as a practical law. The ground of this principle is: *Rational nature exists as an end in itself.* This is the way in which a man necessarily conceives his own existence.[21]

One does not have to be a kantian in normative ethics to hold to this kind of view. It would be more difficult to adapt this kind of view to the basic unit of the pragmatist, but there is no reason not to apply it to almost any theory—supposing it is the best account of the connection between nonmoral and moral predicates.

A view often associated with the "necessary connection" view is the corresponding account of our knowledge of the basic unit. A clear statement of this kind of view is found in the following passages from Sidgwick and Ross, respectively:

> The supreme rule of aiming at the general happiness, as I had come to see, must rest on a fundamental moral intuition, if I was to recognise it as binding at all.
>
> The Utilitarianism of Mill and Bentham seems to me to want a basis: that basis could only be supplied by a fundamental intuition.[22]

---

[21] Immanuel Kant, *The Moral Law: Kant's Groundwork of the Metaphysics of Morals*, trans. and analyzed by H. J. Paton (London: Hutchinson University Library, 1948), 96.

[22] Henry Sidgwick, *The Methods of Ethics* (London: Macmillan, 1962), xxix–xxi.

> That an act, *qua* fulfilling a promise, or *qua* effecting a just distribution of good, or *qua* returning services rendered, or *qua* promoting the good of others . . . is prima facie right, is self-evident. . . . It is self-evident just as a mathematical axiom, or the validity of a form of inference is evident. The moral order expressed in these propositions is just as much part of the fundamental nature of the universe . . . as is the spatial or numerical structure expressed in the axioms of geometry or arithmetic.[23]

The following passage from H. A. Prichard shows this view has been held by some who are intuitionists:

> The sense of obligation to do, or of the rightness of an action of a particular kind is absolutely underivative or immediate. The rightness of an action consists in its being the origination of something of a certain kind A in a situation of a certain kind, a situation consisting in a certain relation B of the agent to others or to his own nature. . . . But, given that by a process which is, of course, merely a process of general and not of moral thinking we come to recognize that the proposed act is one by which we shall originate A in relation to B, then we appreciate the obligation immediately or directly. . . .
>
> This apprehension is immediate, in precisely the senses in which a mathematical apprehension is immediate, e.g., the apprehension that this three-sided figure, in virtue of its being three-sided, must have three angles. Both apprehensions are immediate in the sense that in both insight into the nature of the subject directly leads us to recognize its possession of the predicate; and it is only stating this fact from the other side to say that in both cases the fact apprehended is self-evident.[24]

It is interesting to note that all three of the authors cited supposed that mathematical truths are not logical truths as discussed in the previous section. Their view is that mathematical and logical claims are descriptive of the world and necessary—but not in the manner now thought to be true of axiom systems. If we give up this view of logical knowledge, it would be more difficult to continue to hold this view concerning moral knowledge.

Causal Connection

People have proposed a variety of causal connections to explain the relation between *F*'s and *M*'s, but usually the causal connections are concerned with an explanation of why people accept something as being right or valuable.

---

[23] W. D. Ross, *The Right and the Good* (Oxford: Clarendon Press, 1930), 29–30. Reprinted by permission of the Oxford University Press.

[24] H. A. Prichard, "Does Moral Philosophy Rest on a Mistake?" in *Moral Obligation* (London: Oxford University Press, 1957), 7–8.

For example, cultural relativism is the view that the cause of our accepting any given moral rule is societal pressure, or training, or enculturation. This does not, of course, establish any normative theory as being correct, as we saw in Chapter 4. The same observation holds when we consider psychological egoism as a causal explanation of a person's holding a given moral judgment to be correct.

Some philosophers have argued that there are no evidential relations between nonmoral and moral predicates at all; there are only causal ones. If one were able to make this view understandable and plausible, then perhaps one could rehabilitate some form of egoism or relativism, but that remains to be seen.

Noncognitive Connection

Some philosophers don't worry about any connection between the parts in the basic moral unit, as such, for they emphasize the decision-making aspect or the emotional state of the *people* adopting some basic moral unit.

> To make a value-judgment is to make a decision of principle. To ask whether I ought to do A in these circumstances is . . . to ask whether or not I will that doing A in such circumstances should become a universal law.
>   . . . If pressed to justify a decision completely, we have to give a complete specification of the way of life of which it was a part. . . . In the end everything rests upon such a decision of principle. [A person] has to decide whether to accept that way of life or not; if he accepts it, then we can proceed to justify the decisions that are based upon it; if he does not accept it, then let him accept some other, and try to live by it.[25]

This is a view put forward most strikingly by the existentialists, who stress the fact that each of us *must* make such decisions, for no one else can make them for us. Even if we choose someone to adopt principles for us, we are responsible for choosing that person, and usually know which principles that kind of person will choose anyway.

When we ask of such a view what is the connection between nonmoral and moral predicates, the answer will be that it is the connection made by our choosing *that* as a principle or *that* as the action we will perform. In this sense, there is no connection between the predicates except the connection made by some person making a decision. The decision is not based on anything else within the area of morality, and for the people cited, it is not based on anything in some other area. It is not our "practical reason" that discovers a connection, or even forges it; it is something else. The explanation of what

---

[25] R. M. Hare, *The Language of Morals* (Oxford: Clarendon Press, 1952), 69–70. Reprinted by permission of the Oxford University Press.

exactly this something else is, though, we shall have to leave for those who hold the position.

A number of views hold that the connection between the F's and the M's is made not by your choosing or my choosing but by some more ideal person or persons choosing.

> Now since laws determine the ends as regards their universal validity, we shall be able—if we abstract from the personal differences between rational beings, and also from all the content of their private ends—to conceive a whole of all ends in systematic conjunction (a whole both of rational beings as ends in themselves and also of the personal ends which each may set before himself); that is, we shall be able to conceive a kingdom of ends which is possible in accordance with the above principles.
>
> For rational beings all stand under the *law* that each of them should treat himself and all others, *never merely as a means*, but always *at the same time as an end in himself*. . . .
>
> . . . This making of laws must be found in every rational being himself and must be able to spring from his will. The principle of his will is therefore never to perform an action except on a maxim such as can also be a universal law, and consequently such that the will can regard itself as at the same time making universal law by means of its maxim.[26]

Here Kant is apparently following up earlier suggestions of Rousseau:

> Each of us places in common his person and all his power under the supreme direction of the general will; and as one body we all receive each member an indivisible part of the whole.
>
> From that moment, instead of as many separate persons as there are contracting parties, this act of association produces a moral and collective body.[27]

The view that somehow human beings become ideal observers or judges when the particular characteristics and concerns are not counted is widespread in the history of philosophy. Sometimes a single being is posited, but usually we are to think of each of us as an ideal judge. This view is still common today.

> In justice as fairness the original position of equality corresponds to the state of nature in the traditional theory of the social contract. This original position is not, of course, thought of as an actual historical state of affairs, much less a primitive condition of culture. It is understood as a purely hypothetical situation characterized so as to lead to a certain conception of justice. Among the essential features of this situation is that no one knows his place in society, his class position or social status, nor does any one know his fortune in the distribution of natural assets and abilities, his intelligence, strength, and the like.[28]

[26]Kant, *The Moral Law*, 101.
[27]Jean-Jacques Rousseau, *The Social Contract* (New York: Hafner, 1964), 15.
[28]John Rawls, *A Theory of Justice* (Cambridge, Mass.: Harvard University Press, 1971), 12.

Rawls sets up the original position and then posits principles of justice that people in that state would legislate. What principles are legislated, or what moral rules—direct or indirect—are promulgated is not the primary focus of the theory. What is of concern here is that when we ask what connection there is between the nonmoral characteristics and the moral characteristics, we are given what looks like an epistemological answer based on the nature of human beings.

What has made Rawls's view so influential is how he has worked in so many elements from other theories and how he has shown how to apply his view to actual situations. The original position, for example, is described in the context of each person attempting to secure self-benefit. In order for me to secure my self-benefit without knowing what abilities or offices in society I occupy requires me to design a society in which everyone will benefit. This aspect, then, appeals to those who think that self-benefit is what we primarily aim at. Since I am a member of a group of similar seekers after the principles of justice behind the veil of ignorance, there is a contractarian element in any decision I and the others in the original position construct.[29] Rawls restricts his use of the original position to the construction of the indirect principles of justice, but others have used it to construct direct moral rules of the sort found in any normative ethical theory.

Rawls himself does not construct a normative ethical theory, though his principles of justice presumably would form part of any complete ethical theory. Because this is a work about ethical theory and not primarily about social or political philosophy, Rawls is not covered at length, and this short coverage does not reflect his importance in contemporary philosophy.

Human beings assert or judge the selected principles when they will as members of the kingdom of ends, or insofar as they are part of the general will, or in the original position. It is in this state or position that the reason of humans properly discovers moral principles. (We could hold a pragmatic theory coupled with this view, but it would be slightly different. It would maintain that any given singular conditional is one that will be willed by a person in such a position.)

Sometimes a single being—the ideal Observer or God—is thought to have certain characteristics that ensure the proper moral judgment, but for our purposes we shall not sharply distinguish this view from the others.

[29]The Gauthier book cited at the end of the chapter, *Morals By Agreement*, is a good statement of a clear commitment to a contractarian approach. The contractarian typically supposes we can make best sense of moral relations in human society by contrasting the society with a perhaps mythical presociety state. In this "state of nature" humans did not have morality as we now know it. When we entered society, though, we agreed to give up our "natural liberty" in exchange for the greater security of collective existence. Gauthier is the most influential contractarian as we near the end of the twentieth century, and he supposes that the Hobbesian framework of self-interest as the primary motivation is correct.

Moral rules would, in this kind of view, be justified as a result of their adoption when we enter civil society. In contrast, one could give a utilitarian justification—see Mill's view in the appendix to Chapter 3.

Moral Connection

What about the view that the connection between moral and nonmoral predicates is a *moral* connection? This is an answer that has to be put into context before it can be understood as making an intelligible claim. When we characterize any connection, we can use terms borrowed from outside the area in which this connection is used. For example, when we explain causal or physical connections, we can talk about similarities and differences between them and logical connections. We can say that when we assert "If any person is cut into pieces, burned to ashes and the ashes scattered in the ocean, then that person is dead," we can say that the antecedent is physically sufficient and not logically sufficient for the consequent. We can say that we are invoking a physical and not a logical law; that it would be physically impossible for the person to be alive but not logically impossible. (It would not be a contradiction to claim that the person was alive, although given what occurred, some physical laws we now think acceptable would turn out not to be acceptable.) We might try to avoid using the term 'physical' or 'logical' by talking about *sufficiency*, as in "The event mentioned in the antecedent is sufficient for the event mentioned in the consequent." However, the *kind* of sufficiency is what we are interested in, and that seems to require some additional word such as 'physical'.

Generally, we can talk about sufficiency in an area and say that it is explained by whatever turn out to be the correct theories in that area. If this is the model of explanation, we can do the same thing in ethics. We can say that a given antecedent is sufficient for a given consequent, given that indirect utilitarianism or some other theory is correct. We could then use the kind of language Mill and Kant use when they talk about the laws of morality. The principle of utility, for example, being the ultimate law of morality, would enable us to claim that it is impossible for a rule to be one that we act from, one that maximizes the greatest good for the greatest number, and yet not be a direct moral rule. This kind of response is pragmatic in its origin and use.

The term 'impossible' requires an explanation in terms of the theory—say, indirect utilitarianism—that is assumed to be correct. This is directly modeled on the claim that, for example, it is impossible for an unsupported body not to fall and it is impossible for something to be red and not red at the same time in the same respect. We refer, in those instances, to what we take to be a correct theory of physics and a correct theory of logic. What kind of sufficiency are we talking about then, in terms of this view? We can say it is moral sufficiency. This may strike you as unenlightening, but it is as enlightening as other answers from other areas. In addition, it allows us to explain the moral connection via the work done in normative ethics. From the point of view taken in this book, that is all right, for we know how to find the correct normative ethical theory.

Other Views of the Connection

Let us now briefly list other views about the connection between the moral and nonmoral predicates, keeping in mind that a full treatment of any view is not possible here. The marxists, or some varieties of that view, hold that the connection between the F's and the M's is explained in terms of the social function of a normative theory. Ethical theories are designed, consciously or not, to reflect the view of the ruling class—specifically to reflect what things they want to maintain. So, the capitalists will adopt moral rules that will tend to keep them in power as a class. Moral basic units are just the devices used by the ruling class in a given society to maintain its position. This is also true of the proletariat, although most marxists "prefer" the rules of the proletariat to those of the bourgeoisie.[30]

We might want to talk about a number of views that hold, in some sense, that it is an "illusion" to apply any moral predicate. Some people say that moral predicates are actually some other kind of predicate. Whenever we say that something is good, for example, we could say the same thing by saying that we like the thing or desire it. People holding this view and others related to it have gone under the names "subjectivist" and "emotivist." One might think a normative ethical theory, according to this view, would be a very simple matter of finding out what you like—this would be a version of egoism as a normative ethical theory. Many who hold such views, though, deny that there are normative ethical theories at all. For those who hold that it is an emotional preference for some rule or even some normative ethical theory, we might refer to Dewey's response to C. L. Stevenson's position, which is of that sort. Dewey insists that any emotive element is subject to cognitive considerations. Furthermore, he thinks it is a

> radical fallacy to convert the end-in-view into an inherent constituent of the means by which in genuinely moral sentences, the end is accomplished. To

---

[30]This is, of course, not an adequate treatment of marxist ethics. There is new and interesting work being done in the field of ethics by marxists now that this view has been freed from its connection with the government of the Soviet Union. Please see some of the entries in the bibliography. There is, though, the additional problem of trying to say what a marxist ethics is. "Marxists, in fact, have failed to develop an original or comparatively coherent view of ethics that can be ranked as a 'type of ethical theory' finding its natural place beside utilitarian ethics" [Eugene Kemenka, *Marxism and Ethics* (New York: St. Martin's Press, 1969), 1].

Engels says briefly what a good number of marxists have continued to say since:

> The Fuerbachian theory of morals fares like all its predecessors. It is designed to suit all periods, all peoples and all conditions, and precisely for that reason it is never and nowhere applicable. It remains, as regards the real world, as powerless as Kant's categorical imperative. In reality every class, even every profession, has its own morality, and even this it violates whenever it can do so with impunity.

[Frederick Engels, "Feuerbach and the End of Classical German Philosophy," in *Karl Marx and Frederick Engels: Selected Works* (Moscow: Progress Publishers, 1970), 607].

take the cases in which 'emotional' factors accompany the giving of reasons as if this accompaniment factor were an inherent part of the judgment is, I submit, both a theoretical error and is, when widely adopted in practice, a source of moral weakness.[31]

So, what is the nature of the connection between nonmoral and moral predicates? A variety of answers has been proposed and many of them have been reviewed here, but we have made no attempt to select one. Given your choice of a normative theory and your commitment to other philosophical positions, one of the views is likely to interest you more than others. For now we can say at least that we see the place of the question's answer in relation to the main task of our work—namely, discovering the best normative ethical theory.

HUMAN NATURE AND MORAL PHILOSOPHY

In a course of choosing a normative ethical theory, we made a number of decisions about human nature. In rejecting psychological egoism and psychological altruism, we denied that humans are entirely self-regarding or that they are entirely other-regarding—at least not by nature. A psychological theory of motivation that proposed only one source of motivation, either to benefit oneself or to benefit others, would not be acceptable. However, this is not to say that someone could not posit a goal to act in either way. It might be that we reserve the term 'selfish' for those who choose to act only for self-benefit and the term 'saint' for those who choose to act only for the benefit of others. Are either of these ways better? That, of course, depends on what has value. The theory of value investigation did not reveal that only one character trait, say, altruism/selfishness, had value/disvalue. If we hold that many things have intrinsic value, then neither of these views of which character trait ought to be cultivated is acceptable.

When we rejected psychological hedonism, we thereby denied that only one goal is sought by human beings. If we had affirmed this view, it would have told us a great deal about human nature, and it would have provided us with a simple model of what human nature is. When we deny any view that suggests that we pursue only one goal, we thereby complicate the model we have of human nature. So from the discussions in theory of value and theory of obligation, we find that we have adopted a view of human nature that takes human beings to be complicated, operating from a variety of motives and pursuing a variety of goals. In short, humans are difficult to describe in any one way.

---

[31] The review, "Ethical Subject Matter and Language," was published in *The Journal of Philosophy*, vol. 42, no. 26 (December 20, 1945). It is reprinted in S. Morgenbesser, *Dewey and His Critics* (Lancaster, Pa.: Lancaster Press, 1977), 678. Page references are to the reprinted version.

The topic of human nature is eternally new, and new theories or new variations on old theories are always being discussed. A recent view is included in the view called *sociobiology*. W. D. Hamilton's discussion of inclusive fitness has given rise to a variety of positions involving that and related notions. The following passages from Irven DeVore gives a flavor of what is being discussed:

> We're learning about many other kinds of behavior that could not be explained without an understanding of adaptation, including a genetic theory of inclusive fitness which Darwin couldn't have known about: essentially, any behavior that leads an individual to leave fewer offspring. Why are there sterile castes of bees and ants, for example? Why would any animal risk its life to help another? Why, when a predator approaches, would an animal give a warning cry to other animals, attracting the predator's attention to itself, rather than just fleeing quietly? . . .
>
> The answers began to come out of a theoretical approach to behavior that was emerging. . . . First developed by W. D. Hamilton in 1965 and quickly picked up by other biological theorists like John Maynard Smith, G. C. Williams, Robert Trivers, E. O. Wilson, and Richard Alexander, it pointed out what Darwin could never have seen; namely, that it is misleading to focus a theory of evolution on individuals or even clusters of individuals. What you are really interested in is the *genes*, because it is only the genes that are passed on to future generations.
>
> . . . We are ultimately concerned not with individuals, but with individual genes and their replicas in other members of the species—what we call an individual's inclusive fitness.[32]

Is it true that our genes are "selfish"? Are we programmed or hard-wired to act in certain ways so as to maximize our genotype or at least create as close an approximation to it as we can secure? This kind of approach, taken by those involved in the movement known as sociobiology, is countered by others in the biological sciences. Herbert Simon, for example, claims the opposite. In the following, he uses 'docile' to refer to the trait of being receptive to social influence. His argument is that altruism among humans would have survival value.

> [T]here may be certain altruistic behaviors that, although costly to the fitness of the individual who exhibits them, have more than a compensating advantage for other individuals in the society.
>
> A society that instilled such behaviors in its docile members would grow more rapidly than one that did not; hence such behaviors would become,

---

[32]Irven DeVore, "The New Science of Genetic Self-Interest" *Psychology Today*, February 10, 1977, 44.

by evolution at the social level, a part of the repertory of proper behaviors of successful societies.[33]

Simon also argues that societies that were altruistic would prosper and that altruism would prosper within such societies. So, within societies, there are evolutionary advantages to the individuals who are altruistic. We don't have to rehearse all the arguments, for those who are interested can follow the continuing debate.

There is not time to explore the implications of such views, but the usual concerns will arise. Shall we add this feature to a theory of motivation? Shall we attempt directly to draw normative conclusions from such theories? One would have a difficult time defending the view that an individual's only motive is to replicate his or her genes in other members of the species. Perhaps the motive is not a conscious motive having to do with voluntary actions at all. How could we set up a scientific experiment to test between the selfish gene theory and the altruistic gene theory of Simon? These are the kinds of concerns we would have to pursue were we seriously to take up this view.

Sometimes we ask if human beings are by nature good or by nature evil. If this is the question of whether human beings, in fact, pursue only what they perceive as good, the answer is apparently no. It frequently happens that we decide, as best we can, what is good (what has the most intrinsic value) in a given set of circumstances and then find that we do not pursue it. This happens, as we say, even when we are free to do so. We think, for example, that it is to our interest not to eat foods high in saturated fats, to cut down on the amount of food eaten, and to get plenty of rest. Yet we find ourselves eating potato chips, pastry, and all manner of other such foods in great quantities far into the night. This is sometimes described as the problem of weakness of will; we fail to act in ways that we apparently know are right and fail to pursue goals that we apparently know are the best in a given set of circumstances.

Many philosophers have claimed there is really no such weakness of will phenomenon, for if we really accepted the action as right and the goal as the best one, then we would act in the appropriate manner. It is difficult, when we concentrate on our own experiences, though, to accept this view. Unless someone provides a theory of human nature that shows such a connection, it would be difficult to accept the theory as stated.

FREE WILL

Related to weakness of will is the problem of free will. Although this is a very difficult issue to be clear about and a difficult one to discuss briefly, here is a try. We would all agree that part of the phenomena is the apparent fact

---

[33]Herbert A. Simon, "A Mechanism for Social Selection and Successful Altruism," *Science*, December 1990, 1647.

that unless people are responsible for an action, they cannot be said to be doing what is right or wrong; that unless they can do and avoid an action, they have no obligation concerning that action. Sometimes this set of claims is stated in a shorthand way as "ought implies can." We can say that unless people are responsible, then no judgments of obligation, including right and wrong, are justified. More schematically, with M standing for any term of obligation, we have:

> If any person a is justifiably judged to have performed an M action, then person a is responsible for that action.

Furthermore, if a person is responsible for an action, then the person is free, in some way, both to perform the action and to abstain from performing it. These are both, as we say, options open to the person before the action is done.

> If any person a is responsible for performing an action, then person a is free to perform that action and free to abstain from performing the action.

When we assert these two if-then claims, we do not thereby assert either of the antecedents or deny either of the consequents. Furthermore, and more seriously, we have not specified the way in which people have to be free for even the if-then statements to be true. Some people assume that in order for someone to be free, the causal order must be "suspended"—the person must act contracausally. If this were not so, such people reason, then we would have to suppose that people are caused to do what they do by education, social pressure, character, and the like. Such causal influences are beyond the power of people to alter, so it is said, and thus no one is free to perform an action or to abstain from doing it if the causal conditions for doing one or the other are present. Others, however, claim that no such contracausal freedom is needed; all that is required is the absence of coercion or force. There is a difference between having a device attached to your hand that exerts a force beyond your physical strength to resist and causes your finger to tighten on a trigger, thus causing someone to be shot and your doing this without such coercive influences. It is the lack of force and coercion that is the test of freedom, and not some contracausal activity.

We shall not attempt to settle this complicated issue here. However, you are directed to the readings at the end of the chapter, which will lead you to fuller discussions that might enable you to make up your mind about the nature of *freedom*. Notice that any ethical theory is correct, and we go about determining whether a given action is right, say, or not, then any decision we reach would be an instance of affirming the antecedent of the first two if-then statements. This would entitle us to conclude that some people are responsible for some actions, and *this* would, in conjunction with the second if-then statement, allow us to conclude that such people are free to perform those actions or to abstain from them. This would lead us to say that it is a moral phenomenon that people are free, although it would not tell us what it is for people to be free. It is at this point that we shall leave the issue.

RELATED NORMATIVE CONCERNS

There are a number of concerns related to our main normative concerns that we have not directly discussed, or discussed only in passing. We shall identify these concerns in this section and, where possible, relate them to tasks already performed.

Skepticism, Amoralism, Nihilism

General skepticism was discussed in Chapter 1, but we found no reason to adopt the view that we know nothing or that we are not justified in asserting anything. The main reasons for holding to skepticism seemed to be the "possibility" argument coupled with the view that what we know cannot possibly be false. However, there are good reasons not to adopt the first position, and no reason to adopt the second. Since we use what appear to be justified judgments (for example, we plot the course of spacecraft to Mars and land the craft on that planet successfully), there is reason to suppose that some of our judgments are justified. The explanation of a judgment being justified was given in terms of a theory explaining a set of phenomena. This explanation applies, apparently, to moral phenomena as well as to any other kind of phenomena. Someone could claim that there is a difference in the relation, but then we would have to see the difference that is supposed to make a difference in terms of justification. Of course, someone may have a special account of how the basic units within the area of morality are to be explained, but, as we saw in the section on the moral connection, that is apparently compatible with any normative theory we adopt. We shall consider, then, the position that we cannot justifiably claim that one normative ethical theory is better than any other or, put negatively, that each fails to be justified. Although this moral skepticism would follow from general skepticism, there is apparently no way to establish the general view.

People sometimes distinguish moral skepticism from amoralism and nihilism. *Amoralism* is the view that moral terms have no peculiar sense, and that all that one wishes to claim by use of moral predicates and terms can be claimed by using other terms. According to this view, morality is in some sense an illusion. Because we cannot discuss all the views that hold that morality is an illusion, I shall try to address a kind of amalgam position. According to this view:

> In the world everything is as it is and happens as it does happen. *In* it there is no value—and if there were, it would be of no value.[34]

---

[34] Ludwig Wittgenstein, *Tractatus Logico-Philosophicus* (London: Routledge, 1955), 183 (6, 51).

There are no moral phenomena at all, but only a moral interpretation of phenomena.[35]

Using the categories of this book, the amoralist thinks that normative ethical theories are all mistaken. It is true, they would be wise to concede, that there is something to explain. We have to explain choices; we have to explain a feeling of what is called "obligation"; and we have to explain a good deal more phenomena of this type. However, the view holds that all the theories that propose the application of obligation and value predicates are mistaken—there is another theory that does a better job than any of those, and it does not use any of the moral notions.

Let us choose one such theory, look briefly at the reasons given, and then respond on behalf of those who suppose that some normative theory does a better job than the nonnormative (amoralist) theory. The theory of amoralism, then, claims:

1. No judgments containing normative predicates (such as *right* and *good*) are justified.
2. Normative utterances have a function—namely, to make society secure and ensure its continuance.
3. All the phenomena normative ethical theories attempt to explain can be explained by the function of moral utterances and perhaps by some theory about the psychological or sociobiological state of human beings.

The claim that all singular moral judgments fail to be justified is not the claim that they are all deficient but that some others might be discovered someday that are not deficient. Such judgments fail to be unjustified for the same reason they fail to be justified. It is part of many Buddhist positions that both the affirmative and the negative judgments are to be rejected as illusions. Some Buddhists apply this view not only to morality but to judgments in all areas. However, let us here understand the view as claiming that there is no justification for this (moral) kind of judgment.

Suppose, as seems to be true, that we no longer believe that such a thing as caloric fluid exists. We suppose that the phenomena concerning fire are explainable without the positing of such a substance. All judgments that have caloric fluid notions in them fail to be justified, except those that claim there is no such thing as that fluid. The judgments internal to the theory are, of

---

[35]Friedrich Nietzsche, *Beyond Good and Evil*, trans. Walter Kaufmann (New York: Vintage Books, 1966), 85. Interestingly enough, as a pragmatist I can agree with this stance. The phenomena of physics do no come labeled as physics phenomena; only when we construct theories that are clearly physics theories can we identify the phenomena these theories explain as physics phenomena. Nothing is lost if we say the same thing about moral phenomena. No phenomena come labeled as belonging to a certain area independently of a theory in that area, so this is no different for normative ethical theories.

course, consistent. We can have a systematic presentation of that theory, but the theory has no counterpart in reality. The ancient Greeks posited a number of gods to account for such phenomena as rain and the growth of plants. They then set forth a description of the relation of the gods to each other. We do not precisely or correctly describe our view if we say that Zeus doesn't rain unless we add that rain has nothing to do with Zeus. Did god x marry goddess y? Was the plot to revenge the death of god x by god y of this type or that? What is true, as we suppose, is that the phenomenon of rain does not require reference to gods at all. So all the judgments about what happens in the internal affairs of the gods is empty talk—it is about nothing. This is the way moral language is viewed by amoralists. Somehow we have gotten off the right track and have constructed elaborate theories about the workings of something called "morality"—but there is really no such thing.

The second claim—that the function of moral language is to serve the interests of society—is easier to understand. There is the phenomenon of the use of moral language, and this has to be explained. We also have to understand why people feel guilty if they do not do what they suppose is morally obligatory, and other action-related phenomena. One way to account for these phenomena is to point to the social function of morality, particularly moral language. When people suppose that they have moral obligations, it is easier to make societies work, for people can be relied on; they are more inclined to work hard, to pay debts, to feed their children; and so on. Amoralists claim to account for this phenomenon—that people believe themselves to have moral obligations—by the supposition of the social usefulness of these beliefs. Chemists draw pictures to help talk about their subject matter; they draw lines and talk about bonds in order to arrive at conclusions. Do chemists believe there are things like lines that bond? People postulate Santa Claus so that their children will behave, but they do not suppose there is such a being. (Even if they do suppose such a being exists, they are mistaken.) We might all find it useful to postulate the existence of Santa Claus if we could find that it prevented war or could bring something good (as we say) into existence. If we did that, we would be doing something of the sort the amoralist claims about morality.

The third claim—that we can explain all the phenomena normative theories handle without the use of normative notions—would really require an extensive investigation of some amoralist theory. However, we have seen something of that kind of explanation suggested in the treatment of moral language and behavior. In addition, we would want to see what kind of theory of motivation is proposed. For the rest of this third part, we can see what would have to be done by offering a critical analysis of the theory as outlined.

The first claim is one that requires comparison with the best normative ethical theories in order to arrive at a decision. We know what the claim of the amoralist is, but is it a justified claim? This question has to be determined in the same way we justify any claim that a theory does a better job than its rivals in explaining a range of phenomena.

The second claim can be handled more directly, for as it is stated, it does not apparently do the job that the amoralist wants. To see this, consider similar claims made about other areas of human concern and a different range of phenomena. Instead of talking about normative utterances, let's talk about human contrivances, the fruits of technology. Such devices have historically made society more secure and have usually ensured its continuance. The use of weapons against animals certainly made society more secure, and the use of dams and other devices ensured a supply of water for crops. Shall we say of technology and all the machines we have built that since they have this social function, they have no reality and that there is no fact of the matter other than the desire of society to be safe and to ensure its continuance? This appears to be a clear instance in which this inference is not justified. However, if it is not justified here, then it would seem that we need some reason why it is justified in the morality instance.

It is not open to the amoralist to insist that there is a difference between technology and morality in that there is some fact of the matter about technology but none concerning morality. At this point, this decision depends on whether amoralism or one of the normative theories is correct. Because this is the case, the claim cannot be simply asserted without some kind of evidence. The simple assertion otherwise begs the question at hand.

It is interesting to note that this move of the amoralist is not open to those who are inclined to take an extreme Buddhist view claiming the inapplicability of any concepts and any theories to anything. We shall return to this kind of extreme view shortly.

The amoralist is apparently committed to claiming not just that normative judgments and actions have a social function, but that the social function is the total explanation of such judgments and actions. Otherwise we could agree that the social function exists, but in addition adopt any one of the normative ethical theories examined in this book. But why should we believe that there is only the social function and none of the other functions described by the normative theories so far discussed? Why should we not think that there is a moral fact of the matter along with facts of the matter?[36] The final answer, again, would have to lie in a comparison of the best amoralist view with what we take to be the best normative ethical theory. We can, though, forestall some bad moves that are not open to any amoralist.

No one can claim, without inconsistency, that the reason we decide to abstain from using moral language is that it is bad for individuals and society. This use of a value notion *bad* is inconsistent with the claims of the theory. This is also true of any claim to the effect that we *ought* not to use moral language. Someone might say, though, that the use of 'ought' in this context means that we are making a mistake because amoralism is the best theory

---

[36]To say there is a fact of the matter is not to presuppose some metaphysical view about the nature of *good* or *ought*.

in the area. Yes, we might say, when amoralism is established, then we will be justified in making that claim. However, the notion of *prudence* might be used to explicate the 'ought'. It might be that the amoralist is saying that the prudential course is not to use such language as 'right' and 'good'. However, this will not do, for prudence appears to have as part of its explanation an aim at good and an avoidance of evil. It is not prudential to walk across the river when it is iced over because the ice is likely to break. If the ice breaks, we shall fall in and drown or, at best, receive an extremely chilling experience. These are things that we suppose have negative value; they are either extrinsically or intrinsically disvaluable.

Finally, the amoralists may be confused about the position and really be aiming to defend some kind of noncognitivism. They may wish to claim that our choice of normative ethical theory is a function of our affective life and not of any rational process. This, though, is a different claim and is discussed elsewhere (see pages 285–286).

So, we are justified in rejecting amoralism pending a reply on the part of some irate amoralist who will accuse us of failing to understand the view properly, or some amoralist who compares his or her view, fully worked out, with some range of the normative theories thus far considered. Perhaps some feel that such views have been presented by the stoics or the Buddhists. We shall see.

Nihilism is usually very much the same view as amoralism, but insofar as it is different, it is the view that nothing has value at all. It is a kind of moral despair rather than a kind of moral skepticism or a replacement theory, as is amoralism. However, once again, whether this is true or not depends on whether any of the theories of value is acceptable, and whether they apply. If they do, as has been argued in Chapter 6, then nihilism is not justified.

The strategy of discussing these kinds of views is to engage them into the mechanism of normative ethical theories. Once that is done, all the results of that area are applicable, and we can use the tried-and-true strategies developed there.

Social and Political Theory

There are a number of concerns that are normative. Ethics is one, but so are aesthetics, philosophy of religion, and social and political philosophy. In the latter areas, we are concerned with the kind of political system we ought to adopt, and the kind of society we should strive to establish. If we use value notions, we should ask which of the many societies we could strive to establish is best, and which political system is best. However we state the normative concern in those areas, it is obvious that we will make use of whatever normative ethical theory we have worked out to answer these questions. This is not to say that ethics is "first" or more important. Whatever normative ethical theory we adopt has to be usable for social and political concerns, and whatever social and political theory we choose will have to be consistent with our ethical theory.

Some political theories seem to go naturally with some ethical theories. J. S. Mill thought that utilitarianism and representative democracy went together quite well, for example. Thomas Hobbes seemed to suppose that a version of ethical egoism and monarchism went together in a natural way. If we were to continue this work into the area of social and political philosophy, we would list the phenomena (as we did for ethics), state the main theories, evaluate them, and finally indicate which of those before us appeared to do the best job in explaining the phenomena. In the course of doing this, we would have to say, for every such theory, how it related to various ethical theories. This is a task that will not, obviously, be carried out here.

Religion

Religion is another normative area we have said almost nothing about, but which is related very closely in many people's minds with normative ethics. We discussed the area of religion when we examined the Ten Commandments theory and the appendix to Chapter 6. It was suggested, negatively, that we cannot suppose that what it *is* for an action to be right, say, is for God to approve or command it. This does not preclude people supposing that God provides guidance in our daily lives or that moral revolutions are divinely inspired. Many moral reformers, such as the anti-slavery people in the United States, for example, supposed themselves to be carrying out a divine mission. The only stake normative ethical theory has here is to point out the independence of the moral correctness of the cause from God calling upon people to carry it out. To borrow from Plato, God calls upon people to perform actions because they are right; they are not right because He calls upon them to carry them out. This is a claim that anyone, theist or atheist, can suppose is true.

One of the roles religions play is to provide models or paradigms of action for people. This is an important feature of our moral lives, and yet almost nothing has been said about it. Philosophers often talk about emulating the life of Socrates, but Christians much more frequently choose the life of Jesus; Buddhists, the life of Gautama. This is a strategy to follow: Select the life of a good person and emulate it so far as you can if you seek to be a good person. This advice, though, requires that we know what a good life is independently of fulfilling the advice, for otherwise we could not rationally choose this life rather than that to emulate. In addition, we must frequently make judgments about how far to depart from the life we emulate. For example, would you choose to wander about the streets, as did Socrates, or would you attempt to get a job and talk with others interested in philosophy in places such as bars? In terms of this view of the role of religion in our moral lives, it is an aid and offers a guide, but it is no substitute for the tasks of normative ethics—especially the task of choosing the best normative theory.

Other Ideologies

The kinds of comments made about religion apply also to various ideological movements. Marxism, existentialism, feminism, and liberalism are movements that frequently have an attendant normative ethical theory, although it would seem that almost any normative theory is compatible with most ideological positions. If you adopt an ideology, you adopt a theory with a very broad scope—one that purports to explain the place of human beings in society, the nature of the relations of people to each other, and frequently many nonhuman phenomena also. Insofar as this is so, these ideologies can play the same role as a religious view in providing a general explanation or theory about how all the phenomena fit together within one coherent theoretical system. You can find your moral paradigm—for example, Lenin—within the ideology, just as one can from religions. If you are an existentialist, of course, you will emphasize the necessity of each person choosing his or her own paradigm.

Some normative ethical theories go well with some of the ideologies and some don't fit very well at all. If you are a marxist, for example, you are not likely to suppose that only pleasure has value, for the value placed on freedom is very high. Similarly, though, many marxists in the past have adopted some form of ethical relativism. This is not so common now, however, as marxists have continued their research into normative ethics.

Pragmatism as a philosophical movement has had more influence on contemporary American philosophy than any other. I consider myself to be a descendant of Peirce, James, Dewey, Lewis, Quine, and others who have worked out the views known as pragmatism. These views have become so much a part of the philosophical landscape, however, that it is difficult to pick out any one aspect that is unique. In normative ethics I hope to have satisfied Dewey's concern about the interconnected nature of means and ends by defining intrinsic value in such a way that something of intrinsic value can always be something of extrinsic value also. By choosing a pragmatic theory, I hope to have realized the claim of Peirce about the changing nature of problems and the flexibility that must be built into any method. Might there not be many different pragmatic ethics? If there is an ideology that is pragmatic, then what I say about other ideologies applies here. However, ethical theories have certainly been developed by pragmatists. Such theories range from a sketchy ideal-observer-type theory developed by Peirce, to James's interest version of utilitarianism, to Dewey's naturalistic theory, to C. I. Lewis's complicated epistemological account. My hope is that the pragmatic view presented here provides another kind of normative ethical theory that is consistent with the basic positions in epistemology and metaphysics taken by those who are most clearly pragmatists.

PARADIGMS

All the talk about moral paradigms in the last section leads me to construct a view influenced by Kuhn's work in philosophy of science. Every society adopts a moral code, describable by an ethical theory, that is suitable for solving certain problems in the society. The code is adopted because some kind of crisis develops in the use of a different code. For example, the Hebrews used the rules of Abraham and their other forefathers right through their stay in Egypt. However, the exodus from Egypt brought on a crisis, due no doubt to the destruction of the structure of their society as it had existed in Egypt. A moral genius, Moses, devised a new moral code, the Ten Commandments, which was able to solve the problems associated with the crisis. This code became the standard and offered a standard way of solving moral problems. Solutions to moral problems were derived from making the appropriate use of this new paradigm.

According to this view, the moral history of humanity is just the history of the replacement of old moralities with new moralities, of old paradigms with new paradigms. We can see, if we accept this view, Christianity replacing Judaism, Islam replacing Christianity, and so on. Of course, the 'and so on' is difficult to make out, for a number of phenomena will be very difficult to account for. However, the exact details of this view should be left to those who are interested in developing it.

The question that interests us here is the relation of this kind of view to the main enterprise of developing a strategy for evaluating normative ethical theories. Insofar as the paradigm view suggests that the only test for the acceptability of any singular moral judgment is a standard accepted by a society, then that view is the same as the indirect relativism view discussed in Chapter 4. The only additional point of interest is the use of the notion of *paradigm* and its application from philosophy of science. However, it does not seem that this notion makes any difference in the acceptability of a normative theory.

It may be that the theory of paradigms makes sense of the change of rules, but notice that this is a view that fits in well with a pragmatic theory. The changing of sets of summary rules may well be described by the paradigm shifts that philosophers are wont to talk about; this kind of explanation would not itself constitute a normative ethical theory, however, but rather a sociological theory offering an explanation of why moral rules are changed. This shift would not by itself tell us anything about the nature of the rules that are given up or adopted. We would have to determine this within the context of normative ethics—and, I hope, the strategies that are usefully within this context have been made clear.

A FINAL WORD

The title of this book, *Ethical Theory: Strategies and Concepts* describes what is contained in it. It does not tell us, though, how the concerns of normative ethics are connected with other philosophical matters, let alone how philosophical matters are connected with concerns in other areas. The development of a more complete philosophical context, a more complete account of all justified judgments and not just justified normative judgments, and a fuller treatment of the many metaphysical issues would help to illuminate the conclusions drawn here. Such an enterprise would not begin with an examination of rival normative ethical theories using a strategy developed for such a purpose but with the exposition of what is taken to be a correct ethical theory and what is required for it. We would need to find out what kind of epistemology and metaphysics is required and what view of science must be supposed. This task is not required for the work in this book to stand, for the two tasks would be mutually supportive.

The final advice for those who have worked their way through this book and have made it to this last paragraph is to be as critical as they can. Don't accept any theory without thinking about why you should. If there are lessons to be learned, they are lessons of methods and not of truths.

RECOMMENDED READING

Ayer, A. J. *Language, Truth, and Logic.* New York: Dover, 1946. The author claims that moral judgments are not true or false but only express or evince emotions.

Barnes, Hazel E. *An Existential Ethics.* New York: Vintage Books, 1967.

Firth, Roderick. "Ethical Absolutism and the Ideal Observer." *Philosophy and Phenomenological Research* 12 (1952): 317–345. This is also to be found in Sellars and Hospers, eds. *Readings in Ethical Theory* (see below).

Gauthier, David. *Morals by Agreement.* London: Oxford University Press, 1986.

Prichard, H. A. *Moral Obligation.* Oxford: Clarendon Press, 1949.

Sellars, W., and John Hospers, eds. *Readings in Ethical Theory.* New York: Appleton-Century-Crofts, 1970. This anthology contains a number of very good articles that will give you a "flavor" of twentieth-century metaethics.

Stevenson, C. L. *Ethics and Language.* New Haven, Conn.: Yale University Press, 1944. This work is one of the most completely worked out noncognitivist theories available.

Wellman, Carl. *The Language of Ethics.* Cambridge, Mass.: Harvard University Press, 1961.

INDEX

Abraham, 297
Acceptance. *See* Knowledge
Addition test, 226-230, 231, 232, 233
   organic unities compared to, 226-228, 233
Ad hoc devices, 25, 229
Agapism
   as theory of obligation, 10, 131, 133, 150-152
   as theory of value, 232
Alexander, R., 287
Allen, J. L., 62n
Alsstatt, L., 61
Altruism, psychological, 50-53, 223
Amoralism, 290-294
Antecedent, defined, 15
Arguments, 19
   deductive, 19, 20, 162
   inductive, 20, 21, 146, 147, 163-65, 172, 173
   knowledge and, 29, 30
Aristotle, 9, 127, 142, 190, 191, 276
Aronfreed, 58, 59

Basic notions, within ethics, 263-271
   contrasted with derived, 267
   in theory of obligation, 211, 218, 219
   in theory of value, 211-218

Basic units
   among areas, 265, 267, 279
   explained, 265, 270, 271
   of nonrule theories, 185, 186, 246-48, 268
   of relativism, 269
   of rule theories, 171
   value theories and, 241, 242
   within areas, 265
Beneficence, 143
   duties of (Ross), 140, 141
   principle of (Frankena), 143
Benefit, 43, 44, 99-101, Ch. 2 and 5 passim
Bentham, J., 102, 105, 184
Berkowitz, L., 60, 97
Biased statistics, 21
Boas, F., 158
Boyd, R., 273, 276
Boydston, J. A., 197
Buchanan, W., 61
Buddhism, 293, 294, 295

Capitalism-egoism, 91, 93, 94
Caring, 96
Categorical imperative (Kant), 153, 154
Categorical rules. *See* Rules, categorical
Cognitive developmental theories, 88-97

299

Cognitivism, 9, 276, 277
Communism, 128
Comparative moral judgments, 244–247
Competitionism, 126, 127
Conditional agreement, method of. See
   Moral negotiation
Consequent, defined, 15
Constitutive rules. See Rules, constitutive
Contracausal action, 289
Contraries, defined, 52, 53
Counterexample, explained, 51, 52
Cultural relativism, 161. See also
   Relativism

Darwin, C., 287
Definitions
   reportive, 32, 33
   stipulative, 31, 32
   theories and, 33
Degler, C., 158
Deontological theories of obligation, 15,
   131–169
   agapism as, 131, 133 (fig.), 150–152
   based on categorical rules, 133 (fig.),
      133–137, 150–167
   based on prima facie rules, 133 (fig.),
      138–150
   compared with nonrule theories, 196,
      197, 246, 248
   compared with a pragmatic theory,
      197
   contrasted with teleological theories,
      14, 16, 131–132
   formalist and nonformalist position
      on, 14, 15, 16
   kantianism as, 133 (fig.), 152–158
   multiple rule, 133 (fig.), 133–150
   relativism as, 133 (fig.), 158–167
   rule theories of, criticized, 202–210
   single-rule, 133 (fig.), 150–168
   Ten Commandments, 6, 9, 135–137,
      150
   See also Nonrule theories, of
      obligation
Derived units, 267. See also Basic units
Descartes, R., 182
Devore, I., 287
deVries, B., 96 n

Dewey, J., 181–186, 274, 276, 286, 296
Direct rules, 17, 18
Disagreement, moral. See Moral
   disagreement
Disbenefit, positive, 76
Distributive justice. See Justice,
   distributive
Disvalue, intrinsic, definition of, 214
Duty, 139–142

Egoism, 39–87, 222–224
   combined with utilitarianism,
      133–135
   compared with utilitarianism, 122,
      123
   connection between psychological and
      ethical, 42, 70–74
   as an ethical theory, 40, 41
   human nature and, 286–288
   as a theory of motivation, 40
   See also Egoism, ethical; Egoism,
      psychological
Egoism, ethical, 41, 64–89
   connection with psychological egoism
      and, 42, 70–74
   direct, 74–77
   evaluated, 77–85
   indirect, 75, 76
Egoism, psychological, 40, 42–63
   compared with psychological altruism,
      50–53
   compared with psychological realism,
      53, 54
   and connection with ethical egoism,
      42, 70–74
   empirical, 45, 57–63
   nonempirical, 46–56
   primary motive version of, 44
Emotive force, 28
Emotivism, 8, 285
Ends. See Goals
Engels, F., 285 n
Enumeration, induction by, 21, 163–165,
   172, 173. See also Arguments,
   inductive
Epistemism, 35
Equality, 127, 128. See also Justice
Ethical relativism, 160–167

Ethics
    political theory, 294, 295. *See also*
        specific theories such as Communism,
        Competitionism
    religion and, 295, 296. *See also*
        Buddhism, God
    social theory and, 294, 295
Evidence, 29, 30
Ewing, A. C., 271
Existentialism, 180, 181, 281
Explanation. *See* Theories, as explanations
    of phenomena
Extrinsic disvalue, 214
Extrinsic value, 213

F, 13
    in deontological theories, 15
    in teleological theories, 15, 211
    in theories of obligation, 14, 15 (fig.),
        211, 220
    in theories of value, 15 (fig.)
Fallacies, 20
Fellner, C., 60
Fisher, S., 107
Fletcher, J., 168
Formalists, 14, 15
Frankena, W. K., 122, 127 n, 132,
    133 (fig.), 143, 144, 147, 203,
    204, 207
Free will, 288, 289
Friedman, M., 126

Garner, R. T., 178
Gautama, 295
Gauthier, D., 283
Generalization argument, 206, 207
General will, 206
Gilligan, C., 39, 95–97
Goals, 212, 224–229, 253, 256–260
God, 135, 137, 151, 206, 257–260
Golden Rule, 154 n, 168
Good. *See* Benefit; Value, concepts of
Gorovitz, S., 99 n
"Greatest good of the greatest number,"
    99, 100
    calculation of, 109, 110
    distribution of and problem of justice,
        118–122

and problem of knowledge, 105–108
See also Utilitarianism
Grusec, J., 96 n

Hamilton, W. D., 287
Happiness theory of value, 228–232
Hare, R. M., 201, 202–208, 281
Hedonism
    psychological, 222–225, 286
    value, 11, 220–230
Hegel, G. W. F., 206
Hitler, A., 179
Hobbes, T., 39, 283
Housman, A. E., 33
Human nature, 286–288
Hypothetical agreement, method of. *See*
    Moral negotiation

Ideology, 296, 297
Indirect rules, 17, 18
Induction. *See* Arguments, inductive
Interests, as motive. *See* Self-benefit
Intrinsic disvalue, 214
Intrinsic value, 212–218
    calculus of, 226, 255
    death and, 229
    defined, 212
    instances of, with arguments for,
        215–218
    meaning of life and, 252–254
    obligation and, 211, 248
    rational choice and, 217–218
    See also Value, concepts of

James, William, 181, 296
Jesus, 295
Journey view, 256
Justice
    communist theory of, 128
    competition theory of, 126, 127
    distributive, 9, 10, 118–122
    duties of, 140, 141, 143, 144
    equality and, 128, 129
    merit and, 127
    Mill's theory of, 125, 126
    Rawls's theory of, 128, 129
    retributive, 118
    utilitarianism and, 118–122

Justified assertion, 30
Justified singular moral judgments, 14, 263. *See also* Normative ethics; Singular moral judgments

Kant, I., 8, 90–94, 152–158, 206, 276, 279, 282, 284
Knowledge
    acceptance (belief) and, 31
    basic units of, 189
    being 'true for' and, 30, 31, 78–89, 160
    conditions for, 29
    evidence and, 29
    justified assertion as, 30, 31
    requirement of, in intuitionist theories, 178, 179
    truth and, 30, 78
    utilitarianism and the problem of, 105–108
Kohlberg, L., 39, 89–94, 159, 209
Kuhn, T., 297

Laws
    civil, 138
    natural, 71
Lenin, V. I., 296
Lewis, C. I., 296
Life, meaning of, 251–262. *See also* Meaningfulness of life
Lombardo, J. P., 61
Love, 10, 131, 133, 150–152, 232. *See also* Agapism

M, 13, 263
    moral antirealism and, 273
    moral realism and, 271, 273
    terms in, 272
    value and, 272, 273
Macaulay, J., 60
MacIntyre, A., 192, 193, 276
Mackie, J. L., 273, 274, 276
Maltruism, psychological, 63
Marshall, J., 60
Marx, K., 128, 296
Masochism, psychological, 63
Mayo, B., 192, 193
Meaning, basic units of, 270, 271

Meaningfulness of life, 251–262
Meritarianism, 9, 127
Metaethics, 263–298
Metamoral (indirect) rules, 17, 18
Mill, J. S., 99, 125–127, 155, 182, 184, 229, 331, 274, 276, 284, 295
Mills, R. S. L., 96 n
MO, defined, 211. *See also* Obligation, definitions of
Modals, defined, 71
Monism. *See* Value, theories of, monist
Moore, G. E., 176, 177, 215, 228 n, 241, 273, 274, 277
Moral connection (moral relation), 277–286
    accidental, 277
    causal as, 280, 281
    emotive as, 285
    logical as, 278, 279
    marxism and, 285
    moral as, 284
    noncognitive as, 281
    nonlogical necessary as, 279, 280
    nonresultant theories of, 277
    See also Moral predicates and nonmoral predicates, connection between
Moral disagreement, 27
    intuitionism and, 180
    pragmatism and, 186–190
    relativism and, 165, 166
    rule theories and, 190
    utilitarianism and, 165, 166
Moral education, 209, 210
Moral negotiation, 187–190
Moral phenomena, 27–29
Moral predicates, nature of, 271–277. *See also* Realism, moral
Moral predicates and nonmoral predicates, connection between, 277–286
    accidental, 277
    emotivist, 285
    logical, 278, 279
    Marxist view of, 285
    moral, 284
    necessary (nonlogical), 279, 280
    noncognitive, 281
    subjectivist, 285

Moral principles, phenomenon of using, 27
Moral properties. *See* Moral predicates,
  nature of
Moral relation. *See* Moral connection
Moral terms
  contrasted with nonmoral, 14
  interdefined, 68-70
  listed, 15 (fig.)
  of value and obligation, related, 248
Mores, 269
Morgenbesser, S., 184
Moses, 297
Motivation. *See* Altruism, psychological;
  Egoism, psychological; Hedonism,
  psychological; Human nature
Multiple-rule theories, 133 (fig.)
  categorical, 133-138, 239, 240
  prima facie, 138-150, 239-246
  in theory of obligation, 133-150, 239
  in theory of value, 239

Natural kinds, 267
Naylor, C., 94
Negation, correct form of, 52, 53
Nietzsche, F., 292
Nihilism, 290-294
Nixon, R. M., 162
Noncognitive connection, 281
Noncognitivism, 8, 281, 294
Nonformalists, 15
Nonrule theories, 171-198
  claims of, 16, 176
  comparative and noncomparative
    judgments in, 244-246
  conditional agreement in, 186-188.
    See also Moral negotiation
  contrasted with rule theories,
    171-175
  existentialism as instance of, 180, 181
  intuitionism as instance of, 176-180
  and moral disagreement, 180,
    186-190
  and moral education, 193, 194
  nonresultant, defined, 241
  normality and abnormality in, 179
  of obligation, 171-198
  of obligation and value contrasted,
    246, 247

position rules in, 178, 179
pragmatism as instance of, 181-190
resultant and nonresultant compared,
  241, 242
of value, 241-248
virtue ethics as instance of, 190-194
Normality (nonabnormality), required by
  intuitionists, 178-180
Normative ethics
  characterized via Scheme R, 14, 15
  main divisions of, 15 (fig.), 16 (fig.)
  place of moral judgments in, 13, 14,
    27, 211
  review of, 12-19
  See also Deontological theories of
    obligation; Nonrule theories, of
    obligation; Obligation, theories of;
    Value, theories of

Obligation
  definitions of, 68
  list of, 15 (fig.)
  MO, 67-70
  Moral and nonmoral terms of, 14
  right action, 64-69
  rights, 68 n
  'right to', 67-69
Obligation, theories of
  basic notions in, contrasted with
    theories of value, 15 (fig.), 211
  general characterization of, 13-18
  instances of *F*, *M*, and *X* in, 15 (fig.)
  nonrule theories of, 246, 247
  rule theories of, 16-18, 133 (fig.)
  teleological theories of, 14, 131, 211
  See also Deontological theories of
    obligation; Multiple-rule theories,
    in theory of obligation; Single-rule
    theories, in theory of obligation;
    see also specific theories such as
    Egoism, Utilitarianism
Oldenquist, A., 207
Organic unities, 226-228, 233
Original position, 283
"Ought implies can," principle of, 28, 289
Overriding, of one rule by another, 142.
  See also Rules, categorical; Rules,
  prima facie

Pain. *See* Hedonism
Paradigms, 297, 298
Paternalism, 157 n
Pederson, J., 96 n
Peirce, C. S., 181, 182, 276, 296
"Perception," 142, 144
Phenomena
  as accepted elements, 24
  counterexamples and, 82-84
  facts and, 23, 25
  moral, 1, 2, 27-29
  of motivation, 42, 43
  theories and, 22-27
Piaget, J., 39, 89, 93
Plato, 39, 192, 193, 241, 295
Pleasure. *See* Hedonism
Pluralism, 239-249. *See also* Multiple-rule theories
Political theory, and ethics, 294, 295. *See also* specific theories such as Communism, Competitionism
Possibility mistake, 47, 48
Pragmatism, 181-190, 241-248, 296, 297
  basic units of, 265
  obligation and value in, 246, 247
Pratt, M. W., 96 n
Presupposition, 203, 204
Prichard, H. A., 178, 179, 280
Prima facie rules. *See* Rules, prima facie
Prima facie rule theories, 138-150, 178, 239-246
  of obligation, 123-150
  of value, 239-246
  See also Rules, prima facie
Promulgation, 206-209
Properties, moral. *See* Moral predicates, nature of
"Pseudo-generalizations," 156
Psychological altruism, 50-52, 223
Psychological egoism, 40, 42-63. *See* Egoism, psychological
Psychological hedonism, 221-225, 286
Psychological maltruism, 63
Psychological masochism, 63
Psychological realism, 53, 54
Putnam, H., 276

Quayle, C. D., 162
Questionnaires
  descriptive ethics, 4-8
  key to, 8-11
  values, 11, 12

Rawls, J., 88, 90, 91, 94, 128, 129, 283
Realism, moral, 273-277
Realism, psychological, 53, 54
Relativism
  compared with utilitarianism, 165, 166
  connection between cultural and ethical, 162-166
  cultural, 161, 162
  ethical, 158, 160-167
  moral disagreement and, 165-167
  value, 234-238
Religion, and ethics, 295, 296. *See also* Buddhism; God; Theological voluntarism
Rescher, N., 119
Resultant theories, 241. *See also* Basic notions, within ethics
Retributive justice, 118
Right action, 68, 69
Rights, 68
'Right to', 67-69
"Ripples in the pond," 110
Rosen, B., 89 n, 178, 201
Ross, W. D., 133 (fig.), 139-142, 144, 178 n, 279, 280
Rousseau, J. J., 206, 282
Royer, J. M., 96 n
Rule deontology. *See* Deontological theories of obligation
Rules
  categorical, 16, 132, 148
  constitutive, 15, 16, 145-148, 172-175
  direct (primary), 17-18
  indirect (metamoral), 17-18
  prima facie, 16, 132, 138-150
  summary, 172-174
  See also Multiple-rule theories; Prima facie rule theories; Single-rule theories

Rule theories
  basic units of, 265, 269
  claims of, 16-18
  classified, 133 (fig.)
  contrasted with nonrule theories, 174, 175, 189
  moral disagreement and, 190
  of obligation, 16-18, 133-168
  See also Multiple-rule theories; Prima facie rule theories; Single-rule theories
Rule theory arguments, 199-207, 209, 210
Russell, B., 176, 270, 271
Ryle, G., 221 n

Sartre, J. P., 180
Satisfaction, 54-56
Scheme R, 13-14. See also Normative ethics
Self-benefit, as motive in psychological egoism, 43, 44
Sharp, F. C., 32, 33
Shroeder, D., 62 n
Sidgwick, H., 279
Simon, H. S., 288
Singer, M., 207
Single-rule theories, 150
  based on categorical rules, 150-158, 220-233
  in theory of obligation, 150-158
  See also Value, theories of, monist; see also specific theories such as Egoism, Hedonism
Singular moral judgments, 14, 27
  constitutive rules and, 173-175
  in nonrule theories, 186, 246-248
Situationism, 168
Skepticism, 9, 10, 290
Slavery, 5, 6, 7, 82, 83, 86, 186, 187, 238, 242-245
Smart, J. J. C., 110
Smith, J. M., 287
Social functions of normative utterances, 291-294
Social theory, and ethics, 294, 295
Sociobiology, 287-288

Socrates, 192
Statistical syllogism, 21, 172. See also Arguments, inductive
Stowe, H. B., 238
Subjectivism, 10, 285
Sufficiency, moral, 284
Summary rules, 172-175
Supererogatory actions, 68

Teleological theories, 14, 16 (fig.), 66, 131, 211. See also Egoism, ethical egoism; Utilitarianism
Ten Commandments, 6, 9, 135-138, 150
Theological voluntarism, 9, 135-138, 257-260
Theories
  ethical, defined, 23
  evaluation criteria for, 24-26
  as explanations of phenomena, 22
Trivers, R., 287
'True for', as acceptance, 30, 31. See also Knowledge, being 'true for'
Truth
  contingent, 30
  necessary, 30
  See also Knowledge

Underwhelming value, 225, 226, 231, 232, 240
"Universalizability" principle, 8, 201-209
Utilitarianism, 86, 87, 99-123
  act (direct), 99, 100
  combined with egoism, 133-135
  compared with egoism, 196, 197
  compared with relativism, 159
  counterexamples to, 113-118
  evaluation of, 112-122
  "greatest good for the greatest number," as goal in, 100
  importance of consequences in, 99
  indirect, 100, 101
  moral disagreement and, 165, 166
  motives and, 110, 111
  notions of *good* in, 103, 104
  problem of justice and, 118-122
  problem of knowledge and, 105-108

Utilitarianism (*continued*)
  rule (indirect), 100, 101
  as teleological theory, 104, 106

Valid argument. *See* Arguments, deductive
Value, concepts of
  addition test and, 226–230
  as basis of our motives, 43, 44
  calculations of, 255, 260
  efficient, 215
  God and, 257–260
  instrumental, 215. *See* Extrinsic value
  isolation as test of, 213
  kinds of things that have, 215, 216
  list of, 15 (fig.)
  meaningful life and, 251–262
  nonmoral (efficient), 215
  phenomena for, 216
  underwhelming, 225, 226, 231, 232, 240. *See also* Benefit; Intrinsic disvalue; Intrinsic value
Value, theories of
  basic notions in, contrasted with theories of obligation, 15 (fig.), 211
  categorical rule, 220–223
  concern of, 14, 15, 219–220
  happiness, 221, 222
  hedonism, 220–230
  instances of F, M, and X in, 15 (fig.)
  monist, 225
  pleasure, 221, 222
  pluralist, 239, 240. *See also* Multiple-rule theories
  pragmatic, 241–248
  prima facie rule, 239, 240
  relativism, 234–239
  teleological theories and, 211
Value relativism, 234–238
Vicious infinite regress, 148
Virtue ethics, theory of, 11, 190–194
Voluntarism, theological, 9, 135–138, 257–260
Voluntary action, 45, 46, 48 n

Walker, L. J., 96 n
Warnock, G. J., 196
Weakness of will, 288
Weiss, R. F., 61
Wiggins, G., 95
Williams, G. C., 287
Willing and wanting, 47
Wilson, E. O., 287
Wittgenstein, L., 291
Wong, D. B., 273, 276
Wrensch, D. L., 107